BROOKLA
BOOKS

F I A T
600 & 850
1955-1972

Compiled by
R.M.Clarke

ISBN 1 85520 247 6

BROOKLANDS BOOKS LTD.
P.O. BOX 146, COBHAM,
SURREY, KT11 1LG. UK

BROOKLANDS BOOKS

CONTENTS

5	The Fiat 600	*Motoring Life*	Mar.		1955
7	Fiat 600 Saloon Road Test	*Autocar*	May	13	1955
10	The New Fiat 600	*Road & Track*	June		1955
12	The Fiat 600 Road Test	*Autosport*	Aug.	5	1955
14	New-Look Fiat 600 Economy Car Road Test	*Wheels*	Dec.		1955
18	Fun with A Multipla	*Motoring Life*	May		1957
19	Fiat Fever	*Auto Age*	Jan.		1956
23	Sedan and Multipla	*Motor Trend*	Sep.		1957
24	Fiat 600 Multipla Road Test	*Autocar*	Jan.	18	1957
28	Dauphine and Fiat 600 vs Volkswagen Comparison Test	*Speed Age*	Sep.		1957
32	Excellence in Minature - Fiat 600	*Car South Africa*	May		1958
34	Fiat-Abarth 750 Road Test	*Road & Track*	June		1958
37	Fiat 600 and Rolls Royce Phantom III - Dignity and Impudence Driving Comparison	*Motor Sport*	July		1958
40	Fiat 600 - A Very Small Four for Four	*Foreign Cars Illustrated*	Aug.		1958
44	Testing the Bialbero	*Motor Trend*	Mar.		1959
48	Fiat-Abarth 850 Road Test	*Road & Track*	Oct.		1960
51	Fun with a Fiat	*Motoring Life*	June		1961
52	Fiat 600D Road Test	*Autocar*	June	30	1961
56	South By 600	*Wheels*	Oct.		1961
60	The Fiat Abarth 850TC Road Test	*Motor*	Nov.	29	1961
64	Fiat 600D	*Road & Track*	Nov.		1961
68	The Fiat-Abarth 1000	*Autosport*	Apr.	19	1963
70	Fiat 850 1,950 Mile Road Test	*Motor*	Nov.	21	1964
75	Fiat 600D Road Test	*Canada Track & Traffic*	Feb.		1962
78	The Fiat 600 and 600D	*Motor*	Dec.	19	1964
80	New From Fiat - The 850 Class	*Autosport*	May	1	1964
82	Two Small Sporting Fiats	*Sporting Motorist*	May		1965
89	Two Bites at Fiat Cherry	*Modern Motor*	June		1965
91	Fiat 850	*Autosport*	June	4	1965
92	Fiat Abarth 1600	*Autocar*	Aug.	13	1965
95	Fiat 600D Road Test	*Foreign Car Guide*	Oct.		1965
99	Fiat 850 Coupé and Bertone Spider Road Test	*Autocar*	June	3	1966
105	The Current Fiat 850 Range	*Car and Car Conversions*	June		1966
109	Shoestring Economy for Four Road Test	*Motor*	Sep.	24	1966
115	Fiat 850 Coupé Road Test	*Road & Track*	Oct.		1966
118	Carlo Abarth's Funny Fiats Driver's Report	*Sports Car Graphic*	Jan.		1967
122	Fiat 850 Spider	*Foreign Car Guide*	May		1967
125	The IWR conversion for the Fiat 850 Coupé	*Autosport*	May	12	1967
126	Slow Down (By Order)	*Motoring Life*	Jan.		1968
127	Fiat 850 Idroconvert	*Autocar*	Feb.	22	1968
129	Fiat 850 Spider Road Test	*Road & Track*	Apr.		1968
132	Fiat 850	*Road Test*	Oct.		1967
138	A Touch of the Exotic	*Sports Car World*	Nov.		1969
139	Fiat 850 Coupé and Spider	*Road Test*	Feb.		1969
142	Fiat 850 Special vs.Sunbeam Imp Sport Comparison Test	*Autocar*	Nov.	6	1969
148	Fiat 850 Sport Racer	*Popular Imported Cars*	May		1970
150	25,000 Miles with a Fiat 850 Coupé	*Autosport*	Mar.	5	1970
151	Fast It Ain't - Fiat 850 Racer Road Test	*Sports Car Graphic*	July		1970
154	Fiat 850 Spider Reader's Report	*Popular Imported Cars*	Sep.		1970
158	Special Commuters: $1600 and Under	*Motor Trend*	Nov.		1970
162	Fiat 850 Special Road Test	*Car South Africa*	Dec.		1970
166	Fiat 850T Utility Brief Test	*Autocar*	Dec.	23	1971
168	Sting in the Tail - Abarth 850TC	*Motor*	Mar.	28	1987
172	Funsize Fiat	*Thoroughbred & Classic Cars*	Oct.		1989

BROOKLANDS BOOKS

ACKNOWLEDGEMENTS

Our aim at Brooklands Books is to make available for the benefit of enthusiasts those magazine articles which tell them about the cars they enjoy. In most cases, this material would otherwise be unavailable or hard to come by, and we are fortunate to be able to draw on a large archive which has been built up over many years.

However, our archive would remain no more than that if it were not for the co-operation and understanding of those who hold the copyright to the original material it contains. With their agreement, we are able to reproduce material in Brooklands Road Test compilations like this one. Those who have made the present volume possible are the managements of *Auto Age, Autocar, Autosport, Canada Track & Traffic, Car and Car Conversions, Car South Africa, Foreign Car Guide, Foreign Cars Illustrated, Motor, Modern Motor, Motoring Life, Motor Sport, Motor Trend, Popular Imported Cars, Road & Track, Road Test, Speed Age, Sporting Motorist, Sports Car Graphic, Sports Car World, Thoroughbred & Classic Cars,* and *Wheels.* We are grateful to all of them.

R. M. Clarke

Fiat's name will always be associated with small economy cars, even thought the company has produced very many cars which are neither small nor economy models. Their most famous line began with the two-seater Topolino 500 of 1936, but by the middle 1950s the company had determined to build a four-seater model within the same overall dimensions which would be just as economical. And so they did: the 600 which was announced at the Geneva Show in 1955 was a quite remarkable combination of packaging and engineering flair, wrapped in a body which was curvaceous and attractive. Rather less attractive, but no less a triumph of packaging and engineering was the estate car variant with which Fiat determined to replace the 500-based Giardinera and Belvedere estates; the 600 Multipla was announced in January 1956 and could accommodate no fewer than six people in a vehicle rather less than a foot longer than the basic 600.

In due course, larger engines and more power arrived for both saloon and Multipla variants of the 600, but Fiat were already considering the introduction of a third baby car to their range. In 1964 they introduced the 850 saloon, stylistically similar in some respects to the 600 but slightly larger overall. Within a year, the 850 had spawned two delightful variants the 850 coupé and the Bertone-styled 850 Spyder. Engine capacity and power were increased again in 1969, and the final 850s - saloons with the original engine capacity - were built in 1974. The 600, meanwhile, had ceased production in 1970, while the Multipla had gone as early as 1966.

By their very nature, baby cars tend to be regarded as cute and sweet, and not to be taken very seriously. But the Fiat 600 and 850 had an enormous impact on the design of the small car, introducing packaging solutions which are still adopted in today's economy cars. Their excellence is easier to appreciate in the words written about them when they were new, and for that reason this book is particularly illuminating. Enthusiasts of the 600 and 850 will enjoy it as a good read in its own right, while others will learn from it just what made these little mass-produced cars so special.

James Taylor

c.c. developing the very useful output of 21½ brake horse power at 4,690 r.p.m. which is to be considered extremely lively when· allied to a mere 11¾ cwts. Valve seats are inset and an unusual feature is the built-in inlet manifold which is cast as part of the head. The Topolino operated with a two bearing crankshaft but the new engine works on a three bearing shaft. A by-pass oil filter is employed and the radiator sits ahead of a turbo-fan which forces air through it at the discretion of a thermostatically controlled shutter

The heated air from the lower part of the radiator is expelled underneath the engine but the air from the hotter (top) section of the core can be piped into the car for heating purposes (and demisting through various ingenious channels) at the whim of the driver.

The engine, gear-box, clutch and final drive arrangements are mounted in unit and can be withdrawn from the car en masse. The whole is attached to the body through the medium of rubber bushes, and Fiat's engineers claim a high degree of silence and vibration-free running for the car.

The transmission is based on a four-speed gear-box with synchromesh on second, third and top. The gear lever is centrally mounted in the

TO appreciate the sensational effects of a new economy car from the House of Fiat one has to realise that Fiat have a reputation for establishing precedents in their approach to small car design. In 1936 they announced the "500", or "Topolino" (Mickey Mouse) as it came to be called and set Europe gasping with admiration for a so-called toy that could go anywhere, keep up with most, stand up to any sort of treatment and still be extraordinarily economical on fuel.

But the Topolino had a limitation of the gravest kind. It was essentially a two-seater only car and never succeeded to the same extent as the later four-seaters such as the Renault 4CV and Citroen 2CV, although it could move just as swiftly, just as comfortably, and was of not much smaller overall dimensions.

Perhaps Fiat were wise not to let the little 500 over-grow itself in the manner that is so prevalent among British makers. Instead they let it die a slow and gradual death while they experimented with THE CAR that would take its place. It is praiseworthy too that Fiat did not allow themselves to be bustled by the well-nigh overwhelming demands for its earlier introduction by hundreds of thousands of impatient Italian and French motorists.

By biding their time the designers of the new 600 have been able to study the mistakes of the others and to finalise on a design that is as fresh and original as an April shower. They have done what many will say was impossible: built a four seater saloon around the dimensions of the old Topolino!

In deciding on a rear engine layout the designers agreed that it offered the advantages of providing the highest possible ratio between internal passenger space and external dimensions. The extraordinary compact-

ness of the water-cooled engine, with the side-by-side location of the radiator establishes new records in this respect and the elimination of the long drive-shaft and rear-axle casing

The FIAT 600

allows for a considerable reduction in weight.

The new engine is a four cylinder overhead valve unit with an aluminium cylinder head in the classical manner. It has 60 mm bores and a 56 mm stroke with a cubic capacity of 633

floor and works through a minimum of linkages. As in the case of the famous Renault the drive passes along a shaft running through the top of the gear-box, and returns via the various clusters to the differential which occupies the same casing.

5

Accordingly, top gear is not a direct drive.

The half shafts oscillate on patented-design universal joints (constant velocity) and it is observed that the lateral location of the hubs is proved by the use of rigid members attached to the car frame. The half-shafts are "fully floating" and consequently exposed.

The rear springing is genuinely independent with coil springs and telescopic shock-absorbers, while the front is semi-independent by a single transverse leaf spring. The designers claim that the front spring combines the duties of a stabiliser in addition to the normal work of dissipating road shocks. There is nothing unorthodox about the steering mechanism which resembles the late 500's worm and quadrant type.

One of the odd things about the tiny Topolino was its separate cruciform chassis, and this has been superseded in the new car by integral body construction on the same lines as the Elevenhundred. The two-door body style is retained and the doors themselves open from the leading edges. The one-piece steel roof has a distinctive strengthening ridge around its periphery in obvious anti-

cipation of a roof rack, and the rear seat folds down into a platform if necessary. There is the usual amount of restricted luggage accommodation behind the rear seat, and under the bonnet, where a large six-gallon petrol tank and twelve-volt battery are also situated.

Braking is by Fiat-Baldwin hydraulic system and the hand brake works — in typical Turin fashion — on the transmission.

Both the windscreen and the rear view window are slightly curved, and the sliding side windows are equipped with draughtless ventilation louvres which are easily adjustable. Instrumental details include: flashing indicators, dual automatically - parking windscreen wipers, interior light, illuminated engine space, water temperature warning light, petrol level "winker" when running on the last half gallon, and the usual switches.

Originality of outlook is further expressed in the door pockets, the outer lips of which act as door pulls. A protective splash-back is located on the inside of the engine compartment lid to protect the various engine components from the rain which might get blown under the ventilating openings.

At this stage the appetite is sufficiently whetted to invite the inevitable question: "How will she perform?"

The authentic answer must await

a road test and *MOTORING LIFE*'s readers may rest assured that they will get the first comprehensive account published in Ireland.

Meanwhile the makers have acknowledged that the 600 will be able to move at a maximum speed of 65 m.p.h. and will be just as economical as the Topolino. In our experience the Topolino could average 47 miles per gallon under all normal conditions of trans-suburban work-home driving, and on a country run could touch 56 miles per gallon without a sneeze. If the 600 can do these things it will be a welcome addition to the small car fold, in which a warming-up of the cold war is under way.

Turin says that the road-holding qualities of the 600 are "perfect under all road conditions and at all speeds." They were not found to be optimistic in their claims with the Elevenhundred.

Those are all the facts about the 600 as are known at present—but our correspondent in Geneva writes with a word of caution to warn interested parties that on first acquaintance the 600 looks no bigger than a miniature, but that this impression is completely alien to the space available when one sits into it. As to its acceleration . . . . we must reluctantly wait and see! ■

Small cars can be shapely. The Fiat 600 styling shows a clever combination of straight lines and curves. The large window area provides a light interior

No. 1567 : FIAT 600 SALOON

AN entirely new car is always full of interest, the more so when it is produced by one of the world's biggest manufacturers; the Fiat 600 is one of those original designs which creates another milestone in the history of motoring.

It succeeds the Fiat 500C, which was developed from the original type 500. The new model, which appeared for the first time at the Geneva Show in March, is notable for its rear mounted, four-cylinder, overhead valve engine and its independent suspension. The front suspension is by a single transverse leaf spring, and at the rear there are coil springs mounted on triangular, fabricated swinging arms. There is a four speed gear box, with synchromesh on second, third and top gears, the latter being a form of overdrive. Brief experience of the car in its native country in severe winter conditions whetted the appetite, and when the first models were received in this country by Fiat (England), Ltd., Water Road, Wembley, Middlesex, acquaintance with the friendly little car was quickly and eagerly renewed.

The 600 does not give the impression of a big car scaled down, and the performance on the road is impressive when the engine size is kept in mind. The new car weighs but 14lb more than the previous model 500C, and the power output is greater by 5 b.h.p. The 600 carries four adults within the same wheelbase that, before, catered for only two persons and their luggage.

The engine of the 600 starts easily from cold with some use of the choke. Both starter and choke controls are mounted, side by side, between the front seats, and they may be operated together by one hand. A hand throttle, a simple and effective device connected to the accelerator pedal, is mounted alongside the steering column, and is useful when warming up. To aid this process in cold weather, the carburettor air intake can be adjusted so that air is warmed by being drawn through a vent placed very close to the exhaust manifold.

Very little engine noise is heard within the body, and at all engine speeds there is an impression of smoothness. Even at peak revolutions in the lower gears vibration is not felt from the power unit, and this is a definite asset in so small a car, when any trace of "fussiness" can cause irritation and fatigue to the occupants. The engine seems to enjoy hard work, and at the end of a day's journey during which the speedometer needle was more often than not hovering on the 50 m.p.h. mark, the 633 c.c. engine was as

quiet and sweet as when it had been started some ten hours before.

An engine of this size is at a natural disadvantage in comparison with a bigger unit, used to move the same number of passengers from one place to another. But where the Fiat scores is with the gear box ratios—once the cruising speed has been reached, and this is governed by road conditions and the driver's preference, the 600 settles down in the delightfully geared-up top to what can be described as an easy gait.

When carrying three or four adults it is necessary, in order to maintain an average cruising speed of about 50 m.p.h., to use third gear quite frequently to carry the car up a long gradient or to overtake slower-moving traffic. Once this has been done, the gear lever can be moved smartly into top, and all the driver hears is what might be described as a quiet, contented hum from the engine compartment. It is quite simple to cover forty miles in one hour, and a time regarded as standard for a sixty mile journey was exceeded by only five minutes in the Fiat 600.

On the Gears

The manufacturer has taken the precaution of marking on the speedometer the recommended maximum speeds in the gears—15½ m.p.h. for first, 25½ m.p.h. for second, and 40 m.p.h. for third gear. These figures appear to be conservative, as was amply demonstrated during our first journey in the car, which took us up and down a tortuous Italian mountain road a few miles from Turin. On that occasion, the car, carrying four adults, was driven extremely hard by an experienced works driver. The remarkable performance was later equalled by the 600 which was used in England for this Road Test.

In top gear the maximum obtained on a level surface was a fraction short of 60 m.p.h.—the makers have marked the speedometer at 59. The top-gear ratio is such that it is possible to cruise with the throttle pedal on the floor without any sign of the engine being overworked. The hum behind the rear seats rises a little, and the note changes according to whether the car is going up hill or down. Bred in the Alps and proved in the high passes and along the *autostrada*, the Fiat shows no signs of overheating or of ill effects from constant full-throttle work. If the cooling water level falls or the water temperature exceeds 100 deg C a warning light appears in the instrument panel.

Clutch action is light, and the drive is taken up smoothly, but there is not enough room for the driver's left foot alongside the clutch pedal. The gear change is one of the best we have tried. The slim, short, central lever is in an ideal position, and the speed of the change depends entirely on the agility of the driver. The synchromesh works well. The spring pressure which has to be overcome to engage reverse gear could be stronger with advantage, to prevent the lever being inadvertently pressed down when changing to third gear. First gear, naturally, is meant to be used on a car with this size of engine, and correct use of the gear box enables the driver to be among the first away after a traffic stop.

Alpine proving shows again in the gear ratios, and the car is no sluggard up gradients of the order of 1 in 10 such as are met on main roads in Great Britain. The brakes, too, are witnesses of the original testing ground. Intensive use when the performance figures were obtained produced no signs of fade or unevenness of operation. Applied repeatedly during full-load descents of several steep hills, the brakes pulled the car up firmly and squarely. The hand brake, which operates on the transmission, has a convenient lever placed between the seats, and the brake itself is very effective.

The suspension and cornering abilities of this remarkable little car are praiseworthy. The worst that can be said is that there is slight fore and aft pitching on certain surfaces. Apart from this, the ride is very comfortable, and a rough, unmade road can be taken at 45 m.p.h. without any appreciable discomfort. There is plenty of weight on the rear wheels, and when the car is cornered quickly the

FIAT 600 SALOON

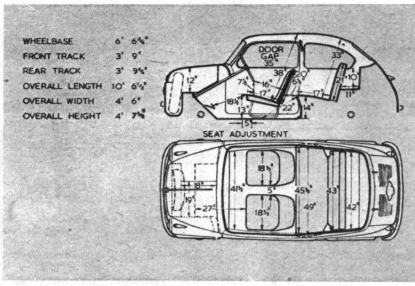

WHEELBASE	6' 6⅜"	
FRONT TRACK	3' 9"	
REAR TRACK	3' 9⅝"	
OVERALL LENGTH	10' 6½"	
OVERALL WIDTH	4' 6"	
OVERALL HEIGHT	4' 7½"	

Measurements in these ⅛in to 1ft scale body diagrams are taken with the driving seat in the central position of fore and aft adjustment and with the seat cushions uncompressed

━━━ DATA ━━━

PRICE (basic), with saloon body, £412 10s. British purchase tax, £173. Total (in Great Britain), £585 10s.

ENGINE: Capacity: 633 c.c. (38.63 cu in). Number of cylinders: 4. Bore and stroke: 60×56 mm (2⅜ × 2⁴⁄₁₀in). Valve gear: overhead, pushrods and rockers. Compression ratio: 7 to 1. B.H.P.: 21.5 at 4,600 r.p.m. (B.H.P. per ton laden 29.4). Torque: 28.9 lb ft at 2,800 r.p.m. M.P.H. per 1,000 r.p.m. on top gear, 13.7.

WEIGHT: (with 5 gals fuel), 11½ cwt (1,288lb). Weight distribution (per cent): F, 39.2; R, 60.8. Laden as tested: 14⅝ cwt (1,638lb). Lb per c.c. (laden): 2.6.

BRAKES: Type: F, Fiat-Baldwin; R, Fiat-Baldwin. Method of operation: F, Hydraulic; R, hydraulic. Drum dimensions: F, 7⅜in diameter; 1⅛in wide. R, 7⅜in diameter; 1⅛in wide. Lining area: F, 33.4 sq in. R, 33.4 sq in. (91.3 sq in per ton laden).

TYRES: 5.20—12in. Pressures (lb per sq in): F, 17; R, 22.8 (normal).

TANK CAPACITY: 6 Imperial gallons. Oil sump, 5½ pints. Cooling system, 7½ pints.

TURNING CIRCLE: 27ft 10in (L and R). Steering wheel turns (lock to lock): 3¼.

DIMENSIONS: Wheelbase: 6ft 6½in. Track: F, 3ft 9in; R, 3ft 9½in. Length (overall): 10ft 6½in. Height: 4ft 7½in. Width: 4ft 6in. Ground clearance: 6⅛in. Frontal area: 16.1 sq ft (approximately).

ELECTRICAL SYSTEM: 12-volt; 28 ampere-hour battery. Head lights: double dip; 40–45 watt bulbs.

SUSPENSION: Front, independent, transverse leaf spring and wishbones. Rear independent, coil springs and swinging arms.

━━━ PERFORMANCE ━━━

ACCELERATION: from constant speeds. Speed Range, Gear Ratios and Time in sec.

M.P.H.	4.82 to 1	7.13 to 1	11.0 to 1	18.2 to 1
10—30	24.4	11.9	—	—
20—40	23.6	13.4	—	—
30—50	31.3	—	—	—

From rest through gears to:

M.P.H.			sec
30	..	..	9.6
50	..	..	35.5

Standing quarter mile, 27.3 sec.

SPEEDS ON GEARS:

Gear			M.P.H. (normal and max.)	K.P.H. (normal and max.)
Top	..	(mean)	57.5	92.5
		(best)	59.5	95.7
3rd	..	..	38—40	61—64
2nd	..	..	23—25	37—40
1st	..	..	12—15	19—24

(Maximum recommended by manufacturer)

TRACTIVE RESISTANCE: 53.3lb per ton at 10 M.P.H.

TRACTIVE EFFORT:

			Pull (lb per ton)	Equivalent Gradient
Top	..	..	105	1 in 21
Third	..	..	170	1 in 13
Second	..	..	290	1 in 7.6

BRAKES:

Efficiency	Pedal Pressure (lb)
80 per cent	100
72 per cent	75
60 per cent	50

FUEL CONSUMPTION: 49 m.p.g. overall for 725 miles. (5.77 litres per 100 km.) Approximate normal range 45–57 m.p.g. (6.2–4.9 litres per 100 km.)

WEATHER: Dry surface, light cross breeze. Air temperature 47 deg. F. Acceleration figures are the means of several runs in opposite directions. Tractive effort and resistance obtained by Tapley meter. Model described in *The Autocar* of March 11, 1955.

SPEEDOMETER CORRECTION: M.P.H.

Car speedometer:	10	20	30	40	50	60
True speed:	8	18	28	38	48	58

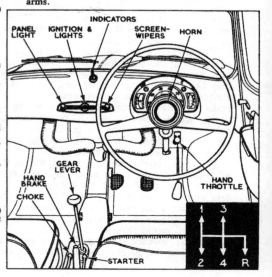

tyres grip; there is no swinging out of the back of the car, and it goes round as required. And it will corner very quickly and safely indeed. There is little or no heeling over except on hairpin bends, when rear passengers feel it desirable to use the hand straps provided. There is no tyre scream, and wet roads make no difference.

The car can be parked in a space little greater than its own length, and it will turn in an average-width suburban road in one movement. The steering is light, and the car is controlled easily at all speeds. Strong side winds have some effect on directional stability; they do so affect most cars of this size and weight. The wheel is placed at a good angle, and because of the short bonnet, forward visibility is extremely good.

At night there is a cosy, intimate atmosphere about the car. It hums along very smoothly, the road ahead well lit by the comparatively small-diameter head lamps. The driving beam is more than adequate for the performance of the car and, in the dipped position, there is light enough to see pedestrians and cyclists. Self-parking wipers are fitted, but the wiper arm spindles appear to be in a position suitable for a left-hand drive car. Consequently, when the screen was wet, the driver of the test car was obliged to lower his head to see through a wiped part of the screen.

The separate front seats are adjustable fore and aft for leg room, and in spite of the wheel arches encroaching into the front compartment, there is sufficient room for large feet. The seat cushions and seat backs provide the necessary support where required, and a tall driver has no feeling of being cramped or shut in after, for example, a non-stop journey of 100 miles or so. If the occupants of the front seats are wearing heavy coats, the driver's left arm is apt to come up against the passenger when changing gear, but for all practical purposes there is adequate width in the

The interior is well finished. Facia equipment is limited to four switches, and the speedometer is shrouded. Large capacity pockets also form door pulls. Large diameter pipes lead to the windscreen demister vents, and the floor is covered with rubber matting

Entry to the rear compartment is made easy by the wide doors, and folding backrests of the front seats. For additional luggage space the back of the rear seat folds forward

body. The back of each front seat folds forward, and this, together with the very wide door opening, makes it an easy matter to reach the back seat.

If only two people are using the car the back rest of the rear seat can be hinged forward, and the resulting space provides room for a considerable amount of luggage. When the seat is occupied, coats and small parcels or cases can be placed behind the seat. There is also room for a few articles in the front compartment alongside the petrol tank. The small tools are stowed here, and the battery and brake fluid reservoir are reached by lifting up the floor covering. Greasing points are limited to six only, on the steering and front suspension.

The engine is well exposed for servicing, when the louvred cover is opened. No lock is provided on this handle. There is a small light to aid attention at night. Out of sight beneath the radiator is the shutter for controlling the interior heating. A small lever in the rear compartment, easily reached from the driving seat, opens or closes the shutter and, according to its position, warm air is forced along the tunnel in the floor, through holes close to the occupants' feet and also ducted to the windscreen vents.

Small cases and parcels can be accommodated in the forward compartment. The battery is kept here and also the brake fluid reservoir. The tool roll tucks away beside the spare wheel

1920

1955

IF YOU think that General Motors is a monster in the United States, consider Fiat of Italy. This one company produces 90% of Italy's total automotive output and they control, through interlocking directorates, virtually every phase of car manufacture, from raw materials to the finished product.

Since 1951, engineering and development work has been underway to design a new model to replace the world famous Topolino (the little mouse). The Topolino, or model "500", always suffered from being only a two-seater, though the later 500-C models were available as a 4-passenger "station wagon". Accordingly, the goals set-up for a replacement car included seating for 4 adults combined with (if possible) lower

first cost, improved performance and better economy.

About 35 million dollars have been spent on plant modernization, and tooling and production of the "600" actually began in November of 1954. The announcement was held back for the Geneva show, since Switzerland is a vital and critical export market situated approximately in the geographical center of Europe.

The new "600" is actually smaller, lighter and cheaper than the "500-C". It is 5" shorter, 1" lower, 3.5" wider and weighs 1232 lbs or 11 lbs less than the 500 C. Its list price is about $950, in Italy, plus tax and license fees. Top speed, with four passengers, is given as "over 95 Km" or 59

mph, plus, on a long level road.

To achieve a lighter, yet roomier package the body and frame are fabricated as a unit and the engine has been placed behind the rear wheels. Sliding windows in the two doors give extra elbow room and there is space for modest luggage in front (by virtue of a side-mounted fuel tank) and at the rear just behind the seat.

The suspension system is completely new and independent at both front and rear. In front the most interesting feature is the use of a "full-floating" transverse leaf spring. Mounted and retained by a pair of widely spaced rubber blocks the design is both simple and ingenious. Since the center portion of the spring is free to move, it

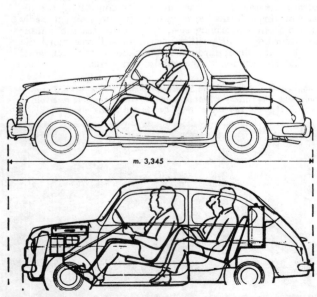

m. 3,345

This comparison of the old with the new shows how four adults are neatly fitted into a wheelbase of only 78.74 inches.

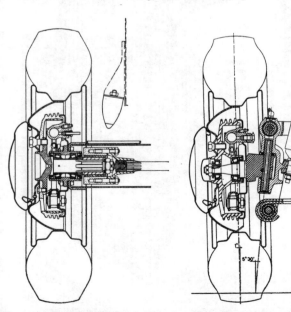

The rear wheel hub design is shown at the left. Drawing at the right shows the clever i.f.s. with detail of one of the spring mountings.

NEW
600
economy car

Allemano

Boano

Pinin Farina

Vignale

Custom bodied Fiat 600's were shown at the 1955 Geneva Show!

imparts extra flexibility and also adds to roll resistance during fast cornering.

At the rear, a swinging axle design is used, with a difference. Each wheel is forced to describe a path determined by a single wishbone which at first glance appears to be similar to the early type Lancia Aurelia. However, the wishbone pivot axis, extended, passes thru the universal joint centers on each side of the differential. This avoids the necessity of employing spherical ball type covers around the universal joints on each side of the differential. Coil springs are used, but unlike the Lancia, there are no universal joints at the wheel hubs. Instead, a bonded rubber coupling of cylindrical shape is used to take care of minor discrepancies which might appear—possibly up to one or two degrees. This coupling is shown in the cross-section view and it should also provide some worthwhile drive-cushioning effect.

The water-cooled four-cylinder engine is fairly orthodox with over-square dimensions (60 x 56 mm) pushrod operated overhead valves and a 3-main bearing crankshaft. The cylinder block is cast iron with siamesed cylinders and the head is an aluminum casting with valve seat inserts and a com-

pression ratio of only 7 to one. Bhp is 21.5 at 4600 rpm. The radiator, cooling fan and water pump are located on the r.h. side of the engine and ducting is provided to divert heated air from the radiator to the body interior, when required.

The unit transmission and differential assembly constitute a unique and well-engineered design. Shown in one of the cross section drawings, there are 4 speeds forward, all indirect and with 3 syncronized. All gears are helical, except first and reverse and the outboard mounting of the 2nd speed pair of gears is noteworthy, though not new. The differential side gears are extra large so that the two universal joints can be located inside, for operation at as small an angle as possible. The joints themselves are the "pot" type to eliminate the need for telescoping splines.

The final drive gears are spiral bevels with a ratio of 43/8 (5.375 to 1). However, the overall ratio in 4th gear is modified by the rearmost pair of transmission gears, the "overdrive" ratio being .896, so that the actual ratio is 4.816 to 1. At 60 mph the engine revolutions are 4500 rpm, equivalent to a piston speed of only 1650 fpm.

Brakes are of course 4-wheel hydraulic and the most interesting features are the

provision for ventilation and the use of bimetal drums at the rear only. The mechanical parking brake is at the extreme front of the transmission. Pressed steel wheels are 12" x 3.5" and mount tires of 5.20" section. Ground clearance as a result is only 6.3".

Obviously the Fiat "600" design has been influenced to some extent by the success of the German Volkswagen. Smaller and more austere than the VW, it is perhaps a better approach to the problem of a "peoples car" than its German counterpart—at least in Europe where the "600" is cheaper in first cost and much more economical in fuel consumption. Gasoline in Italy for example costs about 83 cents per gallon and wages are very low. But in the booming U.S.A., we see little or no demand for a car such as this. Even the most enthusiastic VW owners are clamoring for more speed, power and performance.

Nevertheless the Fiat-Mirafiori Works have never caught-up with their back-log of orders on the 1100 model and are currently claiming title to being the 5th largest auto producer in the world. About 700 cars per day, of all types, are being produced at the present time. ●

The Fiat 4-speed transmission.

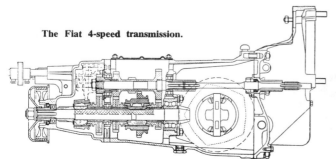

Small 5.20-12 tires allow toe-boards to be located well forward.

NO CLUE to the rear position of the engine is given in this aspect of the Fiat 600, which offers remarkable body space within its 6 ft. 6¼ ins. wheelbase.

At first sight, a saloon car with an engine capacity of only 633 c.c. might seem an odd sort of vehicle to choose for an AUTOSPORT road test. Certainly, our quota does perhaps tend towards the ultra-fast and even the super-expensive. Nevertheless, Britain's curious little roads, with their vast burden of heavy traffic, do encourage the use of very small cars. In fact, a large machine with a two-miles-a-minute maximum may, on occasion, be soundly trounced by a vehicle of small physical dimensions that is capable of extremely rapid changes of direction.

Such a car is the Fiat. It has a body-cum-chassis structure in the form of a

JOHN BOLSTER TESTS THE FIAT 600

A diminutive four-seater rear-engined saloon which combines ease of handling with lively performance and fuel economy

two-door four-seater saloon, and at first sight the passengers and luggage seem to occupy the whole envelope. Eventually, one discovers a tiny engine, hidden behind the cushion of the rear seat. It is an over-square unit, with pushrod operated valves in a light alloy head. Its 21.5 b.h.p. are transmitted to a four-speed gearbox of the all-indirect variety, via a single dry plate clutch. The engine is behind the rear hub line, and the gearbox ahead of it, the drive coming back to a spiral bevel and differential between the two units.

The rear suspension is one of those variations on the swing axle theme, in which a trailing link gives a diagonal movement. The articulated shafts have two universal joints, and the suspension medium is helical springs with telescopic dampers. In front, the classical transverse leaf and wishbone layout is modified by a wide-base spring mounting that confers extra roll resistance. The worm and sector steering gear gives an exceptionally small turning circle.

The body gives adequate accommodation for four people, on two bucket seats and a bench at the rear. The lateral width is generous, but a very tall

driver may tend to encroach on the rear passengers' leg room when adjusting his seat. There is useful luggage space behind the rear seat squab, which also folds forward to make the car a two-seater with extra room for impedimenta. The backs of the front seats pivot down on to the cushions to give reasonably easy access to the rear compartment. The front bonnet takes more luggage, but the petrol tank and spare wheel occupy a considerable proportion of this space.

Unconventional cooling by a radiator alongside the engine is featured. The draught is inspired from behind, and forced forward by a large fan which shares its shaft with a remote water impeller. A short belt drives the dynamo and a second belt takes the power to the fan pulley. Ahead of the radiator, a central duct, built into the body, carries heated air forward for demisting the screen. The screen wipers are offset and self-parking, and though a little noisy in action are notably effective.

The rear side windows are fixed, but there are a pair of sliding panes in each door, allied with an ingenious draught deflector. Even in extremely hot weather, the ventilation is surprisingly effective. The roof has a plastic backing which takes the place of a normal head lining. It is adequate against drumming, though the interior becomes hot when the car is stationary. The all-round visibility is very good.

On the road, the Fiat provides practical transport for four adults on a fuel consumption approaching 50 m.p.g. With an enterprising driver at the wheel, it can more than hold its own in a normal traffic stream, and one is seldom passed on anything except a long, clear straight. The steering is very good, and the cornering power quite high. There is absolutely no oversteering tendency whatsoever, and it is literally impossible to "feel" the rear engine.

In those respects, the "600" is at least the equal of a full sized vehicle. It would be absurd to pretend, however, that so small a car has no disadvantages compared with its bigger brothers. First of all, as one would expect, the ride is definitely hard. The front suspension is unusually stiff, in the interests of freedom from roll and of controlability; consequently, rear seat passengers enjoy the best ride. The very small wheels tend to feel the bumps, and a choppy, up-and-down movement manifests itself on certain surfaces. The faster the car is driven, the better the ride becomes, and there is a marked absence of roll. One feels that the designer decided that he must have superb controllability at all costs, even if it meant abandoning American standards of riding comfort. Of course, he was right.

The other point is that the car's performance depends entirely on the full

EVIDENCE that the Fiat has an engine is afforded by the louvres in the tail of this intriguing and lively little car.

PHANTOM FIAT: The 600 "ghosted" to reveal its body-cum-chassis structure and disposition of main components.

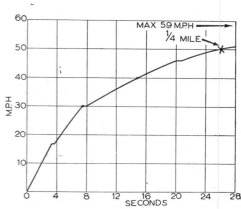

employment of the gear lever. As is usual with over-square engines, there is no "punch" at low revs., and the type of driver who hangs on to top speed will get a very poor response. The lovely little four-speed gearbox is simply made to be used, and it is a pleasure to handle the rigid central lever. One should run up to 25 m.p.h. on second speed and 40 m.p.h. on third, whereupon the diminutive machine becomes quite lively. The brakes work well, but tended to squeal at low speeds on the test car.

The engine is delightfully smooth, and will attain very high crankshaft speeds with no sign of valve bounce. It is far from noisy, only the fan and the gearbox being heard inside the car. The hum from the latter component, though audible on all gears, is by no means unpleasant. Road noise only obtrudes on certain types of rough surface.

The Fiat 600 is an entirely practical car for long journeys. I left Aintree during the evening after the Grand Prix, for instance, and drove all the way to Kent. My cruising speed of an indicated 60 m.p.h. (about 54 actual) was sufficient to cope with most of the opposition, and I was not overtaken more than half-a-dozen times during the whole trip. To be honest, I sometimes had the "clock" well past "70" on slightly favourable gradients. The car seemed to prefer to

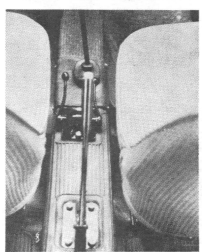

ALL IN A ROW: Positioned between the seats, on top of the control tunnel, are the gear lever, choke and starting controls and the handbrake.

be driven that way, and the fuel consumption did not fall below 48 m.p.g.

This fuel economy makes the car a most attractive proposition, and though it is a useful family hack, the handling qualities render driving a pleasure for solo flips. The cloth upholstery and rubber floor mats are functional, as is the very simplified dashboard. I do feel, however, that there would be a market for a de luxe model. This is just the sort of little machine that many a big car owner could find room for in his garage. As a second string to a big, luxury car, though, the interior has perhaps a touch of austerity, albeit the seats are comfortable and rubber mats are accepted for quite expensive cars on the Continent.

Comparisons are odious, but it is instructive to compare the performance of this car with the "babies" of a few years ago. To drive all the way back from Aintree in one of those would be a fate worse than death. Furthermore, the Fiat is so proportioned that it will outlast several of them without major repairs. Truly design advances, and in the small car sphere perhaps most of all.

The car tested was submitted by the Fiat agents, J. Davy, Ltd., Kensington High Street, W.8.

FORWARD - FOLDING rear seat squab (left) reveals a useful space for luggage.

STOWAWAY: (Above) Packed away in the rear boot, as if by an afterthought, is the very willing little 633 c.c. four-cylinder o.h.v. engine and its auxiliaries.

Wheels road test and analysis of the—

New-look
FIAT 600
Economy car

The Fiat "600" seats four comfortably, cruises at 50 m.p.h. and gives better than 40 m.p.g.

FIAT'S 600, released to car-hardened Europeans early this year at the Geneva Motor Show, has already startled doubters with its remarkable features of smoothness, economy, comfort—and above all its good performance.

There is no denying these features. The "600" seats four comfortably, has some room for luggage and occasional parcels, will cruise between 50 and 60 m.p.h., and will return an economical petrol consumption of better than 40 m.p.g. under hard use; yet, excepting the new popular European cabin-scooters, it is the smallest orthodox car made.

It is also relatively cheap: its Australian price is approximately £756 including Sales Tax.

The little "600" is the brain-child of Fiat designer Dr. Dante Giacosa, who searched around nearly three years ago for a small car to replace the familiar Fiat 500, or as it has been affectionately called, the "Mouse".

His early researches included front and rear-engined cars and front and rear-wheel drive. He examined air-cooled and opposed engines. Five different cars were built incorporating these ideas.

The one decided upon was the "600" as we now see it. It has a conventional water-cooled in-line-four engine which was rear mounted and drove the rear wheels. This model was tested for two years and then released to the public.

Those expecting a radical design must have been downcast because, except for the rear engine which has been common in Europe for years past (e.g. Volkswagen, Renault, Tatra etc.), the "600" is conventional in ideas right through.

In fact, the "600" resembles a scaled-down orthodox big car even to details.

The "600" is a two-door saloon. At first glance it looks as though it is a front-engined small car but the protruding bonnet is filled with a fuel tank, battery, and suspension layout. There is also space for a few small parcels under the bonnet.

The interior of the car is spacious enough to seat the front passengers in a reasonable degree of comfort and the rear ones to a lesser or more respect, depending on the positioning of the adjustable front seats. Access to the rear is over either front seat, which both have hinged squabs.

These seating positions are well up to travelling standards and no one should be unduly cramped on long journeys. There is enough room for moderately large drivers but a very tall one may find that the steering wheel will foul his knees.

We noticed that, while the steering wheel was set parallel to the centre axis of the car, the foot pedals were set considerably off centre to the left. This offsetting of the pedals is a little awkward at first but is something that is forgotten after a few miles.

Other controls are set between the two front seats. There is a floor mounted gearshift lever which is handily placed for fast use; behind it are two pull-up levers which control the starter and the choke; farther back again is the hand brake.

The engine is mounted behind the rear seat in the space usually reserved for a luggage boot. It is a small water-cooled unit which resembles that of the earlier Fiat 500. Hiwever it has a larger capacity and develops more power.

It develops 21.5 b.h.p. (an increase of 30% over the "500") and has a short stroke, essential in small-car engines if they are to be driven fast with reliability.

Its piston speed at 60 m.p.h. in top gear is only 1,860 ft./min. (2,500 ft./min. is generally accepted as the maximum piston speed for safe continuous operation.) This is a reduction of 170 ft./min. from the "500".

A final yardstick of comparison is that on a laden basis, the "600" produces 30 b.h.p. per ton compared with the "500's" 23 b.h.p. per ton.

Thes figures point up that on paper the "600" is a far livelier car than the "500." This is borne out on the road and, in fact, the "600" exceeds the performance one expects from such a small car.

The top speed was a true 60 m.p.h. on level road; acceleration for a standing ¼-mile at 26.9 (fastest) was good.

The "600" showed it was very comfortable cruising at 50-55 m.p.h. and could maintain this pace on all normal highway gradients. On several occasions we wound it up on a long downgrade and had no trouble exceeding the speedometer calibration. Even under this severe use the small engine gave no signs of distress.

We found that the car gave its best performance when driven on the gears to the speeds marked on the speedometer. These are: 1st, 15 m.p.h.; 2nd, 27 m.p.h.; and 3rd, 40 m.p.h. There is no gain in going over these speeds because the engine quickly loses power when they are exceeded. We drove the "600" at these recommended speeds on the gears throughout the test without any sign of distress.

Since the "600"'s power to weight ratio at 30 b.h.p. per laden ton is not high, speed falls off in top gear on steeper-than-average highway gradients. However, maximum speed can be maintained in 3rd gear even on quite steep grades, while 2nd gear will deal with almost any hill.

The "600's" road behaviour is lively, as one would expect from a small car, but is never troublesome.

It wanders on the straightway when buffeted by a gusty wind and oversteers willingly when thrown into tight corners. Both characteristics can be stopped readily with the light and sensitive steering. It is no trouble keeping the car

LUGGAGE OR PASSENGERS: If only two people are carried, the spare space can be used for luggage by folding down the rear squab. Notice how it forms a flat platform with the shelf.

THE WRAPS OFF: The 600 made its appearance at the Geneva show this year. It was a sensation — because small, get-up-and-go cars are popular in Europe.

ORTHODOX, BUT: Suspension, water cooled engine, control layout are all time tried. But Fiat weren't frightened to try a rear engine in combination with these.

be needed in the Fiat than in many other cars, because the hydraulic four-wheel system fitted gives independent braking on front and back wheels in the event of a hydraulic line or cylinder blowing out.

Pedal pressures needed for the hardest of stops were light, a point a woman driver will appreciate.

In addition, they were smooth. Progressive application of harder foot pressures brought an even increase in braking power. There was no sudden lurching stop with a fraction more pressure, as in some layouts.

Under our test we could induce no fade, a welcome feature and one expected from a car designed for Italian enthusiasm on steep mountain passes.

The car also turns in a phenomenally short circle which should make it a delight for women drivers in the suburbs or when shopping.

We were impressed with the "600's" good overall finish and the check-patterned cloth trim which gave the interior a light and airy look.

The headlamps are adequate for all night driving within the car's speed although the dipped position is a little cut off for fast speeds against oncoming traffic. We have noted this point with several other Continental cars but feel it is acceptable in the case of the "600" because its top speed is not high enough to get a driver into trouble. Nevertheless, we feel that speed should be slackened when dipping for oncoming cars.

Th car's tools are very complete even down to a metal chock for holding a wheel when the car is jacked on a hill. The car's construction is simple and service points are open enough not to trouble a person who intends to do his own maintainence.

straight and, once one is accustomed to it, the oversteering tendency can be ignored.

The "600" seems a far better car on loose gravel surfaces than it does on bitumen, possibly because the wheels tend to dig before adhesion is lost. It is stable in a straight line and there is no untoward tail sliding on corners. We had no trouble in driving the car flat out over many miles of loose country roads.

The suspension dealt well with all normal potholes and corrugations on back country roads and would not bottom unless the car was being driven obviously too fast for the circumstances.

However there was a characteristic nose and tail pitch of a short wheelbase car when cruising at steady speeds on a bitumen surface. This pitching is lively but never reaches sufficient amplitude to become bothersome. It disappears on gravel roads.

The "600's" general noise level is low but there is some wind when the car is cruised around 50 m.p.h. This wind noise is mainly caused by buffeting around the sliding windows when they are partly open. The noise is absent when the windows are closed.

These sliding windows are similar to the ones on the earlier "500" but open further and do not impede hand signals. A fair amount of wind blows into the car when they are fully open, but the rear passengers are protected by transparent plastic quarter-panes which are attached to the rear of the doors. The side windows at the rear are not adjustable.

It is worth noting that, like the earlier "500", the air seal is so good in the "600" that it is difficult to slam a door when the windows are closed. The doors are shut by pushing them to, which allows enough time for the air to escape from the body.

No dust whatever entered the car when it was driven on loosely pow-

dered roads, and the car is one of the two best in this respect we have ever tested.

A point we very much liked with the "600" was the roomy pocket for maps or even small parcels in each door.

We also liked the good seal of the forward mounted petrol tank. This is brought about mainly by circular baffles inside the tank which prevent surge. However, the tank has to be slowly filled to avoid throwback.

Another good point about the "600" was the braking. The handbrake was a real stopper, taking less than 50 feet to bring the car to rest at 30 m.p.h. Oddly, this comforting reserve is less likely to

TWO PLUS TWO: The manufacturer's pamphlets saying "room for four" mean what they say. These men are big and hefty, still have room. Two more can sit behind.

SPECIFICATION:

MAKE:
Fiat 600, 2-door, 4-passenger saloon. Our test car from Devon Motors Pty. Ltd., Queens Bridge Street, South Melbourne.

PRICE AND DELIVERY:
£769 (incl. Sales Tax); Immediate.

DIMENSIONS:
Overall: Wheelbase, 6' 6¾"; track: front 3' 9", rear 3' 8½"; length, 10' 6½"; width, 4' 6½"; height, 4' 4¾"; clearance, 6½"; dry weight, 11 cwt.

ENGINE:
4-cyl. ohv, 60 x 56 mm., capacity 633 c.c., comp. ratio 7.0 to 1, 21.5 bhp at 4,600 rpm, 1.23 bhp/sq. in. piston area. Single Weber carburettor with maze air-cleaner, full-flow oil filter. Radiator, 7¼ pt.; sump, 4¼ pt.; petrol tank, 6 gal.

TRANSMISSION:
Single dry-plate clutch; four-speed gearbox with synchromesh on top three ratios operated by central floor-mounted lever; spiral bevel final drive, ratio 5.375 to 1. Overall ratios: 4.82, 7.18, 10.05, 18.2, rev. 23.0. Top gear m.p.h.: 12.8 at 1,000 rpm; 80.5 at 2,500 ft./min. piston speed.

CHASSIS:
Platform chassis and welded all-steel body.

SUSPENSION:
I.f.s. by eccentrically clamped tranverse leaf and wishbones; i.r.s. by coils and swing axles. Telescopic shock absorbers.

BRAKES
4-wheel hydraulic operated by Fiat-Baldwin system; independent braking on front or rear wheels in the event of failure; mechanically operated transmission brake from central floor lever. Friction lining area, 67 sq. in. Ratio: 103 sq. in. per laden ton.

STEERING:
Worm and wheel; 3⅛ turns from lock to lock; turning circle 26½ ft.

ELECTRICAL:
12-volt ignition; 28-amp. hour battery; flashing light trafficators; automatic courtesy light; 40/45-watt headlamps.

WHEELS:
Pressed-steel disc wheels with four-stud attachment; 5.20-12 tyres, recommended pressures 17/23 lb/sq. in. front and rear.

PERFORMANCE:

TOP SPEED:
Average of test runs .... 59.8 m.p.h.
Fastest one way .... 60.0 m.p.h.

MAXIMUM SPEEDS:
At 5,800 rpm max.: 19.65 mph; 2nd, 35.67 mph; 3rd 49.9 mph; *Recommended shift points*: 1st, 15 mph; 2nd, 27 mph; 3rd, 40 mph.

MAXIMUM ENGINE PERFORMANCE:
18.7 bhp at 4,684 rpm (equivalent top gear speed, 60 mph); 25.5 lb/ft. torque at 2,342 rpm (equivalent top gear speed, 30 mph).

ACCELERATION:
Standing ¼-mile: Average of test runs, 27.0 sec; fastest one way, 26.8 sec.
Acceleration through gears: 0-10 mph, 1.8 sec; 0-20 mph, 4.6 sec; 0-30 mph, 9.2 sec; 0-40 mph, 17.0 sec; 0-50 mph, 30.3 sec.
Top gear acceleration: 10-30 mph, 15.6 sec; 20-40 mph, 13.7 sec; 30-50 mph, 14.0 sec.

BEST HILL CLIMBING:
Top gear: 1 in 13.9 at constant 28 mph.
3rd gear: 1 in 8.9 at constant 25.9 mph.
2nd gear: 1 in 6.5 at constant 20.5 mph.
1st gear: 1 in 5.5 at constant 14 mph.

BRAKING:
Footbrake at 30 mph in neutral, 35.2 ft.
Handbrake at 30 mph in neutral, 48.4 ft.
Fade, Nil.

SPEEDOMETER ERROR:
10 mph (indicated) — 9.4 mph (actual); 20 mph — 18.8 mph; 30 mph — 27.8 mph; 40 mph — 37.5 mph; 50 mph — 46.9 mph; 60 mph — 56.0 mph.

TEST WEIGHT:
Driver only, full tank, and gear, 13 cwt.
Distribution: Front, 5.6 cwt; rear, 7.4 cwt.

PETROL:
Hard driving, 44.5 mpg; highway cruising, 46.4 mpg. Premium grade fuel used.

FUN WITH  A MULTIPLA!

THE line of cars stopped, I stopped, but the chap behind was caught on the wrong foot. He motored briskly into my tail-lamps and shunted me into the car ahead. A rapid survey indicated that I would be without my car for a few days.

Alternative transport was essential, and I hastened to the establishment of the estimable Mr. Ryan. I had decided that it was time I renewed my acquaintance with the Fiat 600, but alas, all Mr. Ryan's 600's were bespoke, "except," said his deputy, "for a 600 bus, and that would hardly suit you." On the contrary, I felt, a bus might suit me quite well, and might even be fun. So it was that some twenty minutes later I sallied forth at the wheel of a Fiat Multipla six-seater.

The curious sensation induced by sitting over the front wheel, my feet about two inches from the front bumper, took about a mile to wear off, and soon I was handling my bus as nonchalantly as any of my colleagues of C.I.E., greatly aided by the fabulous forward vision. When I glanced over my shoulder I beheld umpteen cubic feet of space, while away in the distance the tiny engine hummed contentedly.

Apart from its unusual aspect, the driving position is quite satisfactory. The steering wheel is nicely placed, and the pedal positions, if not ideal, hardly justify criticism in a vehicle of this nature. The steering column passes between the driver's legs, but this causes no annoyance at all. I would prefer to be an inch or two further away from things, but the bench front seat is not adjustable, though the slope of its squab can be altered. The only detail which really irritated me was the low level of the top of the windscreen, a fault common to all current-model Fiats.

The most serious failing of the Multipla is one that might easily be guessed—lack of power. Just how the 21 b.h.p. engine can move the outfit at all is a mystery; it is only to be expected that it doesn't move it very rapidly. Admittedly, my Multipla was very new, and running-in speeds had to be observed, but even within this restriction it was evident that the performance is moderate. A maximum speed of some 55 m.p.h. is available, but the acceleration rate is such that in most circumstances the cruising speed will not greatly exceed 40.

The lack of power would not matter so much, but for the deficiencies of the gear-change. The gearbox itself is as good as Fiat boxes always are, with four perfectly chosen ratios, but the lever travels a considerable distance between gears, and on my machine the movement was stiff and rough. This became annoying, when one had to put in so much time at the lever —going home one evening, I counted 23 gear-changes in five miles, including two traffic-light restarts.

But, as readers of previous dissertations of mine will be aware, my standards of judgment are not everybody's, and most potential Multipla owners will be more interested in its utilitarian virtues. Here, it is difficult to restrain enthusiasm. Never before in motoring history has a maker produced a vehicle with so high a ratio of living space to total space as is achieved in the Multipla, and on this ground alone it would appeal to me, as I am growing increasingly averse to cars with great bulbous bonnets and wings, containing only air. In the Multipla there is not an inch of waste space, and the machinery occupies an incredibly small amount of room.

I believe that the Multipla is available with alternative seating arrangements; mine had, behind the bench front seat, four single seats, quite comfortable and with ample room for legs, elbows, heads and the like. These seats folded down to form a clear space about five feet long by four feet wide. Access to the rear is by two huge doors, and one could almost walk through the thing; indeed, as a friend of mine remarked, you could hold a party in there.

The steering is high-geared, accurate and pleasant. It is a little too lacking in sensitivity, too "dead," for my taste; this is probably due to the damping effect of the tortuous linkage required to get backwards to the front wheels. The roadholding and handling are excellent. The polar moment of inertia is high, the driver at the front being utilised by the designer to balance the engine at the rear. As a result, the car is very steady on the straight, with no tendency whatever to wander. Further, it is reasonably free from pitching, the centre seats, "Row B," as it were, being best in this respect. On corners it imparts a reassuring feeling of security, due to a faint understeer and negligible roll. A full house of people did not affect its stability.

I cannot recall having driven a four-wheeled vehicle which was more manœuvrable. The turning circle is small, the steering gear lends itself to full-lock work, and the visibility in all directions is amazing. When parking, you can virtually see your front bumper as it touches the bumper of the car ahead!

The Multipla is not particularly silent, but the noise level is quite acceptable. The gearbox can be heard, especially in the lower ratios, and there is considerable body drumming over cobblestones. But there were no rattles whatever in my example, nor, incidentally, were there any draughts. The bodywork appears to be sturdily built, and the standard of assembly, upholstery and paintwork was really good.

I understand that in Italy sales of the Multipla have not come up to expectations. Two reasons have been advanced for this, its ungainly appearance and its low safety factor on head-on collisions. I think that it has the true beauty of functionalism. It is built to do a job, and where ever style has clashed with fitness-for-purpose, style has given way. The result is a sensible and efficient vehicle, and to my weary eye the Multipla is far better-looking than some of the gilded palaces which cruise past it.

It is true that the driver is exceptionally well-placed to observe the effect of a collision, but somehow I wasn't perturbed by this. It seems to me that you don't stand much chance in a head-on crash these days, no matter what sort of car you are driving. In this regard, the modest performance of the Multipla may be a hidden blessing.

I was pleasantly surprised by my mileage-per-gallon, but I shall not reveal the figure. I didn't cover enough miles to permit an accurate check, and my model was new and tight. Suffice it to say that one could hardly get less than 40 m.p.g., and main-road cruising, lightly laden, should produce well over 45.

I would advise those who are in the market for a station wagon to take a good look at the Multipla, and to those who sell Multiplas I would suggest that they take their prospect for a trial run of at least fifteen miles. A brief run will leave an impression of a curious, fussy, little machine; a little longer is needed to appreciate its many admirable virtues. Perhaps the best comment on this enchanting barouche was made by a friend who said: "Don't you wish you had the sort of job which would justify buying one?" a remark with which I heartily agreed

—PADDY HALION.

Fiat Fever

In spite of stiff competition, the 600 and 1100 Fiats are in demand all over Europe. Here's why.

PHOTOS COURTESY OF F.I.A.T.

By D. M. BARTLEY

NINE OUT OF TEN cars sold in Italy last year were Fiats. As the most expensive automobile the company produces costs about $4,-700, and accounts for less than ½ of one per cent of their sales, one can't say people buy Fiats for prestige purposes. Yet "prestige" people drive them—presidents of major companies, diplomats, movie stars. Although Fiat hasn't had anything to do with racing cars from 1924 until its agreement this fall to help finance Ferrari's "scuderia," the heads of both the Maserati and Ferrari firms, as well as any number of race drivers, drive Fiats.

When one begins to look for the reasons for the incredible success of this generally unspectacular-looking line of automobiles, it's easy to find many people who can give you

all sorts of negative ones. They say, "Fiat is by far the largest auto manufacturer in Italy, the only one which really mass-produces cars according to American standards, so they don't really have any competition." This is partially true, but there are some 15 other established auto makers in the country. Some of them are undeniably very small, highly specialized firms making what amounts to "custom" cars. Nonetheless, they continue to flourish but not at the expense of Fiat . . . their total output is only 11 per cent of the total market.

Then you'll be told, "Fiat is government subsidized." This is not true. It is a privately owned company, with a stockholder's setup similar to that of Chrysler or GM.

"Italian import duty on foreign-

made cars is so high that no one can tell whether or not they'd actually be able to compete with American, British or French-made cars," someone else might tell you. The Italian foreign-car import tariffs are astronomically high, but no higher than those of the other nations mentioned. There is also the inescapable fact that every single Fiat which is *exported* is snapped up as soon as it's available. There is a six-months' backlog of unfilled orders in some countries. This means that Fiat *is* competing with foreign-made cars in their own countries and at a price hiked high enough to include the import taxes and transportation as well as a normal dealer profit.

The smallest and newest Fiat, in production less than a year, has already proved it can handle compe-

Tiny "600" (10½ ft. over-all) has light-weight (238 lbs.), sturdy, easily-accessible engine at rear, is superb on steep mountain roads.

Maximum utilization of space permits all passengers to sit cradled between the front and rear wheels. Extra-wide doors give easy access.

Fiat test driver, G. Peyrolero, takes "600" through 90° corner at almost 40 mph with surprisingly little lean and easily-controlled drift.

Compact design and good engineering make "600" a natural for special bodies. This one, seen at Turin Show last spring, is by Pinin Farina.

tition from such established sturdies as Volkswagen, the 4 CV Renault and even the new 2 CV Citroen in the economy-car field. In spite of sizeable export activities elsewhere, though, top company officials will readily admit that it isn't worth the trouble involved to them to set up a sales and servicing organization in the United States. They don't need —and maybe can't even supply cars for—U.S. sales.

Do they make cheap cars? Not relatively speaking. For example, the Fiat 600, their lowest priced car, costs $945. The 2 CV Citroen, nowhere nearly so nicely finished or neatly styled, costs $976 in France.

How, then, can one explain the success of Fiat? As it is almost impossible to locate any new model Fiats in this country, this was one of the many things we went to Europe to find out. A call to the main Fiat factory in Turin was our first stop in Italy. On the flat plains of the Po River valley and in the rugged mountains which rise, sudden and sheer, from the floor of the valley to circumscribe a giant ring around this busy, clean city which is the Detroit of Italy, we put in a substantial amount of driving time on the two lowest-priced—and most popular—Fiats, the "600" and the "1100." And we found plenty of answers.

Having read a number of rave notices about the new "600," our first reaction on getting into the car was to try to ferret out its flaws. It was pretty fallow ferreting. The two front bucket seats are comfortable, adjustable and give adequate support. The positions of all controls are excellent. The ignition and a choke are located on the low drive-shaft ridge between the seats and so set up that they can be used simultaneously with one hand. The short stick shift is just forward of the starter, and the hand brake behind it is more accessible than most.

Dash controls are sparse though adequate and come easily to hand. Pedals are not miniatures as they are on some other small cars, and are, except for rather meager room for the left foot between clutch pedal and the front, left wheel housing, very well placed.

Possibly the most surprising aspect of the car to an American accustomed to the 17- or 18-ft. length of our cars, or to anyone familiar with the Fiat Topolino, predecessor of the "600," is to climb into this tiny bug which is only 10½ ft. long overall and realize that there is plenty of room—leg room, ceiling height, arm room and even a sense of room to breathe. One is neither cramped nor does one have any sensation of being so.

Driving the "600" on flat terrain is a pleasure. The four-forward-speed shift is responsive enough to make quite fast changes, and the synchronizing and overlapping ratios assure that, with proper clutching, they are almost unnoticeable except for a slight change in engine hum. The car's top speed is something just around the 63 mph figure (speedometer error is very small), which seems slow when one thinks of the 100+ mph of our cars, but keep in mind that you can cruise for hours at maximum speed in this 1,200 lb. buggy. We drove the car flat out for some distance and can easily believe that the engine could be used in this way for 10 or 12 straight hours day after day without any trouble of any kind.

Another surprising aspect to the "600" is the lack of noise—wind, gear or tire.

Acceleration from 0 to anything is not, of course, spectacular (we made 0 to 30 in 9.2 sec., 0 to 50 in 34.5 sec., and 30 to 50 in 30.5 sec.) but is quite amazing in terms of the 21½-hp engine. The excellent gearing, a result of long testing in the north Italian mountain passes and the long, flat *autostrada* of the valley plains, largely contributes to the "600's" more-than-adequate-for-practical-purposes performance in this area. One can get away mighty fast in first gear from a dead stop, can accelerate even while climbing relatively steep grades, and by shifting down to 3rd, can move up nicely to pass at speed. With a fully loaded car, road variations, even on low terrain, may require shifts down to third to maintain a 60 mph cruising speed, but speed can be maintained, and shifts are smooth as mink.

Just for the record, I tried the "600" along about one straight mile of mountain climbing, which included gradients varying between 10 and 20 per cent, without leaving third gear. She kept going, losing a very little bit of speed at the steepest points but never really laboring.

Latest variation of stock "1100" is this handsome, open "TV" (fast tourer) roadster, only recently available. Engine has been "hotted."

Lowest-priced "1100" sells for equivalent of $1,473 in Italy, offers exceptional handling, maneuverability, comfort, economy and long life.

Small edition of American station wagon is "Family 1100" with its 5 doors, greatly increased rear-seat space and fold-down backrest.

Fiat Fever

One of the things which is most bothersome when driving some "economy" cars in the mountains is that one must lose such great amounts of speed in negotiating the innumerable hairpin bends—and it is, of course, impossible to regain such losses as the gradient remains steep. The marvelous cornering of the "600" completely eliminates this problem. You can scoot around the sharpest bend, even to the point of a little breakaway, but maintain speed and absolute control with ease. Bumps, bad surfaces, wet pavement? No hindrance at all! And in spite of the enormous difference in size, placement of controls, hp, etc., within a half-hour I felt as if I'd driven the little hot-shot for years.

Along with the gearing, the brakes contribute largely to one's confidence in the "600." Coming down some miles of steep mountain roads, I applied the brakes repeatedly and hard. Each time they pulled the car up firmly and evenly, and after many applications, there was absolutely no sign of fade. The hand brake, which is on the transmission, is also good.

Steering is quick (with 3½ turns lock to lock) but not too much so. It is light enough to compare favorably with American power steering, probably as a result of a number of things—its high and overlapping steering ratios, shorter wheelbase, low over-all weight, and light front end weight. Rear-engined, the Fiat 600 is naturally a little tail-heavy, its weight distribution being 39.2% front and 60.8% rear. But a particularly ingenious rear-suspension set-up gives it a degree of rear-end steering which counteracts the slight oversteer tendency which is innate in any rear-engined car.

Along with good performance, durability, adequate space and all of the other features mentioned above, for your $945 you also get a very fine finish with attention given to paint and trim and interior good details (we especially liked the large door pockets, the top rims of which serve nicely as inside pulls), an excellent defroster, heat and ventilating system, sliding windows with draft deflectors, a rear seat which folds down flat to provide enormous luggage space if desired, and a well-arranged front compartment which contains luggage space, the battery, spare tire, and filler cap for the fuel tank. (The six gallon tank capacity will take you some 275 miles without a refill as the "600" goes about 47 mpg.) And the rear engine is so positioned as to make it as easy to get at as that of a Model T.

The "1100" proved to be more of the same good thing in a sort of grown-up, "middle-size bear" edition. There was, of course, substantially more room for passengers, the stock four-door we drove comfortably seating five adults. The fully upholstered banquette seats, more extensive dashboard controls and dials, plenty of back-seat leg room and steering column gear shift are some of the interior details which make one aware that this is far from an austere "economy" car. Whereas it is always necessary to keep in mind the small size and relatively tiny engine capacity of the "600" when singing its praises, no such qualification need be made for its big brother.

Everything favorable said thus far about the "600" holds true to a larger degree with the "1100." The latter is, of course, faster (top speed is a true 75 mph for the model B "1100," a rousing 85 mph on the "1100 TV"), more spacious and somewhat more luxurious, as has been mentioned. A conventional front-engine car, the "1100" has not the slightest oversteer tendency, at least so far as we could tell in the relatively short time spent in the car. In almost all other aspects—comfort, good ride, sure, long-lasting brakes, light, responsive steering, durability (we have yet to meet an *unhappy* "1100" 'owner), economy (Fiat, which, like all Italian car manufacturers, underrates its products in top speed, acceleration, gas mileage, etc., claims — miles per gallon for the "1100"), and just plain good engineering of all components from the chassis to the location of the dashboard turn indicator, the "1100" just can't be seriously criticized. It might also be worth mentioning that the top speed and cruising speed of the "1100" are, as they are on the "600," the same.

Once one has accustomed oneself to the larger size and new control locations of the "1100," there is really only one area where the driver is made sharply aware that he is no longer in the smaller car—available power.

Over the same flat, then mountainous terrain that we had traveled in the "600," we went with the "1100.' Most startling, especially when you consider its somewhat mediocre acceleration figures (0 to 30: 5.5 sec.; 0 to 50: 16.7 sec.; 0 to 75: 50 sec.), was the ability of the "1100" to power straight up to the steepest imaginable mountain roads. For example, with one of the excellent Fiat test drivers, G. Raimondo, behind the wheel, the "1100" maintained a steady 70 kph (almost 44 mph) in third gear for the entire distance of a seven-kilometer-long climb, including any number of completely unbanked hairpin turns, at least one of which was on a 22 per cent grade. The fact that Mr. Raimondo was thoroughly familiar with every bump in the road doesn't detract from the performance of the car.

Why are Fiats successful? It would be difficult to obtain a more definite answer than our several days with Fiat provided. The cars sell well because they are good quality, reasonable in cost, economical to use and maintain, superbly engineered, exceedingly comfortable, beautifully finished, and, in a price range which is within sight for great numbers of people, provide every necessary convenience. ●

SPECIFICATIONS—FIAT 600

ENGINE: 4 cylinder, overhead valves; bore, 60 mm; stroke, 56 mm; total displacement, 633 cc (38.63 cu. in.); max. bhp, 21.5 at 4,600 rpm; maximum torque, 28.9 lb./ft. at 2,800 rpm; compression ratio, 7 to 1. Single downdraft carburetor; ignition, 12 volt. Mph per 1,000 rpm in top gear, 12.79.

TRANSMISSION and STEERING: Dry, single-plate clutch; over-all gear ratios: top, 4.88; third, 7.13; second, 11; first, 18.2 to 1. Hypoid bevel final drive, ratio 5.37 to 1. Worm and sector two-piece track rod steering, 28-ft. turning circle.

SUSPENSION: Front, independent transverse leaf spring and single wishbones; rear, independent coil springs and wide-angle, semi-trailing links; telescopic hydraulic dampers front and rear.

BRAKES: Hydraulic; drum diameter front and rear is 7.28 in.; width front and rear, 1.18 in.; lining area front and rear, 33.5 sq. in.; transmission parking brake on rear of gearbox.

DIMENSIONS: Wheelbase, 78¾ in.; front tread, 45 in.; rear tread, 44⅜ in.; over-all length, 126½ in.; width, 54 in.; height, 52¾ in.; dry weight, 1,274 lbs. Tires, 5.20x12 in.

SPECIFICATIONS—FIAT 1100

ENGINE: 4 cylinders, overhead valves; bore, 68 mm; stroke, 75 mm; total displacement, 1,089 cc; maximum hp, 36 at 4,400 rpm; compression ratio, 6.7 to 1; single downdraft carburetor; ignition, 12 volt.

TRANSMISSION and STEERING: Dry, single-plate clutch mounted on flexible hub; 4 forward speeds and reverse; rear axle ratio, 4.3 to 1. Worm and roller steering with independent symmetrical steering rods for each wheel.

SUSPENSION: Front, swinging radius arms, helical springs, hydraulic, double-acting, telescopic shocks, stabilizing bar; rear, flat leaf springs, stabilizer, same shocks as front.

BRAKES: Hydraulic, 4-wheel; emergency hand brake on transmission.

DIMENSIONS: Wheelbase, 92 in.; front tread, 48 in.; rear tread, 47¾ in. length, 148½ in.; width, 57⅓ in.; height, 55¼ in.

sedan

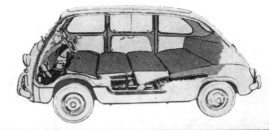

SOME OF THE NEWEST contenders for a slice of the rapidly growing market for small cars in this country have been tossed in the ring by the Fiat organization of Italy. This manufacturer is no neophyte in the car building business, and a brief inspection and short ride in one of these unique little vehicles should convince the most skeptical that this is a serious and well-founded effort to get on the bandwagon.

Our first inspection of the 600 Standard two-door sedan made us immediately aware of the high level of workmanship which is incorporated into this car. The doors close with a satisfying clunk, body panels fit, and there are no rag-tag ends on either the exterior or interior such as loose seals and trim. The entire keynote seems to follow a functional simplicity which avoids austerity because of the excellent finish.

Opening the rear engine compartment should provoke loud cheers from mechanics, service station attendants and do-it-yourselfers. The usual under-hood clutter is pleasantly absent. The radiator is conveniently offset to one side and service points are probably more accessible than in any other car. The engine is an ohv four displacing 38.6 cubic inches which develops 22 bhp at 4600 rpm. The transmission and differential are mounted as a unit with the engine, and the final drive is direct to the swing rear axles and independently sprung wheels.

One of two big surprises we got from the 600 was the ride. It might be expected that a car with a wheelbase of less than 79 inches and with 12-inch wheels would offer something less than ideal. If we cannot describe this ride as ideal, we can honestly say it is great. It is firm enough to avoid sloppy wallowing and yet it smooths out really rough roads. Sharp and deep chuck holes that you might expect would bounce you against the roof are disposed of with a gentle little thump. There is practically no dive during hard braking and the body stays level in the sharpest corners.

A second surprise comes in the handling. The car is admittedly no bomb and it is doubtful that you would attempt power slides and other such driving capers in it. Cornering at full throttle leaves you with a sense of control and security. In tight corners it is possible to set up a gentle but controllable drift. If you break the rear wheels loose in a gravel road turn, corrective action on the wheel is positive and responsive.

To sum it up, this is a fine little car that puts many of its bigger brothers to shame in many departments including the 39 mpg we averaged under definitely uneconomical driving conditions.

THE MULTIPLA is available as a six-passenger station wagon or a four- to five-seater, sleeper-type vehicle.

FRONT SEAT passenger space looks crowded but there is ample toe room under inside mounted spare and tools.

multipla

ONE OF THE CRITICISMS leveled at very small cars has been that they lack interior space for the comfortable seating of passengers and the stowage of luggage or other impedimenta. Fiat solved this space problem and went several steps further in the forthright and functional design of the 600 Multipla. As its name connotes, this is an all-service vehicle which seats four to six adults, and can fulfill most of the requirements placed on a station wagon or camper-type vehicle.

With minor modifications, the Multipla chassis is similar to that in the 600 sedan. Despite ███████ weight distribution resulting from the seating ar███████ unable to detect any departure from the s███████lling qualities which enthused us in the se███████ was covered with just the driver aboard ███████g on all types of roads ranging from sea███████75 feet. We vote for this one as a happ███████f machinery.

PHOTOS BY BOB D'OLIVO

DRIVER'S SEAT is directly over front wheel in Multipla, with high position affording excellent all-around vision.

23

FIAT 600
MULTIPLA

The coachwork is unusual but effective. The front compartment has doors opening at their forward edges, and entry must be made by stepping up over the front wheels : but the wide rear doors enable bulky objects to be loaded with little difficulty

FIAT'S Multipla is one of the most original and ingenious small car designs to appear since the war. Within its limited overall dimensions, it provides more interior space than any other vehicle of comparable size ; one cannot say "more than any other similar vehicle," because in many respects this design is unique. It may be described as a small station wagon in which, because the engine is at the rear, the loading doors have been placed at the sides. On the other hand, in the absence of a power unit in the nose, the front seats can be located over the front wheels, leaving the maximum space behind them for seating or goods as desired. The floor area is large, low and uninterrupted by tunnels or frame members, and is a part of the platform frame.

In elevation and plan the outline of the Multipla is no more than a modified rectangle, yet the car has an attractive, chunky look, appearing neither outlandish nor even particularly unconventional.

When in use as a family car—and not only Italians have large families—five or six children may be seated in quick-release chairs, available as optional extras, behind father and mother. During the week, with the seats removed, and carriage of goods the main concern, father's cheese, wine, pottery or other goods can be loaded easily through the wide doors on each side. Getting into the high front seats is not quite so convenient, because it entails climbing over the front wheel arches,

but the doors are just wide enough to make this practical for the ordinary person. These frontal arrangements resemble closely those of much larger lorries and commercial vehicles with buried engines and flat fronts, familiar in most countries.

The standard seating arrangement, as fitted to the car tested, provides a rather more comfortable folding rear bench seat for two or three, and there is considerable luggage space behind it.

For good reasons of standardization, the 600 c.c. power unit and transmission components of the Multipla are largely in common with those of the Fiat 600. The two little vehicles are intended for different purposes; however, as one is a utility version of the other in many respects some comparison is justified so that it may be seen to what extent the Multipla buyer may lose in performance and m.p.g. as a result of plumping for extra space.

Such differences in performance and economy as exist are to be expected, having the different characters of the models in mind. They amount to no more than 3.5 m.p.h. in top speed, but the m.p.g. range is 38.3 to 45 with the Multipla, as against 45 to 57 m.p.g. with the normal saloon, and the acceleration difference from a standing start to 50 m.p.h. is slightly more than 15sec.

Of necessity the steering arrangements are different, the steering column of the Multipla being universally jointed at mid-point, to carry its drive back under the driver's seat.

The amount of glass provides good visibility for all occupants. The fuel tank as well as the engine is at the rear, the lockable filler cap being near the waistline. The two-colour finish helps to reduce the humpiness of the appearance. Twelve-inch wheels are fitted and they carry 5.20-in tyres

The lower section of the column is placed—not altogether conveniently—between the driver's feet. The front passenger's leg room is limited because the spare wheel is mounted over his or her lap. (One special-bodied Multipla has the wheel outside and encased on the nose; this seems to be a practical rearrangement.)

Because heavier loads can and are expected to be carried on the Multipla, additional braking capacity is provided and the independent front suspension has been redesigned.

In attempting to form an impression of the Multipla, it is well to bear in mind that, despite its tiny engine, the

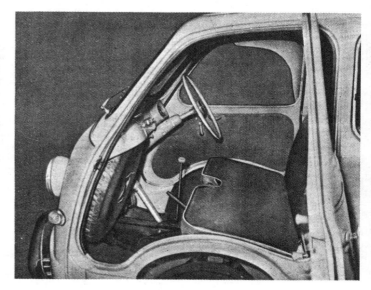

The forward seating position for the driver has made necessary an unusual steering column layout, with the lower section passing rearward between the driver's feet. The spare wheel is mounted inside the front compartment, and within its cover dusters and other oddments can be stowed. There is no provision for housing personal oddments

The side lights are incorporated in the head lamps, below which the winking indicators protrude so that they are readily seen from the side. Deep, strong overriders anchored at top and bottom give good protection. The radiator grille takes in air for the heating system

The engine is the now familiar unit as used in the 600 saloon. All items checked in routine servicing are easily reached. The radiator and cowled fan are mounted on the right

vehicle is designed as load carrier—not as touring car. In the light of this consideration its performance, normally laden, on long journeys becomes all the more surprising. With its low axle ratio, it has not the top gear maximum speed of the normal saloon; on long, straight stretches, therefore, its cruising speed is also lower. But its top gear performance—hill-climbing, acceleration and low speed pulling—is good. Inevitably one needs to use the gear box frequently in hilly country or when in a hurry even when lightly laden.

Seating is comfortable, and the driver and front seat passenger have excellent forward vision. With the engine tucked away at the rear, one appreciates the feeling of remoteness from mechanical devices. Whatever the pros and cons of a forward mounted engine as a protection, some front occupants of the Multipla may feel a little vulnerable until they have become accustomed to the design (as do the occupants of commercial vehicles). The interior is light, roomy and adequately furnished.

Occupants of the front seats do, in fact, suffer somewhat from pitching on a poor surface—owed to the positioning of the front seats almost directly above the front wheels. The motion is not troublesome, and on good roads one is not aware of it. It takes a very short time to become accustomed to the unusual driving position, and after a few miles one realizes that the Multipla can be cornered just as accurately as any other car with an orthodox driving position.

After a short stretch of open road the driver finds that being "out in front" does not affect his control of the car —even in slippery conditions. In spite of its relatively high build the car shows very little tendency to roll, even when fully laden. In dense traffic it comes into its own, the forward visibility enabling one to wriggle the Multipla through narrow gaps, and take advantage of every opportunity that offers; parking in congested areas, too, becomes much easier.

At normal speeds, particularly when laden, the Multipla shows a degree of understeer, but this does develop into slight oversteer when the sharper corners are taken fast. The transition is not caused by pronounced roll-oversteer and is not sudden. It is unlikely to worry the driver once he has become accustomed to it. The steering is light and accurate, and the lock is particularly good.

The gear lever is centrally mounted, on the floor. As with so many rear-engined cars, the movement of the lever is so smooth and precise that one is not reminded of the fact that it is several feet away from the gear box itself.

Occasionally, engagement of first gear at a standstill was a little sticky, but otherwise gear changing is quick and easy—an important point in mountainous regions where the gear lever has to be used frequently. There is synchromesh on the upper three ratios.

On the car tested there was a noticeable gear whine at almost any speed. The high-pitched sound was not loud, but sufficiently persistent possibly to irritate the occupants of the car on a long run. This slight noise is the more noticeable because of the remoteness of the engine and lack of sound from this quarter. The little four-cylinder unit proved an easy starter in all conditions, but it took longer to warm up than most. Even when cold, it did not spit or hesitate, but the pulling power was modest until the running temperature had been reached.

The four forward ratios are well chosen. In first gear, a heavy load can be taken—slowly—up the steepest gradient, and in this gear the car gets away smartly. Very nearly 30 m.p.h. is available in second, although the average driver would change up at about 22 m.p.h. The most satisfactory cruising speed is a little over 40 m.p.h., and this is reached quickly in third—although, here again, the average driver would probably make his change at 30 m.p.h. or thereabouts.

On the speedometer are lines that indicate the recommended maximum speeds in each of the gears. Allowing for speedometer inaccuracy, these marks are at true speeds of 15.5, 20 and 33 m.p.h. on first, second and third. They seem well within the capabilities of the engine, and are reached quickly on level ground, even when the car is carrying four people.

The car's all-out maximum speed is in the region of 55 m.p.h., and though it takes a little time to reach, the car is perfectly happy at this pace, even on indifferent road surfaces. When the car is carrying no more than the driver,

FIAT 600 MULTIPLA

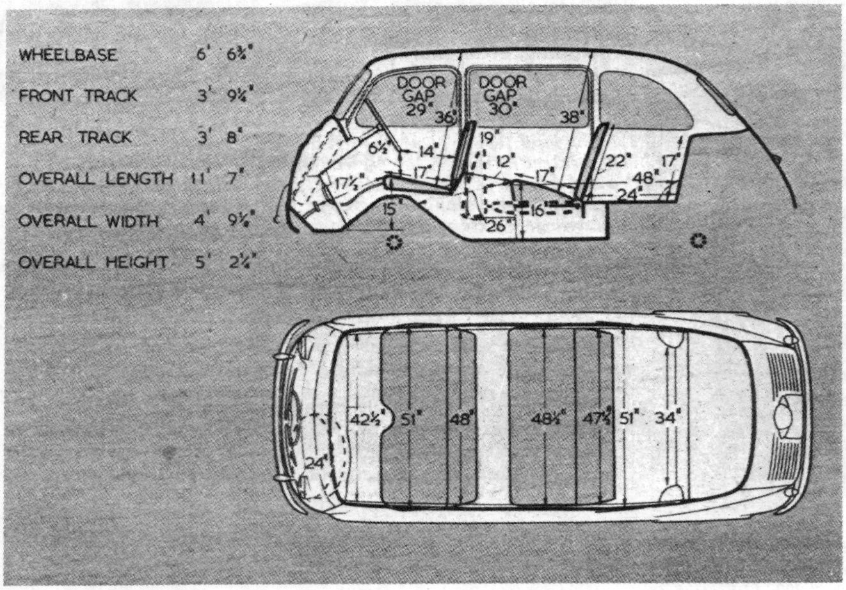
WHEELBASE 6' 6¾"
FRONT TRACK 3' 9¼"
REAR TRACK 3' 8"
OVERALL LENGTH 11' 7"
OVERALL WIDTH 4' 9⅝"
OVERALL HEIGHT 5' 2¼"
DOOR GAP 29"
DOOR GAP 30"

Measurements in these ¼in to 1ft scale body diagrams are taken with the driving seat in the central position of fore and aft adjustment and with the seat cushions uncompressed

PERFORMANCE

ACCELERATION: from constant speeds.

Speed Range, Gear Ratios and Time in sec.

M.P.H.	5.38 to 1	8.22 to 1	13.21 to 1	21.75 to 1
10—30..	22.5	12.0	—	—
20—40..	23.8	17.2	—	—

From rest through gears to:

M.P.H.	sec
30	12.3
40	23.8
50	50.7

Standing quarter mile, 29.7 sec.

SPEEDS ON GEARS:

Gear		M.P.H. (normal and max.)	K.P.H. (normal and max.)
Top ..	**(mean)**	54.0	86.9
	(best)	55.0	88.5
3rd ..	.. ..	31.0—43.5	49.9—70.0
2nd ..	.. ..	22.0—29.0	35.4—46.7
1st ..	.. ..	12.0—18.0	19.3—29.0

TRACTIVE RESISTANCE: 50 lb per ton at 10 M.P.H.

TRACTIVE EFFORT:

	Pull (lb per ton)	Equivalent Gradient
Top	85	1 in 26.4
Third	163	1 in 13.4
Second..	255	1 in 8.75

BRAKES:

Efficiency	Pedal Pressure (lb)
36.1 per cent	25
65.1 per cent	50
92.85 per cent	75

FUEL CONSUMPTION:
39.4 m.p.g. overall for 362 miles (7.2 litres per 100 km).
Approximate normal range 38.3–45 m.p.g. (7.36–6.3 litres per 100 km).
Fuel, Ordinary grade.

WEATHER:
Air temperature 49 deg F.
Acceleration figures are the means of several runs in opposite directions.
Tractive effort and resistance obtained by Tapley meter.
Model described in *The Autocar* of January 20, 1956.

SPEEDOMETER CORRECTION: M.P.H.

Car speedometer	10	20	30	40	50
True speed	14	19	28	39	49

DATA

PRICE (basic), **£532.**
British purchase tax, **£267 7s.**
Total (in Great Britain), **£799 7s.**

ENGINE: Capacity: 633 c.c. (38.54 cu in).
Number of cylinders: 4.
Bore and stroke: 60 × 56 mm (2.36 × 2.2in).
Valve gear: o.h.v., pushrods.
Compression ratio: 7 to 1.
B.H.P.: 21.5 at 4,600 r.p.m. (B.H.P. per ton laden 25.8).
Torque: 28.9 lb ft at 2,800 r.p.m.

WEIGHT: (with 5 gals fuel), 14½ cwt (1,624 lb).
Weight distribution (per cent): F, 46.5; R, 53.5.
Laden as tested: 17½ cwt (1,960 lb).
Lb per c.c. (laden): 3.1.

BRAKES: Type: Fiat-Baldwin.
Method of operation: Hydraulic.
Drum dimensions: F, 8.7in diameter; 1.85in wide. R, 8.7in diameter; 1.85in wide.
Lining area: F, 54.6 sq in. R, 54.6 sq in (124.8 sq in per ton laden).

TYRES: 5.20—12in.
Pressures (lb per sq in): F, 24; R, 28 (normal).

TANK CAPACITY: 6 Imperial gallons (warning light when only approx. one gallon left).
Oil sump, 5 pints.
Cooling system, 11½ pints (inclusive of heater).

TURNING CIRCLE: 28ft 10in (L and R).
Steering wheel turns (lock to lock): 3¼.

DIMENSIONS: Wheelbase: 6ft 6¾in.
Track: F, 3ft 9¼in; R, 3ft 8in.
Length (overall): 11ft 7in.
Height: 5ft 2¼in.
Width: 4ft 9⅝in.
Ground clearance: 5½in.
Frontal area: 18 sq ft (approximately).

ELECTRICAL SYSTEM: 12-volt; 28 ampère-hour battery.
Head lights: Double dip; 40–45 watt bulbs.

SUSPENSION: Front, Independent, coil springs. Anti-roll bar. Rear, Independent, coil springs.

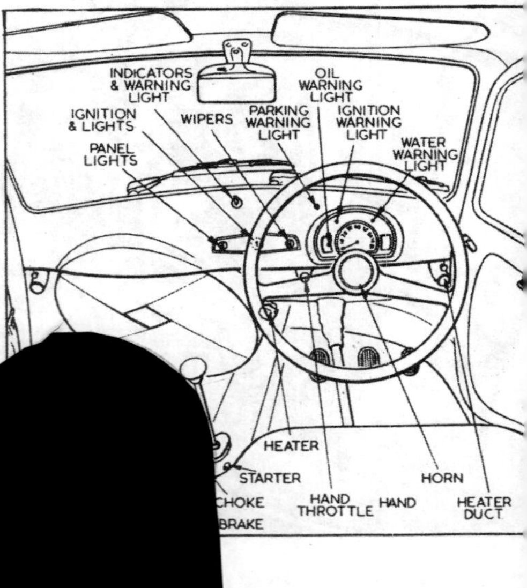
INDICATORS & WARNING LIGHT
OIL WARNING LIGHT
IGNITION & LIGHTS
WIPERS
PARKING WARNING LIGHT
IGNITION WARNING LIGHT
WATER WARNING LIGHT
PANEL LIGHTS
HEATER
STARTER
CHOKE
BRAKE
HAND THROTTLE
HAND
HORN
HEATER DUCT

a speed of 50 m.p.h. can be maintained on main roads of normal gradient.

The car's momentum will carry it up the minor gradients without much loss of speed. On sharper slopes the weight in relation to engine size, coupled in minor degree with the flat front, make the use of the high third desirable if not absolutely necessary. When it is fully laden, however, it is necessary to use third gear even on gentle slopes. This is not surprising, for with so small a power unit the

In its normal position the rear seat can accommodate three people quite comfortably. With the seats stowed to accommodate additional luggage, the total carrying space is extraordinarily good. When the seat is rearranged for passengers there is still considerable luggage room at the rear

great difference between unladen and laden weight is bound to have a marked effect.

Even for maximum retardation, brake pedal pressure need only be light—and this applies equally to the laden state. Response was excellent, and although there was a slight judder occasionally, the car did not pull to either side. The larger brakes fitted to this vehicle, compared with the 600 saloon, include more robust, finned drums. No fade was experienced during the test, and it is likely that braking efficiency would be maintained even when, with a fully laden car, making the best possible time in mountainous country.

Fuel consumption of the Multipla is of particular importance and in this respect the car shows up well. Normal driving gives a little over 40 m.p.g.—a figure which, by suitable driving technique, can be greatly improved; up to 50 m.p.g. could reasonably be expected on a long run with a light load.

In common with the power units of the majority of rear-engined cars, the Fiat engine is wonderfully accessible. In fact, with the engine removed from the car and placed on a bench, the components would not be much easier to work on—and this is important on a vehicle one of whose outstanding attractions is its economy and which, therefore, is likely to be operated by those who prefer to do their own maintenance.

Accessibility

Dipstick, filler caps, plugs and distributor could not be more accessible, and there is plenty of room—particularly to the left of the engine—for wielding spanners. On the car tested there were no oil stains in the engine compartment, and the road dust is kept out by an undertray. The radiator and cowled and ducted fan are mounted over this, to the right of the engine; on the left the exhaust pipe runs down through it, enclosed at this point by a sealing grommet.

It reflects well on the manufacturers that no noteworthy sacrifice has been made, in any important respect, in the effort to keep the price down. The car appears to be strongly built, and the equipment includes twin vizors, twin wipers, leathercloth upholstery and a heater. The last, though of simple design, effectively warmed the feet, demisted the screen, and brought the interior to a comfortable temperature.

The floor covering is of rubber for easy cleaning. It can be removed quickly should a thorough washing be required, and is so moulded that its replacement takes very little more time.

While the brilliance of the side lights is lost in part because of incorporation in the head lamps, the efficiency of the main head light beams is such that maximum speed may be used as safely at night as during the day time. A slight diffusion of light fringes the dipped beam to aid the driver, without bringing reproach from oncoming traffic.

There is little to criticize in this latest version of the Multipla, yet the lack of accommodation for gloves, maps and the like contrasts strangely with the unusual amount of space for normal luggage. And for a go-anywhere working vehicle, the ground clearance is surprisingly modest, especially in a vehicle with independent suspension all round.

Apart from these minor criticisms, however, the Multipla sets out to serve a particular purpose and achieves its aims admirably. As a light delivery van combined with a miniature motor bus, it is ideal. As a multi-seater passenger vehicle it would serve admirably as station-to-hotel transport. And for those who prefer not to tow a caravan around behind their cars, the interior could easily be converted into a two-berth dormitory.

Above all, perhaps, is its suitability for the large family, who may accommodate adequate luggage in addition to themselves. It is up to the task of carrying the average motorist economically about his business when used as an ordinary car, and its qualities are such that it may well become one of the family in the United Kingdom in spite of the burden of import duty which it carries on its purchase price.

John Bentley COMPARES DAUPHINE AND FIAT 600 vs VOLKSWAGEN

Two more European automotive giants challenge the champ, as the free-for-all sales race for a mushrooming U. S. economy-car market shifts to high gear.

Fiat 600 could be called Italy's Model T. Oversize brakes and smooth gearbox emphasize Italian interest in highly roadable cars, even in the economy class.

By JOHN BENTLEY

OF the European manufacturers eager to cut in on the rich economy-sedan market that Volkswagen opened up in this country, none are making more determined efforts than Fiat and Renault. Each will offer the VW stiff competition, but the Fiat 600 and the Renault Dauphine approach the problem from opposite directions.

The Renault, at approximately the same price ($1,645 against about $1,600 for the VW), offers a much more attractively-styled sedan with four doors to the Volkswagen's two, and somewhat better performance from a smaller, more economical engine.

Fiat, in its 600 model, offers roughly the same transportation package as VW for a much lower price, $1,295, achieving nearly comparable performance with an engine little more than half the size of the German cars.

Like VW, both the Renault Dauphine and the Fiat 600 are rear-engine designs of small displacement with pushrod-actuated valves; both are independently sprung all round and feature swing axles at the rear; both are economy machines intended specifically to appeal to the small, budget-conscious family which doesn't see much sense in using up 250 hp with attendant license and insurance costs, gas consumption, tire wear and parking problems, just to drive to the supermarket or railroad station.

The Dauphine, star product of the oldest surviving French automobile manufacturer, is one of a popular line of cars produced and sold in thousands by the vast Renault factory at Billancourt, near Paris. It is a logical (and far better looking) improvement of the Renault 4CV, which for the past few years has had very limited sales in the U.S.

The Fiat 600, an equally big seller in Italy, comes from the 350-acre Fiat plant in Turin. Fiat, too, is a firm dating back to the dawn of the automobile industry and one that, today, has virtually no competition in its own country. A

French designers have managed the impossible with Dauphine—a good-looking economy car which gets performance equal to VW's from even smaller engine.

Winner and still champ of the U.S. economy-car market, the Volkswagen has remained unchanged since 1954. Its workmanship is still unmatched.

COMPARATIVE TABLE

SPECIFICATIONS	RENAULT DAUPHINE	FIAT 600
ENGINE & CHASSIS		
CYLINDERS	4	4
BORE	2.28-IN.	2.36-IN.
STROKE	3.15-IN.	2.20-IN.
DISPLACEMENT	51.5 CU. IN.	38.63 CU. IN.
COMPRESSION RATIO	7.25:1	7.5:1
MAXIMUM OUTPUT	32 BHP @ 4,250 RPM.	22 BHP @ 4,600 RPM.
VALVES	OVERHEAD-PUSHROD	OVERHEAD-PUSHROD
CARBURETION	SINGLE SOLEX F28 IBT DOWNDRAFT	SINGLE WEBER 22 IM DOWNDRAFT
TRANSMISSION	THREE-SPEED (SYNCHROMESH 2 & 3)	FOUR-SPEED SYNCHROMESH 2 3 & 4)
OVERALL RATIOS		
LOW	16.16	18.29
SECOND	7.90	11.04
THIRD	—	7.16
HIGH	4.67	4.81
REAR AXLE RATIO	4.37	5.375
MPH PER 1,000 RPM (HIGH)	15.92	13.85
TURNING DIAMETER	27 FT. 6 IN	28 FT. 7 IN.
STEERING	RACK & PINION	WORM & SECTOR
STEERING WHEEL TURNS (LOCK to LOCK)	4.5	2.75
TIRE SIZE	500 x 15	520 x 12
BRAKE LINING AREA	82.5 SQ. IN.	109.2 SQ. IN.
WEIGHT (CURB)	1,397 LBS.	1,290 LBS
GAS TANK CAPACITY (US GALLONS)	7.75	7.13
DIMENSIONS		
WHEELBASE	89-IN.	78.75-IN.
TREAD (FRONT	49-IN.	45.28-IN.
(REAR	48-IN.	45.43-IN.
OVERALL LENGTH	155-IN.	130.50-IN.
WIDTH	60-IN.	54.25-IN.
HEIGHT	57-IN.	55.25-IN
GROUND CLEARANCE	6-IN.	6.25-IN.
PRICE	$1,645	$1,295
PERFORMANCE FACTORS		
ACCELERATION THRU GEARS (IN SECONDS)		
0 — 30 MPH	7.9	9.5
0 — 40 MPH	11.8 (1 & 2)	17.4 (1 & 2)
0 — 50 MPH	20.9 (1, 2, 3)	30.2 (1 THRU 4)
0 — 60 MPH	31.0	54.1
30 — 45 MPH (HIGH GEAR)	10.6	11.8 (3 &4)
MAXIMUM SPEED (MPH INDICATED)	75	60
MAXIMUM TORQUE (LBS/FT @ RPM)	48.4 @ 2,000	28.9 @ 2,800
BHP PER CU. IN.	.583	.566
LBS PER BHP	43.65	58.63
PISTON SPEED (FT. PER MIN. @ PEAK RPM)	2,585 @ 4,250	1,686 @ 4,600
GAS CONSUMPTION (MPG INCLUDING MEDIUM TRAFFIC AND ALL TESTS)	34.9	38.25

NOTES: Weather dry, clear and warm. No wind. All speeds indicated and uncorrected.

relatively new Italian concept in design, the 600 represents one half of a carefully prepared two-pronged attack on the U.S. small-car market, staged by Italy's No. 1 industrial enterprise. The other is the 1100 sedan, selling for $1,655. This, however, has a conventional front-mounted four-cylinder engine of 67.42 inches displacement.

Both Renault and Fiat are setting up nationwide dealer facilities, following the example of the superb VW organization which finally conquered the American prejudice against foreign cars because of the difficulty of finding parts and service. The French and Italian companies are fully aware of the importance of readily-available, competent service. Fiat's initial sales drive is concentrating on the Eastern seaboard and the West Coast. Florida is next in line; other states will come into the orbit as and when dealers are appointed who measure up to Fiat standards.

It was therefore with considerable interest that, during

Dauphine's unique spare-wheel stowage makes for larger trunk space and simplifies tire changes. Rim-mounted wheels are remarkably light. Trunk is illuminated when hood is opened.

Four-cylinder engine of new Renault develops 32 horsepower from 51.5 cu. in. There is room at sides of rear-mounted plant for tools. Dauphine engine is smaller than Volkswagen.

the same weekend, I took over a Fiat 600 from Hoffman Motors of New York City, the U.S. Fiat distributor, and a Renault Dauphine through the courtesy of Everett Poorman of International Motor Sales of White Plains, N.Y.

The object of these road tests, obviously, was not so much to compare one car against the other or against the VW (as a two-time VW owner I didn't feel another road test was necessary), but rather to find out how each fulfills its purpose. Inevitably, however, since all these spry little machines are pointing their noses at the same market, there are many points of comparison. Here, it is only fair to remember not only that both have smaller engines than the German car, but that the Fiat also gives away nearly 13 cubic inches and some 10 bhp to the Renault, and also that it costs at least $300 less than either of the others. Even so, it shows up remarkably well in terms of comfort, roominess, maneuverability and general finish.

On the grounds of braking and economy, the Fiat is actually superior to the Renault, while its four-speed transmission enables the driver to make relatively better use of available engine power than the Renault's three speeds, and comes surprisingly close to the famous smooth performance of the VW gearbox.

Suppose we get behind the wheel of each of these likeable and interesting midgets which are, in effect, scaled-down versions of conventional-sized cars. As the reader can see from the comparative table, the usual performance factors are all there; but in my opinion, when you are testing a family car with a power unit of under 90 cubic inches, it doesn't really matter whether you take seven or nine seconds in getting to 30 mph, 30 seconds or 40 to reach 60 mph, as the popularity of the "people's car" has long since proved.

The important points are roadability, comfort, roominess, maximum cruising speed without fuss or undue noise, appearance, finish and running economy. Flat-out speed doesn't mean much, either, but the kind of passing speed you are likely to need under average traffic conditions does count for something. In this connection, the Fiat 600 compares very favorably with the Dauphine between 30 and 45 mph, although to compensate for its much lower torque and lesser power-weight ratio, both third and fourth were used to obtain 11.8 seconds, whereas the Dauphine registered 10.6 seconds without shifting. Any VW owner knows, of course, that this situation requires a bit of gear-shift gymnastics.

Let's take the various points that do matter, in the order listed above.

Roadability: Both the Dauphine and the Fiat 600 are very well endowed in this respect. Neither shows any sign of the oversteer usually associated with rear-engined cars, (and for which the VW's notorious) even when taken relatively fast around curves. Of the two, the Fiat, scores slightly with something approaching *under*steer. Despite the rear-poised engine you actually have to steer it firmly around a bend or it tends to pull towards the outside. Both cars give adequate breakaway warning with unmistakable tire squeal; both can be set back on course with a flick of the wheel, though you have to watch the Fiat's very quick steering (only 2¾ turns, lock to lock) which might prove a shade too quick for the uninitiated.

Both cars rode astonishingly well over my favorite stretch of abominable test road, but on severe bumps the Fiat showed up as slightly front-end light. Still, the independent suspensions of these two little cars are nothing short of remarkable in the way they absorb bumps and ruts that would cause much bigger machines to shudder badly.

Comfort: Although this might seem a little far-fetched, I·would embark with the family on a trip to Florida as unhesitatingly in the Fiat 600 as I would in the Dauphine. (The family, besides my wife and elder girl, includes a nine-month old baby.) Admittedly it would take longer, because the Fiat's maximum and comfortable cruising speeds are considerably under those of the Renault, but in taking it by easy stages of, say, 350 miles a day, one would get there just as fresh. The comparative figures in the next paragraph show why. However, the Dauphine has two shortcomings that mitigate against comfort, both connected with the transmission. The shift lever is much too short and located too far forward for comfort; and while the ratios of the three-speed transmission are adequate, there is a crying need for a fourth speed. The Fiat is admirably equipped in this respect; the lever falls very well to hand, its shift action is faster, easier and more positive than that of the Dauphine and you can have as much fun "playing tunes" on the gearbox as you can in a Volks.

Since noise level as well as roominess definitely tie in with comfort, it should be noted that the Fiat has a marked body resonance at around 40 mph on certain types of road. However, in neither car does the engine obtrude at all until over 50 mph. Above this point, the noise level in the Fiat 600 rises more rapidly than it does in the Dauphine. Here again both cars score heavily over the VW, whose air-cooled engine is notoriously noisy.

Roominess: In this department, the Fiat 600 not only compares favorably with the Dauphine, inch for inch, but

Space under hood of Fiat 600 houses gas tank, leaving only a minimum amount of space for luggage. When traveling two-up, back seat can be folded to make a large, flat luggage space.

is in some respects superior, when you consider that its wheelbase is 10¼ inches shorter. For instance, the rear seat width of the Dauphine is 50 inches, compared with 49½ inches for the Fiat; but the latter's seat depth is 19 inches—two inches deeper than the Renault. The Renault scores with four doors, but the Fiat's two doors are 39 inches wide—ample for even the stoutest to get in without discomfort.

In the matter of luggage space, the Renault's trunk (under the hood) has a capacity of nearly five cubic feet, the spare wheel being tucked away in a separate compartment underneath. However, the Fiat's rear seat tilts downward in the same manner as the VW's, to provide an even larger luggage platform when only two people are riding. There is also room for some additional packages in the diminutive "hood" of the Fiat.

Maximum cruising speed: As already mentioned, the Fiat 600 is happiest at around 50 mph, whereas the Dauphine, like the VW, will hold 60 with equal ease. Beyond these points, these cars, too, tend to become mechanically noisy.

Appearance: While Fiat stylists have done well enough with the proportions of so small a car as the 600 for it to deserve being called pert and cute, the Renault is unquestionably the best-looking small sedan on the market. Both cars score heavily in looks over the VW (which will not bother VW partisans a bit). The Dauphine's unconventional wheels are another contributory factor. Tire changes by the way don't require removal of the wheel, but only of

CONTINUED ON PAGE 87

Overhead valve four in Fiat 600 produces 22 hp. at a buzzing 4,600 rpm. It has been used in Italian hot rods with great success. Many have been entered in Mille Miglia race.

EXCELLENCE in miniature

An appreciation of a Fiat 600

by PAUL K. COETZEE

I WONDER if there is a more difficult problem than that faced by the enthusiastic driver who is looking for a suitable car. The expression "suitable car" usually includes consideration of : the individual taste of the potential owner, the suitability of the particular car to be driven in enthusiastic manner, and—a vital factor—the funds available !

Being a driver who does not grumble when a car is not equipped with one of those hushomatic transmissions, I eventually decided to ask for a demonstration run in a Fiat 600. I found the steering to be excellently precise and light, cornering above standard, acceleration lively, and the gear change as positive and sporty as could be. By coincidence, I learned that an old school-mate possessed the second 600 to be imported into Pretoria; after a few brief and inspiring talks (the friend being a driver sharing my enthusiasm), my name went on the waiting list for this car. When I received my 600 my friend's car had just completed 20,000 trouble-free miles.

Concentrated running-in

Being lucky enough to receive one of the first of the detail-modified 1957 models—incorporating, among other things, wind-down windows and steering-column light switches—I decided to do the running-in on a long stretch of road. I am certain that such a "break-in" pays dividends.

After about five months of extensive driving and testing to the limit, the little car covered 10,000 miles and established itself as a permanent member of my garage. In due course a new and bigger car must be obtained, but the 600 will remain—that is for sure !

The Fiat possesses strong personality, while the initial cost and the running costs are extremely low. I feel it is correct to call it an ideal "poor man's sports car".

So far, the garage expenses on my car have been really moderate (excluding two minor crash-repair bills !) and average fuel consumption is about 45 m.p.g. during city use, and between 50 and 54 m.p.g. on the open road.

I often hear the remark from owners of bigger cars "nice little car for the city"; the 600 cruises very comfortably at 55-59 m.p.h. (59 being the recommended cruising maximum) and, as it was bred in the Italian Alps and designed for people who like to drive fast, mountain passes and upward slopes seldom cause its speed to drop below 45 m.p.h.

Average speeds of above 50 are easy to do—and a friend averaged 56 between Warmbad and Pretoria not so long ago. I have completed the trip between Vredefort and Pretoria, via Vereeniging and Germiston, at a 52 m.p.h. average. On arriving at one's destination the engine is as quiet and sweet as it was at the starting point.

The car is free from any vibrations and excessive engine noises. It leaves the impression of smoothness and compactness—especially on the left-front-seat passenger. The seats —especially the rear one—are comfortable, while at the front leg room is ample. I have not yet felt uncomfortable, nor cramped, in my 600, and I have completed journeys of more than 400 miles at a stretch. I may mention that from 1957 onwards the car has been fitted with redesigned front seats, ruling out a complaint regarding the earlier model.

". . . at their own risk"

During a 1,500-mile trip to Magoebaskloof I really saw what the Fiat could do. We travelled via Pietersburg and returned via Mica, Kawyns Pass and Nelspruit to Pretoria; on the stretch from Tzaneen, crossing the Olifants River at Mica, and via the tough Kawyns Pass (in thick mist) to Sabie and Nelspruit, we encountered the worst dust, stone, sand and corrugated roads imaginable. Yet we covered the distance in 5 hours and 25 minutes.

At Magoebaskloof we took every possible and impossible drive in the area and astonished many a big-car driver by totally ignoring such signs as : "Cars proceeding higher than this point should be high-powered" (Wolkberg) and "Drivers descending farther do so at their own risk" (Debegeni Falls). During this tough trip the car not once bottomed on its springs (it was fairly heavily laden).

If asked what characteristic of the Fiat 600 is considered as the best, I would not hesitate to say that it is the handling. I think the Fiat would be an ideal car in which to train would-be competition drivers; controlled slides, high-speed cornering and rapid gear changing (via an excellently situated lever) are among the 600's handling virtues. Four-wheel controlled slides on wet slippery roads are easily executed—and a very light and positive steering, coupled with a very short wheelbase, causes the car to be extremely manoeuvrable. In thick city traffic it is nearly unbeatable

A friend fitted his 600 with an Abarth straight-through twin exhaust system, and a sports coil, with very effective results concerning getaway and top speed. I hope to fit the same accessories to my car soon, and I happen to know of at least another four owners desiring to do the same.

The brakes, being finned, never show any sign of fade or overheating.

Perhaps the best testimonial that the Fiat 600 is a car with a personality of its own is that whenever two meet on the road their drivers greet each other. So far, I have met no less than eleven Pretoria owners who fully agree with me that the 600 is the ideal poor man's sports car. At least one claims that he has reached 70 m.p.h. Most of us, however, claim an honest 65. Although I would not recommend it, 30 is

easily reached in second gear, as is 50 in third gear, without the engine seeming uncomfortable or the valves bouncing.

As far as I can see, the 600 has only one snag. The flow of air through the radiator is regulated by a thermostatically-controlled shutter-scoop and the thermostat may become defective in our tropical climate, with the result that the

engine may overheat (the shutter staying closed). The simple remedy is to fix the shutter in an open position, the car then only needing a slightly longer warming-up period. Another shortcoming is that no temperature gauge is fitted; only a red warning light when the water temperature reaches boiling point. I have not yet had a boiling radiator, so the multi-bladed fan is very efficient.

Looking at the purchase price (£473 at coast), one is amazed to find the car full of functional fittings such as fuel gauge and a fuel-level warning light, a primitive and somewhat noisy but very effective heater and demister, an interior light operated by the right-hand door, flashing indicators with automatic-cancelling switch on the steering column, an excellent system of operating parking, dim and bright lights by a lever situated on the steering column, an engine compart-

ment light, door pockets, and so on. One is not amazed to learn that the 600 was developed since 1945 and that the 1958 models are even fitted with windscreen washers.

Ease of servicing

When the engine compartment at the back of the car is opened the craftsmanship and finish of the 633 c.c. o.h.v. short-stroke engine leaves nothing to be desired, while all essential fittings are prominent and easy to service. In fact, it is a joy to work on the engine and, as it is sealed from below, it is extremely easy to keep spotlessly clean. The 600 is a true enthusiast's car.

Summing up, one cannot but come to the conclusion that the Fiat 600 is a very successful attempt to mass-produce a miniature car providing the man in the street with modern speedy means of transport—and with the cornering ability of a thoroughbred. ●

Wheels and ultra-discreet front fender lettering indicate that this is no 600.

ROAD TEST FIAT-ABARTH 750

IN THE PROCESS of testing and reporting on practically all of the currently available small sedans, we have come up against this question: "What is the minimum acceptable performance for American driving conditions?" There is, of course, no conclusive answer to the question, though it can stimulate considerable argument. On one point we are sure—the performance of the little Fiat-Abarth is not marginal.

What looks, on the outside, to be a very ordinary Fiat 600 turns out to be a veritable tiger on street and highway. Even our somewhat jaded test crew got a tremendous kick out of driving the Fiat-Abarth 750 *derivazione;* in fact, we had the machine for a week, and everyone who drove it for even a few minutes fell in love with it. Undoubtedly a favorite sport of Fiat-Abarth owners will be VW-baiting. The German beetle owners, so used to sneering at the Italian people's car, are in for a surprise when they try a bit of European-style dicing against the Abarth.

The demand for Abarth-converted Fiats is so great that the firm has just opened a new and modern factory build-

ing. The modification process is not simple, or cheap. The first step is to increase the cylinder bore by one millimeter. Not much, perhaps, but in inches it's .03937, which still leaves room for two normal rebores. The crankshaft is completely special, with larger counterweights, and the stroke is increased by 8 mm or .315 inches. Thus the dimensions are 61 x 64 mm, giving 747 cc.

The crankcase is machined at the rear to clear the counterweight, and the valve tappet holes are counterbored to allow for higher valve lift (see illustration). Other machine work, also illustrated, is done to improve oil circulation at the center main bearing, always the most heavily loaded on an in-line 4.

The camshaft is special, not reground, with a higher lift and valve timing of 30°-70°-70°-30° in the usual sequence. Valve springs are, of course, heavier. A larger Weber carburetor (type 32) is used and requires machining a suitable mounting surface on the cylinder head. The head itself has polished ports, and domed pistons supply the compression ratio increase from 7.0 to 9.0:1.

A large carburetor, and an oversize radiator to keep cool.

Clean-lined exhaust manifolding lets it exhale properly.

PHOTOGRAPHY: POOLE

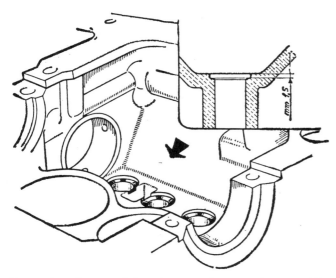

Counterbored tappet holes give cam clearance for more lift.

satisfying Ferrari-like growls from a tiny tiger

Other changes include a lightened flywheel, heavier clutch springs, a larger radiator and a change in the final drive gears from the standard 43/8 combination to 39/8. The Abarth company supply innumerable variations of this engine with outputs from 38 to 47 bhp. They also will supply alternate gears for 2nd, 3rd and 4th, but these are not used in the standard 750, as tested.

Inevitably the question will come up regarding the durability of such a drastically hopped-up engine. In our opinion it will be impossible to prove any reduction in overall life if the extra performance is used with a reasonable degree of restraint. The standard 633-cc engine will take a tremendous amount of abuse, and its output is very conservative at .558 horsepower per cubic inch. The 747-cc Abarth develops .91 horsepower per cubic inch, a reasonable figure in view of the fact that many production engines today run much higher compression ratios and claim closer to 1.00 horsepower per cubic inch. Also, one should note the lower numerical axle ratio, so that, despite a longer-stroke crankshaft (still only 64 mm, the same as a VW) the

Improved oil circulation, new crank and cam are features.

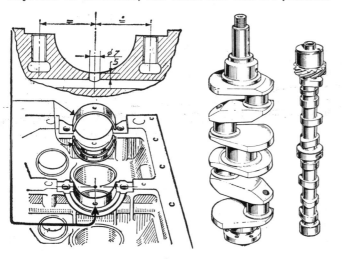

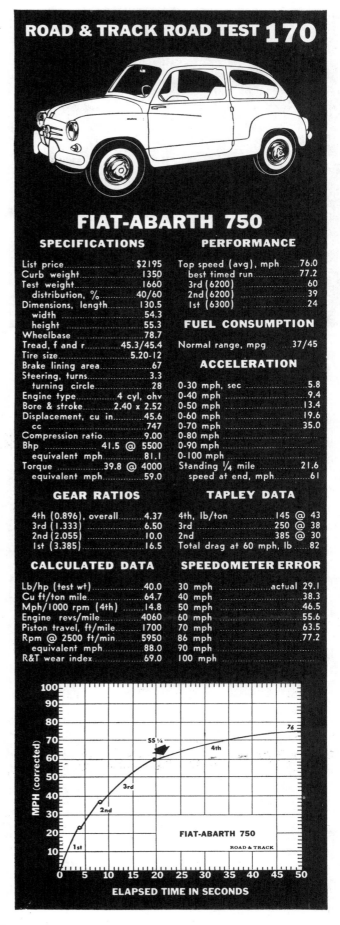

ROAD & TRACK ROAD TEST 170

FIAT-ABARTH 750

SPECIFICATIONS

List price	$2195
Curb weight	1350
Test weight	1660
distribution, %	40/60
Dimensions, length	130.5
width	54.3
height	55.3
Wheelbase	78.7
Tread, f and r	45.3/45.4
Tire size	5.20-12
Brake lining area	67
Steering, turns	3.3
turning circle	28
Engine type	4 cyl, ohv
Bore & stroke	2.40 x 2.52
Displacement, cu in	45.6
cc	747
Compression ratio	9.00
Bhp	41.5 @ 5500
equivalent mph	81.1
Torque	39.8 @ 4000
equivalent mph	59.0

GEAR RATIOS

4th (0.896), overall	4.37
3rd (1.333)	6.50
2nd (2.055)	10.0
1st (3.385)	16.5

CALCULATED DATA

Lb/hp (test wt)	40.0
Cu ft/ton mile	64.7
Mph/1000 rpm (4th)	14.8
Engine revs/mile	4060
Piston travel, ft/mile	1700
Rpm @ 2500 ft/min	5950
equivalent mph	88.0
R&T wear index	69.0

PERFORMANCE

Top speed (avg), mph	76.0
best timed run	77.2
3rd (6200)	60
2nd (6200)	39
1st (6300)	24

FUEL CONSUMPTION

Normal range, mpg	37/45

ACCELERATION

0-30 mph, sec	5.8
0-40 mph	9.4
0-50 mph	13.4
0-60 mph	19.6
0-70 mph	35.0
0-80 mph	
0-90 mph	
0-100 mph	
Standing ¼ mile	21.6
speed at end, mph	61

TAPLEY DATA

4th, lb/ton	145 @ 43
3rd	250 @ 38
2nd	385 @ 30
Total drag at 60 mph, lb	82

SPEEDOMETER ERROR

30 mph	actual 29.1
40 mph	38.3
50 mph	46.5
60 mph	55.6
70 mph	63.5
86 mph	77.2
90 mph	
100 mph	

The Abarth-modified car announces itself to other small car owners with a much brighter, more decorative grille. Poor chrome was evident on the hood ornament, but only there.

FIAT-ABARTH

Positioning of the small tachometer in front of the driver makes up for its size. More chrome than on the standard 600 is again present inside. Spring loading of the shift lever means that 3rd is positioned directly ahead of 2nd for very fast shifts. Vinyl upholstery is $35 extra.

piston travel in feet per mile is only 3.1% more than the stock 600. Engine revolutions per mile are reduced by 9.6%.

Insofar as actual performance goes, it is easier to look at the following table than to describe the results.

	Stock 600	Stock VW	Fiat-Abarth
0-30	9.2	6.9	5.8
0-40	16.8	11.9	9.4
0-50	28.5	18.0	13.4
0-60	54.0	28.0	19.6
Ss 1/4 mile	26.1	23.2	21.6
Max. 3rd	46	62	67
Max. 4th	60.3	70.2	76.0

What the figures do not tell is the fun qualities of the Italian car; this is a small sedan with a genuine sports car flavor. Of course the power output is up, and the weight is very modest (1350 pounds, curb). Even as tested, with driver and observer, the pounds per bhp figure is a healthy 40. It should perform and it does.

What are the drawbacks, the shortcomings, resultant from such a drastic modification? Only one, and that not objectionable to everyone; namely the exhaust note. While not noticeable inside the car, the Abarth exhaust system has a fairly pronounced rap. We liked it.

As reported in the stock Fiat 600 test (Road & Track, July 1957), this is a very pleasant car to drive because of the excellent 4-speed transmission and very smooth-running engine. The Abarth conversion loses nothing in the process and gains quite a lot with its free revving ability. A small but readable tachometer is included with the "package" and is red-lined at 5900 rpm. This engine speed is more than ample for all purposes including Operation Blitzkrieg, but the tiny engine will soar up to astronomical revs without a murmur. We never did ascertain valve float speed—6900 rpm in 3rd gear (73 mph indicated, or 67 mph actual) was as high as we dared go, and there was still no sign or sound of the tappets' not following the cam contours.

Having now enthused at some length over the performance of this car, let us consider the price, or more importantly, the value. At $2195 plus tax and license, the cost per pound is certainly high. Quite frankly it seems like a lot of money to us, though certainly the extensive modifications carried out by Mr. Carlo Abarth and company are worth every dollar. For example, after all the work previously described, each engine is given a dynamometer test run of 4½ hours culminating in a power check at 5800 rpm. This sort of thing doesn't come cheap, and it can safely be said that there is more "hand work" in the Fiat-Abarth than in some of the over-$10,000 cars on the market.

Also, to editorialize a bit, we have always felt that the American market for very small cars (i.e., under 90-inch wheelbase) would be much increased if we were offered fantastic performance, even at some sacrifice in economy. The economy in fuel means very little to us, but the fun qualities of this little car are worth quite a lot.

DIGNITY
AND
IMPUDENCE

The Editor Experiences another Contrast, Driving in Succession a 1938 Rolls-Royce Phantom III and a 1958 Fiat 600

CONTRAST.—Figures that emphasise the difference between these two cars can be gleaned from the tables on page 435.

LAST month it so happened that on the same day I drove the latest Ford Thunderbird and a model-T Unicar, thus changing at short notice from a car of 5,769 c.c. to one of a modest 328 c.c., as recorded in last month's issue. Not long afterwards I was to experience almost as sharp a contrast, on the day on which I stepped from a very imposing 1938 40/50-h.p. Rolls-Royce Phantom III limousine into a new Fiat 600. On this occasion it was a matter of going from 7,338 c.c. to 633 c.c.

The test of the Rolls-Royce arose because I had for some time decided that I would like to gain first-hand experience of a car which many people regard as the last of the " real " Rolls-Royces. Introduced late in 1935, the Phantom III, with its beautiful 60-deg. vee-twelve engine, massive X-braced chassis, automatically-governed coil-spring i.f.s. and ½-elliptic rear suspension with hydraulic driver-control of shock-absorption, and the famous mechanical brake servo, was, and remains, a very impressive piece of automobile engineering, sought after by Rolls-Royce connoisseurs.

I am in possession of the very beautiful catalogue issued by Rolls-Royce Limited about the Phantom III but I had not driven this model. Consequently, I took the opportunity of rectifying this omission when one of these great motor cars became available to us for a few days through the co-operation of Simmons, the well-known Mayfair Rolls-Royce and Bentley copers.

This particular car—3-CM-131— is a 1937/8 3rd series Hooper limousine with electrically raised and lowered division between the front compartment and the elegantly-appointed " boudoir." The latter is sumptuous in the extreme. Upholstery is in soft leather, the floor covered in thick carpets and rug. Companions, concealed behind glass and lit when in use, are let into the rear quarters of the body, the roof has two sunken interior lamps, a Ferranti radio is concealed under the off-side armrest, the folding centre armrest for the back seat contains more make-up equipment, and in the division are stowed two glass-topped tables. There is a telephone with which to speak to the chauffeur and a tiny switch on the near-side seat armrest controls the aforesaid electrically-operated glass division, this rising in ghostly silence at an angle, thus constituting an effective screen should the rear-seat passengers feel draught from the open front screen or sunshine roof, before assuming the vertical and meeting the roof, completely sealing off chauffeur and footman. A small clock and a cigar lighter complete these V.I.P. amenities.

Impressive as these details were, the whole car being in fine condition and bearing the initials " W. P. S." on its doors, I was far more interested in how it would handle and perform. After driving it for more than 300 miles I was even more impressed !

The driving compartment has separate seats, softly upholstered and affording excellent support. Before the driver stretches the long bonnet, terminating in the classic radiator, the shoulders of which stand proud of the bonnet panels. In one's line of vision is the Flying Lady mascot (each one stamped with the magic initials " R.R." and the date in 1911 when this was sculptured by Charles Sykes), without which a Rolls-Royce looks bare and incomplete. The big steering wheel carries those silken minor controls for suspension over-ride, throttle and ignition, the last-named labelled " Early/Late," a pleasing throw-back to a sterner age, when the driving menial could hardly be expected to understand " Advance/Retard " !

The walnut facia carries an imposing yet unobtrusive range of instruments and controls. There is the 110-m.p.h. R.R. speedometer, its white needle swinging steadily round the dial, beyond the red " 30 " digits, as the open road is gained. There is the carburation

control, with spoon-lever, for " Start " or " Normal "; the switch to bring in petrol pumps " A " or " B," or both; the lockable circular electrical panel containing those splendid lamps switches, starter button and the switch whereby each ignition system (twin coils, a total of 24 plugs) can be tested separately, aircraft fashion, as the engine is run up. A battery of six matching switches on the extreme right control twin fog-lamps, facia lighting, heater and wipers. There are a really deep cubbyhole with unlockable walnut lid; cigar-lighter and slide-out ashtray; an accurate petrol gauge reading up to 32 gallons (calibrated every three gallons) and starting at three gallons; combined oil gauge and water thermometer; additional heater and facia lighting knobs; an electric plug; warning lights for low fuel content and dynamo charge; reversing lamps switch and a clock. Behind this dashboard, high in his seat, the Flying Lady pressing onward to the whisper of power unleashed by the big vee-twelve o.h.v. engine, which one likes to think is blood-brother to the Battle-of-Britain-winning Merlin, the driver of a Phantom III feels in command of the road.

The windscreen opens and twin roller blinds are fitted in lieu of sun-vizors. The driver's door possesses a small adjustable armrest

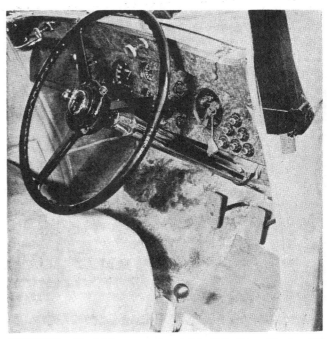

LUXURY.—The driving compartment of the Rolls-Royce Phantom III Hooper limousine, showing the soft carpets, walnut facia and the unobtrusive, precision controls and instruments which confront the driver.

and a divided, plated knob on the steering-wheel centre operates loud or soft audible warning. The front-seat passenger has a grabhandle! Climbing up to drive this Hooper-bodied Phantom III the feet sink again into soft carpets. A driver of average stature finds that he can just see the front wings, or the faired sidelamp on the near-side one.

The first impression, after the silence of the 7.4-litre engine when idling, is the extreme heaviness of the steering when hauling the Rolls-Royce away from the kerb. On the move, however, the steering, which demands just over three turns, lock-to-lock, lightens out and after half an hour's motoring the length and bulk of the car no longer bothers one. But turn it in a cul-de-sac and anyone not in the pink of condition will find himself *panting* from the effort needed on the wheel.

Thanks to the neat, cranked right-hand brake-lever and position of the typically R.-R. right-hand gear-lever entry and egress from the driver's seat can be made with dignity.

It isn't long before an enthusiastic driver becomes enthralled with the performance of the Phantom III. I do not mean so much on account of a maximum speed of some 95 m.p.h. from this very square-rigged 2¾-ton limousine, or on account of useful maxima of over 50 and 70 m.p.h., respectively, in second and third gear, all accomplished in near-silence. What is even more impressive is the top-gear performance, both on account of the car's ability to accelerate effortlessly in this gear from around 10 m.p.h. and because the acceleration from 20 m.p.h. onward is so vivid as to leave noisy, bouncing sports cars gasping.

So flexible is the vee-twelve power unit that I soon developed the technique of getting the wheels rolling in second gear and then going " round the corner " into top gear. These two ratios suffice for all normal motoring. It is fun to slip into third for passing real obstructions, like those 60-foot-long transporters with which the R.A.F. playfully litters our main roads, but top-gear pick-up meets all normal situations.

The other surprising feature of the Phantom III is the manner in which it handles. With the suspension over-ride control, which operates on both front and back wheels, on " hard " the car corners fast with no perceptible roll and can be tucked into traffic gaps with all the *sang froid* of a small sports car. The steering transmits vibration rather than kick-back, unless the front wheels hit a pot-hole, when vintage-car shake of both chassis and steering is felt. Only extremely violent swerves cause the heavy body to affect stability, and then only to a mild degree. Because the Phantom III handles so surprisingly well very fine average speeds are possible on congested roads, in spite of the car's bulk. Cornering is assisted by sensibly mild castor-action on the steering.

Apart from a faint exhaust hiss, a few body rattles after twenty years' use (the near-side front door reminded one that cruising speed had reached 80 m.p.h. by a more pronounced rattle) and rather

IMPRESSED.—The Editor condescends to be photographed with a car which impressed him very much, as a really fast, exceedingly comfortable vehicle, possessing ample performance, sports-car handling and memorable top-gear performance and acceleration.

annoying wind noise round the front-door pillars, this Rolls-Royce travels more silently than a Zephyr, its gears and back axle truly inaudible.

Cruising speed becomes a habitual 80 m.p.h., the Rolls-Royce mechanical servo brakes retarding this heavy car with deceptive efficiency and very light pedal pressure when need arises.

The car I tried had been supplied with a new clutch by Rolls-Royce Limited. This had not bedded in and was somewhat fierce. It is also heavy to hold out in traffic. This brings me to observe that, for all its silent, effortless speed, the Phantom III is essentially a man's motor car. The gear-change, like passing a bodkin through cream cheese if unhurried, can jar the hand if rapid changes are required. Double-de-clutching is called for, up and down, but there is synchromesh to assist the downward changes. Few women below the calibre of Channel-swimmers could park the monster, and, for all its ease of control otherwise, one is conscious of great weight behind the momentum. There is slight front-end shake on bad roads, but no scuttle float to disturb the driver's equanimity.

In traffic water temperature shot up towards 100 deg. C., but soon fell to a normal 75 deg., oil pressure varying between 8 and 28 lb./sq. in. I did not check petrol consumption accurately, but it is certainly at least 10½ m.p.g., possibly improving to about 12 m.p.g. on long runs.

The ride control definitely works, but the engine seemed quite insensitive to ignition advance and retard. The tyres howl quite a lot on slow corners, bearing witness to the weight they carry—with about six gallons of petrol the weight came out at 2 tons 14 cwt. 2 qtr.

Driving a Phantom III turned out to be an even more pleasing experience than I had anticipated, for I never expected the car to handle in keeping with its performance.

Even in the garage this is obviously a possession to delight in and it seems an excellent investment at the £600-£1,000 for which these fine cars are now obtainable. The handsome appearance of the Hooper limousine under discussion was enhanced by Ace wheel-discs, the spare wheel being enclosed in a metal cover on the off-side of the car. For night driving the huge Rolls-Royce-Lucas headlamps are truly effective, and the driver has instantaneous control of the rear-window blind from a control above his head. Self-cancelling direction-indicators are operated by a facia-sill lever. Alas, the doors do not trail; front and rear compartment quarter-windows are opened by means of large knobs, and the front-door window-handles need 7½ turns, the back ones just over two turns, from fully up to fully down. Discreet, covered locks are fitted in both the off-side doors, and the petrol filler-cap locks. It is stating the obvious to remark that the doors shut quietly, with coachbuilt precision. There is a scuttle ventilator, controlled by an under-facia knob, which cools the feet; the control for automatic lubrication of the chassis is adjacent.

Opening the bonnet reveals the engine to be a truly beautiful example of engineering in the true Rolls-Royce tradition. The components are driven in-line on the near side, a dual carburetter with air silencer feeds the two banks of cylinders, and the black stove-enamel finish contrasts splendidly with the perfection of the alloy castings. Incidentally, Rolls-Royce's own electrical components are largely used and the Phantom III has the inbuilt jacking system. Starting handle and jack clip to the bulkhead and the radiator possesses thermostatically-controlled shutters which further enhance the appearance of the car.

POWER DEPARTMENT.—An under-bonnet view of the Rolls-Royce Phantom III, showing the 7.4-litre vee-twelve dual-ignition engine, beautifully constructed, and finished in traditional Rolls-Royce style. No official figures were ever quoted but it must develop some 170 b.h.p.

1938 ROLLS-ROYCE PHANTOM III LIMOUSINE

Engine : Twelve cylinders, 82.5 by 114 mm. (7,338 c.c.) in 60-deg. vee formation. Push-rod-operated o.h. valves. 6.0-to-1 compression-ratio. Approximately 170 b.h.p. at 3,500 r.p.m.
Gear ratios : First, 12.71 to 1; second, 8.44 to 1; third, 5.57 to 1; top, 4.25 to 1.
Tyres : 7.00–18 Dunlop Fort on centre-lock wire wheels; Ace discs.
Weight : 2 tons 14 cwt. 2 qtr., ready for the road, without occupants, but with approximately six gallons of petrol.
Steering ratio : 3⅛ turns, lock-to-lock.
Fuel capacity : 32 gallons. (Range approximately 352 miles.)
Wheelbase : 11 ft. 10 in.
Track : Front, 5 ft. 0⅜ in.; rear, 5 ft. 2⅗ in.
Dimensions : 17 ft. 7 in. by 6 ft. 5 in. (wide).
Used car supplied by : Simmons, 12, Rex Place, London, W.1.

THE FIAT 600 SALOON

Engine : Four cylinders, 60 by 56 mm. (633 c.c.). Push-rod o.h. valves. 7.0-to-1 compression-ratio. 21.5 b.h.p. at 4,600 r.p.m.
Gear ratios : First, 18.2 to 1; second, 10.05 to 1; third, 7.16 to 1; top, 4.82 to 1.
Tyres : 5.20–12 Pirelli Extraflex on bolt-on steel disc wheels.
Weight : 11 cwt. 1 qtr. (ready for the road, without occupants, but with approximately one gallon of petrol).
Steering ratio : 2¾ turns, lock-to-lock.
Fuel capacity : 6 gallons. (Range approximately 282 miles.)
Wheelbase : 6 ft. 6¾ in.
Track : Front, 3 ft. 9 in.; rear, 3 ft. 8½ in.
Dimensions : 10 ft. 6½ in. by 4 ft. 6½ in. by 4 ft. 4¼ in. (high).
Price : (£649 7s. inclusive of purchase tax).
Concessionaires : Fiat (England) Ltd., Water Road, Wembley, Middlesex. (Made in Turin, Italy.)

For this brief, but exhilarating, contact with a good specimen of Rolls-Royce Phantom III I am indebted to Mr. Gerald Shipman, to whom the car has been sold, but who agreed to the loan of it to MOTOR SPORT. He must be pleased with his purchase, particularly because these fine cars, made with watch-like precision—some connoisseurs go so far as to remark that they are as delicate as a watch, and cost more to maintain than the less complex Phantom II—have scarcely depreciated in value since they left Derby. In 1935, for example, the chassis was priced at £1,850 and the complete cars in the region of £2,600.

So interested had I become in Phantom IIIs that I invited myself along to Hythe Road to discuss them with Mr. W. E. Maddocks, Service Manager to Rolls-Royce Limited. A description of " the 12-cylinder Rolls-Royce "appeared in MOTOR SPORT dated November, 1935, from which I find that, massive as the Phantom III chassis appears, it is actually 8 per cent. lighter than the Phantom II frame. The engine has alloy heads, and 14 mm. plugs are used. Power output is 12 per cent. greater than from the Phantom II. The seven-bearing crankshaft is fully balanced and the gearbox is separate from the engine, with synchromesh on all except bottom gear.

Mr. Maddocks told me that the prototype engine was based on an early version of the Merlin aero-engine, from which valuable experience was gained in respect of vee-twelve engine balance, crankcase webbing, etc. Very few modifications were found necessary during the four years the Phantom III was in production, during which time several hundreds were made.

Originally hydraulic tappets were used, in the form of plungers bearing on arms, which ensured zero-clearance at the eccentrically-mounted valve rockers. It proved difficult to ensure complete silence, however, so, in 1938, solid tappets were substituted. Four piston-type, single-jet Rolls-Royce carburetters of the kind used on the late-model 20/25 h.p. cars, were used for the 1935 prototype car only, Rolls-Royce going over to downdraught carburation soon afterwards, so that production Phantom IIIs had a single twin-choke Stromberg carburetter. Later versions had the four-port head, with improved inlet manifold, and the last few made, while retaining an 8/34 axle-ratio, had an overdrive top gear, the gear ratios being : 1st : 11.5 to 1; 2nd : 6.15 to 1; 3rd : 4.25 to 1 (direct) and top : 3.53 to 1 (overdrive).

Rolls-Royce never divulge horse-power figures, but those given in the data table are thought to be approximately correct; the earlier gear ratios are also given. It seems possible that with a free exhaust, were noise no objection, over 200 b.h.p. would be available. Mr. Maddocks recalled the excellence of the i.f.s. system, the coil springs enclosed within oil-dampers. A gearbox-driven oil pump provides automatic adjustment of front and back damping in accordance with road-speed, with additional driver control of front and back dampers, while an anti-roll bar is fitted at the back.

After the Phantom III I immediately took over a little Fiat 600 and drove it more than 400 miles in three days. There is no need to describe this bonny little vehicle in detail, because a full road-test report was published in MOTOR SPORT in January 1956.

But I wish to congratulate Dr. Dante Giacosa on his very commendable achievements. In designing the Fiat 600 he has contrived to obtain a very level and comfortable ride, a thing difficult to do in a light car but a major technical victory in a vehicle as small as the little Fiat. Apart from riding comfort, this talented Italian engineer has produced a really roomy baby car by placing the cooling element beside the tiny four-cylinder engine, and similar clever expedients; to comfortable suspension he has allied real excellence of control, so that less oversteer is experienced in this rear-engined car than in many front-engined vehicles.

A companion who accompanied me on a long Sunday's motoring in the Fiat 600 remarked that there is more space within it than in a certain well-known 1,172-c.c. saloon and that the ride is better. He further remarked that, driven hard, the car in question does only 28 m.p.g. Making no attempt to conserve petrol, the Fiat 600 gave 47 m.p.g., including a number of stops and starts.

I noted that the Fiat's speedometer indicates a third-gear maximum corresponding to the speed which our dim politicians deem the safe limit on many of Britain's arterial motor roads. In fact, the very smooth little engine will run happily to beyond 40 m.p.h. in third gear, and this, coupled with lively acceleration, a cruising speed of around 60 m.p.h., and very handy overall dimensions, make the Fiat 600 an admirable proposition for our congested roads.

If the Rolls-Royce had a temporarily fierce clutch, that on the Fiat possessed the same shortcoming; I think due to faulty adjustment. Otherwise, no complaints, and the " quick " steering is a joy to use, rendering the Fiat safe when the actions of a traffic clot call for sudden evasive action. The driving position lives up to Fiat's reputation in this respect but the left-hand stalks controlling lamps and direction-flashers could be slightly better placed. These controls are new, likewise wind-up windows in the doors, with anti-draught shields, these shields more effective for rear-seat than front-seat occupants. Five-and-a-quarter turns of the window-handles are needed, from closed to fully open.

The Fiat 600 fulfills a very definite demand in modern motoring. It is probably of only *academic* interest to the majority of readers that it should be possible, after a diligent search, to buy a used Rolls-Royce Phantom III for the Fiat's purchase price in this country of £649 7s. inclusive of purchase tax—such is the difference between a petrol thirst of 11 and 47 m.p.g. !—W. B.

EVEN the largest Fiat is a small car, so when we say that the 600 is the small Fiat, you may be sure it's not just relatively small. It's tiny. And small too is the engine powering it. The 600 carries the smallest conventional power plant of any of the cars we've tested, exceeding in size only a few of the two-stroke air-cooled midgets. Under the engine deck at the rear is a perfect replica of a four cylinder, four stroke, water-cooled ohv unit displacing 633 cc. To give you a ready reference point, this is half the displacement of the old MG TD Midget. This baby mill is called upon to do a man's work, and with few reservations, it succeeds. After we've considered the externals and the physical details of our test cars, we'll return to the engine, and to the performance that goes with it.

Designed as a successor to the ubiquitous and world-famous 500 Topolino, the 600, as yet without a nickname, is a diminutive rear-engined two-door sedan. It has an overall length of ten feet, seven inches, which must border on the minimum for a four-passenger automobile. The remarkable part of it is that the four people it carries, unless they are unusually corpulent, will have more headroom, hiproom, and shoulder room than they are ever likely to need. And the glass area of the little car is phenomenal. Claustrophobia is not likely to be a problem here. The only evident lack is legroom, with the wheel wells biting a sizable chunk out of the front compartment, and the rear seats of necessity a little close to the front. Despite this, however, there is no doubt that the Fiat engineers know how to build a remarkably roomy body around a very small chassis. With both doors open, the car looks almost vast inside.

Interior interest centers around the floor tunnel, the function of which, in a rear-engined car, is a bit puzzling at first. It is small, but why, you wonder, have it at all, when there is no drive shaft? A little study shows that it carries the shift linkage to the rear-mounted transmission, as well as the handbrake cable, and the warm-air duct from the engine to the heater and defroster. A potential thief will go crazy trying to find the starter and choke, unless he has advance information that these are the two toggles mounted behind the gearshift, which is also on the floor tunnel. Damper controls for the rudimentary heating and defrosting system

FCI
ROAD
TEST
19

FIAT 600 · A VERY SMALL

are likewise on the floor tunnel. In truth, it can be said that in this car, the control center has been moved from the dash to the floor tunnel, and we're not at all sure it isn't better located there.

The remote shift to the four-speed transmission couldn't be better positioned if it grew out of the driver's hand. It moves effortlessly through the narrowest H pattern we've ever seen. We defy anyone to tell by looking whether the shift is in first or third, or whether it's in second or fourth. Yet there was never any mistake when going through speeds. They seem to follow each other as though pre-selected. The dash still contains the instruments, consisting of a canopied cluster incorporating speedometer to 70, odometer, fuel gauge and lights for generator, oil pressure, and water temperature. There are separate lights on the dash for high beams, parking lights on and directionals on. Lights are controlled by a neat little lever on the steering column, just below the directional lever. A small panel on the dash houses the ignition lock, the wiper switch, and a toggle to turn off the instrument lights. From stem to stern, from top to bottom, the little car shows meticulous workmanship and flawless finish. There isn't much there, but what there is couldn't be improved upon.

The room for improvement, as might be expected, lies in the field of performance. When you have a tiny engine, you may make the car lighter, but this can be carried only so far. And people still weigh the same. In order to match the power-to-weight ratio of even the weakest current American product, the cameo-like Fiat engine would have to be pushing two pedestrians in bathing suits. With two aboard, the Fiat's power-to-weight ratio is a chilling 70 to 1! The wonder here is not that the car performs poorly, but that it performs so well under the circum-

1. Unique performance from this minute 633 cc engine is due largely to oversquare design. Bore diameter is larger then length of stroke.

2. Rear windows of Fiat are permanently fixed—do not roll down. Tiny wheels can be carried under arm all day if need be.

3. Trunk space is taken up largely by fuel tank which holds little more than seven gallons. Spare fits into recessed well at front.

4. This is an honest-to-goodness 15 mph curve—almost 35° Fiat came around at 38 mph indicated without losing rear, but sliding.

FOUR FOR FOUR

SPECIFICATIONS CHART
FIAT 600

PERFORMANCE:

0-30	8.2
0-40	16.0
0-50	24.5
0-60	
Standing ¼ mile	27.0
Speed at end of ¼	50
Top speed	60.4

SPEEDS IN GEARS:

I	0 to 20
II	5 to 32.6
III	11 to 50
IV	20 to Top

SPEEDOMETER ERROR—

Indicated	Timed
30	31.6
40	42.0
50	52.9
Braking	Excellent

FACTORY SPECIFICATIONS:

ENGINE:
No. of cyls. 4
Arrangement ....In-line
Carburetor ....Single down-draught Weber
Valve system ......Overhead
Bore and Stroke ....60 x 56 mm. (2.36" x 2.20")
Displacement ....633 cc. (33.63 cu. in.)

Comp. ratio ....7.5 to 1
Max. bhp @ rpm ....22 @ 4600 rpm
Torque @ rpm ..29 lbs.-ft. @ 2800 rpm

CHASSIS:
Rear axle ratio ....5.4 to 1
Wheelbase ....78¾"
Tread front ....45¹⁵⁄₃₂"
Tread rear ....45⁷⁄₁₆"
Suspension front ....Transverse leaf, telescopic shocks
Suspension rear ....Independent swing axles, coil springs, telescopic shocks
Steering turns, lock to lock 2⅞
Turning circle ......28' 6.5"
Tire size ....5.20 x 12

BODY:
Height ....53¹¹⁄₃₂
Width ....54¹¹⁄₃₂
Length overall ....126⁹⁄₁₆"
Weight (wet) ...1243 lbs.
Fuel Capacity ...7.13 Gals.

MILEAGE:
(hard driving) ...28.8 mpg.

PRICE: $1298.00

Fiat frontal area is quite blunt, offers some resistance to airflow especially at the higher speeds.

Instruments consist of speedometer, oil pressure light, fuel gauge, ammeter light and direction signals.

The small one has plenty of room inside. Seats are not luxurious but adequate for comfortable seating.

stances. Top speed is a whisker over sixty, and the car will cruise at about forty-five. You will note that, although the car will reach that speed, we have included no 0-60 time in the specifications. This is because too great a build-up is required to reach a true 60, and we feel it would present a distorted picture of the car's potential performance. Acceleration is not at all brisk, but the car feels lively, and its agility and small size effectively prevent it from holding up traffic. To properly evaluate the 600, you must consider its limitations, and balance these against its virtues.

Riding on four 12 inch wheels spaced about a 79 inch wheelbase, you couldn't expect a smooth ride, and you won't be surprised. Parkway driving is effortless, but bumps and potholes are definitely to be avoided. The 600 will ride as well as anything built, on smooth concrete, but smooth concrete usually goes with long stretches, and long stretches don't go with the 600. Legroom, as we said, is limited. You can stretch your legs forward fairly well up

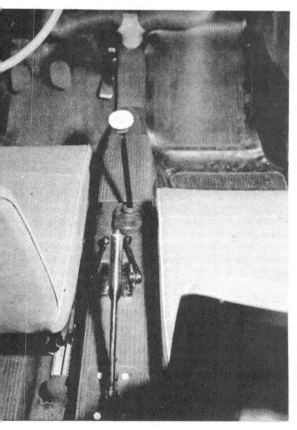

Fiat is independently sprung at rear by huge wishbones. Size of brakes in relation to car is large.

Those unacquainted with the Fiat would be hard pressed to find the starter. The lever on the right when pulled hard fires the engine, the other lever is the choke.

Fender wells cut deeply into passenger compartment, restricting legroom. Position shown here can be tiring after a while.

front, but because of the wheelwells, there's no room to shift them sideways. The seats are also too hard for prolonged riding. And while the engine is quieter than the more common air-cooled jobs, it is kept quite busy, and the lack of insulation lets you know, in no uncertain terms, that it's there. The heating system works off the radiator fan, and is quite basic, at best. It probably would not do in sub-zero weather. Cruising, the car will deliver astonishing mileage, but when it is pushed, the economy curve drops precipitously—as witness our hard-driving figure of 28.8 mpg. Where the car really glistens like a jewel we shall detail.

Because of its size, the 600 will park in spaces that few cars, even economy cars, would regard as spaces, and this with room for four passengers. With a turning circle diameter of 28 feet 6 inches, you could make the proverbial U-turn on a mountain road. The swing axles of the rear give it remarkable roadability. The car has far more handling than its speed will ever let it use. The brake drums

are no larger than beer coasters, but they stop the car as well as those on the 1100, and that is praise indeed. There is a second gear that is all but perfect for town use, and lugging in the 600 is almost unheard of. Luggage space is limited to a small compartment in the "hood" up front, but the rear seat folds to leave enough space for a steamer trunk, which the wide-swinging doors would probably permit you to load. Insulation and padding are limited, but the all-welded unit body and frame will give a lifetime of rattle-free service. Visibility over the stubby front-end, and all around, is fantastic. Finally, combining line and workmanship of the highest order, the little car is really pretty. The 600 has a number of limitations which keep it out of the touring-car category, but if you want a really low-priced, economical car for short runs about the city or in the suburbs, one that's fun to drive and painless to keep up, one that will carry four in comfort, albeit for short distances, you'll have a hard time beating the 600. ◼

43

TESTING the BIALBERO

"...the most beautiful toy ever built for grown-ups."

NOW I KNOW WHAT IT FEELS LIKE to travel in a moon rocket: the noise, the surge of power, the acceleration, the confined space, the sensation of looking at the world from an unusual angle ... and the difficulty of stopping. I got my introduction to the sensation of space travel the easy way, in what has been described as "The most beautiful toy ever built for grown-ups," the *Bialbero*. To give it its full description, this "toy" is the Abarth-Fiat 750 with Zagato body and twin overhead camshaft engine.

This tiny projectile is only hood-high to an Alfa Giulietta sedan, which itself is no windjammer. After the initial gymnastics required to force an entry, the comfort is truly surprising. Adroitly shaped seats for two give support in all the right places. There was a clear two inches between my head and the roof. There is legroom for six-footers, but not an inch is wasted.

Screaming down the Italian Autostrada enclosed in this tiny capsule was a unique motoring experience. Drivers of bigger cars rarely saw it coming up behind until I flashed the lights. It could be steered to an inch through gaps where nothing else could survive. If anyone tried to stay with it, he usually got left behind in a mile or two. It weighs a mere 1200 pounds ready to roll. Tucked away in the smoothly rounded tail is a little jewel of an engine that runs sweetly up to 8000 rpm and develops 62 bhp. The combination is irresistible; I tried two of them. One was a flaming red with a 4.55 axle, the other a shiny silver with a 4.33 final drive.

It was a holiday weekend and the Autostrada was choked with holiday traffic. Conditions could not have been worse for testing a fast car and with anything else I should have given up. This fantastic little machine rocketed through the gaps in the traffic, almost unchecked. After checking the speedometers, both of which were highly optimistic, some quick acceleration runs were made. The results are not offered as definitive performance figures because there was no chance to take a sufficient number of runs, but they give fair indication of the amazing potential of this new Gran Turismo miniature.

	4.55 to 1	4.33 to 1
0 − 30 mph	3.2 sec.	3.9 sec.
0 − 50 mph	7.2 sec.	8.2 sec.
0 − 60 mph	10.3 sec.	11.5 sec.
0 − 80 mph	19 sec.	20 sec.

by Gordon Wilkins

Going away is view most motorists will get of tiny rear-engined coupe which accelerates to 60 mph in just over 10 seconds but is docile in traffic. Rear window is almost flat.

Author tries Zagato-bodied, Abarth-modified Bialbero for size, finds it requires agility to enter but retains ample head- and legroom. Car stands hood-high to Alfa Giulietta sedan.

Carlo Abarth, left, who converted Fiat 600 engine to twin-overhead-cam 750cc unit, explains horse-power testing to author. Engine develops 62 bhp, turns a smooth 8000 rpm without bending valves.

TESTING THE BIALBERO

Abarth single-seat streamliner serves as test vehicle setting records on Monza with each new-type engine developed by firm.

Piston, camshaft and crank for Abarth-Fiat 750 are carefully turned out to withstand high revs. New pistons will be die-cast; this one has 9.5 to 1 compression.

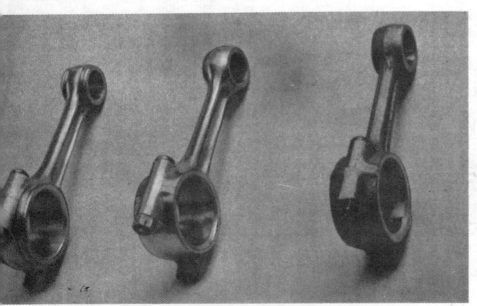

Connecting rod refinements, right to left, from standard Fiat 600 to polished and lightened for Abarth production engines to grooved for twin-cam race engine.

Below 4000 rpm the engine ran smoothly enough, but it is not really getting to work. Above that figure the power comes in with such a rush that it needs a keen eye on the rev counter to prevent it from soaring over 8000. Normal gearshifts are made at 7000. If you should miss a gear there is no great danger until you hit 8400. Then a valve is likely to caress a piston. The engine is incredibly smooth and sweet right through the range. Though no-one could pretend it is inaudible, the snarl from the twin tailpipes, as the car rushes up and down through the gears, is music for the motoring-minded.

Under the prevailing conditions it was not possible to get a series of uninterrupted runs up to a genuine 100 mph, but it seems safe to say that 0 – 100 times should be around 40 seconds. Thanks to this staggering acceleration I was able to snatch a few readings over measured distances which showed a mean maximum speed of exactly 110 mph. Given ideal conditions Carlo Abarth says it should do a genuine 112 mph.

Designed primarily as a competition car it is not particularly cheap (just under $3300 at the works), but it is more than just a temperamental racing machine. It is docile enough to drive in town traffic. On winding roads its high performance and small size are a combination which can defeat most owners of high powered sporting machinery. Steering is sweet, quick and precise. There is a certain amount of oversteer. With the torque available at the rear wheels, taking sharp corners is simply a matter of flicking the wheel and bringing the tail around with the throttle.

The brakes are developed from those of the Fiat 600 which were designed for half the Abarth's speed. Even with competition linings they could not be described as powerful. Putting them on at anything between 80 and 100 mph produces a marked vibration from the front end but no other perceptible result. It takes some quick work with the gear lever if one needs to slow down quickly. The present brakes would probably serve for hillclimbs where this Abarth will be very hard to beat. Something more powerful is needed for circuit racing and fast road driving. It would be relatively easy to fit more effective brakes, possibly discs, yet it remains to be seen whether the suspension would have to be stiffened as a result.

Carlo Abarth has beaten tougher problems than this one on brakes and he has the matter in hand. It is expected that the 750 Bialbero will be homologated as a Gran Turismo car in time for Sebring, where three of them are being entered, for the 12-hour endurance race, one to be shared by Cattini and Poltronieri and another car by Sala and Baghetti.

The engine is directly developed from the standard Fiat 600 unit on which Abarth worked wonders with their push-rods and long stroke crankshaft before turning to overhead camshafts to give him an extra 1000 revs. Much of the design and development was done by a bearded young engineer, Luigi Guerrieri, who until recently was with Bugatti. The standard Fiat 600 block is used with modified oil ways to provide a flow to the valve gear. The head is a Silumin (aluminum-silicon) casting with inlet valves 1.34-inch diameter and exhaust valves of 1.18-inch. Valves are at 80-degrees included angle and are operated through piston-type tappets. The camshafts are enclosed by magnesium alloy covers. A counterbalanced crankshaft is made of the same steel as used by Alfa Romeo and runs in Vandervell copper-lead-indium bearings, but is not nitrided. The camshaft drive is in two stages. The first is the normal Fiat 2 to 1 reduction from the crankshaft to a stub shaft placed where the normal camshaft would be, and from there a second chain takes the drive to the two overhead camshafts.

Standard Fiat 600 connecting rods are used but they are highly polished and lightened by 0.9 — 1.0 ounce. For racing engines there is an even lighter rod where a total of 2.3 ounces has been saved by turning curves around the eyes at each end. The present pistons give a compression ratio of 9.5 to 1 and eventually more weight will be saved by using special die-cast pistons. It was quite a problem to find space for the two twin-choke downdraft Weber carburetors on the tiny cylinder head. They are mounted at an angle to the center line on short curved stub pipes. The angle between carburetor and engine center line is well within the limit recommended by Weber to prevent fuel surge away from the jets during acceleration.

Past experience shows that Abarth horses do not appear for just a few seconds as a flash reading on the dynamometer; they are horses with sturdy legs that stay on the job through continuous days and nights of punishment on the test track, for it has become the rule for every new-type Abarth engine to be put into one of his streamlined single seaters and sent for a long distance record attempt at Monza. The Abarth Fiat 750 recently set up a new series of class records extending from 100 miles at 127.332 mph through one hour at 127.852 mph to 500 km at 128.490.

Indications are that the 750cc twin-engine overhead cam engine should be giving 70 bhp before long. There is a project to install it ahead of the rear axle in a miniature roadster with tubular chassis. This should be a stupefying little machine—dynamite in a small size stick. /MT

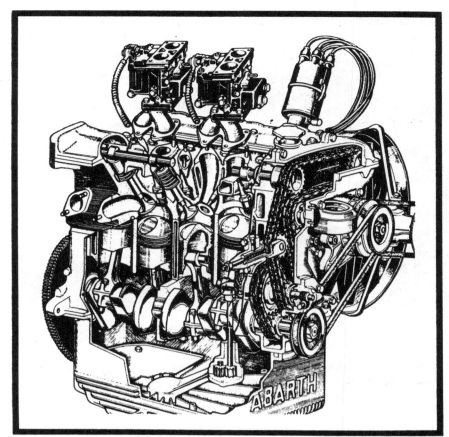

Engine carries two Weber dual-throat carburetors mounted at angle because of limited space. Two overhead camshafts drive valves set at 80-degree included angle.

Photos by Bertazzini and Publifoto

Twin-overhead-cam engine combines reliability with high performance. Currently 62 horses, power may be boosted to 70 hp which should increase already amazing speeds. Engine pulled streamliner 128 mph, will get two-passenger coupe to 112.

FIAT-ABARTH 850

An almost indecently desirable automobile

WHILE UNANIMITY IS RARE among people in general, it is almost unheard of within the ranks of automobile enthusiasts—some dissension existing even among members of the same one-make club. Our staff members are, if anything, more inclined to differ than most, and the arrival of any new test car is inevitably followed by a lively debate. Usually, however, there will be enough agreement on specific points to establish a collective viewpoint and this overall staff opinion becomes a guide for the written report.

In the case of Carlo Abarth's latest creation, the Fiat-Abarth 850, there was no need for prolonged discussion—the car completely captivated everyone. Abarth's various creations on the Fiat 600 chassis are always rather well received because of their extravagantly sporting qualities. However, the new Allemano-bodied coupe is doubly enchanting for it is—in addition to being a fine sporting machine—a completely practical car for day-to-day transportation. This is not to say that the other, Zagato-bodied, cars are totally impractical; but their design is more competition-oriented and therefore less pleasant for touring than the 850.

The highest praise must go to Carrozzeria Allemano for the coachwork that it has created for this new Fiat-Abarth. It is not easy to achieve a balanced design on so small a chassis; the 79-in. wheelbase and tiny 12-in. wheels do not lend themselves to bodywork that is both well proportioned and large enough to accommodate full-size human beings. Nonetheless, this has been done and with such a deft touch that there is more room for people and luggage than in the bulkier-looking Zagato, while visibility is also much improved. Actually luggage space is uncommonly good. There is room for about 3 suitcases behind the seats on a low shelf, and a pair of

very sturdy and handsome leather straps is provided to keep everything tied down.

The exterior finish of the car is excellent, with good-quality paint and a close, even fit around the door, trunk, and engine compartment openings. This is a point that deserves special attention; very small cars must be very carefully finished, for uneven and/or excessive gaps between body panels—items which tend to disappear on the vast flanks of a "full-size" domestic car—

become horribly obvious as the overall size is reduced.

Most of the bodywork on the Fiat-Abarth 850 is steel, but the outer door panels, trunk and engine compartment lids and some of the interior metalwork, notably the instrument panel, are of aluminum. The fenders and the rest of the exterior panels—which must bear the brunt of chance encounters with flying stones and other such air-borne debris—are of steel. While on the subject of assault from without, we might mention that the bumpers, especially those at the front, are probably not quite high enough to fend off the best efforts of the "keep-backing-until-you-hear-glass" type driver. But the Fiat-Abarth 850 is not alone in this and if some care is taken in choosing parking spots, the 850 should collect no more dents than other sports cars.

Getting into the 850 is not a feat that can be accomplished with consummate grace—but with the large door opening provided, it isn't very difficult, either. This is, obviously, the penalty one pays for having a car that is only 47 in. in overall height. Even so, once settled inside, one has room to spare (relative to other sports cars of course). The seats are adjustable, in both the usual fore and aft plane, and for recline—the range of adjustment being so great that just about any driver can find a combination that suits him to the proverbial "T." The seats are of the bolstered-edge, semi-bucket type that have become so common in modern GT machines and are covered with a synthetic material that is almost indistinguishable from, but probably more durable than, real leather. The door panels are done in the same material and a soft carpeting covers the rest of the interior.

The instruments and controls are well arranged and can be read or reached with a minimum of effort. The tachometer occupies the place of honor right under the driver's line of vision and gives the steadiest readings we have ever seen. All of the over-run and bobbling that confuse readings on most of these necessary instruments are entirely missing; the needle follows the engine's speed exactly—no guesswork is required.

Starting the 850 takes just the slightest tug at the starting lever, aided when cold by use of the cold-starting device, and the engine warms to operating temperature rapidly. Only while idling is there any indication of the engine's very high stage of tune. At idle (approximately 1000 rpm) the engine has that peculiar lumpy feeling that only comes with a very "sporty" valve-timing. However, once the car is under way the engine smooths out and, except for its uncommonly thrusty response, feels just like the Fiat 600 engine from which it is derived. A good part of this feeling of smoothness comes from the fact that the

Ready access to gas tank and spare tire, but no luggage space.

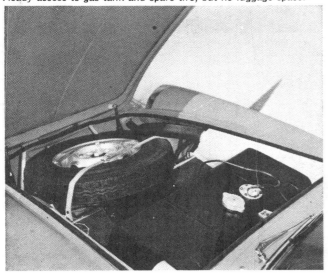

The smooth and powerful Fiat-based 833-cc engine.

engine's power is spread over a very wide rpm range, making it possible to use top gear even at 20 mph.

Driving the Fiat-Abarth 850 is a pure pleasure; the steering is marvellous and, although a high percentage of weight is carried on the rear wheels, only a trace of oversteer is evident. In fact, under most conditions the 850 exhibits a tendency toward understeer. We did discover that lifting one's foot from the throttle while cornering hard would cause the tail to swing out pretty far.

The car showed rare good manners during our acceleration runs; all too often our determined approach to the standing quarter-mile will reveal that a car is prone to all kinds of wheel-shudder, axle-hop and clutch ailments. The 850, however, got under way beautifully every time—the clutch biting solidly and the wheels slipping just enough to keep the engine from bogging down. Only 6000 rpm were used in the gears, as the car was still quite new, and out of respect for this newness we made but one high-speed run. We did find that at speeds above 70 mph the trace of oversteer became more noticeable, but it was never bothersome. The ride was very good (especially for such a light car) and became even better as speeds increased.

Mechanically, this new 850 is almost pure Fiat 600; the chassis is used as purchased from Fiat and only the ring and pinion gears are changed in the transmission/differential case—all intermediate ratios are standard, which is quite all right with us, as the synchromesh is a delight and the spacing of the ratios is perfect. The engine comes more highly modified, with a special crankshaft, pistons, camshaft and several man-hours of special attention to the ports. Meticulous care is taken in balancing and assembling these engines and their smoothness at elevated crankshaft speeds is a tribute to the effectiveness of such techniques. The high percentage of Fiat parts used in the 850 might offend a purist, but those parts have acquired a good reputation for strength and their presence makes the car a lot easier to service than would otherwise be possible. This could be vitally important on a cross-country trip.

As was stated earlier, our entire staff was completely won over by this little jewel and was extremely sorry when it had to be returned to the Abarth distributor. It is not the fastest car in the world, but its fine handling, lovely lines, good finish and inspiring exhaust-note all combine to make this just about the most desirable small sports car that we've seen.

Princely comfort and the sporting look in miniature.

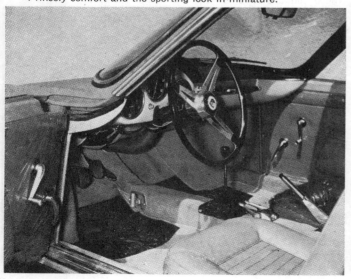

FIAT-ABARTH 850

SPECIFICATIONS

List price	$3395
Curb weight	1345
Test weight	1720
distribution, %	41/59
Dimensions, length	132
width	55.9
height	46.8
Wheelbase	78.7
Tread, f and r	45.3/45.4
Tire size	5.20-12
Brake lining area	67
Steering, turns	3.3
turning circle, ft	28
Engine type	4 cyl, ohv
Bore & stroke	2.44 x 2.72
Displacement, cu in	50.8
cc	833
Compression ratio	9.0
Bhp @ rpm	52 @ 6000
equivalent mph	98.0
Torque, lb-ft	51.3 @ 4500
equivalent mph	73.4

PERFORMANCE

Top speed (mfg), mph	100
best timed run	90.0
3rd (6500)	71
2nd (6500)	46
1st (6500)	28

FUEL CONSUMPTION

Normal range, mpg	32/40

ACCELERATION

0-30 mph, sec	5.0
0-40 mph	7.5
0-50 mph	12.2
0-60 mph	17.6
0-70 mph	28.6
0-80 mph	31.9
0-90 mph	
0-100 mph	
Standing ¼ mile	20.6
speed at end, mph	64

GEAR RATIOS

O/d ( ), overall		n.a.
4th (0.896)		3.88
3rd (1.333)		5.77
2nd (2.055)		8.90
1st (3.385)		14.7

TAPLEY DATA

4th, lb/ton @ mph	165 @ 54
3rd	265 @ 45
2nd	390 @ 38
1st	520 @ 26
Total drag at 60 mph, lb	78

CALCULATED DATA

Lb/hp (test wt)	33.1
Cu ft/ton mile	80.1
Mph/1000 rpm (4th)	16.3
Engine revs/mile	3680
Piston travel, ft/mile	1667
Rpm @ 2500 ft/min	5500
equivalent mph	88.5
R&T wear index	61.3

SPEEDOMETER ERROR

30 mph	actual 29.3
40 mph	37.6
50 mph	46.5
60 mph	55.2
70 mph	64.1
80 mph	72.8
90 mph	
100 mph	

FIAT-ABARTH 850

ROAD & TRACK

MPH (corrected) vs ELAPSED TIME IN SECONDS

FUN with a FIAT

OCCASIONALLY, when the spinning clutch and feeble synchromesh on the domestic Mini-Seven depress me more than somewhat I beg a few days' with the Technical Editor's newish Fiat 600D for the purpose of restoring my flagging belief in the value of a good gear change, and also to show *him* of course, that front-wheel-drive cars need not necessarily have heavy steering and poor turning circles!

As always one is immediately impressed by the air of exuberance about the Fiat 600, and the 600D in particular. The learned owner of the model in question has said more than once that he regards its design as the brightest jewel in the small car treasury, and at these moments of fair exchange I find myself agreeing with him thoroughly.

The 600D still can't outrun a Mini, and the latter pulls away all too rapidly after the drag passes the 50 m.p.h. stage. Yet surprisingly, the Fiat can stick fairly close to the Seven, upto that point and I have read somewhere that its lower maximum speed is more a matter of deliberate planning than accidental shortness of breath. The respective sprint figures anyway are as follows, with the Mini returns in brackets for comparison : —

Zero to 40 m.p.h.	12.5 secs.	(11.5)
,, ,, 50 ,,	20.6 ,,	(18)
,, ,, 60 ,,	36 ,,	(31)
Standing Quarter mile	24 ,,	(23.5)
Maximum Speed (top)	65 m.p.h.	(73)

Piston speeds too are instructive. At 65 m.p.h. the Fiat engine is working at 1,910 ft./min. piston speed while the Mini at the same road rate is achieving 2,090 ft./min. piston speed. The big "but" here is that Fiat designers don't much fancy the idea of their pistons exceeding 2,000 ft./min. at anytime apparently, and therefore stifle things a bit to keep the road speed within that limitation. Figures apart, the 600D seems to *enjoy* its striving no matter how hard-pushed and it is more fun and games to play with. I think that this may be a point involving those built-in safeguards.

The 600's speedometer, by the way, still has red warning circles to advise a conscientious driver when it's time to change up. You are not ordained to observe them although the instruction book says that the Topolino will last very much longer if you do.

The 600D, it will be observed at this juncture, is the lowest-priced multi-cylinder mini-car (now that the term is no longer contemptuous!) on the Irish market ; one doesn't have to pay a delivery charge, or extra for an interior light, winding window trim, heater, over-riders or water temperature signal.

As one steps into it after the Mini, one's thoughts revolve around the incredible surfeit of bric-a-brac space on the Seven and the equally incredible lack of it on the Fiat. You find too, that the real liveliness of metal springs (transverse leaf at front and twin coils at rear) contrasts unfavourably with the more leisurely ride of the Mini's rubber cones. On the other hand, the locational advantages of a transverse

spring when it comes to absorbing front-wheel brake torque appear obvious on the Fiat, for it stops in a much more secure fashion.

That is a further reminder, needless to add, that Fiats — as ever — have magnificent brakes. It is not only a matter of drum design and decent lining-area-to-gross-weight proportions but partially (in the 600 case) it is a case of weight distribution. With two blokes aboard, the Fiat front axle's weight ration of 42.8 per cent may not be related to the ideal for road-holding and cornering, but for braking it's terrific. One understands this better when one reckons that the Mini simply *has* to bleed off a hefty amount of brake effort from the rear wheels, because when you have 77 per cent. of all weight bearing on the front wheels (as for example going down a hill and retarding against the engine only) the back wheels have only a trivial bite left for braking. To prove the point it is necessary to have a run in a 600D for oneself, and to compare its behaviour when braked on a down-slope in relation to the antics of its front-engined competitors.

These, and the astonishing ease of entry and exit, are the things I recall first on our brief changeovers; the abiding recollection also is the bespoke driving position and the Fiat's precise, well-engineered controls. Above all, the gearchange. Without any doubt the 600's stirabout is the nicest thing this side of a Porsche, flattering and bringing the best out of any driver. The synchromesh never does, and never did, make mistakes. Quite an amazing contrast with what I have to contend with normally!

The ratios themselves have undergone considerable revision since the days of Tosca I (which, you will remember, was the T.E.'s last love, now traded like a slave against the D model), but when Mirafiori altered things they did not fall for the obvious, did not just stuff in the more powerful 767 c.c. engine for the sake of stop-watch performance as they might have done, and understandably too. No indeed. The adult-minded Italians dwelt at some length on the less glamorous virtues of economy, durability and refinement. The measure of their success has been amply reflected in the fact that the 600 — due to go out on pension last autumn — has continued to sell so well that nobody now knows when it will retire! As a matter of interest some 1,250,000 have been sold. When you start taking petrol consumption tests you begin to realise why.

Working like blazes the Technical Editor's superbly maintained, but strictly non-modified Tosca II will put 42/48 miles behind a gallon can of petrol with ease. But to be more specific, it will, at a steady 40 m.p.h. on level ground, hum along at practically 60 m.p.g. In fact it used so darned little petrol at a steady 30 m.p.h. that the editorial and very expensive flow-meter (it had already been outraged by the Peugeot diesel the week before) fused and burned out its points! Oh yes, I had already been assured by himself that the speedometer was dead accurate (on speed) upto 50 m.p.h., and 3 per cent optimistic on distance.

CONTINUED ON PAGE 87

1827

FIAT 600D

The 600D is available only in two-door form, of course, but the doors open wide, and both front seats tilt forward to give easy access to the rear seat. Forward-opening doors are retained, but they have sturdy, positive latches

ALTERATIONS made to the Fiat 600 in the six years since its introduction have been confined to details, but the basic model is now supplemented by the option of what may be considered rather more than a de luxe version, called the 600D. Apart from several minor improvements, there are the important differences that a larger, more powerful engine is fitted and the final drive is higher geared.

Both the bore and stroke of the four-cylinder engine have been increased—to 62 and 63.5mm respectively—putting the capacity up to 767 c.c. Comparable figures for the standard 600 are 60×56 mm and 633 c.c. There is thus a useful increase of 21 per cent in swept volume, and a consequent gain in liveliness.

In comparison with the 600 tested in May 1955, the 600D managed a small gain in maximum speed, amounting to 2 m.p.h. for the mean two-way maximum, recording just over 66 m.p.h. compared with 64 m.p.h.; but a much more notable improvement is evident in acceleration. From a standing start, 50 m.p.h. is reached through the gears in 23·8sec, representing a saving of nearly 8sec, and the standing start quarter-mile at 24·9 sec took 2·1sec less.

At any speed the engine is particularly smooth and unobtrusive, and it even pulled without snatch when acceleration was being timed from 10 m.p.h. in top gear—not that one would normally come down so low in this gear. Starting is always reliable, and is immediate when the engine is hot. From cold the choke must be used, and it is needed during the first minute or so after a cold start. In the engine compartment one notices two pipes leading to the air filter, which is of pancake type on the 600D.

One pipe admits cold air and the other supplies air warmed by the exhaust manifold, the choice being made by a flap which may be set for winter or summer use. During our test this was left in the cold weather setting;

the rapidity of warming-up due to this variable hot spot was appreciated. Engine temperature is maintained at the correct level by a thermostatically controlled flap, adjusting the escape of cooling air passing through the radiator.

The extra performance—which is considerably more pronounced on the road than the bare figures suggest—is achieved with a negligible increase in fuel consumption, and indeed the m.p.g. figures at steady speeds of 30 and 40 m.p.h. proved better with this larger-engined version than with the standard 600. The overall consumption figure was 38·0 m.p.g., compared with the 38·8 m.p.g. achieved with the 600, and, of course, in both cases much hard driving with sustained high speeds was included. On M1, where full throttle is used almost inevitably with this car—except for very patient drivers—the consumption fell below 32 m.p.g. A round figure of 40 m.p.g. is the lowest which the Fiat reaches in normal conditions, while with restraint in use of the performance the consumption improved to nearly 50 m.p.g.

Low Fuel Costs

Particularly important is the fact that the Fiat runs very satisfactorily on regular grade petrol; on this fuel there is no pinking or running on, and it would be false economy to use petrol of higher octane values. It saves 5½d a gallon, and the use of fuel costing 4s 2d per gallon puts a target of 200 miles per £1 well within range of the Fiat. The fuel tank holds a fraction under six gallons, and is mounted in the forward luggage compartment. There is no spout for the filler, so that pump attendants can feed in fuel as fast as they like without blowback; when the level is really low the driver can make a visual check to see how much remains. A fuel gauge is the only instrument provided in addition to the speedometer, and it incorporates a small warning light which comes on, flashing at first, when the contents are down to the last gallon. This is matched by a similar light to indicate abnormal engine temperature.

At sustained high speeds the Fiat runs very happily and without protest, and although the rhythmic beat of the rear-mounted engine is clearly audible there is no resonance or roar to suggest that it is revving too fast at high speeds.

Opening quarter lights in the doors and extra ventilating louvres in the engine cover are the sole exterior identifying features of the D version Fiat 600. The rear windows are fixed, as on the cheaper model

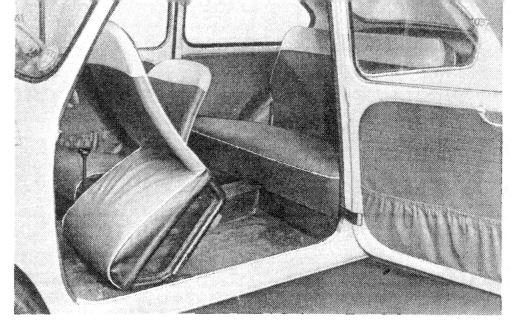

There are map pockets in the doors, and space for parcels is provided in a deep well behind the rear seat. When the car is used only "two-up" the back seat squab may be folded to serve as a luggage platform

With the throttle kept fully open the car's speed fluctuates considerably according to gradient, building up to an indicated 75 m.p.h. on the somewhat optimistic speedometer (69 true) on down grades, and falling back quite a lot on long rises.

The tyre diameter and section are unaltered, but the 600D has a 4·37 to 1 final drive ratio instead of the ordinary 600's 4·82, and the equivalent speed per 1,000 r.p.m. in top gear is raised from 12·9 to 14·1 m.p.h. Even on a long downhill run the engine will not over-rev with this higher gearing, while the effect on the cruising abilities of the car is to combine a useful reduction in noise with the advantages of reduced stress and engine wear when high speeds are kept up over long periods.

Speeds in the gears are increased in proportion to final drive ratio although the same gearbox is used. As is usual practice on the small Fiat cars, the maximum recommended speeds in the three lower gears are indicated on the speedometer, and these are now 19, 28 and 44 m.p.h. respectively, compared with 15, 25 and 40 for the 600. These are rather timid maxima which can be exceeded by a wide margin yet with little or no advantage; thus although an ultimate maximum of 56 m.p.h. is available in third, it was found better to change into top at or near the recommended 44 m.p.h.

Everything about this little car encourages one to make liberal use of its gearbox, which has a really excellent change mechanism. The gear level sprouts vertically from the floor and is conveniently near to the driver's left hand. The change is exceedingly quick, so that the lever can be thrust rapidly and easily from one position to another. In snatch changes the synchromesh remains thoroughly effective, and although bottom gear has no synchromesh, it is easily engaged by a quick double-declutch.

Full engagement of the clutch occurs over a small amount of pedal travel, but the take-up is smooth and readily absorbs full engine power while making fast starts from rest. Yet when the car failed to restart on the 1-in-3 test hill it was clutch slip and not lack of power which held it back. On this exceptionally steep gradient the handbrake would just hold the car, but its lever, conveniently placed between the two bucket seats, had to be pulled up hard and very high to exert the required effort.

In all conditions the footbrake proved very efficient, and the car stops reassuringly in a straight line when braked violently. A pedal effort of only 50lb is enough to produce almost the maximum retardation available—further pressure on the pedal tending to lock the rear wheels. Women drivers, in particular, will like the powerful response of the brakes to light pedal pressures. Relatively slow acceleration of a low-powered car such as the Fiat gives the brakes plenty of respite for cooling down; no brake fade was experienced on British roads. Italian cars, born and bred in a mountainous country, usually are particularly well equipped in this respect.

Easy to park

One feature contributing largely to the Fiat's delightful manœuvrability is its compact turning circle, for which the greatest diameter is 29ft 9in., including allowance for the front overhang to clear walls; and in most city streets the 600D can make a U-turn with space to spare. Parking is splendidly easy, and the car can be tucked readily into kerb-side gaps. Here the lightness of the steering plays its part, and the effort required at the wheel remains exceptionally small even at manœuvring speeds. With 3½ turns of the wheel from lock to lock, the mechanism is quite low-geared, but it is completely free from play or lost movement. In spite of this precision, however, there is a lot of wander on the straight, particularly in windy weather, and this calls for constant correction at the wheel.

To counteract the effects of the weight distribution, with its strong bias over the rear wheels, the recommended tyre pressures have a marked differential from front to back, the respective figures being 14 and 23 p.s.i. With these settings there is considerable understeer on corners, which immediately becomes oversteer if the throttle is released in the middle of a bend. With the front tyres also inflated to 23 p.s.i. there was still a basic understeer. Although a bit

A pancake-type air filter is an exterior distinction of the larger engine. All components, including the radiator filler, are very accessible

FIAT 600D . . .

Space for a small amount of luggage in the front "boot" is shared with the fuel tank and the spare wheel. The luggage locker lid is released by a lever within the car, and has a safety catch

fickle in behaviour, the Fiat remains very easy and good fun to handle on winding roads, and it can be rushed round sharp corners with confidence.

Little body roll occurs even during fast cornering, the transverse front leaf spring being anchored to provide stiffness in roll. The independent rear suspension is by coil springs, and long, semi-trailing links locate the rear wheel assemblies. The ride is generally quite soft and comfortable, and minor surface irregularities pass practically unnoticed.

Partly, perhaps, as a result of the short wheelbase, there is some plunging at the front end, and this is the limiting factor when the Fiat was tried over unmade and deeply potholed tracks. Provided speed was kept reasonably low the car sat down well on its little wheels and the occupants were not much jolted or thrown about. The manner in which the suspension deals with uneven *pavé* is superb, and no road shocks are felt through the steering. On a simulated "washboard" surface, however, there is a lot of vibration—this road condition alone catches the suspension off guard.

Good Forward Vision

Visibility to front and rear is fine, and although the screen pillars are fairly thick the driver does not find his vision unduly obstructed; part of the sloping bonnet and both front wings are seen from the driving seat. The rear side windows are fixed, but those in the doors wind down and are supplemented by swivelling quarter-lights—one of the few external identifying features of the D-type Fiat 600. The left door is locked from inside by rotating a small

catch, but the driver's door may be secured only with the key, which is not the same as that used for the ignition switch. There is no reversing lamp nor provision for fitting one.

The interior mirror is mounted too high to give a view of traffic which is not following closely. A lamp sufficiently bright for map reading is incorporated with the body of the mirror, and is switched on automatically when the driver's door is opened.

A small lamp in the engine compartment, wired in parallel with the sidelamps, is turned on when the engine cover is raised. The usual Fiat lighting controls are retained on the 600D; a small toggle switch on the facia operates the main lighting circuit, which is wired through the three-way ignition switch, and a control on the steering column selects side lamps or headlamps on main or dipped beams. When any driving lamps are on, a small green warning light appears, and this is supplemented by a blue tell-tale for the main beams. These two facia lights and that for the winking indicators are adjustable for intensity by rotating their lenses, a very practical and praiseworthy refinement. Although the headlamps are small they give powerful illumination, and there is a useful pool of light in front of the car on dipped beam, with perhaps too abrupt a cut-off but one which certainly ensures that oncoming drivers are not dazzled.

Tiny pinpoint lights set in the instrument cluster warn of loss of dynamo charges or oil pressure. As in most cars, the latter sometimes flickered at tick-over when the oil was really hot. When one wishes to leave the lamps on while the car is parked, the ignition key is turned to the right, beyond the "off" position, and withdrawn. A feature of the 600D is that the floor-mounted starter control is discontinued, for the starter is now operated by turning the ignition key against a spring. The rich mixture control is still on the floor, as on the ordinary 600.

For a car of this size, rear seat legroom is quite acceptable, and if those on the front seat condescend to move it forward a little, four can travel in commendable comfort. When two are travelling they can set the seats sufficiently far back to allow very ample leg space from the toeboard, and the driving position is comfortable. The driver has to rest his left foot beneath the clutch pedal, but otherwise the pedal layout is ideal, and allows the enthusiast to "heel-and-toe" with the brake and throttle pedals. The seats are rather firm but comfortable and give good support, particu-

Distribution of air from the heater to the front interior is varied by two adjustable shutters near the occupants' feet. There is a vigorous delivery to the demisters with the heater in use

larly in the small of the back. Their springing is pleasantly "dead," and even on rough roads the occupants are not bounced. As extras, buyers may specify front seats with reclining backrests.

For a tall driver the sweep of the wipers finishes awkwardly just in front of his line of vision. There is the usual Fiat provision that the wipers are parked when the wiper switch is pressed down against a spring loading. A simple, direct-pressure type of screen washer is standard.

At the front of the luggage locker are stored the spare wheel, and a tool kit which comprises a pillar jack, a wheel nut spanner and a generous assortment of hand tools. The

lubrication requirement is for attention to eight grease points at 1,500-mile intervals.

Fresh-air heating is provided as standard, admitting air warmed by the radiator. The flap control for the heater was particularly stiff on the test car, and the heater was slow to warm through after a cold start, though it proved really effective when under way.

For its extra performance and gains in quietness and cruising ability alone the D version of the Fiat 600 would be well worth the £32 extra which it costs in this country; and the other refinements mentioned help to make it a welcome new member of the Fiat family.

FIAT 600D

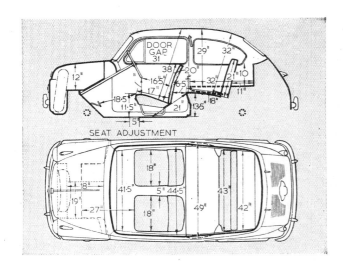

Scale ⅛in. to 1ft. Driving seat in central position. Cushions uncompressed.

DATA

PRICE (basic), with saloon body, **£438**.
British purchase tax, **£183 12s 6d**.
Total (in Great Britain), **£621 12s 6d**.
Extras: Reclining seats **£7 1s 8d** inc. purchase tax.

ENGINE: Capacity, 767 c.c. (46·8 cu. in.).
Number of cylinders, 4.
Bore and stroke, 62×63·5mm (2·44×2·5in.).
Valve gear, overhead, pushrods and rockers.
Compression ratio, 7·5 to 1.
B.h.p. 29 (net) at 4,800 r.p.m. (b.h.p. per ton laden 38·5).
Torque, 40 lb. ft. at 2,800 r.p.m.
M.p.h. per 1,000 r.p.m. in top gear, 14·1.

WEIGHT (with 5 gal fuel): 12 cwt (1,351 lb)
Weight distribution (per cent): F, 37·8: R, 62·2.
Laden as tested, 15 cwt (1,687 lb).
Lb per c.c. (laden), 2·2.

BRAKES: Type, Fiat hydraulic.
Drum dimensions: F and R, 7·28in. dia.; 1·18in. wide.
Swept area: 108 sq. in. (144 sq. in. per ton laden).

TYRES: 5·20—12in. Dunlop Gold Seal.
Pressures (p.s.i.): F, 14; R, 23 (all conditions).

TANK CAPACITY: 6 Imperial gallons.
Oil sump, 6·25 pints.
Cooling system, 8 pints.

DIMENSIONS: Wheelbase, 6ft 6·7in.
Track: F, 3ft 9·2in.; R, 3ft 9·4in.
Length (overall): 10ft 9in.
Width, 4ft 6·2in.
Height, 4ft 7·4in.
Ground clearance, 6·2in.
Frontal area, 16 sq. ft (approx.).

ELECTRICAL SYSTEM: 12-volt; 32 ampère-hour battery.
Headlamps, 45–40 watt bulbs.

SUSPENSION: Front, wishbones and transverse leaf spring. Telescopic dampers. Rear, independent, semi-trailing links and coil springs. Telescopic dampers.

PERFORMANCE

ACCELERATION TIMES (mean):

Speed range, Gear Ratios, and Time in Sec.

m.p.h.	4·37 to 1	6·49 to 1	10·01 to 1	16·5 to 1
10—30	15·9	9·5	6·7	—
20—40	17·4	10·7	—	—
30—50	21·4	19·4	—	—

From rest through gears to:

30 m.p.h.	..	7·8 sec.
40 ,,	..	13·9 ,,
50 ,,	..	23·8 ,,

Standing quarter mile 24·9 sec.

MAXIMUM SPEEDS ON GEARS:

Gear			m.p.h.	k.p.h.
Top	..	(mean)	66·2	106·5
		(best)	68	109·5
3rd	..	..	56	90
2nd	..	..	34	55
1st	..	..	22	35

TRACTIVE EFFORT (by Tapley meter):

		Pull (lb per ton)	Equivalent gradient
Top	..	147	1 in 15·7
Third	..	247	1 in 9·1
Second	..	380	1 in 5·8

BRAKES (at 30 m.p.h. in neutral):

Pedal load in lb	Retardation	Equiv. stopping distance in ft
25	0·30g	100
50	0·83g	36
75	0·86g	35

FUEL CONSUMPTION (at steady speeds in top gear):

30 m.p.h.	55·6 m.p.g.	
40 ,,	48·8 ,,	
50 ,,	38·4 ,,	
60 ,,	34·2 ,,	

Overall fuel consumption for 1,683 miles, 38·0 m.p.g. (7·4 litres per 100 km.).
Approximate normal range 32–49 m.p.g. (8·8–5·8 litres per 100 km.).
Fuel: Commercial grades.

STEERING: Turning circle,

Between kerbs: L, 28ft 7in.; R, 28ft 4in.
Between walls: L, 29ft 9in.; R, 29ft. 6in.
Turns of steering wheel from lock to lock, 3·5.

TEST CONDITIONS: Weather: Dry, breeze gusting to 20 m.p.h.
Air temperature, 50 deg. F.

SPEEDOMETER CORRECTION: m.p.h.

Car speedometer	..	..	10	20	30	40	50	60	70
True speed	..	..	8	18	27	36	45	54	64

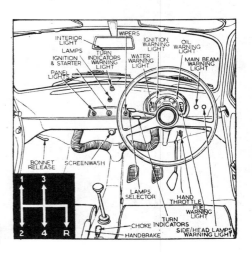

SOUTH BY 600

A long trip in a baby Fiat is something which may not appeal to everyone, but author Kable did the grand Tasmanian tour in ease, comfort and economy.

By MIKE KABLE

MANY of my motoring friends, I'm afraid to say, are still decidedly biased against small foreign cars and stubbornly refuse to recognise their capabilities.

"You'll never make it," they said bluntly.

They were, of course, referring to my forthcoming trip to Tasmania, and for once in my life I was inclined to believe them as the wheels of the Fiat 600 began rolling off the first few miles of a fairly tight 14-day itinerary.

Now that it's over, and the story can be told of just how economical a long motoring journey can be, the most difficult thing is convincing people that we covered some 3000 miles, averaged 45 mph overall at 45 mpg and did not lay a spanner on the car — thanks to the thoroughness of Fiat specialist John Monaghan, who gave it a good preparatory going-over — from the time we left to the time we returned.

Frankly, we did not equal the Morris 850's recent penny-a-mile feat— we did not try to—but in anyone's language 3000 miles for a total cost of £14 for fuel and oil is very, very inexpensive motoring. On my calculations that's a little under twopence a mile.

The tiny Fiat for a start carried two occupants and their luggage. In Tasmania this swelled to four occupants and four sets of luggage, which quite definitely amounted to overloading when you consider that the motive power is just a bare 633 cc. Despite all this the little car kept chugging along merrily without missing a beat.

There's an old saying (which I suspect also applies to a certain South Seas island) that once you've been to Tasmania you'll want to return. It's quite true. My co-driver on the trip, Max Rowling, and I had travelled there a short while after the *Princess of Tasmania* first began operating in October, 1959. The island is absolutely a tourist and motorist's paradise and its people still humane and trusting.

Tasmania's uncrowded highways and roads and bracing air have to be experienced to be believed, and although some magnificent views can be seen without leaving the bitumen the real scenic beauty of this little land is mostly found on secondary dirt roads and bush tracks, where an independently sprung car is almost a necessity. So on this occasion the MG was left at home and the Fiat, a 1959 model with 30,000 miles up, was pressed into service.

Miniature steam locomotives, like this one at Queenstown on the West Coast, have a particular fascination for tourists — and small boys!

Queenstown, a modern-style "wild west" town, is set in Tasmania's rugged West Coast and should be included in any touring itinerary.

Beginning a Tasmanian tour, a Volkswagen drives off the vehicle deck of the Princess at the Devonport terminal.

The very first advantage of taking this small car was that we paid the lowest possible car rate—£18 return—for the sea crossing. This compares pretty favorably with the highest rate of £44 for big cars with trailers or caravans and will mean a considerable difference when the proposed roll-on, roll-off service begins to operate from Sydney to Tasmania.

All booking arrangements were carried out through the Tasmanian Government Tourist Bureau in Sydney and no difficulty was encountered in getting accommodation on the ship, as the period at the end of May is the beginning of the "off season". From October right through to April is another matter, and berths should be booked as far ahead as possible —at least a year, if that's practicable.

Generally one of the most tiresome tasks of any motoring journey in a small car is the constant, twice-daily packing and unpacking of luggage in cramped spaces. However, the Fiat's rear seat folds down in accepted gran turismo fashion and the rubber-covered platform holds an enormous amount of baggage and is reasonably accessible. With this back compartment and the one-suitcase pit under the bonnet well loaded we set off, covering the 130-odd miles from Sydney to Bathurst in three hours, and the long 260-mile hop over the Olympic Highway to Albury in just five and a half hours, including the last 61 miles in half a minute under an hour! Albury to Melbourne was accomplished in exactly five hours, including a stop of three-quarters of an hour for a meal.

Boarding the *Princess of Tasmania* should be a simple task of driving your car on to the ship, parking it and leaving it to be roped down. If you're stuck at the back of the queue

it can be an onerous thing. Families generally get into a state of panic and confusion over their luggage and sometimes there is too much needless argument and rigmarole and too many officious officials at the ferry terminal at Port Melbourne.

The *Princess* is a handsome, gaily painted, 370 ft long ship with a displacement of 4775 tons and fairly adequate facilities for the short, 14-hour crossing. The bottom deck is a flat-bottomed affair which holds 100 cars, a number of semi-trailers and caravans and motorcycles.

Above, the two passenger decks comprise single, double and four-berth cabins and reclining-seat accommodation for some 330 passengers. When the boat is fully loaded the dining room and lounge become painfully small. Bar facilities close at 10.30 pm, three hours after departure time. Since October, 1959, the *Princess* has been regularly making six trips a week to and from the island, and once a year—in July—is stopped for an annual inspection. In the busy Christmas season it makes four trips one way and three the other each week to cope with the heavier tourist trade.

Both dinner and breakfast are served and the menu for each is fairly comprehensive. Waiters also double as bar stewards, but the ship still carries a surprisingly large crew. Many passengers still continue to complain about rough travel, but I feel the majority are inexperienced sailors making their first sea trip— as the *Princess* rides remarkably well and puts out her side stabilisers when seas are rough. Incidentally, I believe the extra drag incurred by these fins

increases the travelling time by as much as an hour.

While Port Melbourne is an exceptionally uninspiring sight, the coastline of Tasmania is a picture, its exotic growth and rich green farm-lands contrasting with the craggy mountain peaks beyond. Devonport, a bright, bustling town on the River Mersey, is the setting-off place for Princess travellers and sets the standard for the immensely picturesque scenery which one encounters on the North-West coast.

As usual our itinerary was entirely unplanned. After berthing we took a quick look at the map and settled on a drive to the Great Lakes. Tasmania in autumn is probably equally as pretty as Tasmania in the spring and there was still an abundance of growth on the way to Deloraine on the Mid-West Highway to Hobart. Soon after turning off at Deloraine we took a gravel road and wound up an awesome mountain range for several miles, eventually coming to a plateau, where the climate changed as abruptly as the scenery. The difference in temperature must have been at least 15 deg—little wonder that the growth was so stunted and windblown! After a three-mile run across the plateau the Lakes—a vast body of blue water—came into view.

From there to Miena, 20 miles away, the road skirts the water and the foreshore is dotted with fishing cabins. Fishermen come from all over to try their skill with the huge trout abounding in the lakes.

Miena is a remote spot which boasts a guest house and a petrol pump. Both were empty, which was a crushing blow, as the petrol gauge

had been registering empty for 18 miles and the nearest garage was at Bothwell, 36 miles away. Several others were in the same predicament and we wheeled away and carried on at a mere 20 mph. The enforced economy run proved needless, as the refill showed we still had three-quarters of a gallon left.

Ten miles further we rejoined the Mid-West Highway and reached Hobart at dusk. From Devonport to Hobart, via the Great Lakes, is a mere 150 miles, even though it constitutes crossing from one side of the island to the other. Hobart is becoming especially tourist conscious and one has a choice of several excellent motels and a number of hotels. The first one encountered, the Motel Derwent, has 32 units and is luxuriously appointed with heated floors, TV, radio, modern decor and —in the "river" suites—panoramic views of the River Derwent. This was our Hobart "home" for three days and a very good one it was, too.

One tourist must around Hobart is a run through the Huon Valley, and this was taken in next day. Certainly it did not look as attractive as before, when it was apple-blossom time, but it nevertheless remained unique and beautiful.

Once in Huon it is a good idea to get off the beaten track. By doing this one is repaid with simply marvellous water views, particularly along the Huon River, that must be hard to equal anywhere. A criss-cross of roads around Lymington and Wattle Grove eventually takes you back on the Channel Highway, which is the alternative return route to Hobart and follows the water all the way. Hobart is spread over a wide area and it is hard to imagine that its population is only about 120,000 people. In peak-hours it has a big-city atmosphere

and, on a much smaller scale, the same traffic problems and choked roads as Sydney or Melbourne. Much of this is due to the many fixed-time traffic lights, which are gradually being changed over to vehicle-actuated ones. There are a multitude of sights to see and if you're in a hurry most of these can be taken in in one breathtaking view from the top of the 4200 ft high Mt Wellington, which towers over Hobart. This is almost rivalled by Mt Nelson, which overlooks the Derwent estuary.

Hobart's attitude towards motor traffic sets an example to road authorities on the mainland. It already has a half-cloverleaf system, opened back in 1959, roundabouts on main intersections and a dual carriageway offering an alternative route from the city. Another new landmark taking shape is the £4 million Tasman Bridge, which will eventually cross high over the Derwent and replace the old floating-pontoon bridge.

On the third day we booked the car in on the rail service from Rosebery to Guildford Junction, which is the only link from the West Coast to the North-West Coast, and whilst in the Tourist Bureau overheard someone inquiring about Queenstown, which was on our route. Subsequently, we had the company on our West Coast excursion of two Melbourne schoolteachers! For the afternoon we had arranged a ferry trip to Bruny Island, off the coast 20 miles from Hobart, but missed it by a bare 30 seconds, and instead spent the time watching boats dredge for scallops, the delicious shell fish for which Tasmania is justly famous.

With the Fiat now loaded to capacity with four people and stacks of

luggage (two suitcases just would not fit and we sent these by road to Launceston to be picked up later) we set off late in the morning of the fourth day to Queenstown, 160 miles away. I had some misgivings as to whether we'd make it. The shock absorbers were down to their last inch of travel and we all had a fair battering after leaving the sealed section at Ouse. For some 40 miles the road consists of stony outcrops and is rough by any standards. However, anything is worth the effort to see the rugged West Coast scenery, and the surface improved before we came into the mountainous country.

There's little on the mainland to approach the absolute grandeur of the Mt King William and Mt Arrowsmith ranges, both favorite spots for bushwalkers, rock climbers and naturalists. It is unspoilt country with a remarkable predominance of purple color and the narrow, winding white gravel road runs right through the centre. Forty miles further on we began the hair-raising descent to Queenstown down a steep, zig-zagging road which, I imagine, would be Australia's equivalent of the famous Stelvio Pass. It was nightfall and pitch dark and we did not try to disprove a tourist-booklet statement that the pass was one of the most frightening in the world.

All Queenstown needs to transform it into a wild-west town of the movies and television is boardwalks. It is a singularly unusual place surrounded by multi-colored hills practically devoid of growth and relies on the Mt Lyell copper and zinc mine and tourism to support it. Vegetation, which disappeared entirely once through the effects of sulphur fumes and tor-

Picturebook views, like this one of the Huon River, are commonplace in scenic Tasmania, a small self-contained tourist gem of an island.

rential rain, is slowly coming back as the rock transforms to soil. One of its fascinating attractions are the miniature steam locomotives which pull minerals to and from the mine and take tourists to Strahan, on Macquarie Harbor, 26 miles away.

Rosebery, 35 miles from Queenstown, is the end of the road, and the ghost town of Zeehan is in between. On the fifth day we took our time and had a good look around before loading the Fiat on to a piggy-back rail truck ready for the journey the following day. There's no ceremony about Rosebery. The small station is about a mile from the town and once you've loaded the car you walk back along the tracks to one or other of the two hotels. Actually, the cars get to Guildford Junction before you do, as they leave on a separate goods train early in the morning four hours before the passenger train departs. It's a two-hour run to the junction and the train then continues through to Burnie.

A start has been made on extending the road through, but construction is being hampered by the rough terrain and it will be probably several years before it is completed.

When we reached the junction our passengers decided to continue their train trip to Burnie. Back to only two occupants the Fiat seemed to simply fly! We drove off to Waratah, another ghost town surrounded by old mine workings, and then headed in the direction of Burnie. We kept up a 50 mph average and on the way drove through a dense rain jungle with hundreds of corners and ferns 20 ft high and providing some of the best scenery found so far.

For some obscure reason Burnie, home of 30,000, is still classed as a town. It is both industrial and rural and the biggest single industry is the huge paper mill. From Burnie to

Devonport is a delightful coastal drive of just 31 miles. So that night it was back to Devonport and a motel ready to begin an assault on the east coast the following day.

The sixth day was a long one and we put in some pretty concentrated motoring, covering well over 200 miles on fairly difficult roads after stopping for a long period in Launceston. The most amazing feature of Tasmania is that the scenery never runs out, and the mountain-pass country between Launceston and Scottsdale is practically beyond colorful description. It changes every couple of miles and on some stretches of winding road your car is never pointing in a straight line. Trying to follow the road and the picture-book scenery is a difficult business. After reaching the coast, and driving for some time in utter desolation, we came upon an oasis in the shape of a luxury hotel/motel complete with all the trimmings—even to a tiled swimming pool. This was at Bicheno, a popular fishing and swimming resort. Judging by the number of young married couples there this must be an especially popular honeymoon resort!

Next morning—the seventh and final day—time did not permit a round trip along the rest of the East Coast to Hobart. In fact, Devonport was more than 170 miles away by the shortest route and we wanted to have a look at the Symonds Plains and Longford motor-racing circuits. The former can be seen from the main Launceston-Hobart road, being built on private grazing property belonging to the Youl family, a group of racing enthusiasts who live about 13 miles from Launceston.

Longford is set in a quiet part of

the countryside and it is difficult to conjure up visions of racing cars roaring along the main street of the peaceful village. However, the control tower, braking signs and grid positions painted on the roadway help to convince you that this actually does happen. Before pressing on we had three sedate laps and a chat with the local innkeeper.

Reaching Devonport again we had the oil changed and the car greased and, just for good measure, took a quick run up to Burnie and back for a last, longing look at the North West Coast. By the time we placed the car on the ship we had packed about 300 miles into the last day. It was a big wrench to have to leave—the weather had been fine for the whole time and the hospitality unbelievable.

Despite its ordeal the Fiat remained completely reliable to the end and is actually performing better now than before. On reflection, though, Tasmania's mountainous grades are surprisingly deceptive and certainly not as bad as they first appear. They are relatively favorable to a small car—we topped most in third gear, with occasional use of second and once or twice struck first when the going became really rough.

I know there are a lot of people who are dubious over taking their small cars on long touring trips. In the first place they have bought them mainly for city use and, when holiday time comes around, they're uncertain about going too far. In fact, a Tasmanian reader has just informed us of a trip he did from Perth to Tasmania in a 600. My advice is to forget all your fears, have your car thoroughly checked and get going!　　　　　#

Make: Fiat Abarth   **Type:** 850 TC

Makers: Abarth & C., Corso Marche 38, Turin, Italy
(Based on 600D Model of S.A. Fiat, Corso IV Novembre 300, Italy)

Concessionaires: Anthony Crook Motors, Ltd., The Roundabout, Hersham, Surrey.

Test Data

World copyright reserved; no unauthorized reproduction in whole or in part.

CONDITIONS: *Weather: Cold and misty, windless initially becoming windy during acceleration tests. (Temperature 38°-45°F., Barometer 29.5 in. Hg.) Surface: Damp tarred macadam. Fuel: Super-premium pump petrol (approx. 101 Research Method Octane Rating).*

INSTRUMENTS
Speedometer at 30 m.p.h.	accurate
Speedometer at 60 m.p.h.	1% fast
Speedometer at 90 m.p.h.	2% fast
Distance recorder	accurate

WEIGHT
Kerb weight (unladen, but with oil, coolant and fuel for approx. 50 miles)	11¾ cwt.
Front/rear distribution of kerb weight	38/62
Weight laden as tested	15½ cwt.

MAXIMUM SPEEDS
Flying Mile
Mean of four opposite runs	93.1 m.p.h.
Best one-way time equals	93.5 m.p.h.

"Maximile" Speed. (Timed quarter mile after one mile accelerating from rest.)
Mean of four opposite runs	91.3 m.p.h.
Best one-way time equals	91.8 m.p.h.

Speed in gears (at 7,000 r.p.m.).
Speed in 3rd gear	70 m.p.h.
Speed in 2nd gear	45 m.p.h.
Speed in 1st gear	28 m.p.h.

FUEL CONSUMPTION
62.5 m.p.g. at constant 30 m.p.h. on level
53.5 m.p.g. at constant 40 m.p.h. on level
45.5 m.p.g. at constant 50 m.p.h. on level
42.5 m.p.g. at constant 60 m.p.h. on level
39.5 m.p.g. at constant 70 m.p.h. on level
35.5 m.p.g. at constant 80 m.p.h. on level

Overall Fuel Consumption for 1,117 miles, 34.6 gallons, equals 32.3 m.p.g. (8.75 litres/100 km.)

Touring Fuel Consumption (m.p.g. at steady speed midway between 30 m.p.h. and maximum, less 5% allowance for acceleration) 40 m.p.g. Fuel tank capacity (maker's figure) 6 gallons.

STEERING
Turning circle between kerbs:
Left	29 ft.
Right	29½ ft.
Turns of steering wheel from lock to lock	3½

BRAKES from 30 m.p.h.
1.00 g retardation (equivalent to 30 ft. stopping distance) with 60 lb. pedal pressure
0.91 g retardation (equivalent to 33 ft. stopping distance) with 50 lb. pedal pressure
0.37 g retardation (equivalent to 81½ ft. stopping distance) with 25 lb. pedal pressure

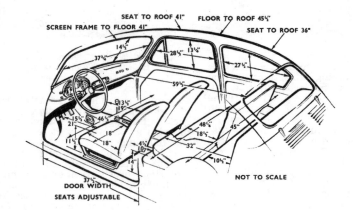

TRACK:— FRONT 3'-9¼"　REAR 3'-8"   OVERALL WIDTH 4'-6½"   4'-4½" UNLADEN
18"   9¼"   GROUND CLEARANCE 3¾"   6'-7¼"   10'-9¾"   FIAT ABARTH 850. TC   19"   10½"

SEAT TO ROOF 41"   FLOOR TO ROOF 45¼"   SCREEN FRAME TO FLOOR 41"   SEAT TO ROOF 36"   NOT TO SCALE   DOOR WIDTH   SEATS ADJUSTABLE

ACCELERATION TIMES from standstill
0-30 m.p.h.	4.1 sec.
0-40 m.p.h.	6.6 sec.
0-50 m.p.h.	10.5 sec.
0-60 m.p.h.	15.0 sec.
0-70 m.p.h.	20.5 sec.
0-80 m.p.h.	31.0 sec.
Standing quarter mile	19.7 sec.

ACCELERATION TIMES on upper ratios
	Top gear	3rd gear
10-30 m.p.h.	—	10.1 sec.
20-40 m.p.h.	18.5 sec.	7.7 sec.
30-50 m.p.h.	15.9 sec.	7.6 sec.
40-60 m.p.h.	16.3 sec.	9.0 sec.
50-70 m.p.h.	16.5 sec.	—
60-80 m.p.h.	18.1 sec.	—

HILL CLIMBING at sustained speeds
Max. gradient on top gear	1 in 11.7	(Tapley 190 lb./ton)
Max. gradient on 3rd gear	1 in 6.5	(Tapley 340 lb./ton)
Max. gradient on 2nd gear	1 in 4.1	(Tapley 540 lb./ton)

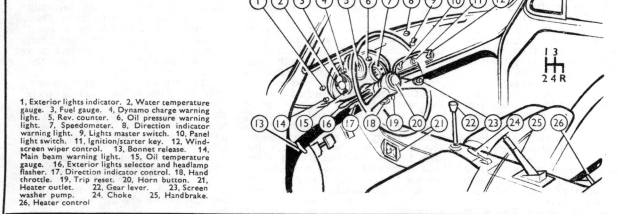

1, Exterior lights indicator. 2, Water temperature gauge. 3, Fuel gauge. 4, Dynamo charge warning light. 5, Rev. counter. 6, Oil pressure warning light. 7, Speedometer. 8, Direction indicator warning light. 9, Lights master switch. 10, Panel light switch. 11, Ignition/starter key. 12, Windscreen wiper control. 13, Bonnet release. 14, Main beam warning light. 15, Oil temperature gauge. 16, Exterior lights selector and headlamp flasher. 17, Direction indicator control. 18, Hand throttle. 19, Trip reset. 20, Horn button. 21, Heater outlet. 22, Gear lever. 23, Screen washer pump. 24. Choke 25. Handbrake. 26, Heater control

The Fiat Abarth 850 TC

Italy's Most Popular Small Car in Over-90 m.p.h. Form

Lowered suspension, different wheels and Abarth's badge on the front "grille" are the only clues to this little Fiat's phenomenal performance.

AT first glance, a price of £1,405 for an extremely small four-seat saloon car of 847 c.c. engine size appears utterly ridiculous. When overtaken by a "baby car" which can accelerate from rest to 60 m.p.h. in only 15 sec., sustains an 80 m.p.h. cruising speed up long motorway gradients without apparent effort, and runs up to well over 90 m.p.h. on request, other motorists are apt to regard the Fiat Abarth 850 TC as a joke in extremely bad taste.

Whilst it carries a certain amount o additional equipment and decoration, this is essentially a Fiat 600D saloon, with major (but virtually invisible) mechanical modifications applied to it by Abarth & C. of Turin so that its maximum speed is increased by more than 25 m.p.h. Enlargement of the engine from 767 c.c. to 847 c.c. results mainly from fitting of a much sturdier crankshaft which increases piston stroke by 5½ mm. yet permits safe use of very high engine r.p.m., there being also a ½ mm. increase in cylinder bore. The existing light-alloy cylinder head is retained with modifications, and a single Solex carburetter of 32 mm. bore replaces the 28 mm. Weber instrument. An Abarth divided exhaust system keeps gas from cylinders 1 and 4 separate from that leaving cylinders 2 and 3 until the silencer is reached. Unseen changes include a special camshaft, reinforced clutch and high-ratio final drive gearing, but there is no change from normal Fiat spacing of the gearbox ratios. Lowering of the all-independent suspension system and fitting of Michelin "X" tyres reduce the car's height by 2¾ in., whilst Girling disc brakes on the front wheels and ribbed rear brake drums provide extra stopping power.

Performance is what causes and justifies this model's high price, so deserves priority of treatment in our test report. A maximum speed of 93.1 m.p.h. is far beyond what might be expected from an 847 c.c. saloon with in-line valves and a single carburetter, yet this speed is attained without the car becoming in any way unfit for everyday use. Below an engine speed of 1,500 r.p.m. a serious flat-spot is evident,

Modifications to the engine are far more drastic than external appearance indicates. A single Solex carburetter replaces the original Weber and a robust crankshaft with greater throw helps to increase capacity by 80 c.c. Accessibility is exceptional.

In Brief

Price £947 15s. 10d., plus purchase tax £457 7s. 3d., equals £1,405 3s. 1d.

Capacity	847 c.c.
Unladen kerb weight ...	11¾ cwt.
Acceleration:	
20-40 m.p.h. in top gear	18.5 sec.
0-50 m.p.h. through gears	10.5 sec.
Maximum direct top-gear gradient	1 in 11.7
Maximum speed	93.1 m.p.h.
"Maximile" speed ...	91.3 m.p.h.
Touring fuel consumption	40 m.p.g.

Gearing: 14.9 m.p.h. in top gear at 1,000 r.p.m.; 32.8 m.p.h. at 1,000 ft./min. piston speed.

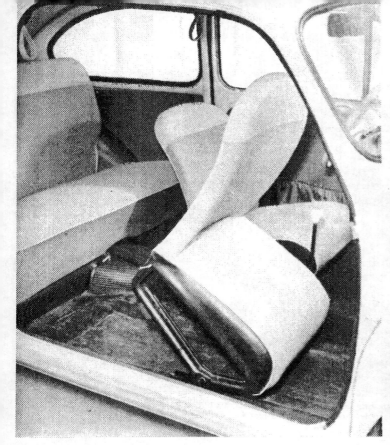

The Fiat Abarth 850 TC

Left: The simple interior furnishings are standard 600D fittings. More lateral support from the otherwise comfortable front seats would be welcome. The heater control is the small lever on the back end of the central tunnel. It is easily reached by the driver.

Below: The instrument nacelle (an Abarth fitting) has a large rev. counter directly ahead of the driver. So smooth is the engine that the needle must be constantly watched when driving hard. The limit is 7,000 r.p.m.

and at speeds between 1,500 and 2,500 r.p.m. it is desirable to open the throttle of a large-choke carburetter gradually rather than to stamp on the accelerator pedal: from this speed right on up the range to 7,000 r.p.m. the little engine pulls hard and is astonishingly smooth, the very large r.p.m. indicator dial being a wise fitment in view of the effortlessness with which the suggested r.p.m. limit is reached. There is power roar from the carburetter and a hearty roar from the twin exhaust tailpipes during hard driving, but none of the mechanical clatter from pistons and valvegear that too frequently accompanies high specific power outputs. Quite a sharp peak in the torque curve helps to produce high readings on the Tapley meter at around 3,000 r.p.m., but this engine's useful speed range is broad enough for touring car spacings between its gear ratios to seem entirely appropriate.

The four-speed gearbox has effective synchromesh on three of its four ratios, the carburation flat spot at low r.p.m. tending to make lack of such aid to bottom gear engagement something of a nuisance around town. Each gearbox ratio (including the geared-up top) involves only one pair of gears running under load, so that all the gears are about as quiet as one another. At 6,000 r.p.m. they provide speeds of 24, 39, 60 and 89 m.p.h. with 1,000 r.p.m. in reserve.

With 7% higher gearing to offset a 10% increase in engine displacement, this Abarth-modified engine with its 9.8/1 compression ratio is remarkably economical of fuel, for example, showing 42½ m.p.g. at a steady 60 m.p.h. whereas a Fiat 600D recorded 35 m.p.g. at the same speed. When temperatures fell to near the freezing mark during our test, the engine needed an exceptionally long warming-up period each morning before it would idle or pull properly, but when the air thermometer rose by 10°F. its per-

sistent hesitancy was almost completely overcome.

On a motorway this diminutive saloon cruises quite naturally at 80-85 m.p.h. with plenty of power in hand, and driving it at maximum speed does not feel to be a strain although oil thermometer readings move up if top speed is sustained for very many miles. A loud booming resonance inside the steel body (sounding to come from the front, although slipping the gear lever into neutral proves that it in fact is excited by the rear-mounted engine) occurs over a range of speeds around 70 m.p.h. which, unfortunately, is more often reached than exceeded on indifferent or crowded roads.

Lowered front and rear suspension systems do not result in this car bottoming audibly if the Fiat Abarth is driven over rough roads when fully laden. The springs are exceptionally firm and powerfully damped, however, so that whilst the car does not seem to be suffering, passengers have a very jerky ride on any but the smoothest roads. To the credit of this taut suspension, one may record a complete absence of perceptible body roll or sway on corners, however vigorously the Fiat Abarth is driven, the braced-tread tyres being most reluctant to squeal.

Sparewheel and petrol tank do not leave a great deal of luggage space in the front boot. The battery and brake fluid reservoir are housed beneath the rubber-matted floor.

Front/rear weight distribution in a 38/62 ratio and what is virtually a swing-axle design of I.R.S. are not features which lead one to expect fine handling qualities, but lowered and stiffened springs in conjunction with Michelin "X" tyres have made this car remarkably controllable. With the appropriate difference between front and rear tyre inflation pressures, a short-wheelbase car which one can feel to wriggle perceptibly on bumps or in gusty winds proves to be perfectly safe at high cruising speeds, needing far less guidance by the driver than first impressions suggest. Adhesion on wet roads is extremely good, and whilst there are conditions of cornering near to the limit of tyre grip in which either sliding of the lightly-loaded front wheels or conversely a power slide of the rear wheels can be induced, this is a nimble model which gives a driver plenty of confidence. Inconsistencies which would invite criticism were they to be exhibited by a larger or heavier car hardly seem to matter when a flick of the wrist suffices to make any necessary correction, and when there is no body roll or side sway to emphasize them.

Fitting of Girling disc brakes to the front wheels means that there is plenty of stopping power available from high speeds. Perhaps because the installation has been designed primarily for racing, however, the front brakes have been set to do a rather large share of the work, and, if passengers or luggage are being carried the front wheels will lock on a wet road surface before full braking effect has been obtained from the well-loaded rear wheels. The ineffectiveness of the handbrake, which acts on the two rear drums, seemed to be largely a matter of adjustment being overdue.

Abarth modifications to the Fiat 600D body shell comprise some extra decoration, and a well-furnished instrument nacelle. The large-dial chronometric r.p.m. indicator dwarfs a speedometer which is itself quite big, and a third dial combines the fuel contents indicator with coolant and oil thermometers—a warning light indicates any loss of oil pressure. The neat individual front seats are comfortable in their simple way, but something giving more lateral support would be welcome. There is enough seat adjustment range to suit a tall driver, but full use of this adjustment diminishes rear seat legroom towards vanishing point.

Rear-hinged doors are retained on this body, and whilst some people fear accidental door opening this layout does provide easy front seat access. There is a small and not altogether rain-proof luggage compartment under the "bonnet" where the spare wheel, tools and 6-gallon petrol tank are also found. As a four-seater, this model has a narrow well for parcels behind its rear seat, or the seat backrest can be folded forwards to form a flat and extremely spacious, rubber-covered floor for luggage, though loading big trunks on to it past a hinged-forward front seat is not easy.

Interior heating, highly desirable in a car which has not got its engine acting as a wind-break ahead of the front floor, is by air ducted up a central "backbone" from the rear-mounted engine's fan and radiator. Like the engine itself, this system was slow to warm up, as if the customary thermostat for restricting initial water circulation was missing, but once the engine got warm the heater was very effective. An on-off valve below the rear seat, and two air outlet shutters (near the driver's and front passenger's feet) which could be closed if all the hot air was required for windscreen de-misting, formed the only heater control system, so that at times when slight warmth would have sufficed for comfort, the body interior tended to become tiringly hot and dry.

By conventional standards, a noisy little 847 c.c. saloon is not worth £1,405. The Fiat-Abarth 850 TC is far from being a conventional car however, its combination of usable high performance with tiny external dimensions making it competitive with some of the world's fastest cars for point-to-point average speeds on many awkward journeys. One can love it or loathe it—but nobody could describe it as dull!

Twin exhausts (which give a loud, crisp buzz) and the Abarth motif identify this 90 m.p.h. Fiat.

Specification

Engine
Cylinders	...	4
Bore	...	62.5 mm.
Stroke	...	69 mm.
Cubic capacity	...	847 c.c.
Piston area	...	19 sq. in.
Valves	...	In-line o.h.v. (pushrods)
Compression ratio	...	9.8/1
Carburetter	...	Solex 32/PBIC downdraught
Fuel pump	...	Electrical
Ignition timing control	...	Centrifugal and vacuum
Oil filter	...	Centrifugal and Fram by-pass
Max. power (gross)	...	60 b.h.p.
at	...	5,800 r.p.m.
Piston speed at max. b.h.p.		2,625 ft./min.

Transmission
Clutch	...	Modified Fiat 6¼-in. s.d.p.
Top gear (s/m)	...	4.084
3rd gear (s/m)	...	6.074
2nd gear (s/m)	...	9.364
1st gear	...	15.42
Reverse	...	19.47
Propeller shaft		None (rear-mounted engine)
Final drive	...	9/41 spiral bevel
Top gear m.p.h. at 1,000 r.p.m.		14.9
Top gear m.p.h. at 1,000 ft./min. piston speed		32.8

Chassis
Brakes	...	Hydraulic, Girling discs at front and ribbed drums at rear
Brake dimensions		
Front discs	...	8.3 in. dia.
Rear drums	...	7.3 in. dia.
Friction areas	...	52.7 sq. in. friction lining area working on 169.5 sq. in. rubbed area of discs and drums (discs 115.5 sq. in., drums 54 sq. in.
Suspension:		
Front	...	Independent by transverse leaf spring and wishbones
Rear	...	Independent by semi-trailing arms and coil springs
Shock absorbers	...	Telescopic
Steering gear	...	Worm and sector
Tyres	...	Michelin "X" tubed, 135-12

Coachwork and Equipment

Starting handle	...	None
Battery mounting	...	In front luggage compartment
Jack	...	Pillar type
Jacking points	...	One socket under each side of car
Standard tool kit:		Bag containing 3 double-ended spanners, sparking plug spanner, screwdriver, pliers, punch, wheel-nut spanner and jack.
Exterior lights:		2 headlamps, 2 sidelamps/flashers, 2 stop/tail lamps, rear number plate lamp.
Number of electrical fuses		6
Direction indicators		Self-cancelling flashers (white front, amber rear)
Windscreen wipers	...	Electrical twin-blade, self-parking
Windscreen washers	...	Manual pump
Sun visors	...	Two, hinge mounted
Instruments:		Speedometer with total and decimal trip distance recorders, r.p.m. indicator, oil thermometer, water thermometer, fuel contents gauge.
Warning lights:		Dynamo charge, oil pressure, lights tell-tale, headlamp main beam indicator, flashers repeater.

Locks:		
With ignition key		Ignition/starter switch
With other key		Driver's door (front luggage boot unlocked from inside car)
Glove lockers	...	None
Map pockets	...	2 inside doors
Parcel shelves	...	Well behind rear-seat backrest
Ashtrays	...	None
Cigar lighters	...	None
Interior lights	...	One in rear-view mirror frame, manually switched
Interior heater:		Warm air from rear-mounted radiator can be directed to floor and to windscreen interior.
Car radio	...	None
Extras available:		Cast light-alloy wheels, special gearbox and final drive ratios to order.
Upholstery material	...	Vynide and fabric
Floor covering	...	Fitted rubber mats
Exterior colours standardized	...	5 (any special colour at extra cost)
Alternative body styles	...	Convertible, or Italian specialist bodies

Maintenance

Sump	...	8 pints, S.A.E. 30 winter, S.A.E. 40, summer
Gearbox and final drive (combined)		2¼ pints, S.A.E. 90EP gear oil
Steering gear lubricant		S.A.E. 90EP gear oil
Cooling system capacity	...	7½ pints (2 drain taps)
Chassis lubrication	...	By grease gun every 2,000 miles to 8 points
Ignition timing	...	10° before t.d.c. static
Contact-breaker gap	...	0.018-0.020 in.
Sparking-plug type	...	Champion
Sparking-plug gap	...	0.025 in.

Valve timing:		Inlet opens 30° before t.d.c. and closes 70° after b.d.c.; exhaust opens 70° before b.d.c. and closes 30° after t.d.c.
Tappet clearances (cold):		
Inlet and exhaust	...	0.008 in.
Front wheel toe-in	...	Zero± .04 in.
Camber angle	...	0° 30′
Castor angle	...	6°±30′
Steering swivel pin inclination	...	7°
Tyre pressures:		
Front	...	20 lb.
Rear	...	26 lb.
Brake fluid	...	Heavy duty
Battery type and capacity		12 volt, 32 amp. hr.

FIAT 600-D

There's no substitute for
cubic inches—or is there?

EUROPE'S MINIMUM-TRANSPORTATION cars, whatever their merits at home, have been something less than an unqualified success here in this country. American traffic conditions virtually guarantee that the mini-car will be flogged along in an absolutely merciless fashion, full throttle every inch of the way and with the engine speed never far short of valve bounce. This is, as you might imagine, an existence well suited to bringing any car's engine to an early and messy demise. Fortunately, there is at least one example of the mini-car that has, if driven with just the least bit of restraint, an adequate service life—Fiat's 600 sedan.

The 600 was introduced in 1955 and was then, as now, an object lesson in getting the most from the least. Even though smaller than its predecessor, the 500 "Topolino," the 600 offered seating for two more passengers, and such advanced engineering features as all-independent suspension and a drive system (engine, transmission, cooling and electrical systems *et al.*) weighing only 238 lb, complete. The car was an immediate success at home and, though it had performance that bordered on being inadequate for our conditions, found many buyers here in America as well. It is, in fact, virtually the sole surviving member of the multitude of mini-cars that were so much in evidence in the years from 1955 through 1958.

This year there is an even better Fiat 600, the "D," which differs from the earlier model principally in engine size, up from 633 cc to 766 cc due to an increase in bore and stroke. In a "big-inch" engine, adding a piddling 133 cc is nothing, but in the 600 it means an increase of 21% and that is very worthwhile. This increase in displacement, and a few other refinements over the original 22-bhp 600, now bring the gross output up to a mighty 32 bhp, for a gain of 45%—certainly enough to warrant acclaim.

Balancing these increases is the change in axle ratio,

from 4.82 to 4.37:1, which gives approximately 11% fewer engine turns per mile and reduces all-out performance (?) a like amount. Nevertheless, there remains a substantial net increase in over-all performance and, perhaps even more important, the car's useful cruising speed and endurance potential are greatly improved.

From the outside, the only things that distinguish the 600-D from the previous model are the pivoting windwings in the door windows and a few more ventilating louvers in the engine compartment lid. Other than that, it is the same boxy but not unattractive sedan that we first saw nearly 6 years ago. We cannot say that the quality has improved, because it always has been nicely, if a smidgen austerely, finished. The panels—which are not very numerous, due to the small size of the car—are of adequate thickness and are assembled with passable precision. The paint, available in several reasonably attractive shades, hasn't the deep gloss that one associates with hand-rubbed lacquer—but it is free of sags, runs and "orange-peel," and that makes it the equal of any mass-produced automobile anywhere. Brightwork, and there is precious little of this, is mostly of durable but not too shiny aluminum. Chromium plate is found only on the headlight bezels and bumpers. These last, incidentally, are very sturdy and securely anchored, and we suspect that they are strong enough to fend off almost anything. A pressure of sufficient magnitude to bend the 600's bumper would simply move the whole car—even with the brakes locked on.

Inside, the 600 is not particularly luxurious, but it certainly exceeds, albeit by the narrowest of margins, what we consider a minimum level of comfort. Four adults of medium-largish size can be accommodated—and, if they can learn not to breathe in unison, will not feel too crowded. Those in the back, however, will be a bit less comfortable than those in front, for they will be perched on a lightly padded bench-type seat, while those riding up forward have separate, nicely contoured, individual seats. All 4 will be short of foot-room, for the front wheel-wells encroach into the space allotted those up front and those riding in the back will have to tuck their feet away in the small spaces beneath the front seats. In cold weather they will all benefit from the blast of warm air available from the heating system, which directs heated air from the cooling system up the "tunnel" that houses the engine control cables and shift rod, to the outlets in the tunnel and/or the ducts to the "defroster" slots under the windshield.

The driver will probably like the car best of all, because it is grand fun to drive despite the low power available. And he will not be confused or distracted by too many instruments; there is only the speedometer—which

FIAT 600-D

was outrageously optimistic in our test car—and a fuel gauge. Colored lights give warning (it says here in the book) should the engine overheat or lose oil pressure, or should the generator stop charging. Also, there are warning lights for the turn indicators, parking lights, and high-beam.

The other controls are more comprehensive and are improved over the earlier 600s to the extent that the ignition key now actuates the starter—instead of the previous floor-mounted toggle lever. The cold-starting enrichment lever is, however, still down on the floor, and it's not really such a bad spot for it at that. Our only complaints regarding the various operating levers are aimed at the steering wheel, placed about 3 in. too high, and the proximity of the pedals to one another too and to the left-hand defroster duct. It seemed almost impossible

for the more "satchel-footed" among us to drive the car without occasionally becoming bound up in things. In fairness to the car's designers we should point out that they haven't much room between the front wheel wells with which to work—but we still wish they would relocate that defroster duct.

Good marks go to the steering action and both the position and feel of the gear shift. Even though the wheel was mounted a trifle high, it was right out there where it encouraged the "Farina straight-arm" driving stance, and the precision with which the car could be aimed should be the envy of every other maker of automobiles. Gear changes—required rather frequently in so low-powered a car—were no bother at all; indeed, we found ourselves stirring the gears about perhaps more than was absolutely necessary just because of the excellent placement of the lever and the matchless meshing action of the synchromesh transmission.

At any speeds we were able to attain, the handling of the 600-D was free of dangerous vices and, at rates of travel that left us with a bit of surplus power, we were delighted to find that the car could be hacked around just like a sports car. Slow to medium-fast bends are taken with a rush and, going in, the 600 actually shows a trace of understeer. Near the apex this understeer disappears as the overloaded (60% of the car's weight) rear wheels begin to slide out and then a quick dash of reverse lock on the steering will bring the car out of the corner with a rush. It's no racing car, needless to say, but it is the best handling rear-engined sedan that we have ever driven. Unhappily, the brakes were not up to the standard set by the rest of the car; the required pedal pressure is much higher than one would think necessary for so light a car and when the brakes are applied hard, they set up a shuddering that is very disconcerting. The car will definitely stop, but the weird pulsing that feeds back through the brake pedal is something to think about while you wait for things to come to a halt.

Road noise is also a definite problem; the presence of so many nearly flat, unsupported areas in the body paneling cannot be helped (without raising the price and weight of the car) but anyone contemplating a long jaunt in a 600 should give either additional sound-proofing or ear-plugs some consideration. Perhaps some of the vibration-damping tapes made by 3M might be used to good effect.

Servicing the 600 will be less bother than with most cars. Almost everything can be reached by simply opening the engine compartment lid and stooping slightly. Fuel is carried up forward, though, in a tank located to the side of the cubbyhole that passes for a luggage compartment. This space is too small for anything but a small valise, but the car's cargo space can be increased by folding the rear seat-back forward—after which the entire rear section may be filled with baggage.

A couple of our staff members own Fiat 600 sedans and they tell us that a question frequently asked them is: Is it practical? The answer is yes, but with some very specific reservations. First off, we should like to say that the new 600-D is a vast improvement over the previous car, being somewhat less marginal in speed and power, and comes closer to being a good "all-around" automobile. However, the car is too small for even a medium-sized family and not quick enough for many people to enjoy driving one for long distances.

On the other hand, as a second car, for use mostly in city or suburbs with an occasional medium-distance trip, it offers unparalleled operating economy and a very low initial cost. And, finally, for those people who are always telling us that they want "a nice plain car without all those frills, and gas economy above all else"—well, by George, this is your chance.

FIAT 600-D

SCALE: 10" DIVISIONS

DIMENSIONS

Wheelbase, in	78.7
Tread, f and r	45.2/45.4
Over-all length, in	129
width	54.2
height	55.4
equivalent vol, cu ft	224
Frontal area, sq ft	16.7
Ground clearance, in	6.2
Steering ratio, o/a	n.a.
turns, lock to lock	3.3
turning circle, ft	28.5
Hip room, front	18.5 x 2
Hip room, rear	50.0
Pedal to seat back	39.5
Floor to ground	8.0

CALCULATED DATA

Lb/hp (test wt)	53.1
Cu ft/ton mile	66.1
Mph/1000 rpm (4th)	14.5
Engine revs/mile	4150
Piston travel, ft/mile	1730
Rpm @ 2500 ft/min	6000
equivalent mph	86.7
R&T wear index	71.8

SPECIFICATIONS

List price	$1295
Curb weight, lb	1350
Test weight	1700
distribution, %	40/60
Tire size	5.20-12
Brake swept area	108
Engine type	4 cyl, ohv
Bore & stroke	2.44 x 2.50
Displacement, cc	766
cu in	46.8
Compression ratio	7.5
Bhp @ rpm	32 @ 4800
equivalent mph	69.4
Torque, lb-ft (est)	38 @ 3000
equivalent mph	43.4

GEAR RATIOS

4th (0.896)	4.37
3rd (1.33)	6.48
2nd (2.05)	10.0
1st (3.38)	16.5

SPEEDOMETER ERROR

30 mph	actual, 29.1
60 mph	55.5

PERFORMANCE

Top speed (4th), mph	70
best timed run	72.0
3rd (5600)	55
2nd (5600)	34
1st (5650)	22

FUEL CONSUMPTION

Normal range, mpg	31/38

ACCELERATION

0-30 mph, sec	7.1
0-40	11.2
0-50	19.0
0-60	32.0
0-70	58.0
0-80	
0-100	
Standing ¼ mile	24.3
speed at end	54.3

TAPLEY DATA

4th, lb/ton @ mph	145 @ 35
3rd	220 @ 29
2nd	335 @ 22
Total drag at 60 mph, lb	85

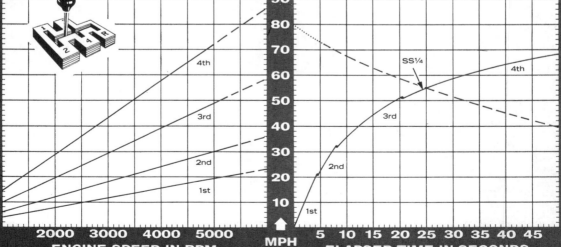

ENGINE SPEED IN GEARS

ENGINE SPEED IN RPM

ACCELERATION & COASTING

ELAPSED TIME IN SECONDS

JOHN BOLSTER

tests

THE

FIAT-ABARTH

1000

T HE performance of Fiat engines, as modified by Carlo Abarth, has for long been held to verge on the supernatural. The reason is that these power units are rebuilt entirely without regard to such mundane things as cost. The racing successes of the twin overhead camshaft engines are well known, but the Fiat-Abarth 1000, which I have just tested, is perhaps of even greater interest, because it competes directly with certain popular British models.

The basis of the car is the Fiat 600 D saloon. This is an extremely small car with a rear engine and independent suspension of all the wheels. The Abarth version has Girling disc front brakes and modified springing. It has all the equipment for which Fiats are renowned and retains the appearance of the 600 D.

The engine is built round a very expensive forged steel crankshaft which is specially balanced, and most of the reciprocating parts of the unit are of Abarth design. The light alloy head has large valves and ports and a sports camshaft is installed. The engine size is increased from 767 c.c. to 982 c.c. and the power goes up from 32 to 66 b.h.p.

First impressions of the car are that the

improvement in performance at peak revolutions is most impressive, but that the extra "punch" in the middle ranges is even more useful in ordinary driving. This is really a very small car, and the low-speed flexibility, allied with instantly available acceleration, render it just about perfect for London traffic.

The little machine fairly scuttles away from the traffic lights, and the gear changes go through very rapidly. Even at its peak speed of 6,000 r.p.m., the unit is well silenced, thanks to its beautiful and highly efficient exhaust system. This quiet running, coupled with an unobtrusive appearance, are valuable when the speedy negotiation of built-up areas is attempted.

Rapid acceleration is one of the car's best features and, somehow, this seems even

more impressive in so small a vehicle. The maximum speed was timed at 86.5 m.p.h., with a strong side-wind blowing, so a few more m.p.h. might be expected under still weather conditions. A genuine 90 m.p.h. was in fact achieved under slightly favourable conditions, during which the speedometer registered 105 m.p.h.

It was noticeable that the riding comfort is much better than that of a standard Fiat 600 D which we tested. Indeed, the absence of pitching, hardness, or up-and-down movement is almost unbelievable in a car of only 6 ft. 6 ins. wheelbase. Many large cars do not ride half so well as the little Fiat-Abarth.

In spite of its rear engine, this car has a very pronounced under-steering characteristic. During hard driving, the rear end can

eventually be made to break away, but the fastest cornering takes place when the rear wheels are only just beginning to run wide. This rather unusual response to the steering is something which one notices less as the miles are covered. The stability is first class at maximum speed, and though sidewinds can be felt, the amount of deviation is very small compared with most rear-engined cars. Bumps and changes of camber never affect the straight running of the Fiat-Abarth.

Fading brakes have in the past been an obstacle to tuning the small Fiats. By

fitting disc front brakes, Carlo Abarth has at one stroke overcome the most serious problem which had to be solved. Rather naturally, the discs are easily able to cope with a 12 cwt. car, though the parking brake is somewhat weak. Excellent fuel

economy is a marked feature, even when the full performance is being used.

The machine is well equipped, in a practical manner that is typically Fiat. The heating system is very simple, but it works particularly well. Another effective piece of equipment is the windscreen washer, which has a rubber bulb instead of a plunger pump and sprays powerfully at the slightest touch. A large rev. counter dominates the instrument nacelle. There is much more leg room than is usual in small cars, and the back seat can carry two adults, though tall people may touch the roof. As a seat for children, the rear bench is adequate for the longest journeys.

With so much performance in so small a compass, this little car is almost unbeatable in traffic. Though no short cuts have been taken in its construction, and much money has been spent on building reliability into the engine, it gives one a splendid feeling of confidence to know that the machinery is virtually unbreakable. The enlarged engine renders the machine even more flexible than a standard 600 D, so as a shopping car it would be difficult to find anything better. This would be the ideal transport for a lucky young woman.

The fact has to be faced that the Fiat-Abarth is a very expensive little car. Yet, there are people who do not have to count the pennies and they may well feel that the excellent quality of the vehicle, particularly in the engine department, makes it worth its price. The sheer impudence with which it trounces bigger cars on difficult roads is something that must endear it to almost anybody who tries it. The farther I drove it the more I liked it, and it was with great regret that I eventually handed it back to Tony Crook.

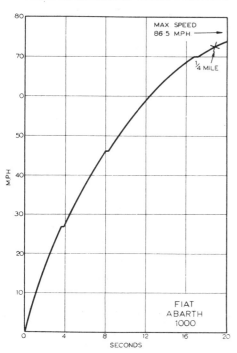

ACCELERATION GRAPH

(graph showing MAX SPEED 86.5 M.P.H., ¼ MILE, FIAT ABARTH 1000, axes MPH vs SECONDS)

SPECIFICATION AND PERFORMANCE DATA

Car Tested: Fiat-Abarth 1000 saloon, price £1,155 4s. including P.T.

Engine: Four-cylinders 65 mm. x 74 mm. (982 c.c.). Pushrod-operated overhead valves. Compression ratio 9.8 to 1. 66 b.h.p. at 6,000 r.p.m. Solex downdraught carburetter. Marelli coil and distributor.

Transmission: Single dry plate clutch. Four-speed gearbox with synchromesh on upper three gears and central remote control, ratios 4.3, 6.5, 10, and 16.5 to 1. Hypoid final drive to swing axles.

Chassis: Combined body and chassis. Independent front suspension by transverse spring and wishbones. Worm and sector steering box with three-piece track-rod. Independent rear suspension by semi-trailing swing axles and helical springs. Telescopic dampers all round. Girling front disc

brakes with drums at rear. Bolt-on disc wheels fitted 135—12 Michelin "X" tyres.

Equipment: 12-volt lighting and starting. Speedometer, rev. counter, oil pressure, water temperature, and fuel gauges. Windscreen wipers and washers. Heating and demisting. Flashing direction indicators.

Dimensions: Wheelbase 6 ft. 6¾ ins. Track (front) 3 ft. 9¼ ins.; (rear) 3 ft. 9⅝ ins. Overall length 10 ft. 9⅞ ins. Width 4 ft. 6⅝ ins. Weight 12 cwts.

Performance: Maximum speed 86.5 m.p.h. Speeds in gears: 3rd. 70 m.p.h., 2nd. 46 m.p.h., 1st 27 m.p.h. Standing quarter-mile 18.8 secs. Acceleration 0-30 m.p.h. 4.2 secs., 0-50 m.p.h. 9.4 secs., 0-60 m.p.h. 12.2 secs., 0-70 m.p.h. 17.2 secs.

Fuel Consumption: 34 to 40 m.p.g.

" ... a taut little car offering its occupants convenience as well as comfort and adequate performance for the unhurried."

Number 46 MOTOR TESTED 1,950 MILES

FIAT 850

PRICE
£453 10s. plus £96 0s. 10d. purchase tax, equals £549 10s. 10d.

How they run...

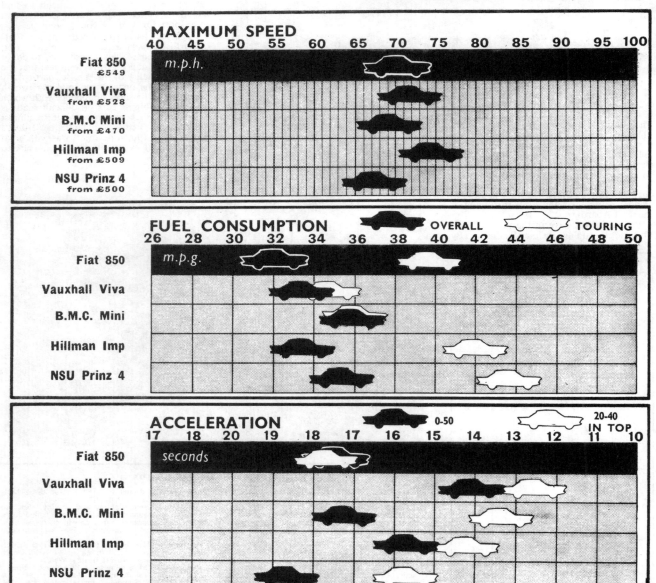

MAXIMUM SPEED

	40	45	50	55	60	65	70	75	80	85	90	95	100

Fiat 850 £549 — m.p.h.
Vauxhall Viva from £528
B.M.C Mini from £470
Hillman Imp from £509
NSU Prinz 4 from £500

FUEL CONSUMPTION OVERALL TOURING

	26	28	30	32	34	36	38	40	42	44	46	48	50

Fiat 850 — m.p.g.
Vauxhall Viva
B.M.C. Mini
Hillman Imp
NSU Prinz 4

ACCELERATION 0-50 20-40 IN TOP

	17	18	20	19	18	17	16	15	14	13	12	11	10

Fiat 850 — seconds
Vauxhall Viva
B.M.C. Mini
Hillman Imp
NSU Prinz 4

Performance figures of 95 cars tested in the past two years will be found in the road test summary on page 112

Stalled in the Common Market: like other foreigners, the Fiat 850's price is
swollen by import duty but the car remains pert, practical and competitive.

THE time has gone when the imported small car was
considered in Britain as an enthusiast's transport. A
certain *mystique* once surrounded foreign designs with
unorthodox layouts, independent suspension and a brisker
performance than the average home product, but times have
changed and small saloons from abroad now have a harder
furrow to plough.

One of the cars that made inroads into the British
"enthusiast" market was the Fiat 600. In May this year,
after this popular car had seen many seasons and many changes
(the engine, for example, grew progressively through the years)
it was supplemented, but not replaced, by the 850. This
followed the pattern of the 600, Fiat's chief engineer Dr.
Giacosa believing that this is still the best arrangement for
very small cars. He emphasizes low weight which he equates
with low cost; passenger and luggage capacity and performance
rate second in the Giacosa scale to economy. Handling and
all-round refinement are important but durability and practicality are paramount. The result is a car which, if it lacks
the sparkle of its competitors, scores in needing less money
(there isn't so much of it in Italy today) to buy and run. It is
a taut little car offering its occupants convenience as well as
comfort and adequate performance for the unhurried. Its
competitors' progress may have made it less of an enthusiast's
car than the 600 was seven or eight years ago, but it is still
good family transport.

Like its predecessor, the 850 has a unitary steel body with
a strong, punt-type floor. The rear engine resembles the 600;
the same block has staggered cylinders and the same stroke,
but a bore of 65 mm. bringing the size to 843 c.c. and making
the proportions over-square. The crankshaft has three bearings, and the water-cooling system is sealed.

The engine lies along the axis of the car and the drive runs
forward through a diaphragm clutch to the all-synchromesh
four-speed gearbox mounted ahead of the rear wheel centres.
Suspension is by semi-trailing wishbones at the back with coil
springs and an anti-roll bar. At the front a broad, transverse
leaf spring serves as a lower wishbone and steering is by worm
and sector. A number of alloy castings are used in the engine/
transmission unit and the battery lives at the front of the car,
but even so, the weight bias remains heavily at the back.
Positioning the petrol tank aft of the rear seat has resulted in
a deeper boot than some rear-engined cars but the inescapable
provision for front suspension and steering lock restricts the
width.

Performance and economy

AN INSTANT starter, hot or cold, the compact Fiat 850
engine with its short, stiff three-bearing crank is smooth all
the way up the speed range. It could be mistaken for a
five-bearing unit and although it can be felt gently rocking
at idling speeds, careful rubber and spring mounting of the
whole engine-clutch-gearbox unit seems successfully to
insulate the passengers from vibration, if not noise. Warming-
up is accomplished unusually quickly; the choke can be
dispensed with after a few hundred yards and the heater
starts work almost immediately. The recommended maximum gear speeds seemed rather pessimistic. They are shown
on the speedometer at 19, 36 and 52 m.p.h. but it was
found, for example, that second gear's maximum could be
exceeded by around 10 m.p.h. before mechanical sympathy
set a limit. As much as 6,000 r.p.m. was used during our
performance tests.

A rather stiff new engine and plenty of driving at or near
the car's modest limits probably accounts for the below average fuel consumption of 33·8 m.p.g. As our computed
touring consumption confirms, 40 m.p.g. should be easily
possible when driven more gently—especially as 850 owners
are likely to be economy minded and therefore drive
accordingly.

FIAT 850

To emphasize the low-cost aspect of motoring in the 850, it will run satisfactorily on cheap (regular grade) fuel.

In both acceleration and top speed, the Fiat lags slightly behind most of its competitors. Top gear is not very high and at 75 m.p.h. the crankshaft speed is nearly 5,500 r.p.m., limiting the potentiality for long-distance " flat out " cruising despite the " over-square " cylinder dimensions limiting piston speeds. The engine will pull smoothly in top down to about 17 m.p.h. Acceleration is adequate, but with a heavy load on cross-country journeys it is better to keep the speed up rather than use the gears to maintain high average speeds.

Transmission

THE REMOTENESS of the lever from the gearbox at the back of the car appears to affect the precision of the change

Austere but practical: rubber matting covers the floor, plastic upholstery the comfortable seats. Both doors have pockets and arm rests.

Plenty of room for two (left) on the smoothly upholstered rear bench, reached by tipping the front seats forward.

very little. Lever movement is short and quite crisp, but less silky than many modern designs. The synchromesh is powerful—almost obstructive—and first was sometimes difficult to engage at rest. Modest torque made the synchromesh on first an asset when traffic restricted speed on hills. The ratios are widely spaced, but well chosen for the power available. Third is useful for overtaking.

The clutch squeaked badly on the test car and has a short, fairly stiff, but not heavy, movement. All the gears are indirect and whine.

Handling and brakes

DESPITE the weight bias towards the back, the handling is not really that of a conventional rear-engined car. The initial impression is of understeer more pronounced in the wet, when the front will break away, although in the dry it follows a firmer line. Opening the throttle even a little is enough to balance the understeer which gives way to slight oversteer as cornering speeds rise. The transition is a gentle one and results in a very safe car indeed. It is also fun to drive; low-speed opposite-lock slides are easy to control with quite progressive breakaway. The Pirelli tyres which are standard equipment have good wet grip but whine on smooth roads.

Roll is negligible and the steering is quick and precise but rather lifeless. The combination of a good driving position and exemplary roadholding compensate on cross-country journeys for small car performance. Another asset for the keen driver to enjoy is above-average drum brakes,

1, petrol filler cap. 2, petrol pump. 3, dipstick. 4, distributor. 5, oil filler cap. 6, radiator. 7, radiator expansion tank. A very narrow bonnet opening makes engine accessibility difficult except for small routine jobs. Access can be improved by removing the bolted-on rear body panel.

Performance

Test Data: World copyright reserved: no unauthorized reproduction in whole or in part.

Conditions: Weather: Dry, light wind, cool. (Temperature 39°–46° F, Barometer 29·97–30·05 in. Hg.). Surface: Dry concrete and tarmacadam. Fuel: Regular grade (89 octane R.M.).

ACCELERATION TIMES

0-30 m.p.h.	..	..	..	6·9 sec.
0-40	..	..	.... ..	11·2
0-50	..	..	..	16·6
0-60	..	..	..	31·9
Standing quarter mile		..		22·3

On upper ratios				Top	3rd
m.p.h.				sec.	sec.
10-30	..	..	..	17·2	9·1
20-40	..	..	..	16·9	8·5
30-50	..	..	..	17·9	10·0
40-60	..	..	..	29·2	—

Fiat 600 ancestry is obvious in the 850's styling (right). There is more room inside than the seemingly narrow body suggests.

The boot is not ideally shaped (left) to take many suitcases: our test luggage totals 4 cu. ft., leaving several unfilled corners.

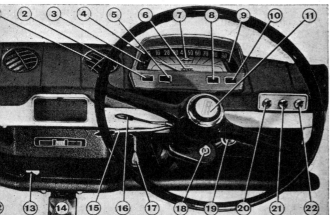

1, air vent. 2, oil pressure warning light. 3, fuel gauge. 4, speedometer. 5, ignition warning light. 6, total mileage recorder (without trip or decimals). 7, direction indicators warning light. 8, parking lights warning light. 9, water temperature gauge. 10, main beam warning light. 11, horn. 12, heater distribution control. 13, heater fan switch. 14, heater air flap. 15, headlight dipswitch/flasher. 16, direction indicator switch. 17, heater temperature control. 18, ignition/starter switch (with accessories position controlling parking lights). 19, screenwasher plunger. 20, lights master switch. 21, screenwiper switch. 22, instrument lights switch. The choke control is on the central tunnel.

Comfort and control

FIRM SUSPENSION and a short wheelbase are seldom compatible with a smooth ride; small, stiffly sprung cars often pitch rather badly. But the Fiat has overcome this very successfully with a ride which is good under all but the most severe conditions at high speed. Big bumps taken fast produce high-frequency pitching, but on most normal roads there is little more than short, well-damped vertical movements. The driving position is comfortable with a near horizontal steering column which is an incidental advantage of the high-mounted worm and sector steering box as opposed to a rack-and-pinion layout, where the steering column has to point more or less at the front wheel axis. Side support on corners is not notably good but the rake of the squabs can be adjusted to several angles or laid flat.

indicating that discs (with the almost obligatory servo) would be a needless complication on a fairly slow, light car. Throughout our test which included the usual proportion of hard driving, they never faded and always pulled the car up straight and quickly. Pedal pressures are notably light and the handbrake gave good stopping power and held the car firmly on a 1 in 3 gradient.

MAXIMUM SPEEDS

Mean lap speed banked circuit..		74·4 m.p.h.
Best one way ¼-mile ..	..	76·4
3rd gear (recommended)	..	52·0
2nd gear	.. ..	36·0
1st gear	..	19·0

"Maximile" Speed: (Timed quarter mile after 1 mile accelerating from rest)

Mean	.. ..	.. ..	72·6
Best	.. ..	.. ..	73·3

BRAKES

Pedal pressure, deceleration and equivalent stopping distance from 30 m.p.h.

lb.	g	ft
25	0·44	68
50	0·93	32½
55	0·95	31½
Handbrake	0·44	68

SPEEDOMETER

60 m.p.h.	..	..	..	3% fast
30	..	..	..	3% fast
Distance recorder	..	..	6% fast

FUEL CONSUMPTION

Touring (consumption midway between 30 m.p.h. and maximum less 5% allowance for acceleration) .. .. 41·4 m.p.g.
Overall .. .. 33·8 m.p.g.
8·35 litres/100 km.
Total test distance .. .. 1,950 miles
Fuel tank capacity (maker's figure) 6·6 gall.

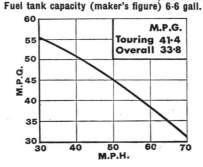

M.P.G.
Touring 41·4
Overall 33·8

STEERING

Turning circle between kerbs:

					ft.
Left	..	..	..	..	29½
Right	..	..	..	..	27½
Turns of steering wheel from lock to lock	..	..	..	..	3½

HILL CLIMBING

At steady speed

			lb./ton
Top	..	1 in 19·5 ..	Tapley 115
3rd	..	1 in 9·6 ..	230
2nd	..	1 in 6·1 ..	365

WEIGHT

			cwt.
Kerb weight (unladen with fuel for approximately 50 miles)	..	..	13
Front/rear distribution	..	..	36/64
Weight laden as tested	..	..	16¾

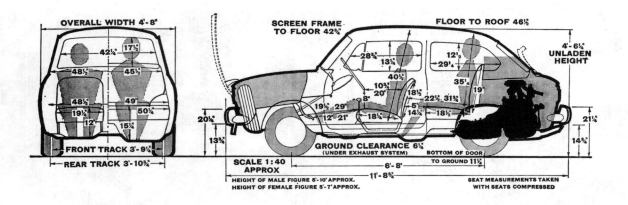

Scale 1:40 approx. Overall width 4'-8". Screen frame to floor 42¾". Floor to roof 46½". 4'-6¼" unladen height. Front track 3'-9¼". Rear track 3'-10¾". Ground clearance 6½" (under exhaust system). Bottom of door to ground 11½". Height of male figure 5'-10" approx. Height of female figure 5'-7" approx. Seat measurements taken with seats compressed.

FIAT 850

Entry to the back is fairly easy, and the front seats remain in the raised position unaided.

Thick screen pillars create some restriction on vision and the rear quarters are invisible from the driving seat. The mirror gives a good spread of view aft and the headlights throw a long, wide beam for night driving.

The heater and demister are outstandingly effective; flaps and shutters control the direction of the flow and the occupants can have warm feet and cool heads, an asset on long journeys. The demisting ducts can be swivelled to give a fresh blow on the face or turned sideways to demist the side windows.

At low speeds, the Fiat is a quiet car, but above 60 m.p.h. road noise and engine buzz combine to fatigue the driver on a long run. Wind roar is subdued.

Fittings and furniture

THE INTERIOR of the Fiat seems unfashionably narrow, a feeling emphasized by the practical, but strictly non-luxury trim. The floor is rubber-covered and the upholstery unpretentious leathercloth, which looks hard wearing and is washable. The plain, metal facia has a plastic top and the instruments are housed in a hooded binnacle together with four warning lights. Switchgear is convenient and simple and the lights are extinguished when the ignition is switched off; an "accessories" position keeps the sidelights on for parking. The choke lies behind the gear lever and the heater controls are fumbly and sensitive to very small movements. A narrow parcels shelf is supplemented by small pockets in the doors but there is no lockable compartment inside the car. The boot is deep and a good shape, carries a reasonable quantity of luggage and is supplemented by a shelf behind the rear seat which is useful for small items but can only be loaded to a depth of a few inches without interfering with vision rearwards. For extra capacity the back seat squab folds flat.

Engine accessibility is poor. The compartment is lit at night (so is the boot) but for anything but purely routine jobs six bolts have to be loosened to remove the back panel. The jack is a robust-looking instrument which lifts the whole of one side of the car.

In the event of an accident, the Fiat has rather a lot of unyielding surfaces inside. Safety belts are offered as optional equipment. The mirror (which incorporates a door-operated courtesy light) has a plastic rim and the parcels shelf is padded. The door locks are safely concealed underneath the armrests.

MAKE Fiat ● MODEL 850 ● MAKERS S.A. Fiat, Corso G. Agnelli 200, Turin, Italy ● CONCESSIONNAIRES Fiat (England) Ltd., Water Rd., Wembley, Middlesex

---

ENGINE

Cylinders	..	4
Bore and stroke	..	65 mm. × 63·5 mm.
Cubic capacity	..	843 c.c.
Valves	..	Pushrod o.h.v.
Compression ratio	8·8:1 (8:1 optional)
Carburetter	..	Weber 30 ICF1
Fuel pump	..	Fiat mechanical
Oil filter	..	Centrifugal
Max. power (net)	..	37 b.h.p. at 5,300 r.p.m.
Max. torque (net)	40·5 lb./ft. at 3,200 r.p.m.

TRANSMISSION

Clutch	..	Fiat diaphragm s.d.p. 6·29 in.
Top gear (s/m)	..	0·964
3rd gear (s/m)	..	1·409
2nd gear (s/m)	..	2·580
1st gear (s/m)	..	3·750
Reverse	..	3·620
Final drive	..	4·625
M.p.h. at 1,000 r.p.m. in:—		
Top gear	..	13·8
3rd gear	..	9·5
2nd gear	..	6·3
1st gear	..	3·7

CHASSIS

Construction	.. Unitary

BRAKES

Type	..	Fiat hydraulic drums
Dimensions	..	7·3 in. dia.
Friction areas	..	67 sq. in. of lining (33½ sq. in. front plus 33½ sq. in. rear) working on 108 sq. in. rubbed area of drum

SUSPENSION AND STEERING

Front	..	Independent by transverse leaf spring with upper wishbone and anti-roll bar
Rear	..	Independent by semi-trailing wishbone/radius arm and anti-roll bar
Shock absorbers:		
Front	..	Telescopic
Rear	..	Telescopic
Steering gear	..	Fiat worm and sector
Tyres	..	Pirelli 5·50—12 tubed

COACHWORK AND EQUIPMENT

Starting handle	..	None
Jack	..	Pillar type
Jacking points	..	One each side of body
Battery	..	Front-mounted under luggage compartment
No. of electrical fuses	..	Eight

Indicators	..	Self-cancelling flashers
Screen wipers	..	Self-parking electrical
Screen washers	..	Manual pump
Sun visors..	..	Two
Locks:		
With ignition key	Starter
With other key	Both front doors
Interior heater	..	Fresh-air, standard
Extras	..	Seat belts, radio, steering lock
Upholstery	..	Leathercloth
Floor covering	..	Rubber
Alternative body types	..	None

MAINTENANCE

Sump	..	5·8 pints S.A.E. 30 winter, 20w, or 10w/30 20w/40 summer
Gearbox	..	3·6 pints S.A.E. 90 E.P.
Steering gear	..	S.A.E. 90 E.P.
Cooling system	..	10·6 pints (sealed system)
Chassis lubrication	Every 1,500 miles to 2 points
Ignition timing	..	10° b.t.d.c.
Contact breaker gap	..	0·017–0·019 in.
Sparking plug type	Marelli CW240L, or Champion N4
Sparking plug gap	0·024–0·028 in.
Tappet clearances (cold)	..	Inlet 0·015 in., Exhaust 0·015 in.
Front wheel toe-in	0·08–0·16 in.
Castor angle	..	9°
Tyre pressures	..	16 lb. front 26 lb. rear

CT&T ROAD TEST

FIAT 600/D

New Zip for Italy's Favourite Bambino

THE CAR

Fiat's breadbox-shaped little 600 has suffered somewhat from anemia in its cooking form. Few of the primarily economy-minded Fiat owners were willing to pay the cost premium for conversion kits to boost the car's punch, but now—at no extra cost—comes the 600-D, offering about twenty per cent more hop.

Besides increased capacity, the 600-D sports pivoting quarter windows on the doors, more louvers on the rear deck lid, self-parking windshield wipers and a key-started ignition to replace the awkward old pull-up floor type.

TECHNICAL

Bore and stroke have been upped to 62mm by 63.5 mm, from 60 by 56 mm, increasing cubic capacity from 632 cc's to 767. Compression ratio is 7.5 to one and horsepower is rated (SAE) at 32 bhp @ 4800 rpm. Suspension, as before, is independent all-round.

STYLING

Cars of the Fiat's size strive for maximum use of interior space, over which the simplest possible shape is then stretched. And most of the 600-D's 11-odd feet of length is interior space; the rear-mounted engine hides in a little compartment too small to be a trunk, and the gas tank and spare tire lie up front in an equally miniscule area.

Styling as such couldn't really be expected to enter into a utility package such as this, but there are vestigial fenders front and rear to offset the boxiness of the over-all shape. Windows seem uncommonly large and so do the two doors.

Relative to its size, cost and purpose the 600-D is a successful design. One feature which seems neither particularly functional nor well thought out is the front-opening door idea. This requires training — you open the door, sort of spin around and fall backward onto the seat. The safety factor is also questionable. If the door is partly ajar, the car has to be stopped before it can be closed. Otherwise the wind will blow it wide open and at high speeds probably rip it right off.

Our test car was very well finished inside and out; there isn't a lot of it, but what there is of the 600-D is soundly put together.

INTERIOR

The benefits of that rectangular outside shape are immediately noticed inside, where despite its tiny dimensions the 600-D doesn't crowd driver or passengers into claustrophobia. In the rear is a bench, the back of which can be folded forward for a station-wagon effect. In front are mounted two chair-type seats with generous fore and aft adjustment and a fairly nonresilient feel to them. They're comfortable enough for the average-sized driver but, we felt, none too spacious and perhaps actually too small for the over-six-foot variety. Seats and door panels are covered in one of those washable materials that could be anything from leather to linoleum.

Instrumentation is hardly complex — a fuel gauge and speedometer, plus lights for oil pressure, battery charge and water temperature, housed in a small cowled cluster directly in the driver's line of vision. Choke and handbrake lie between the front seats. There are small lights for high beam and parking lights, and a soft little under-dash button works the window washers.

A small lever on the face of the rear seat, near the floor, operates the heating system but it's not as complicated as it sounds. You merely reach back between the seats and flip the lever on, off or anywhere in between. It works, too.

DRIVING

Though even cold-weather starts were quick and quiet, using almost no choke, time is needed before the 600-D can get warm enough to run smoothly and use all its power. The warmer it gets, in fact, the better — and faster — the whole car seems to run.

Visibility forward and laterally is excellent and despite our original misgivings, the small-looking rear window affords a good view of what's coming up behind. Pedals are spaced wide enough apart that tangle-footedness isn't a problem unless you have webbed feet, and the small, moderately raked steering wheel feels just the right size. The horn button is where it should be — in the wheel hub — and emits an unusually vigorous toot.

The increase to 767 cc's doesn't noticeably add to top speed. But it does seems to quicken getting there. The added torque will save downshift into third when a burst of thrust is needed, or if you simply must drop down a gear there'll be a noticeable added spurt on hand.

The sporting driver with his passion for shifting can still keep himself contented in this car. A crisp tight-feeling stalk within easy reach proved one of the 600-D's most endearing features. At the other end of the scale, the start-in-second and stay-in-fourth type of driver won't encounter balkiness either.

In the Italian tradition, this is a car meant to be driven and more than willing to be flogged. The useable limit is designated as 5500 rpm's but this little buzzer revs to what seems the low millions quite happily. If you hate noise this will limit your fun,

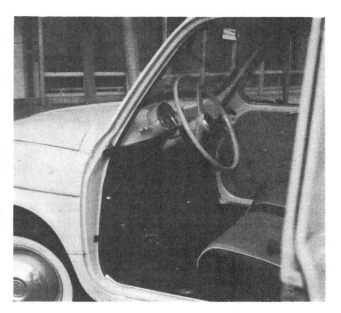

but after a while we noticed the noise was part of it all.

Steering is light, precise and free of any feedback of road jolts. At high speeds (well, relatively high), the car can and should be almost wished through corners. Anything bolder can result in drastic over-steering and resultant slewing in a very big hurry. With a light touch at the wheel and a heavy throttle foot the 600-D can delight the enthusiast within the car's limits, and even these don't seem so limited. Top speed hovers around the 65 mph mark but the car feels smooth and unstrained in this range. Long trips, due to high noise level from engine and wind, might prove fatiguing but certainly aren't impossible.

The Fiat's real forte, however, is congested city traffic and the car is happiest when being revved freely and dodging in and out among the mastadons.

ECONOMY

Our test took in a heavy amount of city traffic, yet under these less than ideal circumstances the 600-D delivered an average of 34 mpg on regular-grade fuel.

STORAGE

A small area behind the rear seat-back, and trunk area well taken up with fuel tank and spare tire, pro-hibit the loading of the family laundry plus passengers in the 600-D. With two up and the rear seat-back folded down there's plenty of room for loads. Elastic map pockets in both doors help stowage of miscellany.

HEATING

Once it's warmed up (which doesn't take long), the Fiat conducts more than enough heat from the rear end around the inside. In fact we turned the heater control to the off position and opened a window on more than fifteen-minute trips.

LAST WORD

Frugal in conception as it is, the Fiat 600-D isn't a humble performer. For people who like to drive it's great fun, with the added benefit of being well built. There is no ashtray provided, but most people will probably be too busy enjoying the drive to notice. With its added zest and the growing reputation Fiat is gaining behind it, the 600-D is better buy now than it's ever been.

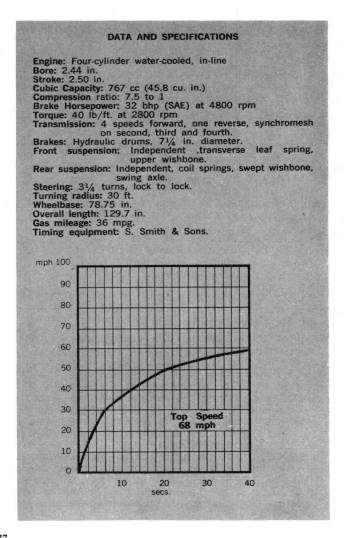

DATA AND SPECIFICATIONS

Engine: Four-cylinder water-cooled, in-line
Bore: 2.44 in.
Stroke: 2.50 in.
Cubic Capacity: 767 cc (45.8 cu. in.)
Compression ratio: 7.5 to 1
Brake Horsepower: 32 bhp (SAE) at 4800 rpm
Torque: 40 lb/ft. at 2800 rpm
Transmission: 4 speeds forward, one reverse, synchromesh on second, third and fourth.
Brakes: Hydraulic drums, 7¼ in. diameter.
Front suspension: Independent, transverse leaf spring, upper wishbone.
Rear suspension: Independent, coil springs, swept wishbone, swing axle.
Steering: 3¼ turns, lock to lock.
Turning radius: 30 ft.
Wheelbase: 78.75 in.
Overall length: 129.7 in.
Gas mileage: 36 mpg.
Timing equipment: S. Smith & Sons.

Top Speed 68 mph

'Motor' tells you
what to look
for under the
skin of that
second-hand car

The Fiat
600 and 600D

SINCE it became available in Britain in May, 1955, the Fiat 600 has proved itself to be a tough little customer and its reputation has grown steadily over the years. Initially, it had a 633 c.c. 22·5 b.h.p. (later 28) engine and, in late 1960, the 600D took over, with a 767 c.c. unit delivering 32 b.h.p. A quick recognition point—the 600D has quarter lights on the doors.

All engines are four-cylinder, over-head valve, with aluminium-alloy cylinder heads and cast-in induction tracts. Gearboxes have four ratios—the units are, of course, rear-mounted.

In typical Fiat fashion, gradual improvements have been made throughout the whole production period and although the new model you can buy today will obviously be better, *in toto*, than a '55 version, none of the modifications is essential for satisfactory motoring. It must be noted that the 600D engine can *not* be fitted to the 600 and will *not* be supplied on a service exchange basis for the smaller unit.

About 2½ million have been made and around 20,000 have been sold in Britain.

● The body
Slipper-dip pre-painting treatment makes Fiat bodies last well and rust is kept at bay. In addition, many parts of the underside and inside the doors are coated for corrosion prevention and sound deadening. The body is, in fact, double skinned and therefore exceptionally rigid. The underside is unusually free from protruding parts and there are no water traps.

Pre-1957 models had sliding side windows instead of drop-down, and, right up to September, 1964, the doors were hinged at their rear edges, the car's only really old-fashioned feature. When this was altered the body

structure was redesigned to cope with the changed stresses.

The battery and spare wheel live at the front and the standard toolkit is such a good one that it is worth checking to see if it is still with the car.

Early seats had tension springs and later ones rubber straps and, in both cases, foam rubber covering. Seat sag is virtually unknown and it is said that the seats become more comfortable with age. From 1961, reclining seats became standard instead of optional.

Uneven tyre wear will indicate faulty toe-in (or toe-out, according to model) and it is important that this measurement is set according to the instruction book for the particular car, as it has been altered over the years, several times. The steering gear itself is massive and unlikely to wear—there are three points of adjustment on the rigidly mounted steering box itself.

● Mechanical
If the engine appears oily, there must be some reason for this, such as a loose oil filter fitting. Oil need not indicate anything seriously wrong, but the unit is, if properly maintained, a clean one.

Valve clearances are set with the unit cold (0·006 in.). When the engine is started up from cold, the valve gear should be quite silent. As it warms, the rockers can be heard but when it is really hot, silence should take over again. These clearances have a considerable effect on performance and many people tend to set them wrongly. Again, it is important to follow the advice in Fiat instruction manuals because the cam form is such that the normal up-and-down setting pattern of rockers does not apply.

Another important point is that, since the rockers are set cold, the push-rods must be forced down hard to

The inside is essentially simple and the seats are comfortable. This is a 600D, identified by the quarter-light window.

squeeze oil from the points of contact in order to get a true reading.

The timing chain (a pattern special to Fiats) should last the life of the engine and premature clatter from this source is unlikely.

● On the road
The gear change and selection should be easy and positive. If not, the most likely cause is lack of lubrication of the link rods. High-melting-point grease must be used as these links run through the heater duct instead of under the car and the lubricant gets rather hot. However, smells which might be mistaken for warm lubricant when the heater is on are usually traced to a slipping fan belt. Difficult

● Specification

ENGINE: 633 or 767 c.c., four-cylinder, o.h.v., rear-mounted.
GEARBOX: Four-speed with synchromesh on three upper ratios.
LENGTH: 600, 10 ft. 6½ in.; 600D, 10 ft. 9¾ in.
WIDTH: 4 ft. 6½ in.
WEIGHT: 11¾ cwt.

● Performance

MAXIMUM SPEEDS: 600, 58 m.p.h.; 600D, 65 m.p.h.
ACCELERATION: 0-50 through gears, 600, 32·5 sec.; 600D, 20·6 sec. 20-40 in top, 600, 27·2 sec.; 600D, 15·8 sec.
TOURING FUEL CONSUMPTION: 600, 44 m.p.g.; 600D, 40 m.p.g.
BRAKING from 30 m.p.h.: 30 to 31½ ft.

● Identity Parade

On sale in Britain as 600, May 1955. Drop instead of sliding door windows, March 1957. October 1959, normal rear-wheel handbrake instead of transmission brake. Sidelamps moved to below headlamps, March 1960. 600D introduced October 1960. 600 discontinued June 1961. Fully reclining seats standard from February 1962. September 1964, forward-hinged doors.

A view of the engine unit few owners see. Note the twin belts for dynamo and pump/fan.

In the front compartment: spare wheel, battery, fuel tank and tool kit.

engagement usually means the replacement of a bush which costs 1s. only, plus three U-plates at 3d. each.

Clutch judder is virtually unknown since 1956, when a modified cable was introduced. The cable runs in a steel tube most of the way and only the final part is flexible. The clutch should be light in operation.

There will be a slight whine when in top gear because this is actually an overdrive ratio instead of the usual 1 : 1 direct. For the car's size, the gearbox bearings are extremely stout and trouble from this quarter is very unlikely indeed.

The brakes should be fully serviced every 12,000 miles, which will result in the linings lasting for up to 40,000 miles in some cases. Neglected adjustment will permit them to wear quite rapidly. Service-exchange shoes with bonded-on linings, profile-ground, cost 8s. 3d. each. Here, again, attention must be paid to the instruction book.

● Servicing points

In addition to items already mentioned where the maker's instructions *must* be followed, there are a few more unorthodoxies.

For example, the engine temperature thermostat operates an air outlet flap (air is discharged through the flap after being blown through the radiator), and if this flap sticks the effect on fuel consumption can be considerable. Therefore, check it for freedom —it is under the rear of the car on the offside. A dashboard light warns of overheating.

The air-cleaner intake has a two-way valve marked green/red or E/I, indicating "summer/winter". In cold weather it is set to use hot air and v.v. in warm weather. It is important that this valve be correctly set as the weather demands, as both fuel consumption and performance will suffer if it is ignored.

The cooling system employs a smallish radiator with a high-velocity water pump and the pipe which runs from the cylinder head to the pump is not a by-pass, but a return bleed which warms the incoming flow after a cold start.

Servicing should include blowing dust and the like from the radiator core; the heater duct contains a gauze air filter which should also be cleaned periodically. The clutch adjuster is accessible after removing the front undertray.

The by-pass oil filter element should be changed at 6,000-mile intervals and the main centrifugal filter cleaned at 12,000 miles. Dynamo and pump/fan belts are separate. The former is adjusted by moving the dynamo, but

on the fan a split pulley is fitted and belt tension is altered by fitting or removing shims between the two halves to change the distance between the faces of the V and, consequently, the effective diameter.

● General

Unlike general practice, the service exchange engines are complete, apart from the starter and clutch, and they are bench tested. An engine bottom half is available on the same exchange basis, as are all other units like transmission, dynamo, brakes, etc.

The workshop manual is an immense volume—more like an encyclopædia— and costs £3 5s., while the owner's handbook is also a model of its kind at 3s. 6d. Spares are 100 per cent available from stock in Britain and there are 359 agents and 43 Fiat distributors in the country, so garage servicing presents no problem.

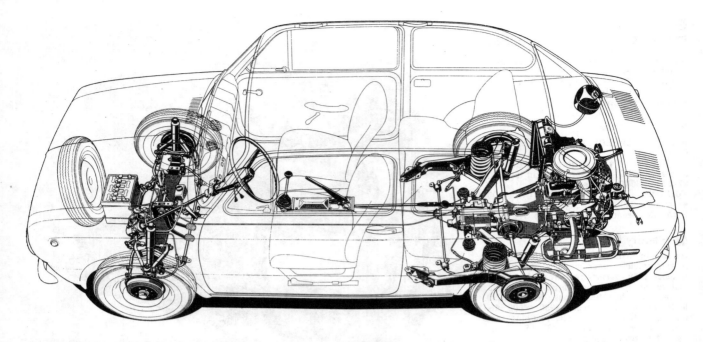

NEW FROM FIAT

JOHN BOLSTER tries an Italian competitor in the 850 class

WHEN a new car is announced by the great Fiat industrial empire, that is news indeed. Always of great interest to the engineer, Fiat cars compete directly with our own on many markets, and "hot" versions are invariably produced by the Italian tuning firms.

The new Fiat 850 fills a gap in the range. Having almost the same fuel economy as the 600, it yet gives greater interior space, particularly to the rear passengers, and the luggage room is really generous. Nevertheless, it is a more compact vehicle than the 1100.

The emphasis in the new car is on safety. The whole structure is designed to protect the passengers in the event of a serious crash, while many safety features are apparent as one examines the machine. Safety is also enhanced by the great attention which has been paid to stability and ease of handling.

A pressed-steel structure, the body is a roomy four-seater with two wide doors. The fuel tank is carried ahead of the engine but behind the rear seat squab, leaving the front bonnet free for the carriage of a considerable quantity of luggage. A very useful luggage space is also provided behind the rear seat, above the tank. The front windows wind down and there are large swivelling panels ahead of them, but the rear windows are fixed. Copious ventilation is provided and a large-capacity heater is supplied with water by a built-in piping system in the backbone of the car.

The engine has a cast-iron cylinder block with three crankshaft bearings, the cylinder head being of aluminium. A chain-driven camshaft operates the valves by push rods and rockers. The dimensions are 65 mm. x 63.5 mm. (843 c.c.) and the engine comes in two states of tune. The standard version has a compression ratio of 8:1 and develops 34 b.h.p. (D.I.N.) at 5,000 r.p.m. or 40 b.h.p. (S.A.E.) at 5,300 r.p.m. The Super version, with a compression ratio of 8.8:1, gives 37 b.h.p. (D.I.N.) at 5,100 r.p.m. or 42 b.h.p. (S.A.E.) at 5,300 r.p.m. Fumes cannot be emitted from the breather,

for they are absorbed through the carburetter when the throttle is open and go directly into the induction pipe under closed throttle conditions, an automatic valve looking after the change-over.

A centrifugal oil filter is incorporated with the crankshaft pulley, the radiator being mounted alongside the rear engine with a two-stage belt drive to the pump and fan. A sealed cooling system is incorporated, with a semi-transparent expansion tank to show that adequate water is in circulation. A diaphragm-type clutch takes the power to a fully synchronized 4-speed gearbox. A bonded rubber sandwich is incorporated in the gear lever linkage, to eliminate the telephoning of vibrations to the car interior.

The suspension is by a wide, three-leaf transverse spring in front, with plastic interleaving. It is rigidly mounted with a separate torsional anti-roll bar, short upper wishbones and telescopic dampers completing the geometry. The worm-type steering gear operates a three-piece linkage ahead of the wheel centres.

Extremely rugged, the triangulated rear suspension arms are not true swing-axles, having a considerable angle of trail. The helical springs are insulated from the body by ingenious rubber buffers. An anti-roll torsion bar and telescopic dampers are again employed. The slip-joints are at the inboard end of the half-shafts, enclosed in the oil-retaining covers of the universal joints. Cast-iron brake drums are used all round for the hydraulic brakes.

I was recently given the opportunity to test the new car thoroughly in Italy. Electronic timing facilities were available and every sort of road surface, from good to atrocious, was provided by the terrain. The machine rides particularly well over rough tracks, while the very quick steering allows rapid corrections to be made. The usual Fiat understeer is not present, and the tail will break away on the tighter corners, particularly if the full power of the S model is applied. This can be controlled with the greatest ease, and the

presence of a rear passenger makes little difference to the handling.

The maximum speed is about 75 m.p.h. for the standard car and 78 m.p.h. for the S. I covered a standing quarter-mile, the car well laden with driver and two passengers, in 22.535 secs. In the S, with only one passenger, I recorded 21.806 secs. There was not much difference at the top end, for the speed, timed over 40 metres at the end of an accelerating kilometre, was 109 k.p.h. and 111.8 k.p.h. respectively. The S feels livelier, however, and can spin its wheels when starting on a dry road.

The gear change is very rapid and about 60 m.p.h. can be reached in third, when one just seems to run out of revs. The insulation of road noise is praiseworthy, while the engine and transmission are quieter than those of previous small Fiats, the S being naturally a little more noticeable mechanically. The brakes are powerful and do not tend to fade.

Of pleasing modern appearance, the 850 is nicely finished and gives a comfortable ride to all four occupants, with a large window area. The test was too short for fuel consumption figures to be obtained, but they are claimed to be highly competitive. As to the safety features, I nearly tested all of them in a head-on collision with an Alfa, the driver of which had been looking upon the vino when it was red!

JOHN BOLSTER tries a FIAT 850 SPIDER and COUPE

WITHOUT any doubt, the new sports version of the Fiat 850 stole the Geneva Show. The very attractive appearance of these little cars, both with the Fiat fixed-head coupé body and the Bertone Spider, caused an appreciative crowd to collect on the maker's stand.

Now I have had an opportunity to put both types through their paces and I can say straightaway that they are even better than they look. In both cases a chassis-cum-body construction is used, only the floor pressing remaining of the standard saloon. Disc brakes are used in front, the independent suspension with a transverse leaf spring being suitably modified for high-speed driving. At the rear the semi-trailing independent suspension arms carry drum brakes. Disc wheels with extra wide rims support 5.20—13 ins. tyres.

The transmission has a final drive ratio of 8/39, to allow the power unit to rev freely. The engine has a new aluminium cylinder head giving a compression ratio of 9.3 to 1, and a special induction system carries a twin-choke Weber downdraught carburetter. The new exhaust manifold has suitably paired pipes, and special camshafts are fitted, that of the Spider giving more power at the expense of a little less bottom end. Gross outputs of 52 and 54 b.h.p. are obtained from the two models, the engine dimensions in both cases being 65 × 63.5 mm. (843 c.c.).

Anti-roll torsion bars front and rear keep the cars on an even keel. Though the seats fold forward for access to the rear space, they lock in their normal position—a worth-while refinement. The Coupé has a seat at the rear for short journeys and the Spider has a rear deck which lifts to allow the hood to disappear. This rear deck is removed altogether when the optional hard top is fitted. Additional instruments are available, including a large electronic revolution counter.

On the road I was at once impressed with the smooth running of the little engine. It seemed capable of unlimited revs without any sign of distress, and I was guilty of attaining 8,000 r.p.m. on both models. The weather was diabolical throughout the test, but it would be fair to say that the Spider will exceed 90 m.p.h. and that the Coupé is 4 or 5 m.p.h. slower. Both types will run in remarkable silence at 75 m.p.h. with an almost closed throttle. For substantially built and luxuriously appointed cars, this performance must be regarded as excellent from 843 c.c. of engine.

The roadholding can only be described as superb. On winding mountain roads in pouring rain, the absence of any rear-engined sensation was astonishing. Initially there is just a suspicion of under-steering, but though violent driving can convert this to mild oversteering it is difficult indeed to provoke a full-blooded rear-end breakaway. The balance is excellent and for sheer fun in driving this car would take some beating. The very quick and positive gearchange, with well-spaced ratios, assists in this, and the brakes are powerful without being fierce.

I drove both cars flat out on an auto-strada in pouring rain, with strong gusts of wind to add to the nastiness. In the Coupé one could feel the wind slightly, but the Spider did not deviate a millimetre, perhaps due to the better penetration of its longer nose. At first I thought the steering was a little bit heavy for so small a car, but on mountain roads I found it was ideal,

TWO MORE SPORTY versions of the Fiat 850 made their appearance at the recent Geneva Show—the Coupé (above) and the Spider (below). The engine (bottom) produces 52 and 54 b.h.p.

the sensation of absolute mastery being altogether delightful.

From the above it is obvious that I am very enthusiastic about the new sports Fiats. At the time when I was testing the cars some very experienced drivers were being given the same opportunities and their enthusiasm was just as great as mine. Not only do the cars handle outstandingly well but they are of delightful appearance and are exceptionally well finished. They are by no means expensive in Italy, but it is impossible as yet to work out their cost in England, for the intentions of our new masters are not yet clear. Even if import duties force up the prices, these Fiats will remain very desirable little cars, but if the Italian figures are not too greatly increased, their impact on our market must be sensational. It is intended that right-hand-drive examples shall be available in England before the Motor Show in October.

The conditions under which we drove the new Fiats can be adjudged from this picture

Two small sporting Fiats

AS briefly reported in our Geneva Show description, Fiats introduced on that occasion two sporting versions of their new 850 Saloon model. So far, no price has been announced for them in this country but it seems certain that they will be on sale at a very competitive figure. We mention the matter of price early in the description of these cars because it is of such fundamental importance to the British market. Fiat now have two sports cars which are well capable of rivalling the small British cars in this field which have done so well, not only at home but in many foreign markets. In the past, so many of the attractive small Italian and other Continental sporting cars have arrived in this country at such an inflated price that they have been of no interest to the British enthusiast. It now seems that Fiats have overcome these problems and the manner in which they have done it is inherent in the technical design of the car.

Both the vehicles are basically the normal 850 saloon model. That is to say basic dimensions, suspension, floor pressings, engine and transmission are all taken directly from the saloon model. The bones of the car are, therefore, able to take advantage of the very high production rate of the saloon car, which is currently achieving one of the highest outputs among small car models in Europe.

Given the bones of the car, the two models, Spider and Coupe, are worked on entirely differently. The Coupe is designed and completed in the Fiat factory whereas the chassis, if it can so be called, for the Spider is mated

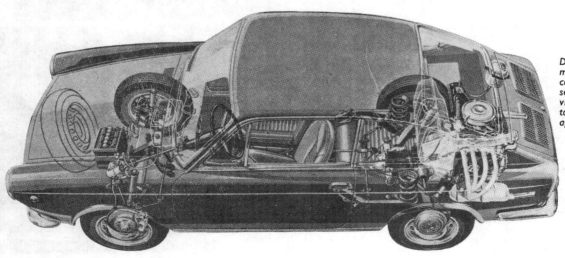

Disposition of the mechanical components can be seen in this ghost view. Their similarity to the 850 saloon is apparent

Coupe and Spider posed together. If the Coupe lacks some of the elegance of the Spider it makes up for it in practicability

with a fully trimmed and equipped Bertone Spider body, designed and manufactured in the Bertone works. As might be expected, the Bertone Spider body comes out a little more expensive—about £60 in Italy or perhaps £90 to £100 more in Britain. The Bertone body also comes out slightly heavier than the works-manufactured one.

The use of the basic floor, engine and transmission of the saloon car means that the two occasional four-seater versions cannot be greatly improved so far as weight is concerned. Indeed, both bodies in practice come out slightly heavier than the saloon. In order, therefore, to provide the additional performance which the owner of a sporting car would normally expect, the output of the 4-cylinder 850 cc engine has been considerably increased. Because it is considered that the Coupe would have a wider appeal than the Spider, the engine characteristics have been made slightly different for the two models. Different cam-shafts, improved breathing, higher compression ratio and flowed exhaust systems have allowed an output of 47 bhp net to be achieved for the Coupe with 44.1 lb ft of torque. The Spider achieves 49 bhp net, with 43 lb ft of torque, the extra power helping to add 10 kilometres per hour to the maximum speed but necessitating much more liberal use of the gearbox to achieve the performance. Doubtless, the noticeably higher maximum speed stems as much from the slicker shape of the Spider as it does from the modest increase in horse-power.

An outstanding feature of both cars is the quality of the finish and the interior trim. In traditional continental fashion they do not boast pile carpet floor covering but what they lack in opulent trimming they more than make up for in careful design and excellent assembly. In order to cope with the higher speeds of which the cars are capable and to accommodate larger discs in the front in place of the small brake drums on the standard 850 model, larger wheels have been fitted and this to some extent impinges on interior space, particularly at the front where pedals have to be substantially offset. Good seats and excellent visibility more than make up for this and the driver immediately finds all the controls falling happily to hand. Controls and instrumentation vary between the two models, those on the Coupe being, if anything, rather superior to the Spider. A rev counter is not fitted as standard but is undoubtedly a most useful piece of equipment since the little engine revs willingly and astronomically. The Coupe provides four seats with no apologies, but there is no doubt that rear seat passengers, unless of extremely small stature, would be most uncomfortable in a run of any length. Nevertheless, it is a practical proposition to get four people in the car and children would certainly be comfortable on the well-upholstered rear seats. Really, the space will be required for luggage when two people are touring since the under-bonnet boot space is large enough for only one suitcase. On the Spider, due to its elongated nose, it has been possible to mount the spare wheel flat in front of the front wheels and this allows a

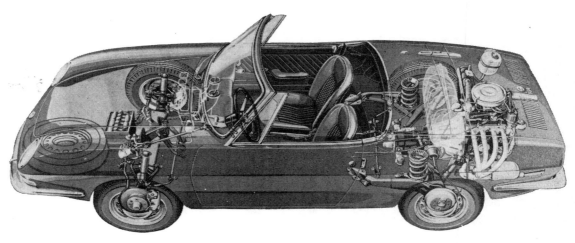

The identical mechanical arrangement of the Spider can be seen by comparing this view with that of the Coupe opposite. Note how the longer nose allows a horizontal mounting of the spare wheel

Neat fascia layout of the Spider. The right hand dial is designed to take the optional rev counter

timed run was just over 80 mph, but the Coupe is said to be capable of 84 mph. Similarly, the Spider in which we achieved 85 mph can, in fact, exceed 90 mph in normal conditions. Acceleration times for the two cars are virtually identical up to 60 mph, achievable in under 20 seconds, whereafter the Spider is slightly superior and reaches 70 mph in just over 30 seconds, amounting to a standing kilometre in 38.5 seconds. Due to the use of generous-sized discs it has been possible to offer light brakes without use of a servo. Braking appeared to be more than adequate for the performance of the car.

After some high speed motorway work, we proceeded through the foothills of the Alps where the cars could be extended over winding roads with surfaces bearing the scars from winter's ravages. It was still raining, and the sort of road which has a drop of a few hundred feet at one side is not the ideal place to experiment with a car's ultimate handling characteristics. It was apparent, nevertheless, that the inherent problems of rear-engined cars have been largely overcome in this model; as would be expected, the traction at the rear was extremely good with the weight bias in that direction, but it was pleasing to find that the front had no tendency to break away first even on full lock with wet polished road surfaces. When the back broke away, it did so predictably and gently. On really rough surfaces, the springing was extremely good and induced no rattles in the bodywork or equipment of the car.

After fairly lengthy acquaintance with the two little cars the predominent impression is that at last there may be some small foreign sports cars to compete with the cheap British models. Their performance is good if not remarkable, and there is undoubtedly scope for further tuning of the engine for the owner who so desires it. But what the cars may lack in sheer accelerative ability they make up for in their pleasing appearance and their quality of construction. Although the Coupe will be the cheaper car and will undoubtedly be the more practical vehicle for England, the Spider is a genuine Bertone jewel—there will be many unable to resist it.

little more space and indeed a little more space is necessary since the hood uses some of the area behind the seats. The hood of the Spider, incidentally, is a very neat solution to an age-old problem. A hinged deck is swung aside to allow the hood to be extracted and clipped in place and the deck is then put back in position, leaving the space below, vacated by the hood, for stowing luggage. If the owner wishes to use a hardtop, the deck can be removed entirely and a genuine GT Coupe results.

Sadly enough, on the day we drove these two intriguing little cars it poured with rain the entire time. We were not, in the unfavourable conditions, able to achieve the times quoted for the cars by the factory, but we came near enough to show that they are genuine, and that the performance of the cars is very creditable indeed. Our best

Very well furnished interior of the Coupe offers good front seats and fully upholstered rear ones, not much inferior to those of the saloon

SPECIFICATIONS—FIAT 850 COUPE and SPIDER

ENGINE:

Four cylinders; bore 65 mm (2.555 in), stroke 63.5 mm (2.5 in). Cubic capacity 843 cc. Compression ratio 9.3:1. Maximum bhp (SAE) 52/54; maximum torque (Coupe) 44.1 lb ft net. Weber 30 DIC dual-barrel carburettor. Camshaft in crankcase. Overhead valves; diaphragm fuel pump (mechanical). Tank capacity 6.6 gallons; 12-volt 48 amp/hr battery.

TRANSMISSION:

Four-speed all-synchromesh gearbox, with Porsche type synchronizer rings; sdp clutch. Overall gear ratios: 1st, 17.7; 2nd, 12.18; 3rd, 6.87; 4th, 4.69. Final drive 4.875.

CHASSIS:

Suspension: front, independent, by transverse-mounted leaf spring and hydraulic, telescopic double-acting shock absorbers. Stabilizer bar. Rear, independent by coil springs and hydraulic telescopic double-acting shock absorbers on swinging arms. Stabilizer bar. Disc brakes at front, drum brakes at rear. Steering by worm screw and helical sector. Pressed steel, bolt-on disc wheels. Tyre size, 5.20-13 in.

DIMENSIONS:

	ft	ins
Wheelbase	6	7.8
Front track	3	9.6
Rear track	3	11.7
Overall length	11	10
Overall width	4	11
Overall height	4	3.2
Ground clearance		5
Turning circle	14	7.2
Kerb weight	$13\frac{3}{4}$ cwt (dry)	

FIAT'S idea about what their customers want are strangely anomalous, for whereas their larger models —the 1100D, the 1500, 1800, and 2300—all offer remarkably high performance in their class, the products below one litre have, until the Coupe and Spider, foregone any pretensions of being fast and concentrate instead on ruggedness, durability, and retention of high secondhand values for ten years and more. Longevity and safety in design do not make the most exciting reading and any lack of enthusiasm for the Fiat 850 should not detract from its ability to do everything a little better than the 600D which has been in production for ten years and earned millions of devotees the world over: they will find the larger car a worthy replacement.

The extra foot on overall length is accounted for by the diminutive bonnet over the rear engine and a longer luggage compartment at the front, these small alterations improving the appearance of the car considerably even though the centre-section and interior are virtually identical to the 600D in appearance and dimension. The engine is bored out to 843 cc and in the process the block was

Road Test: Fiat 850S

lengthened to accommodate a 3 mm bore increase; power output of the 850S (a less powerful version is available overseas) is 37 bhp net in a car weighing only 13 cwt at the kerb, and drive is through a four-speed all-indirect synchromesh gearbox.

Comfort and convenience

Still no more than a four-seater, like the smaller Fiat, the 850 does nevertheless take four adults a distance in more comfort than many of its rivals. It scores considerably as a Turin development in having a lot more luggage space because the area is larger and particularly because the petrol tank has been moved to the rear behind the back seats. Still more space for baggage is afforded when the back of the rear seat is folded forward.

The spare wheel is mounted horizontally in the nose of the car along with hydraulics and the windscreen washer fluid; the latter froze up and remained solid during the cold weather that prevailed, so a de-icer additive is essential in winter-time. Worm and roller steering gear is mounted above the centreline between the front wheels to give a fairly direct steering column angle without introducing universal joints, but this carries the slight penalty of a forward-sloping boot floor. The battery also is hidden under the floor, and does not present itself readily for inspection.

Routine maintenance of the rear engine does not present any special problems, but to tighten the fanbelt or carry out any more detailed work it is necessary to undo four bolts and remove the rear apron; this is a two-minute job.

Inside the car there is an inch more legroom for back-seat passengers, compared with the 600D, an inch more headroom front and rear, and the car is an inch wider inside. This does not add up to more passenger accommodation but there are slight improvements especially in respect of ride comfort. The suspension is softer, but with more powerful damping, and a rear anti-roll bar has been added to the specification. With two inches extra on the wheelbase, the overall effect eliminates small-car pitching and gives a softer ride which is well appreciated on secondary roads. Although the roll factor is low, the driver

is aware when the rear wheels are increasing their positive camber angle and has plenty of warning when oversteer is about to introduce itself.

The interior is simply furnished, with hardwearing rubber floor lining and seats which, with plastic upholstery, look uninspiring but are in fact most comfortable. A simple form of reclining backrest for the front seats is available as a very inexpensive extra, but our car had fixed backrests which were sufficiently reclined to suit us very well.

Visibility from the driving seat is good, despite rather thick windscreen pillars. The front wings are easily seen from the driving seat and although the rear of the car projects beyond the back window by about nine inches, and cannot be seen without an effort, the owner-driver soon

A longer tail was dictated for the 850 as the petrol tank is now behind the rear seat, giving extra luggage space

Simple interior of the Fiat 850 is extremely comfortable

learns how far he can back up. Rubber inserts in the over-riders are a sensible item incorporated in the design.

Fittings and controls

The Fiat 850 is, at a tax paid price of £576, a worthy class competitor because it includes all the "de luxe" items such as heater, screenwashers and headlamp flashers in the specification.

Fresh air for the heating system is taken in through a grille in front of the windscreen, then ducted through the heater and through a pair of swivelling vents on top of the fascia. These are designed to direct warmed or cool air onto the windscreen for demisting, or else onto the passengers' faces. During the very cold weather that prevailed

An extra inch all round increases passenger comfort

Spare wheel and battery (under the boot floor) do not impede the luggage space

the heater was not too effective, even with the booster switched on, and snow on the mats did not melt during a 25-mile journey.

Foot pedals are offset to the left to clear the intruding wheel arch, and are rather close together. Swivelling the left foot on the brake for heel-and-toe gearchanging had its hazards, for a couple of times we "declutched" on the toe of the right shoe, stopping much sooner than desired! The handbrake is in the centre with the choke control alongside.

A binnacle in front of the driver houses the speedometer, petrol and water temperature gauges, also the ignition, main beam, oil pressure and light-operation warning lights. The temperature gauge barely struggled out of the cold sector throughout the test and fell back each time the heater was switched on, which probably accounts for the lack of interior heating.

On the left of the steering column are two stalks of unequal length for indicators and headlight operation.

The door locks were infuriating, demanding to be mentioned because of their habits of being difficult to operate and reluctant to release the key when it has been turned.

Performance

The engine is very low in profile and although the block is cast-iron the cylinder head and most of the ancillaries are made of alloy, keeping weight down to a reasonable minimum. Drive is taken forward through a 6¼ in diaphragm clutch to a new gearbox built with all-indirect ratios, top being an overdrive.

By boring the 767 cc engine of the 600D to 843 cc, the unit has gained oversquare dimensions, ie big bore and short stroke, which are demanded nowadays for long engine life and low piston speeds. The block was lengthened to accommodate the water passages and there is a sloping "roof" above it to drop the engine if the car is struck heavily from the rear. Carburation is through a twin-choke Weber carburettor, and although the maximum power is reasonable at 37 bhp (at 5300 rpm) the torque is not spectacular being 40 lb ft at 3200 rpm. This, coupled with the high top gear, dictates free use of the gearbox at lower speeds.

The engine was easy to start and quick to deliver full performance although, as we have mentioned, it did not reach a proper working temperature in cold weather. On our particular car the clutch was rather fierce and more revs than we would have thought desirable were needed to guarantee a good start from rest. The gearbox is a pleasure to use, having unbeatable synchromesh and positive movement—this is just as well at times for the car's performance is quite leisurely and any delay in gearchanging going uphill would be annoying. Whilst we do not expect every car to have sparkling performance there is a minimum for every driver except the least ambitious, and when laden the 850 is not likely to satisfy drivers who prefer to maintain good progress on their journeys.

The recommended gearchange points, at 19, 36 and 52 mph can be exceeded comfortably without stressing the engine, although at high revs the exhaust system sets up a booming which can be tiring at much more than 60 mph cruising speed.

With two leading shoes, the brakes were light and positive. There is little weight transfer in such a car with the engine at the back, so retardation was sure even on wet and icy roads and in hard driving there was no sign of fade or increased pedal pressure. The lights too are well up to the car's performance.

Handling

Putting up high average speeds in a slow car requires good handling to reduce the need for slowing down, and the 850 is well equipped for the task. Not only is the ride good on main or secondary roads but there is little rolling motion in hard cornering—the car can be placed quickly and accurately even though the steering is somewhat low-geared. The Fiat understeers at all normal road speeds and the final oversteer is predictable. We were surprised to find that it could be driven in snow safely at 50 mph, showing none of the tail-happy characteristics of some older rear-engine designs.

Summary

The Fiat 850 is not an exciting car and does not have any outstanding characteristics; we were indeed disappointed that it is so little better than the 600D and no gain on its older cousin, the Simca Mille. At a really competitive price though, despite import duty, it does offer years of cheap and trouble-free motoring, if we can judge by the smaller cars' records. The 850 is a worthy successor in any garage to a 600D (which continues in production) and is capable of interesting transformation.

SPECIFICATION
FIAT 850S

ENGINE:
Four cylinders; bore 65 mm (2.56 in), stroke 63.5 mm (2.49 in). Cubic capacity 843 cc (51.4 cu in). Compression ratio 8.8:1. Maximum bhp (net) 37 at 5,300 rpm. Maximum torque 40.5 lb ft at 3,200 rpm. Weber twin-choke 30 IFC I carburettor. Overhead valvegear, pushrods and rockers. Fiat mechanical petrol pump. Tank capacity 6.6 gallons. Water capacity 10.6 pints. Sump capacity 5.8 pints. 12-volt 36 amp hr battery.

TRANSMISSION:
Four-speed all-synchromesh gearbox, Fiat 6.29 in diaphragm clutch. Gear ratios: 1st, 3.75; 2nd, 2.58; 3rd, 1.41; top, 0.96; reverse, 3.62. Final drive ratio, 4.625. Gearing 13.8 mph per 1,000 rpm in top gear

CHASSIS:
Integral steel body framework. Suspension: front, independent with transverse leaf spring and upper wishbones, telescopic dampers and anti-roll bar. Rear, independent with coil springs and semi-trailing arms, telescopic dampers and anti-roll bar. Drum brakes all round, 7.3 in diameter. Fiat worm and sector steering. Pressed steel bolt-on wheels; tyre size 5.50 x 12.

DIMENSIONS:

	ft	ins
Wheelbase	6	8
Track, front	3	9½
Track, rear	3	10¾
Overall length	11	8¾
Overall width	4	8
Overall height	4	6
Ground clearance		6
Turning circle	29	3
Kerb weight	13¼ cwt	

PERFORMANCE:

	secs
0 - 30 mph	6.7
0 - 40 mph	10.6
0 - 50 mph	16.9
0 - 60 mph	28.4

MAXIMUM SPEED IN GEARS:

	mph
1st	23
2nd	41
3rd	61
Top	76

Overall fuel consumption: 35.5 mpg
PRICE: £576 including tax

DAUPHINE & FIAT TEST

CONTINUED FROM PAGE 31

the rim, which is secured to a star-shaped plate by five bolts, and spare-tire stowage is spectacularly handy. The spare lies flat in a separate compartment under the front bumper, and was removed with no difficulty at all by my daughter.

Finish: Necessarily, detail finish overlaps to some extent into the area of comfort if we include detailed appointments. Here, each has its distinctive points and its drawbacks. The quality of the paint job on both cars is above average, but neither has quite the fine detail finish of the VW. The Fiat's upholstery is definitely on the Spartan side, and (because of the price differential) instrumentation and appointments are kept down to a strict minimum. For instance, while the Dauphine has a temperature gauge, the Fiat uses a red warning light which comes on when engine temperature rises above the safe maximum. Both

cars also feature warning lights for oil pressure and charging rate indicators—a system which works quite satisfactorily on the Volks as well. The Dauphine scores with such details as glove boxes, a two-note horn, an ashtray and a pull-knob for the radiator blind, but the plastic material used for steering post, turn indicators, dash panel, defroster ducts and door handles appears to be of rather mediocre quality.

Both cars have excellent integral heater and defroster systems. With hot-water radiators, they are perhaps a shade more effective than the VW's, which simply ducts air for heating over the cylinder. Both feature electric windshield wipers, although those on the Fiat are somewhat noisy.

Running economy is self-evident and is one of the main attractions in owning a small car of this type. Under normal conditions, dispensing with peak revolutions required by acceleration tests and speed runs, gas economy is even greater than indicated here. Probably about 38 mph for the Dauphine and 42 for the Fiat 600 would be a fair esti-

mate, compared with 32 for the VW's larger power plant.

To sum up, both the Renault Dauphine and the Fiat 600 fulfill their purpose admirably. If you live four miles from a railroad station, you can make the daily double trip, five days a week, for about 30 cents, in perfect comfort. Or your wife can go shopping with the kids bring back a huge load of groceries with room to spare.

If you want plushier appointments and the 10 extra horses and brisker performance of the Renault's "Ventoux" engine, the Dauphine is your car. If you're primarily interested in getting from A to B and would sooner pocket that $350 difference, the Fiat 600 is wonderful transportation at the lowest list price on the market for a real car.

The question of whether they will be a serious sales threat to VW will be decided only by the event. Both cars stand an excellent chance of making serious inroads into the market, but whether they can win VW fans away from their beloved "beetles" is another story. ●

CONTINUED FROM PAGE 51

I must add that I like the Fiat winking device which warns one when the petrol supply is dropping ("there is still enough in the tank for 40 miles, if you drive easily"). This gadget is additional to the ordinary petrol level gauge, and I wonder why it is not more widely used.

On corners, straightline running and in cross-winds the Fiat gives way heavily to Birmingham, and for my part I must admit that geometrical corrections for tail-heavy aptitudes can be disconcerting. Wise engineers will argue that this is rubbish, and that Porsche and Volkswagen have proved it to be so. Perhaps they are right and I am prejudiced, the Mini is, after all, word perfect in this respect; better even than the Sprite and that is saying a mouthful.

It is primarily on refinement and personality that the 600 scores most, followed in very close order by its excellent traction and rigidity of construction. You could sell the engine sweetness and silence at slow speeds to anyone, but only a competitive drive up the nearest mountainside will indicate how the 600 will keep going when the Mini " grounds " and gets stuck. After the first occasion (when it was returned with a bent wish-bone link), I now find it essential to warn borrowers that my Mini has minimal ground clearance and that no liberties can be taken with gate centre-posts and the like. Similarly, returning again to the Fiat, it

is hard to vend a rattlefree construction on the showroom floor, and I can imagine nothing more indicative of this than the one-piece feel of Tosca I on the day before she was traded — with around 50,000 miles up. Even the redoubtable O'H. was astonished.

Forward-opening doors have their adherents (mostly folks who cannot abide the scrambling exit exercise of the Minis), and their critics. It is plainly more likely that in a crash you will be deposited on the roadway through a forward-opening door than via the rear opening type, but there are always safety belts, and on the 600 under discussion these make life seem so much more enduring. That is probably true of all cars, and Fiat are considerate enough to give you the anchorages anyway.

By 1961 standards, the 600's luggage space is, alas, somewhat inadequate, and the carriage of four adults together with holiday requirements would surely force even me to fit that modern obscenity, the roof rack.

As I said though, re-acquaintance with the 600 in its latest D form is an educational and entertaining experience. It was the forerunner of the mini-car breed and even after six years of unaltered basic design is still remarkably ahead on many points. In personality, refinement, driving position, and very much so in economy, it continues as winner. In many ways I was sorry to swap back . . .

TWO BITES AT FIAT CHERRY

modern **MOTOR** ROAD TEST

MAIN SPECIFICATIONS

ENGINE: 4 cylinders in line, o.h.v.; bore 65mm., stroke 63.5mm., capacity 843c.c.; compression ratio 8.8:1; maximum b.h.p. 42 (gross) at 5300 r.p.m.; maximum torque 42 ft./lb. at 3600; single downdraught carburettor, mechanical fuel pump, 12-volt ignition.

TRANSMISSION: Single dry-plate clutch, 4-speed, all-synchro gearbox; ratios: 1st, 3.77; 2nd, 2.11; 3rd, 1.48; 4th, 1.1; reverse, 3.75. Final drive, 4.453:1.

SUSPENSION: All independent; front by wishbones, transverse laminated spring and anti-roll bar; rear by swing arms, coil springs and anti-roll bar; telescopic shock absorbers all round.

STEERING: Worm-and-sector; 3½ turns lock-to-lock, 29ft. 2in. turning circle.

BRAKES: Drum, 67 sq. in. lining area.

WHEELS: Steel discs with 5.50 by 12in. tyres.

DIMENSIONS: Wheelbase 6ft. 7½in.; track, front 3ft. 9in., rear 3ft. 11¾in.; length 11ft. 8½in., width 4ft. 8½in., height 4ft. 6½in.; clearance 7¾in.

FUEL CAPACITY: 6.6 gallons.

KERB WEIGHT: 13.2cwt.

PERFORMANCE ON TEST

CONDITIONS: Fine, dry bitumen; premium fuel; two occupants; tyre pressures 15/25.

BEST SPEED: 90 m.p.h. (downhill — see text).

FLYING ¼-mile average: 80.2 m.p.h.

STANDING ¼-mile: 22.2s.

MAXIMUM in gears: 1st, 22 m.p.h.; 2nd, 40; 3rd, 60.

ACCELERATION from rest through gears: 0-30 m.p.h., 5.5s.; 0-40, 8.8s.; 0-50, 12.8s.; 0-60, 19.0s.

BRAKING: 30.8 ft. to stop from 30 m.p.h. in neutral.

FUEL CONSUMPTION: 40 m.p.g. over 500 miles, including all tests and city running.

MOUNTAIN CIRCUIT average: 52.75 m.p.h.

HILLCLIMB: 2m. 38s.

PRICE: £832 including tax

FIAT'S 850S is undoubtedly the best small saloon ever produced by the Italian firm. What a pity it took so long to reach Australia.

Douglas Armstrong wrote a glowing report on it in the July 1964 issue of **Modern Motor,** and after driving the car in Italy a few months later I could understand why.

The 850 is beautifully planned; although its wheelbase is only an inch longer than the 600's, it is incomparably roomier inside — and this applies to luggage space as well as accommodation.

General configuration is same as in the Fiat 600 (or 770, as that model has been called in Australia—though not in other countries — since its capacity was upped to 767c.c. a couple of years ago). Four-cylinder engine in the back with radiator at the side, all-independent suspension, battery and spare housed in the front "boot."

The engine differs from the 600 mainly in having a larger bore; but a good deal of "warming" must have been done as well, for the 850S puts out 42 b.h.p. (SAE) from 843c.c., as compared to 32 b.h.p. for the 767c.c.-engined Fiat 600.

Since the 850 weighs only 13.2 cwt. at kerb, the result is a very nippy little car, geared to cruise effortlessly in the 70s. Handling and braking are first-rate, too. No wonder Doug liked it.

Before reporting on my own experiences with two Fiat 850s—a left-hand-drive car in Italy and the right-hand-drive version in Australia — I must point out that only one of the two models described in Armstrong's report is available here.

This is the more powerful 850S (for "Super") model. The 850 "Normale," which runs on 8:1 com-

ACCESS to rear engine with side-mounted radiator is narrow yet most things are easy to reach. Bin around fuel filler (at left) stops any petrol being spilt on engine.

TIGHT cornering round a hairpin puts maximum strain on Fiat's suspension, produces plenty of tyre distortion but little body lean. The car's handling and roadholding are first-class — and it's very nippy, too.

pression instead of the "Super's" 8.8:1, and develops 40 b.h.p. instead of 42, will not be imported—a sensible decision by the Australian concessionnaires (Neal Investments), since most of our small-car buyers go for performance rather than cheap running on standard fuel.

Fiat 850S at Home

My chance to try out the 850S in its home country came during a business visit to Italy last November. Fiat in Turin lent me one for the last fortnight of my stay, in place of the 2300S I had been using.

There were two reasons for this swap: a desire to assess the 850S for Australian conditions — and, frankly, economy. With petrol around 8/- a gallon, and autostrada tolls spiralling with the bigger, costlier cars, the come-down in size meant a very worthwhile saving.

(Next time I visit Italy, I'll make use of Fiat's scheme, whereby you buy an 850—or 600, or any other

Just released in Australia, new 850S is the best small Fiat ever made, says David McKay, reporting findings from two tests — one in Italy, one here

model—and sell it back at a pre-determined figure when leaving; very useful for tourists and businessmen alike.)

Fiat, incidentally, were just as interested as Neal Investments in what I thought of the 850's prospects in Australia. They can't understand why their cars aren't getting more than the present 1.2 percent share of our market and would naturally like to see them do a lot better.

The 850S they lent me was a general factory hack and had some 20,000 kilometres (12,500 miles) behind it. I was somewhat apprehensive about tackling long runs in such a small buggy and had visions of being swamped by high-speed buses and trucks—but by the time I'd driven from Fiat's head office to my hotel

I knew I needn't have worried. The little blue car had plenty of verve and seemed ready to have a go at anyone and anything.

I loaded all my baggage into it next day — my large suitcase going into the capacious nose boot and still leaving room for a couple of squash bags on top—and set out for Milan via the autostrada. It was six years since I'd last battled round Italy, and the difference these super highways have made to Italian life must be experienced to be believed.

Now everywhere seems within easy punting distance, or rather time. For instance, the 80 miles to Milan, which before could have taken a couple of hard hours, was knocked over effortlessly by the 850S in 65 minutes. I began cruising around the 100 k.p.h.

THOUGH little bigger than the 600, Fiat 850 is much roomier inside. Styling is plain—but quite attractive.

REAR compartment is also surprisingly big; but knee-room shrinks if front seats are set full back.

mark (just over 60 m.p.h.), but soon let the needle creep up to 130-140, and with a little judicious slip streaming of a Mark II Jaguar I was able to outrun a Fiat 1100.

Even indicating over 140 k.p.h. (86 m.p.h.), the engine seemed happy and smooth—and after seeing the engines and transmissions assembled at the Turin plant I had no worries about overworking the car.

The engine has three crankshaft bearings, an aluminium cylinder-head, and is fed by a single-choke downdraught Weber. Fiat's customary centrifugal oil filter is attached to the end of the crankshaft, and there's a built-in system for consuming "blow-by" fumes.

Materials and workmanship are first-class throughout, and there are many well-thought-out features, such as the sealed cooling system filled with water/glycol fluid, which gives frost protection down to minus 31 deg. F., and in which the liquid level can be checked through the walls of the translucent plastic expansion tank.

The cooling fan is also plastic. All steering points are lubricated and sealed for life, and there are only two greasing points, so maintenance is brought down to a minimum.

Besides seeing the engines in production, I was reassured by previous experience with Fiats in competition — an 1800, a Nardi 2-litre, a couple of 1500s, and 2300s — all of which used standard cranks, rods, bearings, valve springs, etc., yet performed with never a failure, no matter how hard-pressed.

But back to the 850S. After the flog to Milan and several days of scrambling through the city's appalling traffic, I was beginning to doubt the fuel gauge. I had to keep caning the car in first and second off the lights, or I'd get shunted by those ubiquitous green Fiat taxis and the young Ascaris in 1500 sports (a lovely little car which should be available

here if anyone were enterprising enough). Yet fuel consumption was a steady 35 m.p.g. under such treatment — and on longer runs, including some city running, it was around 40. (I later equalled the latter figure in Australia, on my usually economy-destroying test route.)

Driving mainly on autostradas gave me a wonderful chance to test the little wildcat's long legs, but not its claws—so I went up into the mountains out of Maranello, on the route that Ferrari testers use for LM prototypes and "bread-and-butter" 330 GTs.

Here, in mist and fog, on cobbles, autumn leaves and shiny bitumen, I really enjoyed myself. The 850S was limpet-like in its roadholding, and, try as I might, I couldn't provoke it into any viciousness. This is by far the best-handling rear-engined car I've driven—in fact, it's one of the best-handling cars, regardless of engine layout.

Northern Italy was pretty cold in late November, yet I drove in short sleeves, thanks to the excellent built-in heating system. Movable air ducts (as in the Peugeot 404) make best use of the hot or cold air, and it's a wonder more manufacturers don't follow this lead.

The car was left-hand-drive — no fun driving right-handed in Europe, believe me—and I found myself most comfortable behind the wheel, with everything to hand. Only complaint was that my left leg was cramped by the left wheel arch; otherwise the pedals were perfectly laid out. Steering, suspension and braking were all well above average, and well-chosen ratios—with synchro on first—made the gearbox a delight.

A couple of criticisms could be levelled at the rather short rearward vision, due to the sloping roof line— it was necessary to duck a little for a good look aft—and the rather too-accessible lighting master switch. This

operates all the lights, and then you use a stalk control on the column for "parkers," "short," "long" and "flashers." It is possible to fumble the master switch in error for the wipers and plunge you into sudden darkness.

And in Australia . . .

After returning to Australia I borrowed a new 850S from Neal Investments' Jack Williamson and covered 500 miles at high speed— high for 850c.c. that is — putting 60 miles away in every hour.

The m.p.g. worked out at 40 again, and this included my mountain test course and hillclimb. After my Italian experience I expected as much; but I'll admit I was surprised at how quickly I overtook cars, and at the fact that 90 m.p.h. came up on the speedo on one long down-slope.

A suggestion that this might have been a "tweaked" version from Turin to influence the concessionaires was vigorously denied, and other 850Ss I drove here later went just as hard. But what really interested me was whether the car had lost any of its characteristics in the change-over to right-hand drive.

I found the pedals—moved to the right of the chassis backbone — were decidely offset, and again there was no comfortable resting-place for my left foot. I thought the gearbox wasn't quite the joy it had been in the hills behind Maranello; this could have been because of sitting on the other side of it and having to push the lever through a different angle. Moreover, the lever was hard against my thigh and could become annoying on a long run.

Rearward vision was as before, and I felt that a slightly longer mounting bracket for the mirror would improve things. But these are minor criticisms, and the way the little wildcat went

CONTINUED ON PAGE 161

GEARBOX, steering are excellent, but pedal layout is cramped by wheel arch. Note air vents set in dash.

FRONT boot takes fair amount of luggage, despite spare, and its front-hinged lid cannot blow open.

Road impressions of the

FIAT 850

By JOHN BOLSTER

WHILE I was waiting for a Fiat 2300S coupé, this obliging firm kindly lent me a little 850 saloon. This was not, of course, one of the glamorous Coupé or Spider models that I recently went to Italy to test, but a perfectly normal four-seater saloon. Nevertheless, I soon found that it was a far better car than I expected, and I parted with it most unwillingly, for I had enjoyed a happy week.

Three things particularly endeared the 850 to me. I was getting rather tired of rear-engined cars because they generally wriggle about in a side wind on the motorway. The Fiat remains remarkably stable, perhaps because the engine is very light. Another thing about rear-engined cars is that their heaters are usually very feeble, somewhat noisy, or they smell of hot metal. The 850 has an unusually powerful heater that is easy to control, for which I gave it top marks. The third attribute of the little car is its fuel economy. We have had full four-seaters that recorded 40 m.p.g. before but this one can still achieve such a figure when driven hard on the motorways.

How fast is this Italian people's car? The makers claim 125 k.p.h. and my stopwatch said 79 m.p.h., which is a shade faster. Under slightly favourable conditions

I timed the machine at 84 m.p.h. in one direction, and the speedometer showed a rather optimistic 90 on occasion.

The new sporting models have disc front brakes but this standard saloon has drums all round. I found the stopping power to be entirely adequate, but I didn't have to negotiate Italian mountains, of course. The gear ratios are better spaced than is often the case with such bread-and-butter cars, acceleration from a standstill taking 5.2 secs. to 30 m.p.h. and 12.2 secs. to 50 m.p.h. The changes go through very rapidly and the synchromesh on all four speeds is unbeatable, the central lever being very rigid and direct in action.

The Fiat corners well and rides remarkably comfortably, only pitching a little on very bad roads. The seats, with adjustable reclining backs, are comfortable too, even for tall drivers. The headlamps seem remarkably powerful for so small a car, and the detail work is well thought out. The squab of the rear seat folds forward for the carriage of goods, or of two large dogs in my case. For the man or woman who wants a tough and economical small car, this 850 has a lot of character and is somehow "different". Priced at £575 10s. 5d., including P.T., with £6 extra for the reclining seats, the Fiat 850 is cheap to buy, cheap to run, and fun to drive.

● Impressions by **BERNARD CAHIER**

S IGNOR ABARTH, who seems always to have the magic touch, has taken a Fiat 850, removed its 36 b.h.p. engine, put in reinforcement here and there, added disc brakes to make it stop, and has squeezed into the engine compartment a 1,600 c.c. twin-cam power plant giving 175 b.h.p. The result is a rather crazy little car which leaves you speechless. Its performance is so outstanding that it really does not make sense.

This O.T. 1600 (O.T. means *Omologato Turismo*) is immensely fast for a midget-sized touring car only 11ft 8in. long, and the miles I did behind its wheel shook me more mentally than those in any other fast car I have driven recently.

First, let us see what is left of the Fiat 850. This will be short: the body frame, steering (now made more direct), the suspension (modified and reinforced), and the name. Obviously, the list of Abarth's modifications is longer, and here it is: The track has been widened 1·5in. at the front and 4·5in. at the rear, while the standard 12in. pressed steel wheels have been replaced with 13in. dia. magnesium ones, with 5·00-13in. Dunlop racing tyres at the front and 6·00-13in. at the rear. To help keep the 1,600 c.c. twin overhead camshaft engine cool, the radiator has been moved to the front of the car, with an oil-cooler alongside it. The standard 4-speed 850

FIAT ABARTH 1600

gearbox was considered too weak to withstand 120 lb ft and this is replaced with the type used on the Abarth 1300. Inside, the fittings have been completely redesigned, with a special instrument layout, light-weight bucket seats and a wood-rimmed steering wheel. Parallel-action wipers are fitted and a 20-gallon fuel tank is installed in place of the back seat.

Altogether, this list of modifications is certainly impressive and it is no surprise that the Italian price tag of £500 for the 850 Fiat has been changed to one reading £1,420 for the O.T. 1600.

The driving position, thanks to a

→

well-made racing bucket seat, is extremely good and the steering wheel is at a proper angle. However, the pedal arrangement was not of the best in the car I drove, as it was practically impossible to heel-and-toe. The dashboard is very business-like and the instruments well placed. All the gauges are there—rev counter, oil pressure, oil temperature, water and fuel. In the car I tried the speedometer was in front of the passenger, no doubt to inspire him.

As soon as you fire the engine all kinds of things seem to happen, and you feel as if you are in a busy little factory. The aggressive sound of the engine fills the interior convincingly with noises belonging only to racing cars. The car trembles, and as you start moving it sort of shakes, grinds, breathes hard and loud, and you can almost hear the poor thing saying: "Don't you think you have given me too much?"

Despite the tune of the engine I did not have any trouble in getting across Turin, and in fact the twin-cam engine had enough flexibility that you could drive the car at 35 m.p.h. in top gear. The clutch was progressive enough so that you could always make smooth take-offs, and the all-synchromesh 4-speed gearbox was quick and pleasant to use although it did have a slightly spongy feeling. A 6-speed gearbox is also available for the car, but with all that torque and power I am not sure that it would be the ideal thing to have, at least for most competitions. In the 4-speed gearbox I had, the gear ratios were high but well-spaced, with first going to 45 m.p.h., second to 75, and third to 100 m.p.h. The red line was set at 7,800 r.p.m., but this twin-cam 1600 is such a smooth, free running engine that you can easily take it up to 8,000 and even more, the absolute limit being around 9,000 r.p.m.

Leaving Turin we first took the O.T. 1600 to our favourite *autostrada* at Ivrea where we nearly always make our speed and acceleration runs. These runs were very successful, the car being surprisingly good at high speeds. The mean maximum speed I recorded was 132 m.p.h. but Abarth's chief tester Klaus Steinmetz told me that the O.T. had done as much as 136 m.p.h., which I believe. Still, I thought that 132 m.p.h. was far from being slow for a Fiat "850." In acceleration I recorded 0 to 50 m.p.h. in 5·4sec, 0 to 60 in 7·2sec, 0 to 80 in 13·6sec and 0 to 100 in 20·8sec. The standing quarter mile was covered in a fantastic 15sec and the standing kilometre in 27·6sec. These figures are really

shattering for such a car and I was very impressed to see how well the car behaved during many hard take-offs during those acceleration tests.

At maximum speed the car wanders a bit and you have the feeling of being in the cockpit of a plane ready to take off, this impression being nicely completed by the roar of the engine which makes any conversation limited. It does not actually feel out of hand but is sensitive to any side winds or irregularities of the road, which is not too surprising at more than 130 m.p.h. After all, the Fiat 850 was only made by its engineers to do 75 m.p.h. The brakes are without fault, except for being almost too powerful if you push the pedal hard, in which case this 6ft 9in. wheelbase car becomes twitchy.

Incidentally, as well as the O.T. 1600, I drove the new Fiat Abarth 1000 which is a modified version, brought to 1,000 c.c. of the same new Fiat 850. After the O.T. 1600, the 1000 feels infinitely more peaceful with its 60 b.h.p., and it is a very nice little car to drive, smooth, comfortable and very spirited. In top gear I recorded 95 m.p.h. For accelerations, I got 0 to 50 m.p.h. in 8·6sec and 0 to 60 in 13·2sec, while the standing quarter mile was done in a very excellent 18·4sec. Actually those figures are better than the standard Mini-Cooper, and not too far away from those of the Mini-Cooper S. The Fiat Abarth 1000 is sold at a low price of about £640 in Italy, where it should be a terrific seller as well as a worthy successor to the ageing Fiat Abarth 850 and 1000 built around the body components of the Fiat 600.

After our speed and acceleration tests we took the O.T. 1600 for open road driving, notably over the many twisting, hilly roads surrounding Turin. Exciting moments marked those runs, especially when the car was pushed hard over curvy, bumpy roads. It was over these types of roads that I found out that much work remains to be done in the handling department of this flying scorpion. The car I drove, at least, had such a strong understeering behaviour that when going fast you frequently had the feeling that even at full lock you were not quite going to make it around the corner. Nearly always it took more room than expected. One of the reasons is that the car has such a wide rear track with its fat tyres sticking way out that at first you had the natural tendency to judge the width of your car by what you saw in the front, which is noticeably narrower than the rear. The result was that one time my rear right tyre brushed some sharp edges on the side of the road, there was a loud bang as it burst and after a graceful spin the car was brought under control without further trouble.

The steering, which seemed adequate during our speed tests on the *autostrada*, felt less pleasant on wind-

Top: Wide Dunlop racing tyres, large twin exhaust outlets and the finned oil sump hint at the performance offered. Centre: This front view shows how much more the rear tyres stick out than do those on the front wheels. Bottom: Parallel action windscreen wipers are a practical addition

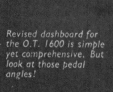

A 1,600c.c. twin cam engine is not such a tight fit as might be expected

Revised dashboard for the O.T. 1600 is simple yet comprehensive. But look at those pedal angles!

For the high-speed test runs an air spoiler was added above the engine compartment

ing bumpy roads. The large tyres used seemed to emphasize the kick-back reaction of the road, and generally speaking you did not really feel the car sometimes the way you should with the sort of machine built for speed and competition.

As I said earlier, the handling and steering can be much improved, but I am sure that Abarth will soon solve this problem, as he did with his 2-litre G.T. At first this was tricky to drive on mediocre roads, and we still have a lot of those in Europe. In spite of some defects due to the youth of the car (only three had been made at the time of my test) I returned the car to Abarth convinced that they had made a competition-type touring model capable of running away from most of Europe's hottest, and this with 1,600 c.c.

Two main problems remain to be solved. First, the car must be homologated as a touring car and this may take time, for Abarth will have to built 1,000 O.T.s before this takes place. Second, reliability and handling should be closely allied to the outstanding performance.

The O.T. 1600 was immensely exciting to drive. It is not a hot-rod like the Mini-Buick, the VW-Chevrolet and so on, but is a serious and extremely well made competition car with many remarkable features. Abarth created it at a time when everyone was crying in Italy because business was bad, and the more credit should go to him. Another wild scorpion is born and I think that this one will be a lot of fun to watch in the open. ∎

ABOVE: One of the strong points (literally) of this little car are the solid front bumpers with ample overriders. A weak point is miniscule trunk space which is not quite completely filled by small boy.

LEFT: The 46.8 cubic inch engine has enough urge to maintain speed on long hills, but a shade over 70 mph is all it can do, even with the wind behind it. Accessibility is not bad, and performance is just right for an errand running car. Back bumper is also ample.

ROAD TEST

Fiat 600D

By THE EDITOR

The least expensive of the imports, this $1262 Fiat is a unique car.

▶ Although I'd first seen Fiat 600s years ago, my reaction on receiving the test car was the same as that of many current VW lovers on seeing their first Beetles—you're kidding. But they weren't kidding at all. There the little thing sat, the engine was running, and I got in, fiddled with the controls to find out which did what,

and took off into New York City traffic.

The Fiat 600D looks small and it is small, but it is also a real car, not a toy as you might at first suppose. The steering felt much heavier than necessary for so small a car, but it also felt solid. As I've come to expect from Italian cars, the brakes were

The biggest change in the new version of the Fiat 600D is hinging the doors at the front rather than the back. This makes the car safer, but a slight bit harder to get in or out of.

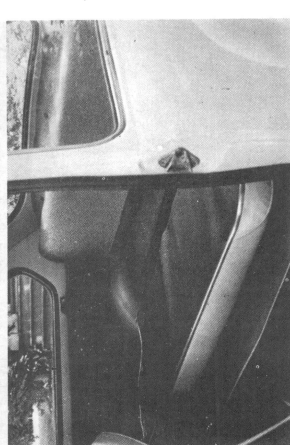

Bumper is a shade higher than VW's, and over-riders are big enough to protect finware.

FIAT 600D

right there and gave it great stopping power. This is a definite case of the car being built for the kinds of people who will drive it, and every Italian thinks he is Nuvolari and drives accordingly. With fuel prices and car taxes high, salaries low, this is the car they drive, and what it lacks in size or performance it more than makes up in brakes.

Once we got the car out on a highway, it turned out to be a pleasant surprise. It went. Not like a bomb, but it went as a good little economy import should. On a 60 mph road it happily went along at 60. On a longish, steepish hill it held its speed about as well as a VW Beetle and even picked up a few mph with two adults aboard. Not bad.

Parking in the city, this car really comes into its own. It could thumb

its nose at VW-sized parking spaces because it is nearly three feet shorter. Overall length of about 11 feet (131½ inches) lets it squeeze in almost anywhere. Even more useful, adequate bumpers with big, solid overriders, mean that you can afford to risk it in places where you know any other small import would stand to pick up a dent. (Thinking along these lines, I made a point of looking at the older Fiat 600s that were running around. Few if any of them showed the

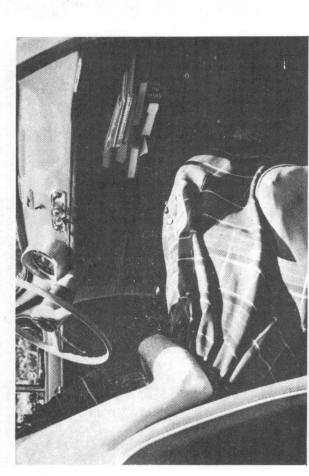

There is no glove compartment, but a handy parcel shelf is good for errand running like taking back library books. Front seat passengers have enough room, but it's cramped in back.

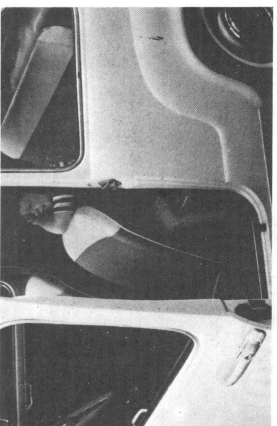

Package space behind rear seat is big enough only for a small suitcase, and rear-seat legroom is not great. Five-year old has ample room, but even his knees hit the back of the driver's seat.

Rear seat folds flat for luggage carrying, almost a necessary feature for a car which otherwise would be able to carry little. For a weekend trip with baggage, this becomes a two-man car.

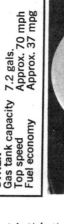

Rear drum is even fancier than the front being larger and made of aluminum for better cooling.

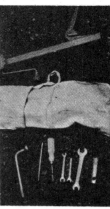

Tool kit includes easy-working jack, screw-driver, wrenches, and wheel lug wrench.

FIAT 600D—SPECIFICATIONS

BODY TYPE — 2-door, 4-passenger sedan

ENGINE

Engine locations	Rear
Cylinders	4-in-line
Bore and stroke	2.45 in. x 2.50 in.
Piston displacement	46.8 cu. in.
Compression ratio	7.5 : 1
Output (S.A.E.)	32 hp
Corresponding RPM	4,800
Cooling system	water

DIMENSIONS

Wheel base	78.75 in
Over-all length	131.5 in.
Width	54.25 in.
Height	55.32 in.
Ground clearance	6.3 in.
Shipping weight	1,331 lbs.
Turning circle diameter	28 ft. 6 in.
Tire size	5.20—12

OTHER

Gas tank capacity	7.2 gals.
Top speed	Approx. 70 mph
Fuel economy	Approx. 37 mpg

that are different from those in most other cars. For instance, there is a small toggle switch right in the center of the dashboard which energizes the stalk-type light control lever on the left of the steering column. Unless this switch is turned on, no juice and therefore no lights. Cute, but what for? I couldn't find out either. The windshield washer is a small rubber button which works like the floor mounted rubber-ball type squirters. I found that it worked well and I liked it. It would easily adapt to non-squirt-equipped cars and should make for a very neat and efficient installation. The hand choke control is a lever next to the handbrake like the heater controls on the 1965 VWs. This also seemed an odd way to do it, but with a rear engine it means a shorter control cable, and it does work very nicely.

Taken all-in-all, the Fiat 600D makes good sense in the U.S. market. It offers a minimal, but complete car at a minimal price ($1262 East Coast POE) and gives it a useful bumper so you can park it anywhere without worrying. As a second car here it makes just about as much sense as it does for a first car in Italy where it's been a best seller for years.

Close-up shows how fuel tank fills front trunk leaving little room for luggage.

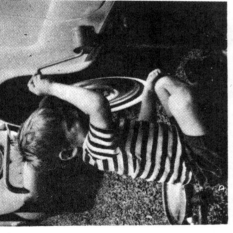

RIGHT: Worm-gear jack has so great a mechanical advantage that even a small boy can operate it easily, both up and down.

FIAT 600D

BELOW: Italian cars are famous for their brakes and this little one is no exception. Cast iron front drum has radial cooling fins.

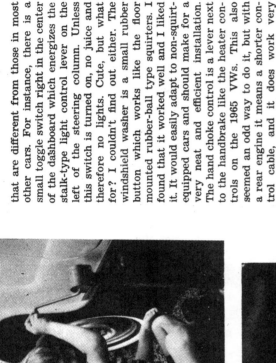

rumpled fenders and pushed in ends common to city-parked small cars.)

This is a car that takes quite a bit of getting used to. In Italy it is not the innofensive little animal it appears to be on these shores. In Rome, Fiats whiz around and intimidate pedestrians. In this country it is a different kind of a car. Here it is sold as a second car for short trips and running errands. For this use either in the city of suburbia, it is in its element. In the week we had it, and the several hundred miles we drive, the 600D managed to endear itself to the whole family. A first car it is not, an only car it is not either by U.S. standards, but as a second car it would certainly shine.

It has a couple of neat little gadgets

Autocar Road Test 2082

MAKE: **FIAT**

TYPE: **850 Coupé**
and Bertone Spider

Speed range, gear ratios and time in seconds

m.p.h.	Top (4·69)	Third (6·87)	Second (10·02)	First (17·72)
10—30	18·7	10·2	6·1	—
20—40	16·7	9·0	5·9	—
30—50	16·5	9·5	7·1	—
40—60	19·1	11·0	—	—
50—70	25·4	13·9	—	—
60—80	38·6	—	—	—

WEIGHT
Kerb weight (with oil, water and half-full fuel tank):
14·4 cwt (1,607lb-732kg)
Front-rear distribution, per cent. F, 37·8; R, 62·2
Laden as tested .. 17·4 cwt (1,943lb-885kg)

TURNING CIRCLES
Between kerbs .. L, 31ft 6in.; R, 28ft 5in.
Between walls .. L, 33ft 5in.; R, 30ft. 5in
Steering wheel turns lock to lock .. 3·8

PERFORMANCE DATA
Top gear m.p.h. per 1,000 r.p.m. .. 14·0
Mean piston speed at max. power 2,580 ft/min
Engine revs at mean max. speed 6,200 r.p.m.
B.h.p. per ton laden 54

OIL CONSUMPTION
Miles per pint (SAE 30) 1,000

FUEL CONSUMPTION
At constant speeds
30 m.p.h. 48·8 m.p.g. 60 m.p.h. 38·5 m.p.g.
40 ,, 47·2 ,, 70 ,, 32·5 ,,
50 ,, 42·6 ,, 80 ,, 26·9 ,,
Overall m.p.g. 32·5 (8·7 litres/100km)
Normal range m.p.g. 28 to 38 (10·1-7·4 litres/100km)
Test distance (corrected) .. 1,106 miles
Estimated (DIN) m.p.g. 31·8 (8·9 litres/100km)
Grade .. .. Premium (96·2-98·6 RM)

TEST CONDITIONS
Weather Dry and sunny with 0-6 m.p.h. wind
Temperature .. .. 13 deg. C (55 deg. F)
Barometer .. .. .. 29·5in. Hg.
Surfaces .. .. Dry concrete and tarmac

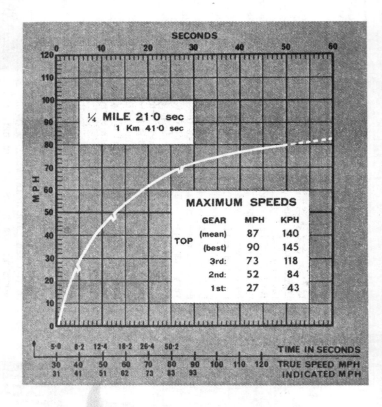

¼ MILE 21·0 sec
1 Km 41·0 sec

MAXIMUM SPEEDS

	GEAR	MPH	KPH
TOP	(mean)	87	140
	(best)	90	145
	3rd:	73	118
	2nd:	52	84
	1st:	27	43

5·0	8·2	12·4	18·2	26·4	50·2				TIME IN SECONDS
30	40	50	60	70	80	90	100	110	120	TRUE SPEED MPH
31	41	51	62	73	83	93				INDICATED MPH

BRAKES

	Pedal load	Retardation	Equiv. distance
(from 30 m.p.h.	25lb	0·38g	120ft
in neutral)	50lb	0·78g	39ft
	70lb	1·00g	30·1ft
Handbrake		0·42g	72ft

CLUTCH Pedal load and travel—20lb and 5in.

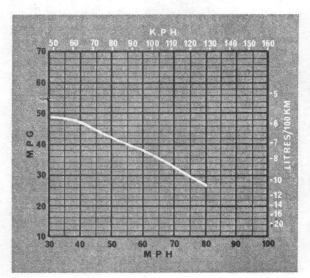

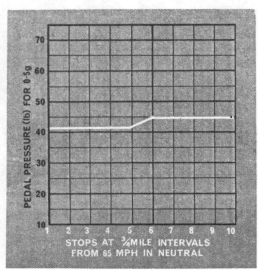

STOPS AT ¼ MILE INTERVALS
FROM 65 MPH IN NEUTRAL

Fiat 850 Coupé and Bertone Spider

843 c.c.

AT A GLANCE: Two rapid rear-engined sports cars based on 850 saloon. Coupé more refined than Spider, but not quite as fast in ultimate top speed. Light, fade-free brakes with discs at front. Lively ride, good road-holding with few of the usual rear-engine characteristics. High standards of finish for small car.

MANUFACTURER:
Fiat S.p.A., Corso Marconi, Rurin, Italy.

U.K. CONCESSIONAIRES:
Fiat (England) Ltd., Northdale House, North Circular Road, London, N.W.10.

PRICES:

Basic	..	..	..	£702 0s 0d
Purchase Tax	..	..	£147 16s 3d
Total (in G.B.)	..	..	£849 16s 3d

EXTRAS (INC. P.T.)

Radiomobile	..	..	£40 1s 6d

PERFORMANCE SUMMARY

Mean maximum speed	..	87 m.p.h.
Standing start ¼-mile	..	21·0 sec.
0-60 m.p.h.	..	..	18·2 sec
30-70 m.p.h. (through gears)		21·4 sec
Overall fuel consumption		32·5 m.p.g.
Miles per tankful ..	..	..	215

WHEN the Italian economic recession hit their motor industry in 1964, it was hard to see how anything but trouble could come out of it. But at the Turin motor show that autumn the whole of the special coachwork hall appeared to be turned over to derivatives of the diminutive Fiat 850, as a gesture of encouragement to the general belt-tightening decreed by the government. Buyers were then able to see that little coupés could be as stylish as big ones and much, much cheaper.

The parent factory of Fiat (aptly dubbed "the mother of Italy") was the first to realize the potential of a small specialist car, so two diverse plans were laid down to cover both ends of a large potential market. For what the publicity and ad. men might call "the discerning masses," Fiat began to build the 850 Coupé in their own works; for those wanting something even more special, they backed a very pretty little open Spider designed by Bertone, marketing it through their usual dealers. These two cars made their public debut at the Geneva show in the spring of last year, and we visited Italy to drive them briefly just before their introduction.

By the end of last year right-hand-drive Coupés were being imported here at the remarkably low price of £850 including tax, duty and import

surcharge, and the Spider was available in left-hand-drive form only, at the more "exclusive" price of £1,000. This test deals with both, because in addition to carrying out our full set of measurements on the Coupé and driving it for some 1,100 miles, we ran the Spider for 520 miles and timed its acceleration and top speed for comparison.

Mechanically the two cars are very little different, and both are substantially modified versions of the saloon. Power output of the 843 c.c. rear engine is raised from the saloon's 37 b.h.p. net at 5,100 to 47 at 6,200 for the Coupé and 49 (also at 6,200) for the Spider. To achieve this gain the compression ratio is increased from 8·8 to 9·3 to 1, a twin-choke Weber carburettor and four-branch exhaust manifold is substituted and a revised camshaft fitted. The gearing of both cars is not changed significantly; although bigger, 13in. wheels are needed to clear the front disc brakes, lower-profile tyres compensate.

Before the engine tuners got to work on the B.M.C. Mini, a high-performance saloon with an engine of only 843 c.c. was unheard of, and it is important to remember the tiny size of the engine when assessing the Fiat. Yet even so, both cars proved capable of 90 m.p.h. with brisk ▶

The Bertone Spider can be specified with either a soft folding hood or a detachable hardtop, as shown here

acceleration and an incredible willingness to rev very highly indeed.

This Fiat engine is one of the most remarkable in recent times, for with only three main bearings and quite conventional pushrod valve gear it runs to 8,000 r.p.m. when really thrashed and feels as though it could go on and on for ever despite being abused in this way. It is smooth right through the range, except at its rather lumpy idling speed, when the body seems to pick up a resonance and to boom uncomfortably. Below about 3,000 r.p.m. there is very little bite to the performance, but from then on the torque comes (as one tester put it delightfully) scampering in like a bouncy puppy. Of course, such a willing engine needs a rev counter and Fiat provide an exceptionally clear and legible dial to match the speedometer with a steady pointer and red warning mark starting at peak power (6,200 r.p.m.).

When first taking the performance figures we tried using this mark as a limit, but later improved our standing-start times by 8sec to 80 m.p.h. by running well "into the red" to about 7,500. It is always satisfying to find that a designer has worked his sums out right (the Italians seem particularly good at this), and at maximum speed the little Coupé exactly reaches the peak of its power curve in top. The Spider, with less frontal area, is even faster, and reaches speeds well into the 90s (95 m.p.h. best, 92 mean) but our car began to lose oil pressure when held flat out on motorways for long periods.

After the difficulties we had in getting full performance from the 500F because it was too new, Fiat made sure the Coupé was well run in and it came to us with nearly 10,000 miles behind it, 1,551 of them clocked up during a 24-hour endurance run at Snetterton last February. Despite

what can only have been a hard life for any demonstrator, the little car felt taut and in the prime of condition with no rattles nor any signs of deterioration.

The Spider engine was not so loose, with only about 5,000 miles behind it, and could not quite match the acceleration times of the Coupé. Less attention appears to have been paid to sound deadening on the Spider and there was a kind of gravelly exhaust noise all the time; this open version never felt as refined as did the Coupé. Although the Spider has slightly more woodwork on its facia, we preferred the plain layout of the Coupé and considered it to be the better-finished car.

The gearbox is all-indirect, with synchromesh on all four. While the box itself works precisely there is some loss in feel introduced by "give" in the long linkage. At rest,

There are very few differences between the engines of the Coupé (right) and Spider (left). Both have dipsticks so close to the manifold that they are too hot to touch. On the Coupé the fuel filler is under the rear bonnet, with a splash guard, whereas on the Spider it is on the tonneau deck outside

Standards of finish in the Coupé are excellent. The radio fills most of the parcels shelf and there is no glove locker. The back seat can take two adults, but legroom is restricted

FIAT 850 COUPÉ AND BERTONE SPIDER ...

first gear often baulks unless one is rather brutal and stabs the clutch quickly, snatching the gear before the layshaft has stopped. There is quite strong spring-loading across the gate towards third and top which makes the second-to-third change easy and incredibly fast if one simply bangs

On the Bertone Spider there are more supplementary instruments, and a drop-down locker under the passenger's grab handle

the lever forwards without sideways pressure. At no time was there the faintest crunch from the synchromesh, not even when trying to gain every tenth of a second on our standing-start times.

First is rather low compared with the upper three, which make a close

and well chosen set; but then the Coupé managed to restart on a 1-in-3 test hill without difficulty so there has most likely been a compromise. The handbrake, by the way, held easily with the car facing either way on this gradient.

The 850 saloon has drum brakes back and front, but on the Coupé and Spider, large diameter discs (the same as on the new 124, incidentally) are fitted to the front wheels, working on the new Bendix-Lockheed single-piston principle. They proved to be light and sensitive with practically no fade during our repeated stops from three-quarter maximum speed. When used lightly in traffic there is sometimes a scraping noise, but this disappears when the pedal is pushed harder and may only have been caused by a light coating of rust on the disc faces.

HANDLING

The days of unstable, oversteering, rear-engined cars are over and the handling of the Fiat is a good example of the progress that has been made. Despite a rear weight bias of 62 per cent there is no noticeable oversteer on the road, quite the reverse in fact, with the car taking a naturally wide line that can easily be tightened by the steering as required. It feels best to judge the corner early and set the car up without changing one's mind, for it can become "untidy" if one decides to alter course half-way through. On the M.I.R.A. road circuit we explored the handling to adhesion limits and found there was a gradual and very controllable transition to oversteer which could be incited by "tweaking" the

Fastback styling seems to suit rear-engined cars particularly well, and the Fiat is one of the prettiest of all

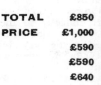

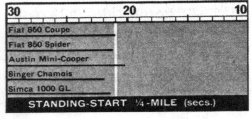

HOW THE FIAT 850 COUPÉ AND BERTONE SPIDER COMPARE:

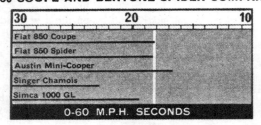

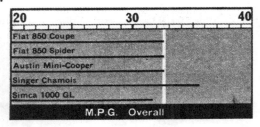

steering wheel, as with a good rally car set up for quick response.

Often rear-engined cars become extraordinarily skittish on wet surfaces, but this Fiat maintains very well indeed its good manners and seems reluctant to wag its tail even when spinning the wheels on particularly greasy surfaces.

The steering, like all the controls, is very light and the car responds quickly. At speed it does not become oversensitive, and although one can feel the disturbances in cross winds they seem to be damped out immediately by the corrective influences built into the car.

It is probably the very uneven weight balance that causes the ride to be distinctly choppy; in this respect the Coupé is considerably better

than the Spider. This trait did not show up particularly on our close-set concrete waves at M.I.R.A., but on the road the front of the car seems to get bucked about on the small irregularities encountered everywhere. With luggage under the front lid the ride improves considerably, and the "dead" springing in the seats prevents the occupants from bouncing in sympathy, so the feeling is not unpleasant even if it can never be forgotten entirely.

SEATING

The firmness of the suspension helps to reduce body roll and the Fiat corners on a very level keel. Seat shaping also helps keep one in place, with almost a comfortable padded

"well" to sit in, and good wrap-round backrests for shoulder support. On the Spider the angle can be adjusted over an adequate range by means of a thumb-screw stop at the base of the backrest, but on the Coupé it is fixed in what we found to be the right position, to accommodate the locks required as a safety feature under Italian law. For access to the rear compartment a button must be pressed to release the backrest.

In the front one sits rather skewed round to face the offset pedals. Rear-engined cars inevitably displace their passengers farther forward between the front wheel arches, and these intrude into the pedal and foot areas. On the left-hand-drive Spider we felt our feet slightly cramped, while on the right-hand-drive Coupé one's shoes

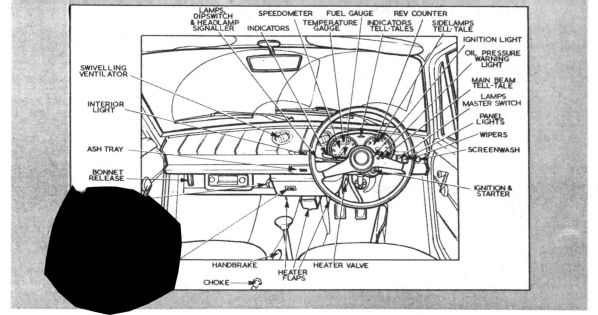

LAMPS, DIPSWITCH & HEADLAMP SIGNALLER
INDICATORS
SPEEDOMETER
TEMPERATURE GAUGE
FUEL GAUGE
INDICATORS TELL-TALES
REV COUNTER
SIDELAMPS TELL-TALE
IGNITION LIGHT
OIL PRESSURE WARNING LIGHT
MAIN BEAM TELL-TALE
LAMPS MASTER SWITCH
PANEL LIGHTS
WIPERS
SCREENWASH
IGNITION & STARTER
SWIVELLING VENTILATOR
INTERIOR LIGHT
ASH TRAY
BONNET RELEASE
HANDBRAKE
CHOKE
HEATER FLAPS
HEATER VALVE

FIAT 850 COUPÉ AND BERTONE SPIDER ...

must *overlap* to work two pedals at once. Actually Fiat have done a good job in converting the car for the British market, and the brake pedal pad is very slightly angled to tilt one's right foot over one's left when braking and declutching simultaneously. There is a narrow rest for one's foot beside the clutch, but any shoe size over a narrow No. 8 could find no way to reach it. In fact, none of our big-footed testers had trouble in getting at the pedals when they wanted them.

Both front seats have a long range of sliding travel, spring-loaded forwards and moving easily on well-greased runners. The steering wheel diameter is a compact 15in., and the polished spokes do not reflect in the screen at night. It is angled to a comfortable, semi-straight-arm position with the robust gear-lever near one's hand (left or right depending on the layout). Through the wheel on the Coupé the driver sees two big circular dials containing all gauges and warning lamps; on the Spider slightly smaller main instruments are supplemented by separate gauges set into a wooden facia panel.

A neat set of rocking switches carry symbolic labels, and twin levers on the steering column work the indicators and lamps (including main-beam flasher) with firm, precise movements. Fiat do not subscribe to the idea that a small car needs only a small horn and so on these two cars it sounds a deep, and rather rude, raspberry, with melodious overtones. The wipers sweep big arcs rapidly and on right-hand-drive cars they are offset to the correct side. The ignition switch is below the facia on the steering column, although on the Coupé there is no additional lock for the steering. A separate key is needed for the doors.

To get into the back of the Coupé one or other of the front seats must be slid forward and the backrest folded

▶

Luggage space is scarce on both cars. The Coupé is on the left and the Spider on the right. With the spare wheel horizontal under the floor there is really only room for a slim over-night bag in the Spider

down. One extra adult can sit here half-sideways quite comfortably, but two children would fit in much better. The rear backrest does not fold forwards to make a platform for extra luggage, but then quite a big suitcase will fit in under the front lid; only the spare wheel lives here, the fuel tank being at the back.

After creating their neat little baby Coupés, Fiat trim them very smartly in the latest stretch p.v.c. that practically passes for pigskin. There is an air of luxury inside that one seldom sees in small cars unless they are given the expensive coachbuilders' treatment after delivery. A good deal of attention has been paid to sound deadening (much more in the Coupé than the Spider) and the little power unit only begins to buzz when the revs are wound well up the scale.

On a recent Continental trip we were surprised to see 850 Coupés all over Italy, Switzerland and even France and Germany. Now that we have tested one we can understand why such a model has become popular so quickly. It has chic looks, brisk performance with economy and a tasteful interior that changes remarks like "That's nice" to "Yes, it *is* nice" on closer acquaintance. ∎

SPECIFICATION : FIAT 850 COUPÉ AND SPIDER, REAR ENGINE, REAR-WHEEL DRIVE

ENGINE
Cylinders	4, in-line
Cooling system	Water, sealed with pump, fan and thermostat
Bore	65mm (2·56in.)
Stroke	63·5mm (2·49in.)
Displacement	843 c.c. (51 cu. in.)
Valve gear	Overhead, pushrods and rockers
Compression ratio	9·3-to-1
Carburettor	Weber 30 DIC
Fuel pump	Weber mechanical
Oil filter	Fiat full-flow centrifugal
Max. power	47 b.h.p. (net) at 6,200 r.p.m.
Max. torque	44 lb. ft. (net) at 3,600 r.p.m.

TRANSMISSION
Clutch	Single dry plate, diaphragm spring, 6·3 in. dia.
Gearbox	4-speed, all-synchromesh
Gear ratios	Top 0·96; Third 1·41; Second 2·06; First 3·64; Reverse 3·62
Final drive	Hypoid bevel, 4·87 to 1

CHASSIS AND BODY
Construction	Integral with steel body

SUSPENSION
Front	Independent, transverse leaf spring, wishbones, telescopic dampers, anti-roll bar
Rear	Independent, semi-trailing arms, coil springs, telescopic dampers, anti-roll bar

STEERING
Type	Worm and roller
Wheel dia.	15in.

BRAKES
Make and type	Fiat-Bendix disc front, drum rear
Servo	None
Dimensions	F, 8·9in. dia.; R, 7·3in. dia. 1·18 in. wide shoes
Swept area	F, 136·4 sq. in.; R, 54 sq. in. Total 190·4 sq. in. (218 sq. in. per ton laden)

WHEELS
Type	Ventilated pressed steel disc, 4·5in. wide rim
Tyres	Pirelli Sempione tubed—size 5·20—13in.

EQUIPMENT
Battery	12-volt 48-amp. hr.
Generator	
Headlam..	
Reversi..	
Electric..	
Screen ..	
Screen ..	
Interior..	
Safety b..	
Interior..	
Floor co..	
Starting ..	
Jack	
Jacking points	sills
Other bodies	

MAINTENANCE
Fuel tank	6·6 Imp. gallons (warning lamp) (30 litres)
Cooling system	13·2 pints (including heater) (7·5 litres)
Engine sump	5·6 pints (3·25 litres) SAE 30 Change oil every 6,000 miles; clean filter element at engine overhaul only
Gearbox and final drive	5·6 pints SAE 90EP. Change oil every 18,000 miles
Grease	2 points every 1,500 miles
Tyre pressures	F, 16; R, 26 p.s.i. (all conditions

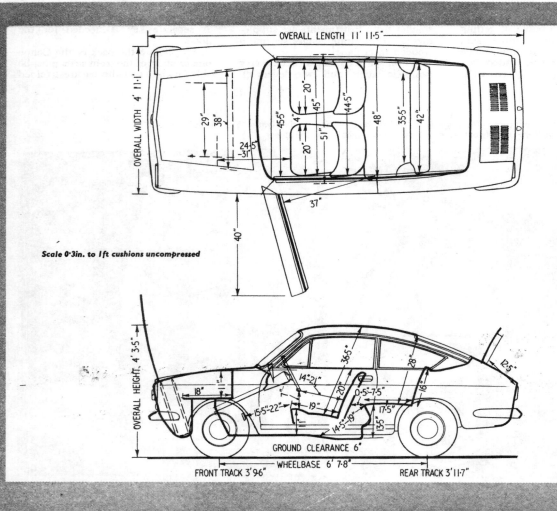

Scale 0·3in. to 1ft cushions uncompressed

OVERALL LENGTH 11' 11·5"
OVERALL WIDTH 4' 11·1"
OVERALL HEIGHT 4' 3·5"
GROUND CLEARANCE 6"
WHEELBASE 6' 7·8"
FRONT TRACK 3' 9·6"
REAR TRACK 3' 11·7"

THE CURRENT
FIAT 850 RANGE

ONE FOR EVERY PURPOSE

ONE FOR EVERY POCKET

A BIT over twelve months ago Fiat followed up their then recently-announced 850 saloon with a couple of alternatives—the coupe and the spider—which made this sort of middle-of-the-road line, sandwiched between the tiny and the medium-sized models, a pretty complete sort of range. We've just been pedalling about the countryside in all three, with an Abarth version of the saloon lent to us by Radbourne Motors and thrown in for good measure. Now, we motoring scribes get long looks of envy from all our friends (whenever we see him) because of the motors we get to drive, but it isn't always fun: it's true to say that there are practically no bad cars made nowadays, but there's a heckuva lot about the place which, for all their appeal to us personally (and very likely to most of you too) might just as well be barrage balloons. Not so the 850 Fiats: we've hardly ever been as impressed by a bunch of tiddlers in our little innocent lives. Call 'em roller-skates if you must, but drive any one of them for a few miles and you'll find the proof of the saying that the Italians understand all about the sort of motor-car which people like us like to drive.

With engines of 850 c.c.—all of them except the Abarth churning out under 55 horse-power, they don't exactly set the road afire. Nor could you expect them to. But they keep up very well with the traffic, keep ahead very easily of quite a lot of it and make all the right noises and do nearly all the right things: some of them do *all* the right things. And don't go sneering at those power figures, either—the saloon's total of 40 b.h.p. is better than the score for, say, the 850 Mini, and the coupe and spider, at something in the low-to-middle fifties, approach pretty close to the figure achieved by (for instance) B.M.C. in the 1100 range. And these are only eight-fifties.

Top: Standard saloon, in a park.

Centre: Spider, in a hurry.

Bottom: Coupe, in a shower.

Starting at the bottom, as you might say, we come first to the 850 saloon. This is the cheapest of the lot at £550, and joined the Fiat range in the spring of 1964, so that it hasn't got anything like whiskers on it yet, a respect in which it differs from the smaller and older 500 and 600 models. Like the two real tiddlers, it is rear-engined, the four-cylinder unit being a bored-out version of the 600 engine; new dimensions of 65 mm. × 63·5 mm. give a total capacity of 843 c.c. and the bore is, in fact, increased by three millimetres—the stroke remains the same. The cast-iron block has an alloy head, with overhead valves operated by pushrods, and a compression ratio of 8·8 to 1. The three-bearing crank has a centrifugal oil-filter and there is a sealed cooling system—a popular feature nowadays, but for the sake of your piece of mind they throw in a plastic tank which is transparent, so that you can tell at a glance if you've run out of water provided you can see through the clouds of steam. The cooling fan, which is of pretty generous dimensions, as you might say, like most rear-engined cars, has plastic blades.

This is mated up to a four-speed gearbox with Porsche-type synchromesh on all the forward gears, and the ratios, although some people might find them all a bit on the low side, match up well with 42 b.h.p. performance and are much better spaced than on most small cars. If we were being rude today we would say that they are much better, too, than we might of expected of Fiats, who haven't been famous for this sort of thing in the past. But we're not, so there.

As you might expect, all four wheels are independently suspended, with swinging arms and a transverse leaf spring in front and coil springs and triangulated radius arms astern. Telescopic dampers, and anti-roll bars, are fitted at both ends. The brakes are drums, all round.

Inside the car is complete and adequate but, like a lot of continental small cars, a bit sort of spartan. The seats are pretty rudimentary, when all's said and done, although they are comfortable enough, the controls, apart from the gearlever and pedals, boil down to three switches and a dial, with a few warning lights in it, and so on. It is, nevertheless, adequate, this sort of thing—the warning lights are for charge, low fuel level, oil pressure and side-lights, as well as the usual turn and main beam warnings; the speedometer isn't aesthetically the most pleasing shape but it tells you how fast you're going, which is all you can reasonably ask, and there are adjustable fresh-air vents on the top of the facia which will direct cooling streams of air straight into the driver's eyes but which are less enthus-

iastic about demisting the windscreen. But we can't have everything.

The going makes up for all this, really. Once you've started the engine you get the feeling that this is a small saloon you can really enjoy driving, and so it is. The engine is almost unbelievably willing to rev—the speeds we got in the gears are far higher than Fiat's published estimates—and it seems to thrive on really hard work. It isn't particularly noisy inside, for a small car, and the gearbox is pure joy. The changes can go through as fast as you like to move the lever—we never once caught it out—and if you keep the revs up you start going places. At the top end of the scale the engine makes the most delightful overhead camshaft noises—odd when you come to think of it, 'cos there ain't no o.h.c. on this mill, mac. But it makes the noises nevertheless—built-in enthusiasm, we assume.

Handling? It's all right. The worst thing you can do is to expect too much of it. One must remember that this is an ordinary, common or garden rear-engined small saloon, and it was never designed to scoot round the corners like a racer. Nor will it, but you can get it round remarkably quickly without a lot of wild drama. It carries four people without losing all its urge, too, although you naturally tend to find that the hills are that much steeper when four strapping Anglo-Saxons sit where only lightweight Italians were intended to. It'll take all your baggage, too—the rear seat backrest folds forward like an estate car, or a Hillman Imp, to supplement the boot under the bonnet, and there are two or three different sorts of parcels shelves scattered about the inside.

Speeds are not all that frantic—the Abarth version, tested and reported on elsewhere in this issue, goes a lot more quickly—but they'll get you there. We got a top speed of 76 m.p.h., accelerating figures of from rest to fifty in 16·9 secs and from rest to sixty in 28·4 secs, two up. In the gears, the thing simply goes on revving, and kindness of heart alone really stopped us from going further than 23, 41 and 61 in first, second and third.

So much for the saloon. Next in line so far as price alone goes is the 850 coupe. We reckon there is only one better-looking car in the small motor field, and that's the 850 spider, but we'll get to that a bit later. For the time being it's the coupe we're talking about, and this will set you back £850 in this country—a daft price, of course, for a small car however good, but it isn't Fiat's fault. The basic price is £702, thanks to import duty and what not, and purchase tax takes care of the rest. Which is a shame, because it will probably mean that you'll never see many of them about

If you want an attention-getting device that you can still park, in say, Mayfair, then get a shufti at the Spider then pawn all you own to buy one.
By the way, this specimen was painted a sort of hellfire red. Wow!

Top: Simple austerity, Standard saloon.

Top centre: Simple luxury, Coupe.

Bottom centre: Engine as installed in Spider.

Bottom: Beautiful seating as in Coupe.

and the car parks and traffic jams of this sceptred isle would benefit immensely if there were more of 'em.

Mechanically, it is similar to the saloon except that the head is modified, there is some very sexy manifolding on both inlet and exhaust sides with revised porting to match. A dinky little Weber carb gets the gasworks credit, and the compression ratio is upped to 9·3 to 1, which means another dozen horse-power—52, to be precise. Downstairs it stands on bigger wheels than the saloon which apart from anything else has the effect of increasing the overall gearing by a small amount—nothing, though, to signify, as we say.

The body is Fiat-designed and built, and is a neat little two-seater, with strictly temporary-accommodation rear seats fitted beneath a sharply raking roof line. On this and the spider the Fiat badge is circular—just like they used to be in the days of the works racers, which is a nice touch: there is fuller instrumentation, with a nice little binnacle in front of the driver containing a rev-counter and a speedometer: the latter incorporates trip and total mileage recorders and a fuel gauge, and the tachometer dial is punched with little 'oles which come on to tell you whether or not you have your side-lights on, your headlamp main beams on, too little oil pressure or no charge at all. Another light flashes at you to say fill up now or walk to the nearest garage—it starts coming on when there is just over a gallon left.

We liked this little car immensely. The body is one of those which doesn't look its best until you see it alongside something alleged to be smart and sleek from another maker, and when you see it like that it is gorgeous. Not that this matters a lot, of course, to the chap who's actually driving it, although it's very good for the old ego to be admired by all the bus queues. The main thing is that it can be driven. The suspension set-up is to all intents and purposes the same as that of the saloon but, of course, the things which help to make it better include a lower centre of gravity and the bigger wheels. At least, we think these must help. At any rate, you can chuck this little car about like nobody's business: its top speed isn't all that high, but it is nevertheless what can only be called high enough in view of the car's capability to cruise very close to it, and to go through bends as fast as almost anything else outside the real racer class.

In actual fact it will do an honest 85 however you like to look at it, and Fraser-limit apart you can cruise all day, and for that matter all night, at a good old eighty. At this sort of lick the revs are close enough to the peak of the power curve for main road mountains not to knock too much off this, while a fuel consumption of 36 m.p.g., even under these conditions, helps, to say the least. Acceleration? Lively, although without taking the rubber off the back tyres, as you might expect from fifty-odd horsepower. From rest to fifty wants around a dozen seconds—four or five seconds better than the saloon—and you can get to sixty in just over seventeen. From this point on the acceleration tails off more than somewhat because at max revs you will only get something in the low sixties in third gear, which is a bit of a snag, particularly when it comes to wanting a bit of smart urge to overtake in safety. The gear ratios, all a bit on the low side, are pretty nicely spaced, though, with maximum speeds of 22, 42 and 63 m.p.h. which suit the car's medium performance quite nicely.

Steering is faultless, and the handling very likeable. Every ounce of movement on the front wheels can be detected, and when the tail slides—which is what goes first—there is plenty of warning. A small twitch on the wheel and the situation is back under control, which is just the way it ought to be, and the steering ratio is high enough to eliminate the necessity for frantic shuffling on roundabouts.

So much for the coop. The spider is the same only different, if you follow. For a start, they manage to squeeze another couple of horsepower out of the works and this helps to propel the extra bits and pieces there are about the place: the inside, for instance, is much more swep' up than the coupe, and you get such refinements as two-speed screen wipers, better seats, a cigar lighter and a few more dials to watch, which replace some of the blinking lights. It must also be a better shape, since it went quicker than the coupe (and achieved a quite horrifying number of revs in the process). The body, which really is quite beautiful, is a Bertone job, and looks a bit like an Elan without the pop-up lights. The one they gave us had a sleek and very with-it hard-top, whereas the open version has, obviously, a soft-top which when the sun shines folds away invisibly behind a panel at the back. Unlike both the coupe and the saloon, you stick the fuel in through a cap on the outside of the car instead of under the rear bonnet, and it has particularly neat door handles and other touches which all go to take away the feeling of extravagance you might otherwise get if you had shelled out a thousand quid for it—which is what, unfortunately, all the taxes and import duties make the total price come to.

The hard-top includes a highly technical ventilation system which makes it possible to breathe without opening all the windows, and once again it is a Bertone effort.

Inside it is, as we said, all pretty plush and everything is nicely laid out, in the proper manner for a miniature G.T. car. Performance, so far as acceleration is concerned, is pretty well identical to the coupe, such small variations as there are in the times for acceleration from rest being put down to differences in the cars' total mileage and in the weight of the editorial foot on the relevant day. Top speed, however, is a long way up provided you let it rev the way it wants to: the tachometer is red-lined at six-two, but the car simply doesn't want to stop at that point, and although we felt it might be unkind to a thousand quid's worth of someone else's motor-car to do it often, it didn't show anything but pure Italian delight when the needle advanced enthusiastically into the red in top gear. For maximum

The end. How we all wish that it was just the beginning. We all really fell for the 850 Coupe. Only wives (and bank managers) put an end to what could have been a beautiful affair.

speed it went rushing up to seven thousand, which is just about ninety m.p.h., and felt delightfully hard and lively as it did so, with no nasty vibrations or untoward activities.

We all liked the handling—the way you could flick the tail in and out is something you find only too rarely, and its controllability is tremendous—but, as with the coupe, we're less enthusiastic about the gearing. This is the same as the coop and has the same problems, in that third is only good for 63 miles an hour if you keep to the rev-limit, which makes it a rather low sort of dog—sorry, cog. There isn't too much noise even at maximum r.p.m., it goes well over thirty miles on a gallon of go-juice and is a pretty desirable little motor car. Both pretty and desirable.

Cars on Test

FIAT 850 SALOON, COUPE and SPIDER

Engine (saloon): Four cylinders, 65 mm. × 63·5 mm.; 843 c.c.; single Weber carburettor; pushrod-operated overhead valves; compression ratio 8·8 to 1; 42 b.h.p. at 5,300 r.p.m.
Coupe: 52 b.h.p.; **Spider,** 54 b.h.p., with revised cylinder head; compression ratio 9·3 to 1; revised manifolding, etc. Otherwise as saloon.
Transmission (all models): Four speed and reverse gearbox with synchromesh on all forward gears.
Suspension (saloon): Front, independent, with wishbones, transverse leaf spring, telescopic dampers and anti-roll bar; rear, independent, with semi-trailing arms, coil springs, telescopic dampers and anti-roll bar. Tyres 5·50 × 12.
Coupe and spider: As saloon except for 13 inch wheels.
Brakes (all models): 7·3 in. drums front and rear.
Dimensions (all models): Overall length, 11 ft. 8 in.; overall width, 4 ft. 8 in.; ground clearance 5¾ in.; overall height (saloon) 4 ft. 6½ in.; (coupe) 4 ft. 3 in.; (spider) 4 ft. 1 in.

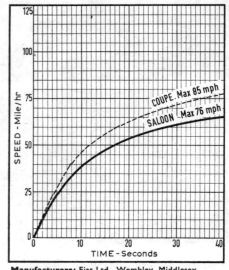

PERFORMANCE	m.p.h.
MAXIMUM SPEED (Saloon)	76
Mean of two ways	75
MAXIMUM SPEED (Coupe)	85
Mean of two ways	85
MAXIMUM SPEED (Spider) See text	90
Mean of two ways	87
SPEEDS IN GEARS (All models) First	22
Second	43
Third	63

ACCELERATION		
Saloon	Coupe	Spider
secs.	secs.	secs.
0–30— 6·7	0–30— 5·4	0–30— 5·0
0–40—10·6	0–40— 7·4	0–40— 7·9
0–50—16·9	0–50—11·9	0–50—12·3
0–60—28·4	0–60—17·3	0–60—17·3
	0–70—28·0	0–70—28·0

Manufacturers: Fiat Ltd., Wembley, Middlesex.
Prices in U.K.: Saloon, £550; Coupe, £850; Spider, £1,000.

Shoestring economy for four

''. . . unfashionably tall and austere . . . not quite so cramped as its size might suggest . . . will buzz along at 60 m.p.h.''

THERE are only three four-wheel cars on the British market listed at under £500 tax paid. Two of them, despite import duty and freight charges from Italy, are Fiats. At £417, the diminutive twin-cylinder Fiat 500 is the cheapest of all by a long way. Then comes the quicker and more roomy BMC Mini at £478 followed closely by the Fiat 600D at £493. When the bigger and faster Fiat 850 was announced, it was widely thought that the 600 would become redundant. For a time, sales did fall but after such a long production run the car had become very reliable and many people found the relationship between performance, economy, accommodation and price more favourable than that of the two other small Fiats. Aided by the credit squeeze, it is again one of Fiat's top sellers and total output is now approaching the three million mark.

We last tested a 600D five years ago and while there have been no drastic changes since then, normal development and rationalization have brought lots of detail improvements like bigger headlights, front-hinged doors, anti-burst door locks, safety belt

anchorages, and so on (Fiat, incidentally, were one of the first European car manufacturers to do extensive crash-testing research on their cars). Although unfashionably tall, narrow and rather austere inside, the car is not quite so cramped or uncomfortable as its size might suggest. Moreover, despite its highly competitive price, it is well equipped for basic family transport, standard fittings including a heater, screen washer, tool kit, and several thoughtful warning lights. On paper, the car's performance is poor: in practice it can be scuttled through busy town traffic (or parked in pint-size gaps) while bigger, faster cars queue behind. Out of town, it will buzz along at 60 m.p.h. and only when overtaking or struggling uphill with a load does the available horsepower seem inadequate. The compensation is exceptional economy, for it runs on the cheapest petrol and does 40-45 m.p.g. providing you do not drive hard.

Performance and economy

With only 767 c.c., the 600D has one of the smallest four-cylinder car engines made in Europe. Its output of 29 b.h.p. (net) is near the bottom of the scale too so performance is hardly in the neck-

---

PRICE: £400 plus £93 7s. 9d. purchase tax equals £493 7s. 9d.

Fiat 600D

straining class. Lightly laden, it will keep up with (and often beat) normal stop-go traffic stream by accelerating hard through the gears, but with four people up you tend to put aside all competitive motoring and settle for the inside lane—especially if there is an adverse headwind or hill. It works the other way too, of course, For such low power, the car has quite high gearing (14.2 m.p.h. per 1,000 r.p.m.) so nothing is going to burst if you take advantage of a helpful tailwind or downhill. Speeds of well over 70 m.p.h. (over 80 m.p.h. on the optimistic speedometer) can be reached like this so motorway travel in the right conditions can be almost as fast as the law allows. At high speeds, the engine hums away quite smoothly and fairly quietly apart from a resonant period around 50 m.p.h.

Overtaking sometimes demands careful anticipation since the car can be exposed in the wrong lane for quite a long time: one then tends to ignore the suggested intermediate maximum speeds marked on the speedometer. The handbook promises long engine life if you stay within indicated limits of 19, 28, 44 and 68 m.p.h. in the gears but since these figures correspond to relatively modest engine speeds, no immediate damage will result from exceeding

them. We had no trouble starting the engine; it always went first-time from cold with the floor-mounted choke open.

The top-gear fuel consumption curve shows just how economical this Fiat can be on the cheapest low-grade petrol. If you cruise at 50-55 m.p.h. the overall consumption will be in the mid 40's: even 50 m.p.g. would be possible with really gentle driving. On the other hand, if you keep your foot hard on the throttle nearly all the time—as most of our drivers did—the consumption becomes relatively heavy. Our first consumption check—which included an abnormally high London mileage—worked out at a disappointing 33 m.p.g. Even by our standards, this seemed unfairly low so, just before these pages went to press, we embarked on a special 250-mile country tour, driving briskly (55-60 m.p.h.) but avoiding very high revs and full-throttle cruising. The Fiat returned 41.5 m.p.g. for this journey, bringing our overall fuel consumption up to 35.5 m.p.g.

Transmission

The sturdy floor-mounted gearlever is spring-loaded to the right which makes upward changes from second onwards quick and usually effortless: they need to be quick, too, since the engine revs fall rapidly on a closed throttle. It needs a firmer hand to change back from third to second. Unless you do it gently, each gearchange is accompanied by a metallic clonk from the lever as it

---

Performance

Test Data: World copyright reserved; no unauthorized reproduction in whole or in part.

Conditions
Weather: Overcast, 0-15 m.p.h. wind
Temperature 58°-62°F. Barometer 29.28 in. Hg.
Surface: Tarmacadam and concrete, sometimes damp.
Fuel: Mixture 94 octane (R.M.).

Maximum speeds

	m.p.h.
Mean lap speed banked circuit	67.3
Best one-way ¼-mile	73.1
3rd gear	40.5
2nd gear	26
1st gear	18

see text

"Maximile" speed: (Timed quarter mile after 1 mile accelerating from rest).

	m.p.h.
Mean	65.7
Best	68.7

Acceleration times

m.p.h.	sec.
0-30	7.4
0-40	12.6
0-50	21.0
0-60	36.2
Standing quarter mile	24.5

m.p.h.	Top sec.	3rd sec.
10-30	—	10.3
20-40	16.1	10.7
30-50	21.0	16.1
40-60	48.1	—

Speedometer

Indicated	20	30	40	50	60
True	19	28	37½	47	57
Distance recorder				3.2% fast	

Hill climbing

At steady speed		lb./ton
Top	1 in 14.9	(Tapley 150)
3rd	1 in 8.6	(Tapley 260)
2nd	1 in 5.8	(Tapley 380)

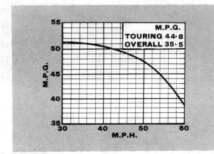

M.P.G.
TOURING 44·8
OVERALL 35·5

Fuel consumption

Touring (consumption midway between 30 m.p.h. and maximum less 5% allowance for acceleration) . . . . 44.8 m.p.g.
Overall . . . . 35.5 m.p.g.
(=7.96 litres/100 km.)
Total test distance . . . . . . 1,200 miles
Tank capacity (maker's figure) . . . . 6.8 gal.

Steering

Turning circle between kerbs: ft.
Left 28
Right 28.5
Turns of steering wheel from lock to lock . 3.1
Steering wheel deflection for 50 ft. diameter circle . . . . 0.8 turns

Brakes
Pedal pressure, deceleration and equivalent stopping distance from 30 m.p.h.

lb.	g	ft.
25	0.27	111
50	0.94	32
Handbrake	0.38	79

Fade test
20 stops at ½g deceleration at 1 min. intervals from a speed midway between 30 m.p.h. and maximum speed (=48.6 m.p.h.)

	lb.
Pedal force at beginning	34
Pedal force at 10th stop	36
Pedal force at 20th stop	36

Weight
Kerb weight (unladen with fuel for approximately 50 miles) . . . . 11.8 cwt.
Front/rear distribution 39/61
Weight laden as tested . . . . . . 15.5 cwt.

Clutch
Free pedal movement . . . . =1.2 in.
Additional movement to disengage clutch completely . . . . =2.3 in.
Maximum pedal load . . . . =35 lb.

Parkability
Gap needed to clear a 6 ft. wide obstruction parked in front

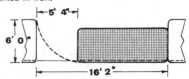

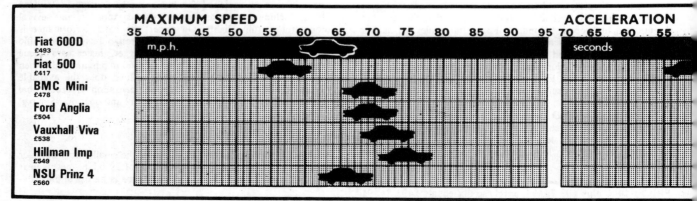

	MAXIMUM SPEED	ACCELERATION
Fiat 600D £493		
Fiat 500 £417		
BMC Mini £478		
Ford Anglia £504		
Vauxhall Viva £538		
Hillman Imp £549		
NSU Prinz 4 £560		

Parking the 10 ft. 10 in. 600D is very easy—you don't really need to back into a meter bay like this.

Although the seats are small (below) and simply upholstered, they are anatomically shaped and quite comfortable. Gearlever and handbrake are well placed and the driving position good, even for tall people. Rubber matting covers the floor.

Only if the front seats are pushed well forward is there sufficient legroom behind for tall people. The heater control can just be seen at the back of the "transmission" tunnel.

The rear squab (below) folds forward to make this large luggage platform. With the seat in place, there is still a small luggage well behind.

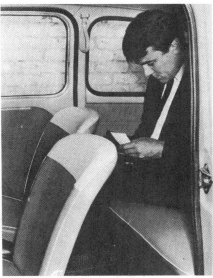

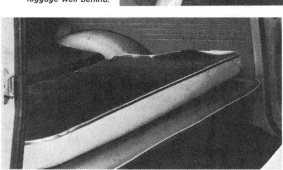

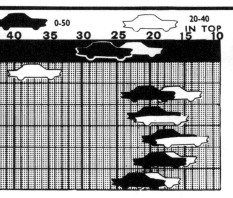

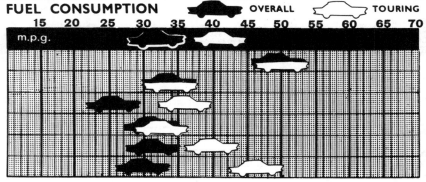

FUEL CONSUMPTION

111

Fiat 600D

smacks the gate, and all the ratios, including top which is indirect, whine loudly. Synchromesh on 2, 3 and 4 is unbeatable and sometimes strong enough to be obstructive—the lever on our test car occasionally needed an extra hard nudge to get it in. First is a "crash" ratio that can only be engaged on the move by accurate double de-clutching. Less skilled drivers will either crunch it in or settle for second instead which is not ideal for a quick getaway from walking pace. First was sometimes reluctant to engage when the car was at rest.

The clutch bites without any judder but for such a small car the Fiat's is not especially light; the effective part of the medium-length travel is also small so it needs a delicate foot to start off or change gear without a jerk.

Handling and brakes

The steering on the 600D and 850 Fiats has a dead and rather stiff feeling which most people find odd at first. There is very little castor action on gentle turns so that the steering wheel—which can almost go "over-centre"—must be consciously unwound to straighten up, rather than just allowed to slip through the fingers. Happily, the sharper the corner and the higher your cornering speed, the more alive and lighter the steering becomes so that "feel" is most acute when most needed.

Despite the heavy tail, the 600D has been made to understeer quite strongly which makes it rather a safe-handling car in unskilled hands. Except on very slippery roads, there is never enough power surplus to provoke a tail-slide so you don't have to treat the throttle with any respect. If you suddenly lift off when cornering hard, the nose tucks in suddenly (just as it would on many front-wheel cars) because the reduction in speed leaves you with more lock applied than was necessary a second before when countering understeer. Even on a wet road, there is unexpectedly little tendency for the back wheels to slide.

Unassisted drum brakes on all four wheels stop this lightweight car quite well enough from 70 m.p.h. Fade was negligible during our usual test (admittedly from only 48 m.p.h.) and pedal pressures generally light. What we did not like was the fierce way in which a little extra pressure produced a lot more braking: this unprogressive action often resulted in an unintentional crash stop guaranteed to upset the driver behind.

Comfort and controls

Although it feels a bit claustrophobic at first, the 600D is not uncomfortably cramped inside. Inevitably, you sit close to the door (which can be used for cold-shoulder side support) and elbows might overlap a bit in the middle. But generally there is room for a six-foot driver who has inches to spare between his head and the hard roof lining. Anyone taller will probably want the seat to go farther back in order to disentangle his knees from the steering wheel. The floor-hinged pedals are off-set well to the left because of intruding wheel arches and the brake and accelerator are so close together that the brake must be operated with an airborne foot. Unacclimatized drivers found this both awkward and potentially dangerous because a sudden jerk could sway your hovering foot from the small pedal pad; there is also the possibility of working brakes and engine against each other—in fact it was difficult *not* to heel and toe. There is comfortable space to rest the left foot between clutch and brake on the sloping toe-board. Luggage accommodation is less satisfactory: you can squeeze a hold-all into the front boot and several slim items behind the rear seat but you can't really carry four people *and* a large suitcase.

The front seats, though small and spartan, slope and bulge in the right places and most people found them more comfortable than they look. Side support is quite good. Both front seats tip

The 6.8-gallon petrol tank (with screw-on cap) allows a range of up to 320 miles. The battery is under the "luggage" space.

All this luggage can be carried if there are only two people in the car. The two smallest boxes (1 cu. ft.) just about fill the front boot: the two beneath (1.6 cu. ft.) fit snugly behind the back seat: the pile on the right (6.5 cu. ft.) fills the luggage platform (made by folding the rear seat squab forward) without obscuring rearward vision. Total, 9.1 cu. ft.

17½ x 13 x 6
14 x 11 x 5
21 x 15 x 7
17½ x 13 x 6
28 x 21 x 9

Safety check list

1	**Steering assembly**	
	Steering box position	Ahead of the front axle line but well behind front of car
	Steering column collapsible?	No
	Steering wheel boss padded?	No, but horn button large and flat
2	**Instrument panel**	
	Projecting switches, etc	All central toggle switches and ignition key
	Cowls, etc.?	Yes, instrument cowl behind steering wheel
	Effective padding	Probably
3	**Ejection**	
	Anti-burst door latches?	Yes. Designed to withstand 30g
	Child-proof locks?	No, but only two doors.
4	**Windscreen**	Zone toughened
5	**Door structure**	
	Interior handles and winders	Projecting
	Front quarter light catches	Projecting
6	**Back of front seat**	Firm perimeter frame but otherwise very soft. No lock to prevent front seats tilting
7	**Screen pillar**	Beading over metal but not really padded
8	**Driving mirror**	
	Framed?	Yes, heavily
	Collapsible?	Probably
9	**Safety harness**	None, but anchorages built-in

forward (not a good safety point) making access to the back unexpectedly easy but the wide doors have no keep-open catches and a slight wind will slam them shut as you enter. The back seat has generous cushion area and squab height and again proved quite comfortable: it would be better still if the cushion sloped more to give better support under the thighs—a deficiency emphasized by the poor leg room. Surprisingly, three small adults can sit abreast on the back seat because the wheel arches to not steal any valuable space.

By small car standards, the ride is acceptably comfortable though certainly not good. Vertical movement is fairly low—on a good road the car travels quite smoothly—but wavy sections make it pitch to and fro (especially under braking) and it thumps over troughs and holes. At night, the pitching makes dipped headlights flash up and down.

The heating system is not only standard equipment but built into the car. Heated air is force-fed from the engine along a central tunnel to outlets under the facia and on to the screen—a simple ring grab opens the foot warmers. At the back of the tunnel, just in front of the back seat but within reach of the driver, is a stiff three-position lever. This admits air to the tunnel (which takes some time to warm up) and, on its third setting, admits a further stream through the luggage space behind the rear seat. This simple arrangement has three shortcomings: it will not feed cool air to the car in hot weather (the windows are the only ventilators) and output is dependent on engine speed which means that fine adjustment is difficult to achieve. With the vent fully open there is also a prominent hissing noise from the outlets though the car hardly goes fast enough for wind roar to become excessive. Accelerating hard, the engine is pretty noisy but it settles down to a more isolated hum for main-road cruising.

With quite a small turning circle (at 28½ ft., 2 ft. larger

Continued on the next page

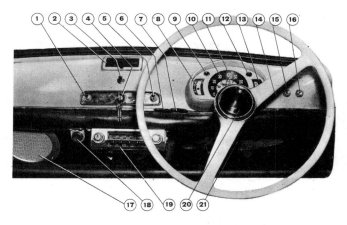

1, panel light. 2, ash tray. 3, master lights switch. 4, ignition/starter. 5, wipers. 6, dip and main beam. 7, indicators. 8, space for water thermometer. 9, ignition light. 10, speedometer. 11, mileage recorder. 12, oil pressure warning light. 13, petrol gauge (including low-fuel warning light). 14, main beam tell tale. 15, parking light indicator. 16, indicator tell tale. 17, radio speaker (non-standard). 18, screen washer bulb. 19, radio (extra). 20, horn. 21, hand throttle.

Specification

Engine

Cylinders	4
Bore and stroke	62 mm. x 63.5 mm.
Cubic capacity	767 c.c.
Valves	o.h.v. pushrod
Compression ratio	7.5:1
Carburetter(s)	Weber 28 ICP3
Fuel pump	Mechanical
Oil filter	Full flow centrifugal
Max. power (net)	29 b.h.p. at 4,800 r.p.m.
Max torque (net)	28.9 lb. ft. at 3,000 r.p.m.

Transmission

Clutch	6.1 in. s.d.p.
Top gear (s/m)	0.896:1
3rd gear (s/m)	1.333:1
2nd gear (s/m)	2.055:1
1st gear	3.385:1
Reverse	4.275:1
Final drive	4.87:1
M.p.h. at 1,000 r.p.m. in:	
Top gear	14.4
3rd gear	9.8
2nd gear	6.3
1st gear	3.8

Chassis

Construction	Unitary body/chassis

Brakes

Type	Hydraulic drums.
Dimensions	7.3 in. diameter.

Friction areas:

Front		37.3 sq. in. of lining operating on 54.4 sq. in. of drum.
Rear		37.3 sq. in. of lining operating on 54.4 sq. in. of drum.

Suspension and steering

Front	Independent by transverse leaf springs and wishbones.
Rear	Independent by semi-trailing arms, swing axles and coil springs.
Shock absorbers:	
Front	} Telescopic
Rear	
Steering gear	Worm and sector
Tyres	Pirelli 5.20 x 12.
Rim size	3½J

Coachwork and equipment

Starting handle	No
Jack	Pillar screw with fixed handle
Jacking points	One each side
Battery	12-volt
Number of electrical fuses	6
Indicators	Front, side and rear flashers, self-cancelling
Screen wipers	One-speed electric
Screen washers	Rubber-bulb manual pump
Sun visors	Two
Locks:	
With ignition key	Ignition/starter
With other key	Doors
Interior heater	Hot fresh air ducted from engine fan to interior and screen
Extras available	Reclining front seats
Upholstery	Vinyl
Floor covering	Rubber matting
Alternative body styles	Convertible

Maintenance

Sump	5.6 pints S.A.E. 10W/30
Gearbox and rear axle	2.7 pints S.A.E. 90 EP
Steering gear	Fiat W90 oil
Cooling system	7.6 pints (drain taps two)
Chassis lubrication	Every 1,500 miles to 2 points
Minimum service interval	1,500 miles
Ignition timing	10° advance from t.d.c.
Contact breaker gap	0.018 to 0.020 in.
Sparking plug gap	0.24 to 0.028 in.
Sparking plug type	Champion L7
Tappet clearances (cold)	Inlet 0.006 in. Exhaust 0.006 in.
Valve timing:	
Inlet opens	4° b.t.d.c.
Inlet closes	34° a.b.d.c.
Exhaust opens	29° b.b.d.c.
Exhaust closes	1° a.t.d.c.
Front wheel toe-in	0 to 2 mm.
Camber angle	1° ± 20'
Castor angle	9° ± 1°
Kingpin inclination	5° 30'
Tyre pressures	14 p.s.i. front, 23 p.s.i. rear

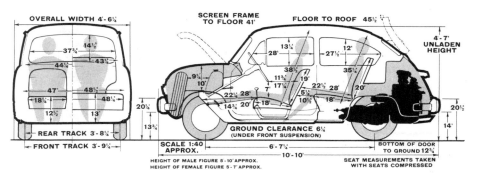

Fiat 600D

than that of the last Fiat 600D we tested) and good forward visibility over the stubby, sloping bonnet, parking is very easy: you can usually slip into a gap, especially a parking meter bay, forwards though reversing is not troublesome because there is very little invisible overhang beyond the back window. Strong rubber overriders protect the bumper.

Fittings and furniture

Large areas of painted metal, rubber matting on the floor and plain plastic upholstery make the inside very non-de luxe in appearance. This might be a showroom handicap but in practice we found it quite habitable. It is easy to wipe clean (though not to sweep out because of the raised door sills) and there is no essential item missing from the equipment which includes a rubber-bulb screen washer, a dash-top ashtray, six warning lights and grab handles for the rear passengers. There is also a hand throttle which would be more useful if placed nearer the driver's hand than his knee.

The instruments and switchgear look like afterthoughts but they are easy to see and reach and the separate nacelles can be easily removed for repairs. The two column stalks (lights and indicators) are genuine finger-tip controls. Although the shin and knee padding on the scuttle looks effective, the small "bladed" toggle switches in the middle of the facia would almost certainly injure before snapping off if a passenger were thrown forward in an accident. On the other hand, the mirror is so thickly framed that it looks like one eyepiece from a pair of fashionable spectacles. Behind it is a reading light.

There is more space for oddments than in many larger cars. Besides the full width front shelf (most of which had been lost to a radio and speaker on our test car) there is a small flexible map pocket in each door and a narrow but deep well behind the back seat. The technique is to drop your shopping in at the top and then pull the squab forward to unload. Alternatively, the squab can be folded flat, estate-car fashion, to make a surprisingly large luggage platform: this, of course, is at the expense of passenger space.

Servicing and accessibility

Most of the jobs listed for routine attention should be done every 6,000 miles. Unfortunately, there are a couple of nipples on the kingpins which need a squirt of lubricant every 1,500 miles: most owners would probably prefer to do this chore themselves rather than lose their transport to the garage. Otherwise, there is very little lubricating to do and none at all on the suspension. For routine attention, engine accessibility is excellent—ancillaries like the fuel pump, distributor, coil, oil filler, dip-stick, dynamo and (once the air cleaner is off) carburetter are all within easy reach. Moreover, the full width lid lifts right out of the way and supports itself, and there is automatic illumination at night.

The pillar-screw jack is operated simply by turning a fixed handle which raises the car quickly and easily. It is housed in the front boot along with a neat set of tools in a plastic box, the spare wheel and battery. What little space remains can be used for luggage. The boot lid is also supposed to be self-supporting but would oscillate gently up and down on its catch for several minutes before slamming shut.

Maintenance chart

1 **Engine.** Check sump level (every 300 miles); check radiator water (300); change engine oil (6,000); check tappet clearances (6,000); clean air cleaner (6,000); check carburation (6,000); clean crankcase breather system (12,000).

2 **Transmission.** Check oil level (6,000); change oil (18,000).

3 **Steering.** Grease kingpins (1,500).

4 **Wheels and tyres.** Check tyre pressures (300); grease front wheel bearings (12,000); grease rear wheel bearings (18,000).

5 **Electrical.** Check electrolyte level of battery (1,500); lubricate distributor and check contact breaker gap and condition (6,000); clean and re-set sparking plugs (6,000); check battery terminals for tightness and coat with vaseline (6,000); clean dynamo commutator, check brushes for wear, and lubricate (18,000); clean starter commutator, check for wear, lubricate free-wheel components (18,000).

6 **Brakes.** Check fluid level (6,000). **Miscellaneous.** Lubricate door hinges and check body-mounted suspension and engine retaining bolts for tightness (12,000).

1, carburetter. 2, radiator filler cap. 3, coil. 4, voltage regulator. 5, petrol pump. 6, dip stick. 7, distributor. 8, oil filler. 9, dynamo. 10, water pump. 11, fan.

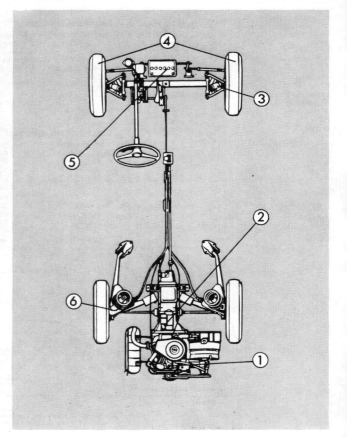

MAKE: Fiat. **MODEL:** 600D. **MAKERS:** S.A. Fiat, Corso G. Agnelli 200, Turin, Italy. **CONCESSIONAIRES:** Fiat (England) Ltd., Water Road, Wembley, Middlesex.

FIAT 850 COUPE

One of the handsomest, best-balanced designs ever seen on a small car

To THOSE WHO appreciated the nimbleness and economy of the Fiat 600, but wanted additional power, better brakes, handsomer lines and a more attractive interior, the newly-imported 850 Coupé will be more than welcome. The 850 sedan, introduced in Italy in the spring of 1964, was a scaled-up 600 incorporating the familiar layout: 2 doors, 4 seats, all-independent suspension and a rear-mounted water-cooled 4-cyl engine. It was an immediate success, but man does not live by bread alone, so the Coupé and its sister, the Bertone-bodied Spider, were designed to capture the small-displacement sporting market in Europe. They did so with such unexpected success that production has lagged far behind demand, and the Coupé is just now becoming available in the U.S., more than a year after its introduction. The Spider, produced at the rate of about one for every 20 Coupés, may not be marketed here for some time.

It is not hard to understand the popularity of the 850 Coupé. Following the current rage for fastbacks, but producing an all-new body rather than simply adding a sloping roof to the existing sedan, Fiat has come up with one of the handsomest, best-balanced designs we've seen on a small car. Achieving elegant simplicity on a 79.8-in wheelbase is no easy task. Clichés and gimmicks have been avoided, the closest thing to this being the Ferrari GTB look of the neatly chopped-off tail. This favorable first impression is backed up by the interior, with a very attractive vinyl upholstery that

would be fitting on a car costing $1000 more. Although most staff members thought the wood veneer on the dashboard was useless (and unsuitable on *any* modern automobile), the large, round speedometer and tachometer are exactly right for the sporting character of the car. Besides the usual warning lights, there are fuel level and water temperature gauges, but none for oil pressure. There is no glove box, but a shelf under the dash and door pockets are useful for small objects.

FIAT 850 COUPE
AT A GLANCE...

Price as tested	$1834
Engine	4 cyl, ohv, 843 cc, 52 bhp
Curb weight, lb	1590
Top speed, mph	86
Acceleration, 0–60 mph, sec	18.0
50–70 mph (3rd-4th gear)	15.6
Average fuel consumption, mpg	29.7

FIAT 850 COUPE

A wide seat adjustment range suits drivers of all heights, and the steering wheel position is very good. The same cannot be said for the pedals, however; only the smallest, best-trained feet can work comfortably in the space available, which is limited by the intruding wheel wells. The rear seat is strictly for children, as the shortest member of our staff found his head grazing the roof even when hunched forward. Nevertheless, families with two small children will be well accommodated. We felt the fold-down rear seat of the 600 would be useful for extra luggage in the 850 Coupé, since normally only two persons would be carried. The regular luggage compartment under the hood also houses the spare wheel and battery (below a quickly removable panel), while the fuel tank is at the back, behind the rear seat.

The engine starts instantly from cold and warms up quickly, the floor-mounted choke being neeed only briefly. Like all Fiats, the 850 Coupé is extremely maneuverable, and a joy to drive on winding roads and through light traffic. Steering is initially a bit vague, but more precise at higher speeds where it counts. As with other light rear-engined cars, the 850 is susceptible to side winds, but there is no problem keeping it in line. Adhesion is good in all attitudes, and it is obvious that Fiat has gone to great lengths to eliminate oversteer. Under most conditions the car understeers, with a gradual shift to neutral characteristics as cornering speeds increase. Only by entering fast turns at near maximum can the tail be hung out, and this is easy to anticipate.

Despite its 843-cc capacity, the engine is extremely willing if kept above 4000 rpm. Using maximum revs in every gear, it surpasses quite a few cars of greater displacement in acceleration and top speed, and cruises easily at 70-75. More power is wanted when climbing steep grades or passing slow cars on the highway, as the 850 does not recover lost ground quickly. A third gear which only goes to 61 mph (at recommended revs) complicates this situation. While the acceleration and cruising speeds come easily, and an occasional 7000 rpm doesn't seem to bother the engine, the continued use of high rpm to maintain this performance level is not conducive to long engine life, even if the Fiat unit gives every indication of robust construction. The speedometer and tachometer on our test car were both very accurate, steady and easy to read, the former actually being a trifle slow, in contrast to the usual optimistic Italian instruments. The all-synchro gearbox functions better the

harder it's used. Making slow, casual shifts, the action is a little chunky and first gear is sometimes hard to find, though it is always right there when the lever is moved decisively.

Riding comfort is good for such a small car. The pitching which occurs on major bumps and dips is well damped, and the overall comfort level is high. A valuable feature is the locking mechanism of the backrests, preventing them from pivoting forward on braking.

The brakes are well up to the job, stopping the car quickly and smoothly with no loss of control. Repeated use brought no fade or appreciable increase in pedal pressure. Some earlier Fiats have been under-braked, but the fitting of discs to the front has transformed the cars in this department.

Considering how hard the engine works, it is a remarkably smooth and quiet unit; at idle it can hardly be heard at all, and it purrs along unobtrusively at moderate speeds. In the 5000-6500 rpm range its note changes to a satisfying, sporting growl. While this sound is suited to fast acceleration, it is not so enjoyable at cruising speeds, especially with the windows rolled up. This is a consequence of a small engine and a low final drive (13.5 mph/1000 rpm); it sounds as though it wants another gear for continuous cruising above 60 mph. The structure of the car is very rigid and rattle-free.

Although we had no opportunity to call upon the heater, the ventilation system is excellent, delivering cool air where wanted through swivelling ducts on the dashboard which serve as defrosters when turned toward the windshield. A two-speed blower insures an ample supply under varying conditions.

Several technical features should be mentioned which are normally not apparent in the operation of the car. A sealed year-around cooling system, using a mixture of water, glycol and rust inhibitor, gives protection to minus 31° Fahrenheit. Sudden losses of coolant can be remedied by adding water to the expansion tank, but permanent coolant is required for major replenishment. The engine incorporates a crankcase vapor recirculation system to reduce exhaust emissions. Gases are conveyed from the valve cover through the air cleaner to the carburetor, with a valve to restrict the return of most vapors at idling speeds. Fuel consumption was expectedly low, and even lower than expected during the flat-out performance runs at 25.7 mpg. Under ideal cruising conditions 36-38 mpg should be obtainable.

The Fiat 850 Coupé is an excellent car in the Sprite class for those wanting stylish good looks and space for children in addition to the excellent performance. Driven moderately it should be a durable car as well. Considering the many sophisticated features it offers, its price of $1834 is almost too good to be true.

FIAT 850 COUPÉ

SCALE: 10" DIVISIONS

PRICE

Basic list	$1834
As tested	1834

ENGINE

No cyl & type	4-cyl, ohv
Bore x stroke, mm	65 x 63.5
In	2.56 x 2.50
Displacement, cc/cu in	843/51.4
Compression ratio	9.3:1
Bhp @ rpm	52 @ 6200
Equivalent mph	85
Torque @ rpm, lb-ft	45.6 @ 4000
Equivalent mph	53
Carburetors	1 Weber 30 DIC 1
No. barrels, dia	1 x 1.18
Type fuel required	premium

DRIVE TRAIN

Clutch type	single plate, dry
Diameter, in	n.a.
Gear ratios: 4th (0.96)	4.68:1
3rd (1.41)	6.87:1
2nd (2.06)	10.00:1
1st (3.64)	17.73:1
Synchromesh	on all 4
Differential type	hypoid bevel
Ratio	4.87:1

CHASSIS & SUSPENSION

Frame type	unit with body
Brake type	disc/drum
Swept area, sq in	n.a.
Tire size	5.50–13
Make	Pirelli Sempione
Steering type	worm & sector
Turns, lock-to-lock	3.5
Turning circle, ft	31.5
Front suspension: independent with unequal A-arms, transverse leaf spring, tube shocks, anti-roll bar.	
Rear suspension: independent with semi-trailing arms, coil springs, tube shocks, anti-roll bar.	

ACCOMMODATION

Normal capacity, persons	2
Occasional capacity	4
Seat width, front, in	2 x 19.0
Rear	47.5
Head room, front/rear	36.5/29.2
Seat back adjustment, deg	0
Entrance height, in	48.7
Step-over height	14.7
Door width	40.8
Driver comfort rating:	
Driver 69 in. tall	80
Driver 72 in. tall	80
Driver 75 in. tall	80
(85–100, good; 70–85, fair; under 70, poor)	

GENERAL

Curb weight, lb	1590
Test weight	1950
Weight distribution (with driver), front/rear, %	39/61
Wheelbase, in	79.8
Track, front/rear	45.6/47.7
Overall length	142.0
Width	59.0
Height	51.1
Frontal area, sq ft	15.1
Ground clearance, in	5.3
Overhang, front/rear	27.6/34.6
Departure angle, deg	19
Usable trunk space, cu ft	4.3
Fuel tank capacity, gal	7.9

INSTRUMENTATION

Instruments: 100-mph speedometer, 8000-rpm tachometer, odometer, water temperature, fuel level.

Warning lights: high beam, parking lights, turn signals, fuel tank reserve, oil pressure, generator charge.

MISCELLANEOUS

Body styles available: coupe as tested

Warranty period: 12 mo/12,000 mi

CALCULATED DATA

Lb/hp (test wt)	34.8
Mph/1000 rpm (high gear)	13.5
Engine revs/mi (60 mph)	4525
Piston travel, ft/mi	1890
Rpm @ 2500 ft/min	6000
Equivalent mph	79
Cu ft/ton mi	69.6
R&T wear index	85.6

EXTRA COST OPTIONS

Seat belts, outside rear-view mirror, radio

MAINTENANCE

Crankcase capacity, qt	3.5
Change interval, mi	6000
Oil filter type	full flow
Change interval, mi	30,000
Chassis lube interval, mi	1500

FUEL CONSUMPTION

Normal driving, mpg	28–35
Cruising range, mi	220–280

ROAD TEST RESULTS

ACCELERATION

Time to speed, sec:

0–30 mph	4.8
0–40 mph	7.8
0–50 mph	12.0
0–60 mph	18.0
0–70 mph	27.4
50–70 mph (3rd–4th gear)	15.6

Time to distance, sec:

0–100 ft	4.5
0–500 ft	11.3
¼-mile	21.0
Speed at end, mph	63.7
Passing exposure time, sec:	
Car ahead going 50 mph	9.9

SPEEDS IN GEARS

High gear (6300), mph	86
3rd (6500)	23
2nd (6500)	41
1st (6500)	61

BRAKES

Panic stop from 80 mph:

Deceleration, % G	78
Control	good
Parking: hold 30% grade	yes
Overall brake rating	good

SPEEDOMETER ERROR

30 mph indicated	actual 30.8
40 mph	41.0
60 mph	60.5
80 mph	80.2
Odometer correction factor	1.001

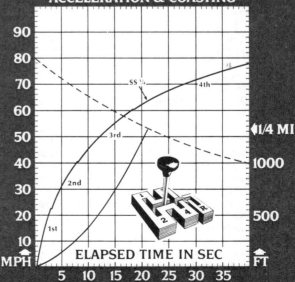

ACCELERATION & COASTING

ELAPSED TIME IN SEC

MPH — FT

1/4 MI — 1000 — 500

OTS COUPE
SPIDER
BERLINA CORSA 1000

Carlo Abarth's FUNNY

Abarth's conversions may be beautiful
Or they may be ugly
But they go, good grief they go!

AS PER OUR LAST EXPERIENCE WITH JOHN RICH MOTORS, this latest one turned out to be full of pleasant surprises. It started out to be a road test of the new Fiat Abarth OTS 1000, and wound up including two other exciting new Abarth creations — the sexy little 1000 Spider and an absolutely unbelievable Group 2 sedan called the Berlina Corsa. The OTS is the most easily recognized of the trio, being a 150 cc enlargement of the Fiat 850 coupe we tested in the October 1966 issue. In bringing the engine up to one-liter form, Carlo Abarth has performed his usual tricks of engine modification, to bring power output to roughly 80 hp at 6400 rpm. In addition, there has been an improvement in spring and shock rates, a re-location of seats (to provide more room for tall drivers), and some external trim added to denote that it is a special model. Unless you're an experienced Abarth follower, it may come as a shock to you to find this rework increases the price over the 850 by roughly $1200. If you are, however, you know the kind of excitement the versatile Italian puts in his conversations.

The OTS is not a sizzler. Its zero-60 mph time is 18.6 seconds. Its real forte is maneuverability, and it has enough power and rev range to be far from handicapped in this department. With only a slightly firmer ride, the wheelhop we described on extreme cornering with the 850 coupe has been eliminated. The steering, with this firmness, seems quicker and more responsive and, depending on your driving background, will either seem a joy or frighteningly touchy. So, combining this responsiveness with a top speed of 100 mph, you wind up with a vehicle that doesn't need brute acceleration to get places in a hurry. Gas mileage in excess of 26 mpg is a surprise bonus that helps you make the payments. To be sure, there are drawbacks. The biggest we found in this instance was increased engine noise. Much of it was from the valve train, so it's possible that tappet

clearance was too wide on our test car, but the Abarth exhaust lets itself be strongly heard in the passengers' compartment, too.

To sum up the concept of the OTS 1000, it's sort of the Italian answer to the difference between a standard Mustang and a GT350; i.e., taking an inexpensive production-line model and making more of a GT out of it, without horrendous sacrifices in tractability and so on.

Next up was the Spider 1000 Coupe. Very attractive, modern, and almost exotic in appearance, it is nonetheless based on the 850 platform, power train, and suspensions. It has 9.8-to-1 compression ratio, compared with the 11.5-to-1 figure for the OTS, an identical weight of 1610 pounds at the curb, but a zero-to-60 mph time a half-second better due, undoubtedly, to its better streamlining and smaller frontal area. For its price ($3195) it would seem that the sleek convertible should have more performance to back it up, as the suspension seems relatively soft and it lacks the cat-like qualities of the OTS. In this case, however, the attention has been focused on the body ... with excellent results, as the accompanying pictures bear out. The engine was, however, also noisy in this unit, suggesting that Abarth leaves this factor out of his considerations. It was even more out of place in the somewhat plush surroundings. Seat designs and location are better than they are in the coupe-based model, handling is excellent except for quite a bit of wind-wander when there are gusts blow-

All three Fiat Abarths handled well and had little body roll, top left, under hard cornering. The Spider, top right, drew much attention on the streets because of its sleek lines. The cockpit of the Spider is attractive, rich-looking, and functional. The red OTS 1000 coupe has the same body as Fiat's 850, but similarity ended there. Though not powerful, the OTS is a refined, improved version of the 850. The Berlina Corsa in its homologated form, bottom, looks like an ugly duckling next to the OTS. But don't let looks fool you, it's a real winner.

FIATS

By Jerry Titus

FUNNY FIATS

ing. The major features of the Spider are discernible to the eye of the beholder. We really liked it, but felt it would be a far more logical package with 20-percent more power, even at an increase in price.

Saving the best for last, the Berlina Corsa is probably the ugliest car we've seen in many a season. Abarth apparently could care less. Its job is racing as a Group 2 sedan. We trailered it to Willow Springs for a track test. We took only three laps for an evaluation. The last lap was some seven seconds faster than anything recorded for Class D Sedans, which it's in, and some two seconds faster than anything in Class C. As a matter of fact, it was embarrassingly close to our best times in a Class B BMW!

Understand, before we describe the car, that if any nationality has inherited talents, the Italians all seem to have one for legal homologation. Abarth has, again, exercised this talent well. Based on the old 600 Sedan body shell, this one-liter weighs a little over 1200 pounds and develops about 95 hp at a peak of 7500 rpm. John Rich didn't know what the redline was, so we played it by ear and seat of the pants. It was still pulling strong at 8500. We didn't bother with a zero-60

mph time, but it ran through the quarter-mile in just over 18 seconds with two people aboard. It has four-wheel disc brakes. It has a five-speed gearbox, a top speed of 115 mph, and the cornering power of a Formula machine. A fiberglass "front bumper" is an option. It houses an oil cooler — a big one. The rear deck is held permanently open by bracing. Both enhance streamlining as well as insuring proper engine cooling. The interior is, as you'd expect, like a race car, with full instrumentation, large wrap-around bucket seats, and a stripped-out appearance. There are absolutely no frills.

Driving the car was definitely an exciting experience. It just plain flies into, through, and even out of a corner. We don't need to go into much more detail along these lines, however. Suffice to tell you that, two weeks later, we watched Dan Parkinson, Rich's driver, chase the devil out of a pretty quick Alfa GTA at the Tucson Nationals. If you want to absolutely terrorize the Mini Cooper drivers in your Region, the Berlina Corsa can be purchased, race ready, for $4987.

In reading this report over, we must admit it's not the most descriptive we've ever written. The major reason is that there's only one way to get a truly accurate picture of an Abarth product — drive it. In the case of the Berlina Corsa, all you have to do is watch it in action. That's a thrill in itself!

Photos: Pat Brollier & Gerry Stiles

Two latest additions to the line of Fiat Abarths lack good power, but make up for that with good handling characteristics. Left, the OTS 1000 coupe is mild-looking enough and could be a threat in H Production racing. The Sporty Spider, right, makes driving in the mountains fun.

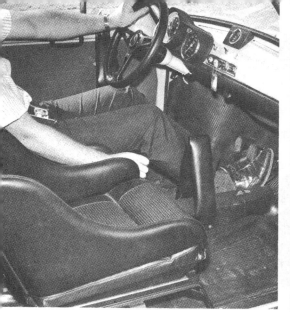

The Fiat Abarth Berlina Corsa is probably the fastest Class D Sedan in this country. Top left, the cockpit is built to hold the driver in place, with wrap-around seats and leg supports. Cornering is best attribute of this ugly little car. Lap times at Willow Springs during the test were better than the C Class Sedan record. Water and oil cooler are mounted in aluminum bumper, top right. The small, and noisy, four-cylinder engine has room to spare in the rear engine bay. Deck lid supports are homologated. Bottom, Berlina Corsa, with two aboard, has enough power to spin track tires during quarter-mile acceleration run.

LEFT: Carb on one side of the head and exhaust on the other makes room for these straight pipes which get the gas out of there in a hurry. This is the hottest factory version of the 850 engine.

BELOW: Nice round dials with white letters on black faces take care of speed, revs, and oil pressure. Heat and amps would be a nice addition, but this makes a very neat and simple panel.

LEFT: This badge tells the tale—specialist coachwork with some rough edges caused by limited mass production in a shop built to handle one-off specials.

FIAT 850 SPIDER

By SLONIGER

DUE IN THE U.S. THIS SPRING, WILL THE FIAT 850 BECOME THE OPEN ROADSTER THIS COMING SUMMER?

ABOVE: The Fiat 850 Spider is even neater than its hard-top brother. Naturally, it looks best top down.

BELOW: Rear-engined Fiat 850 Spider opens wide to show easy access to seats, luggage, and engine.

▶ Some cars are sensible and some cars are fun. If you object to wind in the hair and rain in the face, skip this page because the Fiat 850 Spider is meant to be an open automobile. I decline to comment on their readiness for the puzzle factory but there *are* people who like open cars. Then there are girls with elaborate hairdos. (And no, I don't know why the former always marry the latter.)

I'm afraid I fall into the class that insists, "it never rains into an open car if you keep moving," so don't expect any real objectivity on the practical approach to a Fiat 850 Spider. In 730 miles and two weeks I don't suppose the lid was raised more than twice, including the photo session. If you want a roof, Fiat does sell a hardtop for the Spider— they also sell a 850 Coupe which has

FIAT 850 SPIDER

rear vision and costs less, while going just as fast.

Since you got this far, let's assume you too yearn for the two-people days, when all we remember our sunny jaunts down back lanes—or that you can at least dream about a second car in the two-grand division.

For America this Fiat 850 Spider is the ideal town vehicle in sunny climes (to say nothing of the car all coeds will want at first sight). You can park it in half-spaces, enjoy the maneuverability and all-around vision (top down remember) of a bicycle, get 30 mpg without even trying and have fun, a very special commodity in motoring.

Taking looks first—and why else would you pay that much for two seats?—this has to stand as one of Bertone's better days. For balance, clean lines and just plain prettiness, the Fiat Spider is a hit, with only a hair too much height in the poop if you want to really quibble.

Unfortunately, Fiat themselves lack the capacity to build these Spiders so Bertone does that too. Quality control is not up to conception, as often seems to happen when a speciality shop gets into the mass- or at least semi-mass-production of automobiles. Panel fit could be better (and is on the 850 Coupe which Fiat puts together themselves), and things like that very neat little deck over the folded top need more care.

On the test car it never really hooked in place properly, rattled all the time and generally made a nuisance of itself. As an idea, to hide the folded top, it is superb. The cloth itself can be raised or lowered by one man but he will go quietly frantic with all the niggling catches and buttons to be done up or unhooked. Putting this one down is a little like unhooking the stays of a Victorian virgin.

Once in place, should you bother, the top kept out both wind and weather, while the frameless side windows, rattled on their merry way, but let in surprisingly little air. Incidentally, the basic window design was right because you can drive with windows up and top down without being buffeted in the face. There is a breeze around the back of your

Fuel filler cap on the top deck can present minor problems, the soft top keeps out water if not drafts, and wrap around bumpers provide fair protection.

neck but that's the name of the game isn't it?

Getting on to that driving, entry and exit are aided by wide-opening doors but, naturally, this is a good trick with the top up, thanks to the knee-high proportions and low-mounted seats. Once in, there is leg room for six-footers. I would expect better back rake adjustment in a special vehicle like this. A thumb screw to give a modicum of option, not workable underway, is not enough. Also, any but Italian sizes will want the steering wheel further away when the legs are right, but only if they drive with fairly outstretched arms.

Pedals are better spread than in many Italian cars and they even throw in a dead pedal to brace

against in the bends. Heel-toe maneuvers, the sort of trick you want to play in this car, are very difficult unless you have flamingo leg joints that bend either way. The quickest, tightest-gate shift I know is right wher you want it, the hand brake handy but largely ineffectual.

The dash in wood and leatherette is pure pleasure to look upon and what's more they have five full-value dials with white numerals on black backgrounds. Apart from a speedo with both mileage indicator and resettable trip with tenths wheel, there is a large tachometer plus individual dials for fuel, water temperature and oil pressure. Of course you get the full set of warning lights too, this being a Fiat.

CONTINUED ON PAGE 161

JOHN BOLSTER tries

The IWR Conversion for

the Fiat 850 Coupé

THE Fiat 850 coupé is, without any doubt, the best-looking small car of the present time, and it was Ian Walker's idea to make the car go as well as it looks. Personally, I doubted whether a fairly substantial vehicle could be given an exciting performance with only an 850 cc engine. I run an 850 coupé myself, with which I am more than satisfied, but I secretly wondered whether its performance could be appreciably enhanced without spoiling its good manners and docility.

It turns out that Ian was right and I was wrong. I have recently been using his 850 coupé for some long and hurried journeys and I am still absolutely amazed at the excellence of the car. Very few conversions appeal to me, and I sometimes return them to the owners without writing a word, because I will not give publicity to machines which are noisy, intractable, or which have sticky and unresponsive accelerator pedals, nor will I mention those vehicles which mop up a tankfull of petrol in 100 miles. The IWR Fiat has none of these faults, and I must put it down, straight away, as about the best tuned car that I have yet driven.

When developing the car, the IWR engineers at first found it easy to obtain a vast power increase in the 7000 to 8000 rpm band, with a corresponding loss in the middle accelerating range. Such a car would be useless in 70 mph England, and so they brought the peak down to 6000 rpm and concentrated on improved acceleration.

The work which has been standardized consists of a complete strip down and balancing job. An IWR road camshaft is fitted, the cylinder head is considerably modified, the inlet tract is improved, and the Weber carburetter gets different settings. The distributor is modified with new points, and a set of sparking plugs completes the job, which costs £85. For continuous high speed, an Abarth large capacity sump costs an extra £19 10s 0d. An Abarth exhaust system was fitted to the test car, but this is not really necessary as the standard exhaust system of the coupé is very efficient.

In addition to the work on the engine, the car had been lowered 1½ ins. This small amount, curiously enough, made the body look much longer, the cost of the work being £25 in this case.

On the road, I found that the tuned car was as well-balanced as the one in my garage. There is a little less power at the lowest speeds, but above 3000 rpm the two cars are equal, the tuned one taking the lead around 4000 rpm. At 5000 rpm, the improvement is very obvious, and at 6000 rpm, the little engine is at its best. I normally changed up at 7000 rpm but the Fiat was willing to go higher.

The speedometer of the test car was absolutely accurate at 60 mph. The honest maximum speed seems to be almost exactly 95 mph, but 100 mph can be attained on a slight down grade and then held on the level at about 7300 rpm. This is cruelty, but the car seems very happy to maintain 90 mph indefinitely.

Even more impressive is the fuel economy. A typical journey at a legal 70 mph crawl will give you 40 mpg or better. Quite a bit of town work, followed by a lot of 90 mph *autoroute* cruising and a downhill burst at 100 mph, to impress a fast Citroen driver, gave me an average of 37.6 mpg. In other words, the tuned car is at least as economical as the standard one.

By intelligent use of the gearbox, some fine acceleration figures may be recorded. Obviously, wheelspin is no problem with an 850 cc car, but 0-30 mph in 4.8 secs, including a snatched gearchange, will generally ensure priority at the traffic lights. 0-50 mph may be done in a snappy 10.6 secs, if you play your cards right, and 0-60 mph takes 14.4 secs. For a substantially built 850 cc car, these times really are astonishingly good.

The IWR coupé is as quiet as the normal one, and auntie would not even notice that it had been tuned. She would need a little more throttle when starting from a standstill, to avoid the risk of stalling, but once on the move she would be just as happy as in the standard model.

The lowered suspension gives a slightly harder ride than standard, although all trace of pitching is eliminated. Very bad roads cause the bump stops to touch, but no normal English road would bring this about. The car remains absolutely flat on fast bends and the cornering power, already good, is improved. In the paddock at Oulton Park, I noticed that even this quite moderate lowering operation attracted considerable attention to the Fiat.

Many a good car has been spoilt by the attentions of so-called experts in the conversion business. In the case of the Fiat 850 coupé, however, I can thoroughly recommend the work of Ian Walker Ltd. Almost anybody would greatly prefer the IWR 850 to the standard coupé, and it has literally none of the disadvantages which so many modified cars exhibit. For further details, call at Woodhouse Service Station, 236 Woodhouse Road, Finchley, London N12, or ring ENT 6281.

FIAT 600 (767 cc) £555* Slow Down (By Order)

Maximum 66 mph (50 mph in 21 secs). Average fuel consumption 38 mpg.
Weight 12 cwt (38% front). Tyre pressures 14 lbs F/23R.

Water-cooled. Four-cylinder "square" in-line engine at rear driving through 4-speed (non-synchromesh 1st) gearbox with change on floor. All-independent suspension by double transverse springs at front and swing axles (coil springs) at rear. Self-supporting chassisless body. Three-bearing crankshaft. Full-flow oil filter. Drum brakes. Worm and sector steering. 12 volt lighting.

JUDGING by the manner the four-letter maker's name monopolises this here compendium it is hardly surprising that Fiat today is the largest producer of vehicles in Europe, and the only one with three "millionaires" on the baker's list. The 500 (2¼ million) being the world's lowest-priced, cheapest-to-run car — if we are to believe what the man said a page earlier. The 600 (over 3 million) being the best *value*, and the 1100 (2 million) the oldest. It was while he was busy writing the score for the 600 that Turin's chief apostle of sanity, Dr. Dante Giacosa, tossed off the 500 as a sort of experiment to resolve the air versus water-cooled arguments of the period (1954/5). He didn't visualise that model as a viable commercial proposition, and its eventual marketing and sales successes — which did not follow immediately let us add — came as a surprise. Either way the 600 is Giacosa's masterpiece and the later 850 owes it much.

The 600 has held well to its starting price and general intention. One model only. No extras allowed or allowed for. A shining, shining example of initial foresight and subsequent honesty. The 600 has survived the years without deviation and with fewer major modifications than any we

know. It can't ever have been a high-profitability motor, like the Cortina, Viva, yea and the 850. Herein is no box. This one is fully grown, solid in meaning as well as feel; the weight tells us that. We seek reason and we find double-skinning of the stress-bearing panels. By '68 standards she has got tall, yet you can seat three adults across the back. Not comfortably, but it IS possible.

Such is the basis of sophistication. For our money the 600 is the most highly refined member of the clan. The 500 resembles an ultra-simple putt-putt by comparison, which is probably why so many customers go into Fiat Dealers looking to see one and come out buying the other. Part explanation is that the 600 is infinitely easier to drive. Refinement again. And much more flexible. Nevertheless, 29 bhp at four-eight from a low pressure (7·5 to 1 cc) four-pot, cross-pot, cross-flow, alloy-headed engine is far too modest to be anything if not deliberate. Hard fact No. 1. The 600 is a dull stopwatch actor and confirms the suggestion that Giacosa (and Brass) cling to some kind of dogmatic beliefs about holding small-car paces to what they consider as fast enough for the average small-car buyer to handle with safety. Issigonis (and

Brass?) have the same fixation about "alert" driving positions!

We aren't joking. Set the 600's power-to-weight ratio (49 bhp per ton) against the Mini's 59 or the Imp's 57 and there, you understand now why Sig. Edgar Abarth has been able to earn himself a fortune out of making Fiats go faster for the local Lights Brigade. Certainly, the Methusaleh-like labelling of the speedometer with its recommended limits for the change points of each ratio (44 mph in 3rd!), including a final red-line mark for Top at 66, are little respected south of the snow-line. As the majority will realise, you run no mechanical risk by ignoring these markings . . . not like breaking the seal on the mechanical governor that held back the butterfly intake control on the 600's predecessor during the running-in mileage. In them days bang went your warranty.

By all the rules the Seicento should have retired when the 850 came along. That was the idea, but the public just kept on asking for it. Note that the car is rarely advertised; didn't appear at Earls Court these last two seasons.

Not that its popularity should be any mystery to us. We ran an early version for about 48,000 miles and talked so much about it that the subject had to be banned on pain of becoming a bore. The memory of the powerhouse's smoothness lives on as a treat by any standards; the natural vibration of its three mains crankshaft somehow never getting as far as the body proper, thanks to Fiat's ingenious oil spinner/damper on the shaft's nose and the counter-revolutionary reactions of cantilever-hung engine mountings. As for buzz, the density of the car keeps it in check until after 55. You've heard of people getting punctures in hydrolastic Minis and ruining the wheel because they didn't twig it? We have a better one. You can take the lead off a plug on the 600 and — power-droop apart — it won't show by feel.

We remember too, the way you have to leave the car standing overnight to let the block cool before checking the valve clearances, the subtle engineering touches like the marking of the individual torque settings on to the head of every bolt, the female studs used to hold down the aluminium cylinder head (so as it won't "freeze" against ordinary ones) and male studs — if you please — to keep on the wheels . . . they too being guided into position by little dowels. We remember the mark-

ing-up plate that helps one to get the spark timing spot-on, the high temperature warning on the dash (so very, very essential on a rear-engined, water-cooled type) and the carefully fashioned chock in the tool kit to hold the car when you jacked her.

It isn't all poetry. The ride is pitchy and the rear suspension is inclined to make takeover bids for the steering's job in over-ambitious corners. The rear system, a rudimentary synthesis of swing axle format, works adequately well on the 500—where the weight mass at the back is considerably less. On the 600 it is not quite so idiot-proof. Geometrically you get understeer. In practice it ultimately changes to oversteer.

The slow warm-up, particularly when running on the cheaper grades which the engine ordinarily relishes, is irksome and the 1,500 miles greasing interval is a bind. Special tools are required for most serious jobs and none should ever be undertaken on a Fiat without recourse to the Workshop Manual . . . which on the 600 costs 70/-.

Top marks again, for 38 mpg overall averages on cooking fuel, for first-class braking with bi-metal drums (cast-iron insets to handle the friction and slotted alloy drums to dissipate the heat quickly) and independent front/rear hydraulic lines.

Lesson. The obvious tendency for weight transfer to take place rear-to-front when a car is being halted can be propounded in terms of 60% front to 40% rear braking effect on a rear-engined fellow like the 600. On a front-engined rear-wheel driven (orthodox) car this widens to 70:30% and with a front-wheel-driver to 80:20%. Thus, on a rear-engined car — the condition being that it has sufficient weight mass over the front wheels to make them bite before transfer takes place — you *do* get superior stopping power.

Ferry Porsche planned the gearbox by the way, and even without synchromesh on first, the change is gorgeous.

No wonder they won't let it fade away. In spite of devaluation, pressure from its immediate protégée (850) and a relative absense of with-it glamour the 600 holds well to its Best Value title. After a painfully-slow sales start in Ireland, the assemblers pursued a low-cost spares policy and expanded upon a maker-backed service station at which all Fiat owners are made to feel welcome. These have earned their reward and the 600 has never looked back. ∎

FOR	AGAINST
● Best value	● Anti-burst door locks
● Economical	● Poor performance
● Comfortable	● Restricted boot
● Quiet and smooth	● Deflected by wind
● Easy to drive	● No synchromesh on 1st
● Excellent brakes	● Frequent servicing
● Maker-backed service	● Swing-axle influence

* Price estimated against DV effect. (Pre-DV stocks still available at £525.)
Two-door style only. No variants. (Assembled by Fiat (Ireland) Ltd.)

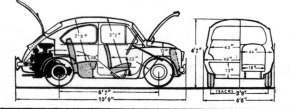

On our 1967 *test car the badge said "Idromatic", but the semi-automatic* 850 *is now called the "Idroconvert"*

FIAT 850 IDROCONVERT

AT A GLANCE: Semi-automatic adaptation of Fiat's top-selling 850. Four-speed gearbox not needed with torque converter multiplication and shift often jerky. Big performance loss and much heavier fuel consumption compared with normal 850. System expensive for a cheap car.

MANUFACTURER: Fiat S.p.A. Corso Marconi, Turin, Italy.
U.K. CONCESSIONAIRES: Fiat (England) Ltd., Northdale House, North Circular Road, London, NW10.

PRICES:

				£	s	d
Basic	..	..	..	453	10	0
Purchase tax (in GB)	..	..	105	12	11
Seat belts (front)	..	..	..	8	8	0
EXTRAS (inc. P.T.)						
Idroconvert semi-automatic						
transmission	..	..	..	73	15	0

LIKE Volkswagen, Fiat have for a long time neglected the trend towards automatic transmissions which has slowly been sweeping into Europe from the USA. Still the 2300 saloon is the only model in the vast range to be offered with the option of a fully automatic gearbox, in this case a Borg-Warner unit from England. Little cars, cheap and easy to drive with a minimum of mechanical complication, give reliable service and have been enough in demand without the enticement of an optional automatic. And, being (again like Volkswagen) committed to rear engine designs (for their smaller ranges at least), Fiat have not been able to buy an automatic box "off the shelf" like Ford or Rootes can, so there have been serious engineering restrictions on what could be installed.

Now, to keep up with the times, the simplest solution has been found by adopting a semi-automatic type of transmission made by Fiat in conjunction with Ferodo. It employs a perfectly standard four-speed synchromesh Fiat gearbox driving through a servo-operated clutch and a torque convertor. Initially the car was called the Idromatic (like the badges on our test car show) but it was later renamed Idroconvert in a fit of publicity conscience; *idro* is Italian for hydro (appertaining to hydraulics), of course.

In every aspect except the pedals, gearlever and driving technique, the Fiat 850 Idroconvert is a typical Fiat 850. There is no clutch pedal and the gearlever knob is bigger and chunkier than normal. Between the knob and the gearlever itself is an electric switch which triggers a solenoid to energize the vacuum servo for the clutch as soon as one tries to move the lever. With the car in gear and the lever left alone, the torque convertor acts as a fluid clutch and enables the car to be driven purely on the accelerator and brake.

Although the torque convertor has a magnification ratio of 2 to 1, each gear has a fixed range much the same as on the normal version. Probably because there is some slight slip and power loss in the torque convertor, even at maximum revs, we were not quite able to match the speeds that we obtained in each gear with an ordinary 850 in 1964. However, the semi-automatic car will pull away from rest even in top gear, and it is necessary to change down only for extra performance—not to prevent the engine juddering or stalling.

Gearchanges are simply a matter of lifting off the accelerator and moving the lever. On the Fiat the synchromesh is stiff, especially when cold, and this effects the precision with which one can release the knob and let the clutch take up. It is therefore all too easy to drive jerkily if one stirs the lever about to get acceleration; if one leaves it in third, say for town use, the step-off and pick-up are extremely leisurely.

Compared with the normal 850 there is quite a performance loss with the Idroconvert. From rest to 60 mph takes over 8 sec longer and top speed is down by 3 mph. More than just this there is a 20 per cent deterioration in fuel con-

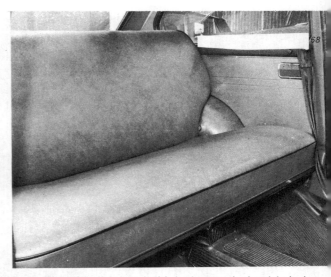

Above left: No clutch pedal and a wider than usual brake are the only clues inside the car. Above right: Upholstery is plain (and easy to clean) and the back seat lets down as a luggage platform.

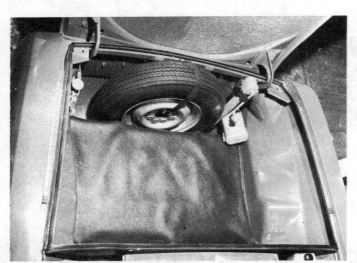
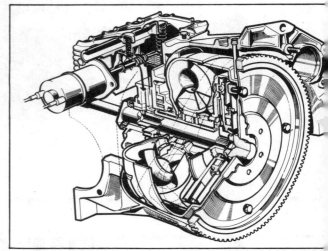

Above left: There is room for a big, square suitcase under the front lid. The battery is beneath the rubber mat in a well. Above right: The hydraulic torque converter forms a neat sandwich between the engine and gearbox, with the mechanical clutch and starter ring almost in their normal positions

PERFORMANCE DATA

Figures in brackets are for the Fiat 850 tested in AUTOCAR of 20 November 1964
Acceleration times (mean): Speed range, gear ratios and time in seconds:

mph	Top		3rd		2nd		1st	
	(4.45-9.90)	(4.45)	**(13.04-6.52)**	(6.52)	**(19.0-9.50)**	(9.50)	**(33.6-16.8)**	(16.8)
10-30	**11.9**	(17.4)	**9.6**	(9.8)	**7.0**	(6.1)	—	
20-40	**15.2**	(17.2)	**10.8**	(9.5)	—	(6.9)	—	
30-50	**20.1**	(17.8)	**14.0**	(10.3)	—		—	
40-60	**25.9**	(22.7)	—	(15.2)	—		—	
50-70	—	(34.5)	—		—		—	

FROM REST THROUGH GEARS TO:

30 mph	. . . .	**7.9 sec** (6.6 sec)
40 mph	. . . .	**13.7 sec** (10.2 sec)
50 mph	. . . .	**20.6 sec** (17.0 sec)
60 mph	. . . .	**35.0 sec** (26.8 sec)
70 mph	. . . .	— (54.9 sec)

Standing quarter-mile 24.2 sec (22.9 sec)

MAXIMUM SPEEDS IN GEARS:

	mph	kph
Top (mean)	**73** (76)	**118** (122)
(best)	**75** (78)	**120** (126)
3rd	**58** (61)	**93** (98)
2nd	**41** (42)	**66** (68)
1st	**22** (24)	**35** (38)

OVERALL FUEL CONSUMPTION FOR 782 miles: 28.2 mpg;
10.0 litres/100km (35.5 mpg; 8.0 litres/100km)

sumption; and over 782 miles with two different examples we could not achieve even 30 mpg. The normal 850 is good for over 35 mpg with 40 mpg within reach on journeys.

It is now over three years since we drove the 850 saloon, so this test gave us a chance to get up to date on the model. It seems a basic car by British standards with plain plastic trim, screwed-down rubber mats and not a great deal of room inside. These economies and the production rate in Italy of 1,000 per day explain how it can be sold here for £20 less than a Mini Super de luxe. In the Common Market where all trading tariffs disappear next year, the 850 is a very cheap car. Yet the semi-automatic option represents 13.4 per cent of the basic price and is a very expensive extra at £74 tax and duty paid.

To those of us conditioned to using a clutch, it seems to be an awkward and not very satisfactory half-way stage to fully automatic control. For someone with a gammy left leg or for a very non-adept learner, it could be the only way to go small car motoring. One of our testers thought it might suit a busy Mum, the kind who regularly gets herself into the wrong gear and never remembers to push the clutch out when she stops. Keen drivers are unlikely to become "Idro" converts, though, and the system can never be much more than a compromise. □

GORDON CHITTENDEN PHOTOS

FIAT 850 SPIDER

As soundly built as it is beautiful

WE TESTED the Fiat 850 Coupé when it first arrived in the U.S.; when the mechanically identical Spider later became available in this country we felt that the performance would be so similar that a further test would be unnecessary. Readers, however, repeatedly requested a

separate evaluation and the Associate Editor's experience with his own 1967 Spider convinced us that the car was markedly different in character if not in actual performance. We waited for a 1968 model, almost unchanged except for the simplest reaction to exhaust emission standards possible:

FIAT 850 SPIDER
AT A GLANCE

Price as tested. $2376
Engine. . . . . .4-cyl, ohv, 817 cc, 52 bhp
Curb weight, lb 1640
Top speed, mph. 84
Acceleration, 0–¼ mi, sec. 21.7
Average fuel consumption, mpg 32.5
Summary: attractive, nicely-finished small-engined sports car . . . good handling, moderate performance . . . low price.

FIAT 850 SPIDER

a reduction in displacement from 843 to 817 cc, just below the 50-cu in. lower limit for engines requiring smog devices. The engine still has the crankcase recirculation system acceptable last year for controlling crankcase emission.

If, as we said, the Coupé was one of the handsomest designs ever seen on a small car, the Spider is certainly the most beautiful. Its carefully fashioned Bertone lines were admired by everyone who saw the car, and more than one owner of a small-displacement British roadster cast covetous eyes upon it. The lovely body is matched by a good-looking and comfortable interior, with black vinyl throughout, a full set of properly round instruments, and simulated wood on the dashboard. The top is of excellent design, easy to raise and lower and nicely hidden by a flush body panel when down. Fit is extremely good and no drumming or flapping was experienced. The heater is capable of toasting occupants when required; it is even possible to make comfortable runs on chilly California nights with the top down. New for 1968 are a pair of sun visors, sorely missed on earlier Spiders, and an optional semi-integral hardtop, which ingeniously replaces the body panel behind the cockpit. So far available only with a new car, the hardtop adds $260 to the price. At the rear, bumper guards and a back-up light have been added this year.

Beyond esthetics, and of course the fact that the Spider is simply a 2-seater while the Coupé is (almost) a 2+2, the major difference between the two is that the Spider is about 3.5 in. lower throughout—top, hood, steering wheel, seats— bringing about a noticeable improvement in both subjective and actual handling characteristics. Although the Coupé's adhesion is good, body lean in hard cornering is apparent to driver and passengers; in contrast, the Spider goes through the same corners flat. Our test car had optional Rader wheels, which increased the track by 1.5 in. and lowered the roll center a minute amount but not enough to be appreciated by the average driver, even in fairly hard cornering.

Since the rims are no wider, the Rader wheels are essentially an appearance accessory for those who want the Chaparral look badly enough to pay $195 extra. We prefer the stock wheels (wide-rim conversions will shortly be another option).

The Spider is about 7 in. longer than the Coupé (all in front) and 50 lb heavier. Because the spare tire is carried horizontally, almost as much luggage space is available; a slight advantage of the long nose is that the weight distribution is not quite as biased toward the rear. Fiat claims the same power output for the 817-cc unit as before (the only change seems to be a decrease in bore from 65 to 63.9 mm) but our test figures would suggest that a horse or two has been lost. In fairness, the test car had barely 1000 miles on it and we limited engine speed to the 6200-rpm redline in the acceleration runs (we went to 6500 in the Coupé). The Associate Editor's 843-cc Spider, with 10,000 miles on the odometer, was run the same day for comparison and reached the ¼-mi mark in about a second less time. The engine will definitely perform better after it is fully broken in. The redline also limits the top speed to 84 mph but with the Spider's better penetration, anyone willing to use 6700 rpm could reach 90 mph. As we said in the previous test, 7000 rpm occasionally (and briefly) won't bother the engine. On the other hand, all-day cruising above 5000 rpm (68 mph) will probably shorten engine life—not a strong point anyway. At 4000 rpm, the engine note is loud, but not unpleasant. Fuel consumption was never worse than 30 mpg, including our speed runs, with a best of 35 mpg on one tank.

Priced $100-250 less than the Mark Three versions of the MG Midget and Triumph Spitfire, the Fiat 850 Spider offers excellent value in terms of esthetics, finish, detail design, ride and handling, but its performance (and probably longevity) suffers in comparison to that offered by its 1300-cc, 65/75-bhp competitors. With suspension geometry that keeps its tail heaviness well in check, the Fiat can be flung about enthusiastically, giving an exceedingly high fun-per-dollar quotient. As soundly built as it is beautiful, the Spider gives every indication of maintaining its appeal over a long period of time. If Fiat can import enough Spiders to meet the demand already created by the car's seductive appearance, the highways will be dotted with them. ⊗

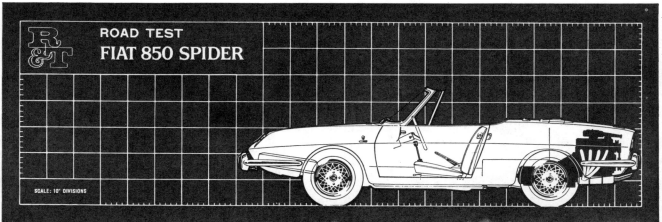

ROAD TEST
FIAT 850 SPIDER

SCALE: 10" DIVISIONS

PRICE
Basic list.................$2109
As tested.................$2376

ENGINE
Type............4 cyl inline, ohv
Bore x stroke, mm....63.9 x 63.5
 Equivalent in.......2.52 x 2.50
Displacement, cc/cu in...817/49.9
Compression ratio..........9.3:1
Bhp @ rpm...........52 @ 6200
 Equivalent mph............84
Torque @ rpm, lb-ft..45.6 @ 4000
 Equivalent mph............54
Carburetion...... 1 Weber 30DIC1
Type fuel required......premium

DRIVE TRAIN
Clutch diameter, in..........7.2
Gear ratios: 4th (0.96).....4.68:1
 3rd (1.41)............6.88:1
 2nd (2.06)..........10.03:1
 1st (3.64)...........17.75:1
Synchromesh..........on all 4
Final drive ratio..........4.88:1

CHASSIS & BODY
Body/frame................unit
Brakes: 8.9-in. disc front; 7.2 x
 1.18-in. drum rear
 Swept area, sq in.........205
Wheel type & size, in....4½ J x 13
Tires....Pirelli Sempione 5.50-13
Steering type.....worm & sector
 Overall ratio............13.0:1
 Turns, lock-to-lock......3.5
 Turning circle, ft..........31.5
Front suspension: unequal A-arms,
 transverse leaf spring, tube
 shocks, anti-roll bar
Rear suspension: semi-trailing
 arms, coil springs, tube shocks,
 anti-roll bar

OPTIONAL EQUIPMENT
Included in "as tested" price:
 seat belts, outside mirror, Rader
 wheels
Other: radio, detachable hardtop,
 chromed disc wheels with wide
 rims

ACCOMMODATION
Seating capacity, persons........2
Seat width..............2 x 18.0
Head room...............40.0
Seat back adjustment, deg......0
Driver comfort rating (scale of 100):
 Driver 69 in. tall............85
 Driver 72 in. tall...........75
 Driver 75 in. tall...........70

INSTRUMENTATION
Instruments: 100-mph speedometer, 8000-rpm tachometer, 99,999
 odometer, 999.9 trip odometer,
 water temperature, oil pressure,
 fuel level
Warning lights: high beam, parking
 lights, directionals, fuel level, oil
 pressure, ignition, generator
 charge

MAINTENANCE
Engine oil capacity, qt........3.5
 Change interval, mi........6000
Filter cleaning interval, mi..12,000
Chassis lube interval, mi.....1500
Tire pressures, psi.16 front/26 rear

MISCELLANEOUS
Body styles available: roadster as
 tested, coupe
Warranty period, mo/mi.12/12,000

GENERAL
Curb weight, lb.............1640
Test weight.................1965
Weight distribution (with
 driver), front/rear, %....40/60
Wheelbase, in...............79.8
Track, front/rear......47.1/49.2
Overall length.............148.9
 Width.....................59.0
 Height....................48.0
Frontal area, sq ft..........15.7
Ground clearance, in.........5.3
Overhang, front/rear....35.1/34.0
Usable trunk space, cu ft.....3.6
Fuel tank capacity, gal.......7.9

CALCULATED DATA
Lb/hp (test wt)..............37.7
Mph/1000 rpm (4th gear)....13.6
Engine revs/mi (60 mph)....4425
Piston travel, ft/mi.........1845
Rpm @ 2500 ft/min........6000
 Equivalent mph...........82
Cu ft/ton mi................65.0
R&T wear index...............82
Brake swept area sq in/ton....209

ROAD TEST RESULTS

ACCELERATION
Time to distance, sec:
 0-100 ft....................4.7
 0-250 ft....................7.7
 0-500 ft...................11.7
 0-750 ft...................15.2
 0-1000 ft..................18.3
 0-1320 ft (¼ mi)..........21.7
Speed at end of ¼ mi, mph....62
Time to speed, sec:
 0-30 mph....................5.7
 0-40 mph....................8.8
 0-50 mph...................13.2
 0-60 mph...................20.0
 0-70 mph...................31.4
 0-80 mph...................46.7
Passing exposure time, sec:
 To pass car going 50 mph....9.5

FUEL CONSUMPTION
Normal driving, mpg.......30-35
Cruising range, mi.......235-275

SPEEDS IN GEARS
4th gear (6200 rpm), mph......84
 3rd (6200)................58
 2nd (6200)................40
 1st (6200)................23

BRAKES
Panic stop from 80 mph:
 Deceleration, % g..........72
 Control.................good
Fade test: percent of increase in
 pedal effort required to maintain
 50%-g deceleration rate in six
 stops from 60 mph.........25
Parking brake: hold 30% grade.yes
Overall brake rating........good

SPEEDOMETER ERROR
30 mph indicated......actual 28.0
40 mph...................37.5
60 mph...................57.5

ACCELERATION & COASTING

Legend:
— Time to distance
-·- Time to speed
--- Coasting

Speed, mph (vertical axis)
Distance, ft (right vertical axis)
Elapsed time in sec (horizontal axis)

Another beauty queen from Italy

FIAT 850

There is no question that some of the finest examples of automotive styling are the work of the Italian coachbuilders. Until very recently, however, it would appear that Fiat and those artisans were not on speaking terms. This is all changed now with the introduction last year of the 850 coupe and the 850 Spider.

Only recently produced in sufficient quantity for testing the 850 Spider is the prime subject for this report although the coupe has also been driven extensively by our ROAD TESTers.

Priced at $2110 for the Spider and $1916 West Coast P.O.E. for the coupe these cars are definitely in the category of economy cars as to initial outlay, and with fuel consumption in the 26 to 29 mpg range, operating economy goes without saying.

Presented as sports cars they have reasonably brisk performance for such small engine displacement, easily outdistancing many of their com-

petitors in getting off the line and at the top end.

Interior appointments are well laid out with driver and passenger comfort in mind. There is minimal luggage space in the Spider and the back seat of the Coupe is best thought of as a luggage and parcel shelf and forget about its use for passengers unless they be midgets or small children.

Careful inspection of workmanship on both cars failed to turn up evidence of careless assembly, painting or detailing.

That the cars have buyer appeal is evident in the demand for the product. Dealers are hard pressed to keep enough vehicles in stock to offer customers a choice of colors. In Southern California there is a waiting list for the Spider and only barely can the factory keep up with orders for the coupe.

The Fiat 850 in either the Spider or coupe configuration has a lot going for it, smart styling, sports car performance (small sports car, true) and economy. Anyone in the market for

a small sports car with appeal would do well to look closely at these new offerings from Italy.

STYLING

With body by Bertone it is hard to fault the lines of the Fiat 850 Spider. Sleek and simple seem the terms best suited for description. There is nothing gimmicky, no unnecessary chrome, in fact what chrome there is consists mainly of bumpers fore and aft which offer little in the way of protection against those who park by ear.

Sports cars, in recent years, have managed to avoid the ghastly appearance they formerly presented with the top up. The 850 Spider has followed this trend presenting a smartly styled appearance with either the soft or optional hard top in position.

The quarter windows, while offering a modicum of wind protection, detract slightly from the otherwise clean balance about the cockpit.

The fine appearance of the exterior is carried on inside with beautifully crafted seats in handsome vinyl that would be a credit in a much more expensive machine. The one touch that seems out of place is the panelling on the dash. Satin finish anodized aluminum or just more of the vinyl would be more in keeping with today's design.

Styling of the coupe is also of a high degree of excellence. The lines again are simple and elegant with the fastback treatment one of the handsomest we've seen.

POWER and PERFORMANCE

Responsive, willing and nimble are easy terms to apply to the 850 power plant because they all fit. The 54 hp (52 in the coupe) are coupled to one of the smoothest of gearboxes, a unit impossible to beat even with snap shifts. The two extra horses in the Spider come from slightly hotter valve timing.

The in-line four cylinder overhead valve engine has a compression ratio of 9.3:1 necessitating the use of premium fuel. Bore and stroke are slightly oversquare at 65 × 63.5 mm. The three bearing crank runs in hardened journals.

An interesting engine feature is the sealed cooling system which employs a combination of anti-freeze, water and rust preventive for year round protection. There is a provision for adding water in case of a leak in the system. However, when the leak has been repaired it is important that the recommended coolant mixture be replaced.

The torque rating is 45.6 foot/pounds at 4,000 rpm, which, incidentally is the proper engine speed area for best performance. There seems to be a gear missing when climbing our favorite mountain road. Second results in excessive engine speed and there just isn't enough pull in third. However, the power plant seems not to mind a bit of high revving now and then.

Front suspension is independent with transverse mounted leaf spring and hydraulic, telescopic, double acting shocks and stabilizer bar. At the

With true sports car suspension the 850 is a thoroughbred in tight corners.

Husky discs with a powerful caliper set-up do an admirable job of halting either of the 850's quickly and in a straight line. Light wheel and tire assembly permit easy replacement even without a locating stud.

rear, also independent, there are coils, similar shocks on swinging arms and another stabilizing bar.

Wheelbase of the 850, both the Spider and the coupe, is 79". Both employ unitized body and frame construction resulting in a pleasantly rattle free package.

Getting off the line in the ¼ mile acceleration runs the Spider turned in a best e.t. of 20.03 and a trap speed of 65.64. We estimate the milder state of tune for the coupe would naturally result in a slightly lower speed. The passing time from 50 to 70 required both third and fourth gears and a hair over 15 seconds.

The warranty is the conventional 12 month, 12,000 mile type and to date we have received no complaints from owners as to service problems.

HANDLING and ROADABILITY

With proper attention to recommended tire pressures the road manners of either of the 850's as sports cars or as touring machines cannot be faulted. With the weight bias 60% to the rear it is important that the rear tires carry about 10 lbs more air than those in front for best cornering. In either coupe or roadster form the Fiat 850 can be hurled into corners with zest since great effort has gone into the elimination of the oversteer often found in rear engine cars. Under most driving conditions there is moderate understeer and even in the hardest cornering attitudes this becomes neutral. There is no feel of body lean under the severest of stresses.

At freeway speeds one is aware of surface imperfections in highways but this is a characteristic of all sports car suspensions and a sacrifice one is happy to make for the excellent adhesion.

Steering is quick at 3.5 turns, lock to lock and only light effort is required.

The engine is a high revving unit showing 4800 rpm at 65 mph indicated. But while the little horses are working hard they are willing to take on more with 7000 producing no feel of valve float or other bothers.

Shifting is quick and positive, which is very good, you'll use the shift lever a lot when traffic bogs down.

BRAKES and SAFETY

In keeping with the 'all new' Fiat 850 Coupe and Spider there are new binders up front to eliminate the complaint against earlier models of insufficient brakes. The presently employed discs do an excellent job, stopping the car repeatedly with no sign of fade or pulling. Conventional drums are used at the rear.

The unit body construction lends to rigidity and strength as well as to rattle free comfort.

On the minus side we find the pedal position quite close for all but the small footed driver and the window crank at five turns up or down is distracting.

The spare tire is mounted at the front ahead of the steering column which adds to the safety inherent in the double U-joints in the column itself.

Where the muscles for the 'mighty mite' live. They move the 850 at a brisk pace without complaint.

Trunk space in the 850's is minimal but there's always the back seat of the coupe and there's space behind the front seat in the Spider.

Seat belt installation is good but the retractors should be discarded immediately. The groping for the retracted belt may cause too many a lazy motorist to say, "to hell with it."

The front seat backs in the coupe have a locking device to prevent their flopping forward on hard decleration.

Four way flashers are standard equipment.

Padding on the dash is at a minimum and combined with the veneer panelling presents an unnecessary hazard.

The wide base rim wheels with 5.50 × 13 tires are felt to be an added safety plus by adding stability.

COMFORT and CONVENIENCE

The first and probably most important comfort feature of the Fiat 850 is the excellent design of the seats. Well engineered, they are deeply padded and give good lateral support.

The rear seat in the coupe might be comfortable for very small chil- dren but there is not enough head- room for an adult of even the short- est stature. Consider this seat a convenience feature for carrying extra luggage.

The instrument package in the Spider is complete with large, easily read speedo and tach. Off slightly to the left are the temperature and amp- meter gauges. The fuel level gauge is centered between speedo and tach and boasts a warning light as well.

Instruments on the coupe are more spartan with only the fuel gauge and the speedometer and the tach. How- ever, both cars feature a resettable trip odometer.

Visibility in the Spider with top up is quite good for a sports car al- though there is the usual rear-quarter blind spot. Viewing from the coupe is superb with great quantities of glass in all directions.

The engine warms quickly on cold mornings with the manual choke needed for only a few moments. This, of course has a helpful effect in get- ting the heating system in operation quickly. Good ventilation is provided

through two ducts at the top of the dash which can be swivelled to act as windshield demisters or defrosters. Ducting of heat can be directed either at the passenger's or driver's feet or both.

While there is no glove box a parcel shelf under the dash provides for a few items. Map pockets in the doors take care of a few more.

Luggage space in the front com- partment is rather small at 4.3 cu. ft. but in the Spider there is additional room behind the seats. In the coupe one has the entire rear seat unless transporting children.

There is no adjustment in seat back position in either car which is un- fortunate. On a long trip variation in seating can be quite restful.

As with most other rear engine cars, especially those of light weight, there is definite wander in cross winds, however, when one learns not to fight it there is no difficulty in keep- ing the car in a straight line.

A thoughtful touch, a convenient rest for the driver's left foot is placed just where it's needed.

Roof line of the Fiat 850 coupe permits easy entry and exit.
Sleek lines at the rear hide the engine room.

CONCLUSION

For the sports car buyer with a limited budget we believe the Fiat 850, either Spider or coupe merits more than a passing glance.

For a modest price he is offered a high degree of styling and neck twisting individuality coupled to brisk performance, handling and roadability in a package that won't bankrupt him at the gas pumps.

In addition to its other qualities the Fiat 850 is a carefully constructed machine with extra care taken in assembly, finish and detail.

Should the owner choose to go racing he will find himself in the Sprite category, H production, and there are enough options allowed to make an already going machine even more competitive on a modest budget.

There is evidence of careful attention to the comfort of the driver and his passenger as well as his safety.

At the price, both in initial outlay and in upkeep it appears to us worth even more than the budget price. ♠

With top erected the Spider becomes a cozy and snug package, secure against the elements.

Full instrumentation tells the 850 Spider driver things he needs to know. The coupe is a bit more spartan.

Push button and recessed pull make for as smooth a door line as possible. Push button contains lock.

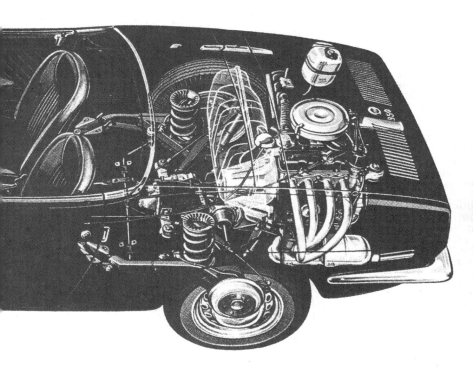

Fiat 850 jack is one of the easiest to use. A wider base is essential when lifting from soft ground or warm asphalt. The plastic 'knock offs' are ornamental not functional.

...A TOUCH OF THE EXOTIC

To be available shortly in this country, a range of sports cars that will have every enthusiast in raptures.

A YOUNG Italian automobile couturier is fast joining the ranks of the almost revered Turin designers. His name is Francis Lombardi, a former aircraft designer now turning his talents to exotic sports cars.

Lombardi created the sleek body for the Abarth Scorpion. Based on the Fiat 124 chassis, the design was so successful it has now been adapted to suit the smaller 850 chassis.

Known as the Lombardi Grand Prix Fiat 850 the cars are being imported by the Formula I organisation of Sydney and will be distributed by North Shore Fiat dealer John Caskey.

We saw our first Lombardi at Caskey's showroom. It's one of those cars that grabs you at first sight, an exotic piece of Latin femininity to be gazed at, but not touched. Such is the regal aura that surrounds this machine.

Lombardi's body has been designed to bolt straight on to the existing 850 chassis. No changes have been made to the base and the unit runs standard 850 running gear and suspension. The body is all metal except for a fibreglass panel at the rear, which can be completely removed for access to the power plant. The whole car is only 11 ft 8 in. long, but because of its aerodynamic lines and roof height of 3 ft 6 in. it looks bigger than it really is.

Even the interior gives the impression of space, yet you still have the feeling of being part of the car, as if it's an extension of your own body. It's the same feeling you get in a well designed racing car. As someone remarked, "you wear it like a glove".

Lombardi has used his aircraft tendencies in the design of the instrument panel. All the gauges, which include an electronic tach, speedometer, calibrated to 110 mph, temp and fuel, are housed in a centre console angled toward the driver. This is extended to the floor and joins another console which houses the short gear lever and handbrake. The standard 850 pedals are retained, but Lombardi has added a 10 in. padded racing style wheel with his emblem on the centre boss. The well padded seats could have come straight out of a Grand Prix open wheeler and provide an excellent lay-back full arm position.

Luggage space is at a minimum, the car has no boot as such. The front compartment is taken up by the fuel tank and spare wheel, while the engine takes care of any space at the rear. However, there is some space behind the seats, but only, and we mean only, for funny shaped soft overnight bags.

Make no mistake about it, the Lombardi Fiat is an enthusiast's car, one that will be rarely seen, except on days without the slightest hint of a cloud in the sky. The Lombardi is purely a status symbol and certainly beats the old line of "Come up and see my etchings". The bachelor with a Lombardi will need a stick to fight the lovelies back.

As well as the 850 based car, the importers

Looking as if it has come straight out of the Turin motor show the Lombardi Fiat sits regally on showroom floor of Fiat dealer John Caskey.

The body is all metal except for a fibreglass panel at the rear. This can be completely removed for access to the rear mounted engine.

have plans to bring in some more exciting Lombardi designed machines. One will be a fuel-injected 903 cc version. Modified by Giannini, one of Italy's oldest engine builders, it will produce 80 bhp and have a top speed of 112 mph. Also there will be a 1000 cc twin overhead cam version developing 116 bhp at 6800 rpm. This will come as a road going car but there will be a racing version with modified suspension and disc brakes all round. Price will be around $5000, which puts them in the same class as the Lotus SE and, while the 850 version sells for $4000, there could be some prospective Lotus buyers taking a hard look at Mr Lombardi's Fiats. #

FIAT 850 COUPE/SPIDER

$1,997/2,178 West Coast P.O.E.

Two of the most delightful little cars available. A buzzy, 843 cc four-banger winds up tight to propel them at preposterous speeds, while excellent suspension allows them to maintain such velocity over any kind of roadway. At $1,900 for the Coupe and $2,100 for the Spider, they represent the greatest fun-per-dollar bargain to be found in the automotive marketplace. Manufactured by Fiat Motor Co., Torino, Italy.

Getting tired of puttering around in that staid ol' VW? Want something that handles, goes like a bomb and has that Italian flair for styling? Should your answer be in the affirmative, why not drop by your friendly Fiat dealer and check out his little 850.

For those who have never seriously considered looking at this pert performer, whether it be the coupe or roadster version, let alone drive one, they're in for a rather pleasant surprise. For what on the surface appears to be a tiny, skitterish pop-gun is anything but a joke.

Make no mistake, the Fiat 850 is as Italian as Sophia Loren, and nearly as curvy. It has been designed and executed with the normal male Italian in mind, which should give you an inkling of what the Fiat 850 is all about. Let's face it, the normal Italian likes to stand on it, under road conditions wholly unlike anything found in the U.S. Thusly, the new 850 coupe and Spider reflect the rationale of the country.

Raw speed and power the Fiat 850 has not, but lithe quickness and fine road holding qualities it has. Figure it out, Italians drive like every day is his last on earth. Therefore a situation close to that of 'survival of the fittest' occurs which makes it necessary for any Italian car manufacturer to build a great amount of agility into his cars. He has to or there won't be many repeat customers.

Engines are small in Italy because taxes on large displacement power plants are high. For example, an owner of a Fiat might pay only a few dollars in taxes on his mighty mouse, whereas the owner of a multi-liter Maserati would find himself coughing up a great deal more. So if the idea of a small-high-revving engine bothers you, think of what those taxes in Italy must do to those would be Nuvolaris. Consequently, Italian automobile builders go to great ex-

tremes to develop high powered, low inch engines. It is no wonder then, that the Fiat 850 is a typical product of this type of thinking. Displacing only 51.5 cubic-inches (843cc), the little screamer is capable of churning out a whopping 52 horsepower, something around a horse a cube, at 6200 rpm.

Another amazing aspect concerning the Fiat 850, especially, when one considers the Fiat's healthy power and dependability, is the fact that this little rascal is manufactured in a rather conventional manner. The aim here is not great precision and hand fitting, but rather a great reduction of unit cost through mass production. The crankshaft in the water-cooled engine is supported on five main bearings. The valves are actuated by the normal ohv system of tappets, pushrods and rocker arms. Handling the carburetion is the ever present Weber unit, of 1.18 inches in diameter feeding premium fuel into

The seats in the little Fiat sportsters are as good as those fitted in many really expensive sports cars. Deep, contoured and with built-in headrest.

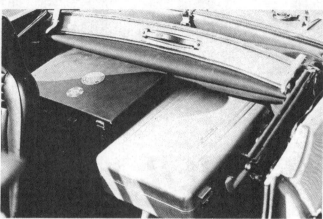

There is room in the soft top Fiat for stowing small items of luggage behind the seats.

Safety dash is padded, switches are recessed and the speedo and tach stare the driver right in the face.

the somewhat high compressioned (9.3:1) four-banger. Torque figures indicate a healthy 45.6 lb/ft at a modest 4000 rpm.

As we said, the Italians *use* their means of motored mania. A peek at the drive line tells it like it is. Starting off with an effective final drive ratio of 4.68:1, the little hummer can really smoke those itty-bitty (5.50 x 13) tires. When you figure that the gearing allows only 13.5 mph at 1000 rpm, by the time you reach the magic 60 mph barrier the Fiat's mill is spinning somewhere in the neighborhood of 4500 revs — it's easy to tell, your eardrums will let you know. Torque multiplication is handled by a four-speed gearbox housing fully synchromeshed gears of 3.64, 2.06, 1.41 and 0.96:1. These ratios will generate top speeds (using 6500 rpm as a guide) of 23, 41, 61, and 88 mph. Obviously the drivers of this high-winding wagon must be inured from the sounds generated by all that tight winding behind him and continue to wham away at the shifter. The harder

one whams the quicker one goes.

Being that the Fiat 850 and its blood relative, the 850 Spider, are what might be termed as Italy's latest form of the automotive art, built for a penny-watching public, when they arrive on our shores, fully taxed, licensed and marked-up, you can expect to plunk out not much more than $1900. For those who like the sportier roadster-bodied Spider, add $200 to your loan policy. It's a bargain any way you look at it, especially if you've got a little of that Latin blood coupled with a liking of banging through the box.

Although having only been imported to the U.S. for the past year or so, the Fiat has has enjoyed great success in Europe, due to its sporty looks, snappy performance and low operating costs. Exterior wise, the 850 coupe features some new body work front and rear, a more pronounced peaked line along the side of the car, dual head and tail lights and the rear quarter window has been placed at a slightly different angle.

Like so many other foreign automotive products, the Fiat 850 and its roadster-bodied brother, the Spider, feature monococque body construction which provides an amazingly rigid and stable platform to hang a fully independent suspension on.

Basic wheelbase lengths for both cars are the same (79.8 inches) as well as the same track (46.6 inches front, 47.7 inches rear). The coupe's overall length is 142 inches, the Spider, due to its greater overhang, is a few inches longer. As for weight, the Fiat 850 coupe tips the scale at a light 1600 lbs., unladen, while the Spider is even a more slender 1500 lbs.

Front suspension consists of an A-arm on top and a transverse leaf along the bottom. Wide-based diagonal trailing arms, on the rear suspension, give the swing axles a very positive location. Although coil springs and telescopic shock absorbers are used, only the front receives the services of an anti-roll stabilizer.

Happily, the earlier Fiat's prob-

It may be tiny but this 850cc engine produces 52bhp and propels the little car at almost 85mph.

Perfectly in proportion, the coupe looks great from any angle. This is the rear-end treatment for 1969.

lems with under braking have been licked with the use of a disc front/drum rear arrangement. Unfortunately, the pointy-shoed Italian fashions have made the pedal size and location rather snug for the 'clod-hopping' footed Americans.

A word to the wise concerns tire pressure. If your driving experience in a Fiat 850 or a Spider is to be a pleasurable one, always keep 10 psi more air pressure in the rear tires. This will allow the Fiat to develop an under, to neutral-steer even though there is a 60% rearward bias. The lack of body lean and horsepower gives this little demon the ability to bang through the bends without getting into the metal mashing stages.

The Italians use the Fiat 850 as a family car despite its petite proportions. The back seat can be used for an auxiliary luggage compartment, and is large enough to accommodate a family if the children are small and possess flexible natures. On the other hand, if you plan to carry more than two of adult size, forget it!

The front seats are another story. Even for a good-sized adult they are very comfortable and have enough shape and padding to prevent over-tiring on long trips. Probably the biggest reason for all this comfort is

the fantastic leg room. A nice little extra feature is a locking device to prevent the seats from moving forward in the event of a panic stop. And for you GP drivers, the steering wheel is positioned in relation to the dash, so you can assume your proper arms-out driving style. Headrests are also included as standard equipment.

Your maps, booze or cigarettes can be placed in a shelf under the dash or in various pockets inside the door panels, although trunk capacity is a slim 4.3 cubic-feet. Many carry extra luggage behind the front seat. Hopefully the people at Fiat will reactivate that fold-down backseat of its predecessor Fiat 600 as a way of providing additional luggage space.

When it comes to gauges, the coupe is a little in need. Only a fuel gauge, tachometer and speedometer are provided. On the other hand, the Spider offers a large tach and speedo, flanked with a small temp, ammeter and fuel gauge. Two adjustable nozzles, on top of the dash, provide interior ventilation and can be swiveled around to ct as defrosters during cold or rainy weather.

Well there you have it. For less than two thousand bucks you can buy yourself a happy bundle of fun, fancy and frugality fittingly found in a Fiat. ♠

Fiat 850 Coupe
Data in Brief
DIMENSIONS

Overall length (in.)	140.75
Width (in.)	56.10
Height (in.)	54.5
Wheelbase (in.)	79.8
Turning diameter (ft.)	29.2

WEIGHT, TIRES, BRAKES

Weight (lbs.)	1437
Tires	5.50 x 12
Brakes, front & rear	drum

ENGINE

Type	4 cylinder
Displacement (cu. in.)	49.86
Horsepower	42

SUSPENSION

Front	leaf spring
Rear	coil spring

Fiat 850 Spider
DIMENSIONS

Overall length (in.)	148.0
Width (in.)	59.0
Height (in.)	48.0
Wheelbase (in.)	79.0
Fuel tank capacity (gal.)	7.92

WEIGHT, TIRES, BRAKES

Weight (lbs.)	1598
Tires	5.50 x 13
Brakes, front	disc
Brakes, rear	drum

ENGINE

Type	4 cylinder
Displacement (cu. in.)	51.4
Horsepower	54.0

SUSPENSION

Front	leaf spring
Rear	coil spring

2 CAR TEST

FIAT 850 SPECIAL
SUNBEAM IMP SPORT

In spite of the growing number of front-engine, front-wheel-drive small saloons, there are still adherents to the other-way-round school. Here we try two leading under-1-litre rear-engined contenders in the slightly-warmed-up "mini" class—the Fiat 850 Special from Italy (£694) and our own Sunbeam Imp Sport (£733). Changing the Fiat's tyre equipment from its standard cross-plies (as tested) to radials partially closes the gap in price.

Description—Fiat 850 Special

Introduced in the spring of 1964 the basic 850 model bridged the gap between the 600 and the 1100. The car broke little new ground technically, but provided a step-up for the person requiring a car slightly better than the 600. When the coupé, styled by Fiat, and the Spider, styled by Bertone, were introduced, they proved an immediate success and these sporting cars were given an increase in engine size from 843 to 903 c.c.

This rather left the former 843 c.c. engine in a void, so Fiat wasted no time in introducing the 850 Special, which at the time was referred to as the 'Italian Mini-Cooper'.

The tag was attached because, although still having the 843 c.c. power unit, with a compression ratio of 9.3-to-1 and a twin-choke Weber carburettor linked to some impressive manifolding both in and out, the unit developed 47 bhp net at 6,400 rpm, some 10 bhp more than the old standard unit.

To accommodate this extra power, several other changes were made, mainly confined to the chassis parts. The wheel sizes were upped by 1in. to 13in. diameter, the front suspension was revised to give greater wheel movement and an anti-roll bar was fitted. Disc brakes were added to the front, and minor improvements made to the internal and external appearance.

The resulting package was an attractive car with a sporting nature, whose engine could be screamed up to 7,000 rpm when needed, yet still potter along at 20 mph or so in top gear. The torque curve is rather peaky with a maximum at 3,600 rpm, and the engine thrives best with plenty of revs but still gives the feeling of being 'unburstable'.

This tends to lead to the car being driven flat-out most of the time, which depresses the fuel consumption somewhat but does not cause any oil to be used.

All the forward gears have synchromesh, with the long, remote linkage from the rear engine position working positively at all times. Brakes are always very definite, with a sensitive feel through the pedal; no servo is fitted.

Loaded weight as tested is 17.9 cwt and overall top gear ratio is 13.7 mph per 1000 rpm (this is with the 'overdrive' top gear ratio of 0.96), on the 145-13 Sempione cross ply tyres. Length of the car is 11ft 8.5in. and width is 4ft 8in.

Description—Sunbeam Imp Sport

The Imp as such, first came on the scene about six year's ago. Its rear engine layout and compact dimensions implied some obvious sporting possibilities although Rootes were not very concerned about this at first. However,

The wide angle lens used for this photograph gives a false impression of the relative size of each contender; there is little to choose between them in this respect

their competition department were very busy behind the scenes and in 1965 produced the Tulip Rally winning Rallye Imp powered by a 998 c.c. engine.

With the introduction of the Sunbeam Imp Sport, however, the 875 c.c. engine was retained, although in a very different form from the standard version. Briefly the differences consisted of new pistons, a new cylinder head with more metal around the ports, larger valves and a different camshaft. Twin Stromberg 125CD carburettors were fitted and a free-flow exhaust system incorporated a straight-through silencer. Further modifications to the cooling system were incorporated and an oil cooler was added, which gave a further touch to the sporting image.

The work on the engine put the power output from the standard car's 39 bhp at 5,000 rpm up to 51 bhp net at 6,100 rpm. The torque figure remained unchanged but the new camshaft lifted the maximum effect from 2,800 to 4,300 rpm, allowing the unit to be revved freely, something which it thrived on.

Gearboxes on Imps are notably good, and so suited the Sport because of the characteristic light and precise action.

In spite of the remarkable tractability of the engine, it still gave a good turn of speed, with 90 mph possible from the 10-to-1 compression ratio, all-aluminium unit.

The suspension is only slightly altered from that of the standard Imp, with stronger wishbones and drive shafts and revised damper settings. Tyres are 155-12 Dunlop SP41s on 4.5in wide rims. Drum brakes were retained for the Sport, but a servo was added which is situated in the rear boot beneath the combined brake and clutch fluid reservoir. Mintex M22 anti-fade linings are used which give impressive fade-free stopping.

Loaded weight as tested is 17.6 cwt and overall top gear ratio is 15.1 mph per 1000 rpm. Length of the car is 11ft 9in and width 5ft 0.25in.

Performance—Fiat 850 Special

As with every other Fiat, you cannot help being aware of what a willing character the engine has immediately you turn the ignition key to start. It sounds eager right from the word go. Equally it isn't quiet, but the noise made is not unpleasant. Its power range is good for its capacity; it will potter along quite happily at 20 mph in top—we were able to take acceleration figures from 10 mph in fourth without protest—and will rev to well beyond its 6,400 peak power rpm, valve-crash occuring at 7,600 rpm. With maximum torque at 3,600 rpm, it pays to rev high for best results; for our acceleration runs through the gears, we changed gear at 25, 45 and 66 mph—about 7,000 rpm. From a standing start, 40 mph comes up in 8.5sec, 60 in 19.0, the ¼-mile in 21.3 and 70mph in 32.6sec.

At 13.7 mph per 1,000 rpm, the 850 Special might seem low-geared, yet its 80 mph mean top speed falls a little below maximum power rpm. Maximum comfortable cruising speed is around 70 mph. The gearchange is good by rear-engine standards and spring-loaded into the 3rd-4th plane, the stubby lever moving positively about the gate. You must push it down to select reverse. Synchromesh is strong. Fast changes are made with a quite audible "clunk" from the lever linkage rather than the box itself. The cable-operated clutch is light, progressive and free from judder, and stood up well to repeated hard treatment during fast standing starts.

Performance—Sunbeam Imp Sport

Here is an engine that needs to be revved even harder to get the best out of it—perhaps not

surprisingly when you remember its Coventry-Climax ancestry. Peak power of this single ohc unit is achieved at 6,100 rpm, similar to the Fiat's, but maximum torque is at 4,300 rpm, considerably higher. In first and second gears it will rev very high—to 8,000 rpm in fact, making the driver well aware of it in the process. The result is a brisk, smooth but noisy performer; from a standstill 40 mph is reached in 7.5sec, 60 in 16.3, the ¼-mile in 20.2 and 70 mph in 23.5sec. We changed gear at 26, 50 and 78 mph, which corresponds to about 7,000 rpm. The Imp Sport doesn't stop after 70mph by any means however. 80mph comes up in 37.2sec and the mean top speed is a creditable 90mph with the result that up to nearly 80 mph cruising is possible, a remarkably good speed for 875 c.c. in a four-seat body. Overall gearing in top is quite high—15.1 mph per 1,000 rpm, so that the Sunbeam does not accelerate well below 20 mph in top, though on a light throttle it will trickle along, without snatch, at 12 mph.

After driving a front-engine car with a good gearchange such as an Escort or Viva, the Imp Sport's change seems a little sticky and notchy. Get to know it better and one comes to like it very much. It is precise and positive, with well-chosen ratios and excellent synchromesh. If in the mood, a keen driver will make very fast changes up or down purely for the fun of it; the hard-revving, quick-to-blip engine encourages enthusiastic driving on a winding road. The hydraulically operated clutch is as light as the Fiat's, but as with the brake pedal the awkward position of the pedal makes it seem heavier.

Performance differences

The Fiat's kerb weight, maximum bhp and torque (net) are 1,546 lb, 47 bhp and 43.5 lb.ft. respectively. Corresponding figures for the Sunbeam are 1,638 lb, 51 bhp and 52 lb.ft.; frontal areas of each are fairly similar. To propel 6 per cent more weight, the Sunbeam has 8 per cent more claimed horse power and nearly 20 per cent more torque, so it is not surprising that it is clearly the faster of the two. Performance figures were taken at 1,500 miles on the 850 Special and 3,750 miles on the Imp Sport; from previous experience of all Fiats, we would suspect that the particular test car would have recorded better figures with a greater distance behind it.

Fuel Consumption

Both cars' test mileage included long journeys. With overall consumptions of 30.9 mpg for the Fiat and 28.9 for the Sunbeam, neither is as economical under varied driving as one might expect. The Fiat's minimum safe range with its 6.6 gallon tank just clears 200 miles, but similarly driven the Sunbeam cannot be counted on bettering 180 miles between tankfuls; the test car had an unusually honest petrol gauge—when the needle said "empty", it meant it. Driven in convoy over a 160-mile route involving London traffic, motorway cruising and fast country roads, the Fiat returned 30.2 mpg and the Sunbeam 29.1 mpg.

On the other hand both cars responded frugally to gentle driving, to a remarkable degree. Over similar 100-mile trips, the Fiat

For what some people might like to call "instant accessibility", the Sunbeam Imp Sport (bottom) is the better-planned of the two. In fact, the back panel of the Fiat 850 Special (below) can be removed after six bolts are undone

TWO CAR TEST...

achieved 36.8 mpg and the Sunbeam 35.9 mpg. As with other consumable things on motorcars, the way each drank very much reflected the way each was driven. In one final respect, the Fiat beats the Sunbeam hands down—oil consumption could not be measured on the 850 Special as the level didn't change during the 1,000-mile test period, whereas the Imp Sport did only 650 miles to the pint.

Ride, Handling and Brakes— Fiat 850 Special

There is a reassuringly strong feel to the way the Fiat rides over poorer roads. The ride is firm but not harsh and suffers only moderately from the nose-pitching tendency common to most rear-engined cars. Damping is good.

Our test car was fitted with cross-ply Pirelli tyres, which are standard equipment. Steering is rather dead, but fairly accurate, with about $\frac{1}{4}$in. of slop at the steering wheel rim. Like most rear-engine cars, the Fiat strongly dislikes side-winds. A blowy day on a motorway calls for constant close attention unless the wind is dead ahead or astern, if one wants to stay in one lane. There isn't much self-centring, but with 3.2 turns lock to lock for a $28\frac{1}{2}$ft turning circle—very useful in towns—the steering is quick enough for any emergency.

Driven hard round a corner the Fiat understeers a little at first, then changes to oversteer as the not-excessive amount of roll builds up. The result is that you tend to take the bend in a series of jerks rather than smoothly. Lifting off one's right foot can bring the tail out a little. The inside front wheel will lift slightly as well. Excellently deep curved backs to front seats are a boon on a winding road for both passenger and driver.

The brakes are more than capable of dealing with any treatment one can mete out to them; in an emergency stop, it is the front tyres which will lock first. The handbrake holds easily on a 1-in-3 slope.

Ride, Handling and Brakes— Sunbeam Imp Sport

Noise is the main drawback of the ride of this model, partly at least because it is fitted as standard with radial-ply tyres which tend to accentuate bump-thump over cat's eyes and other obstructions. The ride itself is firm, somewhat harsh over sharp irregularities, well-damped and again fairly free of the usual nose-pitching common to this sort of car.

In itself, the rack and pinion steering is very good. It is light, accurate and very positive, with very little slop at the wheel rim—less than $\frac{1}{8}$in. There is plenty of feel, but also a fair amount of kick-back over rough surfaces. At just over $2\frac{1}{2}$ turns from lock to lock for a $29\frac{1}{4}$ft turning circle, the steering is really quick, though some enterprising owners would probably like a slightly smaller diameter steering wheel than the $15\frac{3}{4}$in. one which is standard. Self-centring is good.

Any side wind at all tends to blow the Imp off course, just as it does the Fiat. One has to steer it all the time on a windy day, which can become tiring on a long run.

Its quick response to small corrections in a straight line feels like that of a markedly oversteering car, but, perhaps partially because

Both cars corner with little roll, though each will lift an inside front wheel if pressed hard

of the "front-engined public" to whom the Imp had mainly to be sold, Rootes' designers planned the Imp to understeer *in extremis*. It does, with great determination, to the extent where one must respect it on a wet road or when pressing on fast—lifting-off decreases the tendency to plough straight-on, but does not automatically correct it as on a front-wheel drive car. Only a dab of braking on entry really sorts things out, bringing the tail round and keeping the front tyres closer to the chosen line. Provided one does not venture too far, the Imp Sport is perfectly well behaved. There is little roll, even when the inside front wheel lifts during hard cornering. The seats hold one well sideways.

Although of drum type both front and rear, the Imp Sport's brakes work well and do not fade appreciably under any circumstances. Their only shortcomings during the test period was the comparatively long time they took to recover fully after passing through some floodwater. The handbrake proved well up to its job.

Ride, Handling and Brakes—differences

Differences in tyre equipment make direct comparison difficult in ride and steering. Some of the Imp's slightly harsher ride might be put down to having radial tyres. Basically, both ride acceptably well. The slightly sloppier steering of the Fiat is partially due to its less precise steering mechanism; the Sunbeam's steering is marginally the better of the two in most respects.

A stranger to these two or any other small rear-engined car may at first find them apparently a little top heavy, especially if he is used to a Mini. In fact, this is an illusion, both being far more stable than might at first be thought. One can do surprising things with both. The Imp Sport can be cornered rather more smoothly than the 850 Special; both have equal difficulty in sticking to a wind-blown straight line. Brakes are good on both, though it is the Fiat's which are lighter in spite of the lack of a servo.

Noise

The noise level within the Imp is slightly higher than in the Fiat, but only just. The composition, however, is different. In the Imp the noise is made up almost equally of engine roar and wind whistle which comes mainly from the front quarter-lights. The Fiat is commendably low on wind roar, however, the engine causing the majority of the body "boom". It is quite a deep note and not unpleasant. What is surprising is the relatively low wind noise from both cars; this is unusual for what would be classed as cheap cars, showing that the sealing is good on both.

Gear whine is noticeable in the lower ratios on the Imp and a body boom sets up at about three-quarters of maximum revs, but overall noise level gets no worse after 65 mph.

The Fiat is mounted on cross-ply tyres and road noise comes through as a muted roar, with bump-thump relatively muffled; the Imp is a different story, with bump-thump exceptionally harsh, being almost pure bang over concrete divisions (as are frequently found on many of the older dual carriageways).

Engine note from both would be described as sporting, and both clatter somewhat on tickover when hot.

Fittings and Furniture—Fiat 850 Special

In keeping with what we expect of the smaller Fiats, the interior appears somewhat spartan to comfort-conscious people. Closer interest shows that nothing is missing, however, and all that is provided works in a most functional way.

The interior is trimmed neatly in black plastics matched with white paint, to provide a

very smart appearance. The floor is covered with black rubber carpet. The seat squab seems on the hard side to start with and extends well forward to support the thighs, while the seat back is not very high but supports the small of the back well. A novel system allows the seat back to be raked fully if necessary—but not while seated. The combination of adjustments should suit all shapes and sizes, the firmness of the seat never causing any stiffness at any stage. Sitting position is higher than in the Imp, giving a very good view of the road at all times and allowing the four corners of the car to be seen for parking manoeuvres. The interior mirror gives a good rear view, incorporating a courtesy light; it can be dipped at night, but vibrates a little when the car is travelling at speed.

The sloping, padded facia carries two swivelling ventilation outlets and a hooded instrument panel in front of the driver. A small switch panel to the right of the steering column has three switches; for lamps, panel light and windscreen wipers. The windscreen washer operating plunger is just below the panel.

Other lamp controls and the direction indicator lever are mounted on the steering column.

The hooded instrument panel contains the speedometer, fuel gauge—calibrated full, half and a warning flashing light when the fuel level is getting low—and water temperature gauge, in addition to four warning lights.

These warning lights seem to indicate that Italians are rather unobservant, as the lights are very large and particularly bright at night. Their function warns that the main beam is on (blue), the side lights are on (green) and two red ones indicate generator charge and low oil pressure. The main offender is the green light which for obvious reasons is always on after dark and reflects from the steering wheel rim on to the windscreen, directly in the driver's line of view.

The steering wheel has an imitation wood rim, the two spokes are drilled, giving a sporting appearance, and have a crackle black finish.

The door opening levers are conveniently placed beneath the arm rests on the doors with the window winders (low-geared, anti-clockwise for up) high up to the front.

A full-width, padded-edge parcel shelf below the facia takes the odd package, other parcel accommodation being a shallow tray on the centre tunnel and elastic-edge map pockets on the doors.

Fiat on the left, Sunbeam on the right: the ability on both cars to fold the back seat squab forward increases versatility usefully. On the Sunbeam one can also open the back window

TWO CAR TEST...

All the passengers have grab handles set into the white headlining, those at the rear incorporating coat hooks.

Control pedals are pendant for the clutch and brake and floor mounted for the throttle. Heel-and-toe changes are possible, the wheel arch providing a convenient right-foot rest.

Heater controls consist of a lever to admit fresh air and one to admit hot air or direct it through the facia vents for screen demisting. A blower switch on the centre console is noisy in operation but very efficient, and great quantities of hot air could be obtained soon after starting from cold.

Luggage accommodation is larger than the Imp's, two reasonably sized suitcases together with some soft bags sharing the space with the vertically mounted spare wheel. The battery is located under the front luggage compartment, well away from any engine heat, and readily accessible beneath a flap.

The engine compartment looks larger and neater than that on the Imp, but to gain the same accessibility the back panel needs to be removed. This is very easily accomplished with six bolts.

Fittings and Furniture— Sunbeam Imp Sport

First impressions of the interior implied greater luxury with the fully carpeted floor, two-spoke padded steering wheel (padding fell off during course of test) and "fully instrumented" facia panel shrouded in recessed padding to prevent glare. Closer examination of the instruments, however, reveal only two true gauges, the 100 mph speedometer and fuel gauge (gauge

calibrated, full-6 gallons, half-full with a division for three-quarter-full and a red section when approaching empty).

The remainder of the gauges (with two blanked holes) consist of warning lights, which show battery charge, water temperature and oil pressure (too high or low respectively).

Seats and door panels are trimmed in matching plastics material, the seats having a good range of backward adjustment. The seat back is rather high and supports the shoulders to promote an armchair feeling. This low position causes the arms to point slightly up-hill if holding the wheel at "ten to two", and might cause early fatigue. The low position does not reduce ability to read the instruments, however, and still affords very good all-round visibility. The interior mirror is rather inadequate and mounted too high up for complete rear vision through the back window. There is a wide parcel shelf behind the rear seats, with access through the rear window, which can be hinged upwards.

Other controls for lamps and windscreen washer-wipers are to the right of the steering column along with the ignition switch. Direction indicator lever and horn, and headlamp dipping is controlled by levers protruding from the right and left hand side of the steering column respectively.

The gear lever is conveniently mounted almost vertically, with the pull-up choke control in front of it on the floor. The clutch, brake and throttle pedals are all pendant type. The clutch pedal has quite a long travel but is only operative over a short portion. The brake pedal effort is reasonable, with plenty of feel, and the throttle pedal position allows for heel-and-toe changes in addition to being close enough to the wheel arch for this to act as a foot steady.

On the passenger side of the facia panel, a large drop-down tray can accommodate more than the odd pair of gloves and both doors have 5in. deep, full-width shelves for maps and the like. The door opening lever and window winders (high geared, clockwise for up) are rather low down, however, and could foul a book which had slid along the shelf.

No grab handles are provided for passengers

The Fiat interior is neat and functional with plenty of open shelf space; wiper switch is some way from the windscreen washer which is mounted under the facia

PERFORMANCE FIAT 850 SPECIAL

PRICE £694 (total including purchase tax)

		Maximum speeds
rpm	**mph**	
5,850	80	Top
7,200	70	3rd
7,200	45	2nd
7,200	26	1st
		Acceleration
Ind. mph	**sec**	**mph**
32	5.0	0-30
42	8.5	0-40
52	12.9	0-50
62	19.0	0-60
72	32.6	0-70
83	—	0-80

21.3 sec 62 mph		Standing ¼-mile
Top (4.93)	**3rd (7.22)**	**mph**
—	9.5	10-30
16.3	9.0	20-40
16.6	9.4	30-50
19.4	11.2	40-60
26.3	10.3	50-70
—	—	60-80

30.9	**Overall mpg**
32	**Typical mpg**
Neg. consumption	**Oil—miles per pint**

REAR ENGINE, REAR-WHEEL DRIVE

ENGINE
Cylinders	4, in line
Main bearings	3
Cooling system	Water; pump, fan and thermostat
Bore	65.0 mm (2.56 in.)
Stroke	63.5 mm (2.50 in.)
Displacement	843 c.c. (51.4 cu.in.)
Valve gear	Overhead; pushrods and rockers
Compression ratio	9.3 to 1 Minimum octane rating 98RM
Carburettor	Weber 30 DIC I
Fuel pump	Fiat mechanical
Oil filter	Centrifugal
Max. power	47 bhp (net) at 6,400 rpm
Max. torque	43.5 lb.ft (net) at 3,600 rpm

TRANSMISSION
Clutch	Fiat diaphragm-spring, 6.5 in. dia
Gearbox	Four-speed, all-synchromesh
Gear ratios	Top 0.96
	Third 1.41
	Second 2.05
	First 3.63
	Reverse 3.61
Final drive	Hypoid bevel, 5.13 to 1

SUSPENSION
Front	Independent, wishbones, transverse leaf spring, telescopic dampers, anti-roll bar
Rear	Independent, semi-trailing arms, coil springs, telescopic dampers, anti-roll bar

STEERING
Type	Fiat, worm and sector
Wheel dia.	14 in.

BRAKES
Make and type	Fiat, disc front, drum rear, no servo
Dimensions	Front 8.9 in. dia.; rear, 7.3 in. dia. 1.18in. wide shoes
Swept area	Front 136.4 sq.in.; rear, 54 sq.in. Total 190.4 sq.in. (276 sq.in./ton laden)

WHEELS
Type	Pressed steel disc. 4-stud fixing. 4.5 in. wide rim.
Tyres—make	Pirelli or Michelin; Pirelli on test car
—type	Sempione cross-ply/tubeless
—size	145-12 in.

Maximum speeds

	mph	rpm
Top	90	5,950
3rd	82	7,500
2nd	56	8,000
1st	30	8,000

Acceleration

mph	sec	Ind. mph
0-30	4.9	32
0-40	7.5	42
0-50	11.1	52
0-60	16.3	62
0-70	23.5	73
0-80	37.2	83

Standing $\frac{1}{4}$-mile	66 mph	20.2 sec
mph	3rd (5.70)	Top (4.14)
10-30	10	—
20-40	9.1	14.7
30-50	9.7	15.0
40-60	10.4	17.5
50-70	11.9	21.2
60-80	—	27.6

Overall mpg	28.9
Typical mpg	30
Oil—miles per pint	650

REAR ENGINE, REAR-WHEEL DRIVE

ENGINE
Cylinders . . . . . 4, in line
Main bearings . . . 3
Cooling system . . Water: pump, fan and thermostat
Bore . . . . . . 68.0 mm (2.68 in.)
Stroke . . . . . 60.4 mm (2.38 in.)
Displacement . . . 875 c.c. (53.4 cu.in.)
Valve gear . . . . Single overhead camshaft
Compression ratio . 10.0 to 1 Minimum octane rating 98RM
Carburettors . . . Two Stromberg 125 CDS
Fuel pump . . . . AC mechanical
Oil filter . . . . . Tecalemit, full flow, renewable element

TRANSMISSION
Max. power . . . 51 bhp (net) at 6,100 rpm
Max. torque . . . 52 lb.ft (net) at 4,300 rpm
Clutch . . . . . . Laycock, diaphragm-spring, 6.25 in. dia.
Gearbox . . . . . Four-speed, all-synchromesh
Gear ratios . . . . Top 0.85
                    Third 1.74
                    Second 1.83
                    First 3.42
                    Reverse 2.85
Final drive . . . . Hypoid bevel, 4.86 to 1

SUSPENSION
Front . . . . . . Independent, swing axles, coil springs, telescopic dampers
Rear . . . . . . Independent, semi-trailing arms, coil springs, telescopic dampers

STEERING
Type . . . . . . Rack and pinion
Wheel dia. . . . . 15.75 in.

BRAKES
Make and type . . Girling drums front and rear, vacuum servo
Dimensions . . . Front 8.0 in. dia. 1.5 in. wide shoes
                 Rear 8.0 in. dia. 1.5 in. wide shoes
Swept area . . . . Front 75 sq.in.; rear 75 sq.in.
                 Total 150 sq.in. (170 sq.in./ton laden)

WHEELS
Type . . . . . . Pressed steel disc, 4-stud fixing, 4.5 in. wide rim
Tyres—make . . . Dunlop
     —type . . . SP41 radial ply/tubeless
     —size . . . 155-12 in.

---

and a centrally located heater control takes the form of a flap which provides plenty of air, but the control position was indeterminate. The front luggage compartment will hold a reasonably sized suitcase plus small soft bags, in addition to accommodating the spare wheel, which is housed upright in the front. Much of the compartment is obscured by trunking over the wheel arches, which makes the remaining space rather an odd shape.

Engine accessibility at the rear is fairly good, the engine compartment housing the brake servo, oil cooler and battery.

Fittings and Furniture—differences

The Fiat seems stark in comparison with the carpeted comfort of the Imp. This is more of an illusion, as the function of the Fiat fittings could be described as "clinically efficient" more useful items being provided. The Imp, with its sporting pretentions, is very deficient in what it appears to carry in the way of instrumentation.

Location of simple things like door handles is much more convenient on the Fiat, the whole giving the feeling of having been planned as a complete exercise.

This theme extends to the outside styling as well, with the minimally functional Fiat lines contrasting starkly with the cluttered appearance of the Imp.

There seems to be more room to move around inside the Imp, giving a less claustrophobic impression. This could be accounted for, however, by the difference in seating positions; in the Fiat one is perched high up and in the Imp sunk down into the high-backed seat.

Personal Opinion

A difficult choice for me, as I think that both cars would make much more sense with engines, transmissions and driven wheels at the other end. Taking them as they are, I prefer the Fiat's looks by a long way. It is neat and functional, even pretty in bob-tailed wrennish sort of way, whereas the Imp Sport comes from the rear-engined bath-tub school of stylist, for whom I do not care. On the other hand, the Imp Sport's performance is a great draw—it does

go remarkably fast for its size—and the gearchange is excellent. I prefer the Sunbeam's steering, but do not like the handling of either very much. And this wavering nose in a side-wind is very irritating on both. The Imp fits my 6ft far better than does the Fiat; both have comfortable enough seats. If pushed to a decision, I would settle for the Sunbeam —just. **M.S.**

Personal Opinion

Once the basic points have been analysed it seems to be quite a fair comparison of two cars in this class. The Imp Sport hardly has enough to justify its claim to use the description 'Sport', while the Fiat makes no sporting claims, calling itself 'Special'.

This is very modest, especially when it proves to have more to offer of a sporting nature, including that "instant" sporting accessory— the "wood rimmed", spoked drilled and crackle black finished steering wheel. Also it needs no oil cooler or brake servo.

While the Imp has many attractive features, including an incredibly tractable engine (very nice even if it takes a long time to get "worked up"), I do not like it *in toto*. Least of all do I care for the appearance of the "instrument panel".

The excessive understeer of the Imp, together with its somewhat indefinite steering, did not help to build my confidence either, but it is quite at home on motorways.

It should not be very difficult to read between the lines and see that the Fiat is much more my sort of car. The seat I found to be one of the most comfortable that I have met in a small car on a long journey. Good support for the small of the back really shows up after much wheel twirling through sharp bends, something which it takes very easily in its stride in spite of front end stiffness; this only causes the bonnet to bounce up and down without any drama.

On almost all counts, therefore, I find the Fiat more suited to my needs; it would make a good second car (should the occasion arise); it is functionally efficient with stark, clean styling; it feels unburstable and performs equally well on twisting or open roads, all for nearly £40 less. **C.J.H.**

Sunbeam interior, which with its carpet looks superficially the more luxurious of the two. Door pockets are much valued for odds and ends. Like the Fiat, the only instruments it has are the speedometer and fuel gauge. The wiper switch and washer plunger are combined

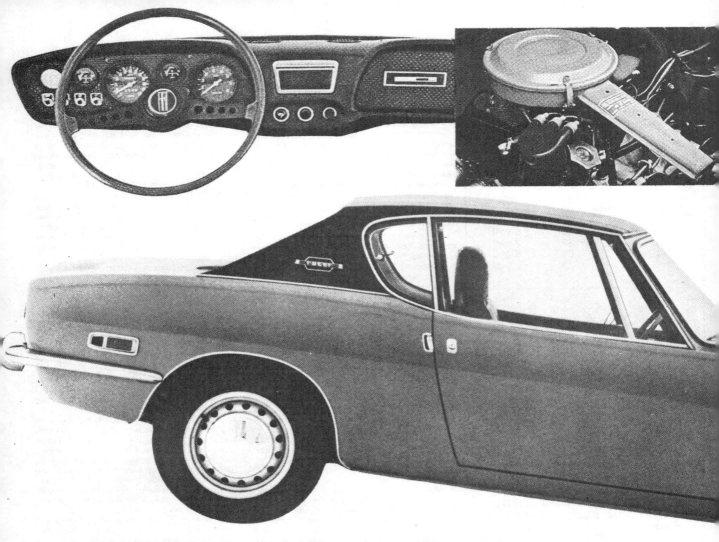

THE STYLING IS AS FRESH AS TOMORROW BUT THE ENGINE IS ONE OF THE SMALLEST AROUND. IT WORKS HARD JUST TO HIT 60 MPH.

■One look at this sleek little car and you are immediately convinced that you must have one. Start to get into it and you begin to have misgivings. Once behind the wheel, with your feet on those tiny pedals, your eye catches the neat dashboard arrangement with its reasonably large speedometer and tachometer, and you think perhaps you've been too hasty. The headroom is adequate and there is plenty of legroom, too. You turn the key and the engine comes to life behind you. It sounds good and as you push the clutch, you feel yourself getting ready for a week or so of real fun behind the wheel. You whip around the first corner, go for second gear and it is right about then you notice that the tach's red-lined somewhere around the 7000 rpm mark. You know then that you'll have to "burn" it constantly to get anywhere. The Fiat 850 Sport

Racer *is* a fun car but it's not going to be everybody's cup of tea.

We had a big snow in our area a day or so after we picked the car up for test. The first thing we discovered was that the racer was slung so low that the belly pan kept touching the snow (just about four inches) and that the front wheels tended to slide down into the ruts made by the big domestic cars. We had literally folded up a passenger in the space behind the driver and passenger seats. This, of course, noticeably increased the difficulty of steering on the slippery roads because it made the front end light and upset the delicate balance the Sport Racer offers.

We drove all during that bad weather without ever getting stuck although many cars out at the same time did. This Fiat seemed to have a

special proclivity for pushing itself away from the sidewalk and out into the main stream of traffic, but it had a frightening knack for stuffing snow into the front wheel wells until the tires rubbed. The clearance behind the front wheel and the body is extremely limited. We also found it a little hard to start in cold weather once you had let it sit over night. First of all, the manual choke was positioned between the seats and had to be pulled forward as well as up. This proved to be extremely difficult particularly for the "lady of the house." You had to wait several minutes until the car warmed up a bit before driving off or it would stall.

It was a couple of days before the roads were cleared of the snow and one could drive more than thirty-five miles an hour. The fun part came

FIAT 850 SPORT RACER

Bertone touched this one and it came out with an eye-catching beauty. It's still strictly a two seater, though, and difficult to get into at that. The little engine is a high-winder in the true sense of the word developing 58 horsepower at 6400 rpm. The get the best out of it you have to "put your foot into it" and keep it there. Once you get it up to speed, however, it clings to the road like a much heavier car.

then—almost. Only once in our whole test period did we get the Sport Racer up to sixty miles per hour and then the engine sounded as if it was working its heart out. This sound gave the impression that you were pushing the little car along some thirty miles an hour faster. As a result we found it much easier on our nerves to cruise along with the needle on the 50 mph mark.

In all honesty, this whole bit was a little disappointing because the car has some nice things going for it in addition to the beautiful styling. The seats were extremely comfortable and the visibility all around just great. The handling left nothing to be desired even for an 80-inch wheelbase job like this one. The brakes were better than average and all the controls were positioned so

that they could be reached easily. The windshield wipers functioned perfectly either in snow or rain and the defroster cleared up the windshield in a most reassuring manner. The heater was too much—really too much. We drove around most of the time with it off and just turned it on periodically. In a few moments the interior of the car was too hot and it did no good to just open the windows because your feet roasted even with the heater vents under the dash closed. We never had to use the heater fan at all.

Alright, let's face it. The term "Racer" in this car's name is a misnomer. It might be all kinds of funs in rallys or gymkhanas where you don't need top speeds constantly, but our test car just didn't seem to want to do more than sixty. We've

driven Fiat 850 coupes that moved out with much less effort. The Sport Racer will run about $2400 in the American market. We would rather dig down into the old bank account and come up with several hundred additional dollars for a Fiat 124.

Summing up, the Fiat 850 Sport Racer with its Torino emblem on the dash and "Racer" medallions on the sides is a truly beautiful little car. The black vinyl top adds to its appearance. It is comfortable for two but it is nowhere as exciting to drive as it looks. We can't see how winding that little engine out to 6400 rpm's constantly can do anything more than cause a trip to your friendly dealer before the first year is out. Frankly, it's underpowered. A body like the Racer's should have more than a 900 cc's engine pushing it around town. ●

25000 MILES WITH A FIAT 850 COUPE

By JOHN BOLSTER

BECAUSE I nearly always have at least one road test car in my garage, I make little use of my personal vehicle. Nevertheless, it is necessary to keep one's own motor carriage, even though its annual mileage is quite small. As I usually have to be coldly analytical in my articles about cars, perhaps I may be excused, just this once, for mentioning a few of my personal whims and prejudices in choosing my means of transport.

Prior to the Fiat, I ran an AC Aceca coupé, and I loved it dearly, because it was so pretty and was beautifully made. I parted with it for two reasons, the first of which was the 70 mph limit; I test fast cars abroad but I have given up rapid motoring in England, for what is a professional driver without his licence? The second reason was that the AC was a hobby-car, demanding careful maintenance if it were to give of its best. As I have a 1903 Panhard, a 1911 Rolls, and a 1390 house, my few leisure hours are already fully occupied in tinkering!

When I was invited to go to Italy for the preview of the Fiat 850 Coupé, I immediately fell for another pretty face. I detest live axles and cart springs, but as this little car was all-independent, it satisfied my mechanical scruples. I was doubtful about the roadholding of a rear-engined machine, but an impassioned assault on some mountain passes removed any worries on that score. I dislike noisy cars, and most small ones are unbearable on that account, but the Coupé proved to be quieter than many models double its size. Performance was of practically no interest, and a timed run in the region of 90 mph was more than adequate for one condemned to drive in Wilson's paradise.

Delighted

So the little Fiat came to live in my ancient barn. I had chosen a chaste shade of gunmetal grey and I was delighted with its appearance. I cannot stand elaborate plated decoration or nasty shiny writing on a car, but the 850 Coupé is completely plain and unadorned, relying on its exquisite Italian shape for effect. Above all, the interior is most attractive and in the very best taste; why should one spend hours inside a car that looks like an over-decorated bathroom? I admit that I attach great importance to the looks of a car, both outside and in, and I am prejudiced against those vehicles which have an untidy mess under the bonnet, for engines should be beautiful, too.

In the correspondence columns of some motoring magazines, disgusted owners write of their experiences with the new cars they have bought. It seems that it is far from unusual to take delivery of a car that is on the verge of falling to pieces, and terrible things can happen during the first weeks of ownership. In my case, there were no faults on delivery and the only replacement under guarantee was a bulb for the instrument lighting.

After the car was run in, I found that it would return as much as 40 mpg in 70 mph England, which fell to 36 mpg on a trip to Monza. During the first two or three thousand miles, an occasional half-pint of oil was added, after which the consumption fell almost to zero, where it has remained ever since. The engine revs very freely, like all Fiats, and there is not much performance unless one uses this facility. I normally change up at 6000 rpm in everyday driving, but it pays to go up to 7000 rpm if maximum performance is required. As all the gears are indirect, the efficiency of the transmission is the same whichever ratio is in use.

For 11,000 miles the reliability was absolute, but then I heard a grinding noise from the front brakes. When I sent the car in for its 12,000-miles service, I was horrified to learn that the pads were worn out and that the surface of the discs had been damaged. Worse was to follow, for at 18,000 miles the brakes were found to be in trouble again. I pride myself on being light on brakes, having driven some of my cars for several years without relining—a 20 hp Rolls-Royce gave me over five years without touching the brakes, and it was very secondhand

40-10-15

when I got it. Perhaps I am expecting too much, as friends with other disc-braked cars have had similar experiences, and I note that Patrick McNally suffered the same defect with his Ferrari.

The only other important mechanical replacement has been the clutch, which began to show slight signs of slipping after 20,000 miles. It pays to replace a slipping clutch immediately, or other damage can be caused and they never cure themselves, as many people hope they will. The car is normally serviced—and very well too—by Fiat (England) Ltd, but at the first suspicion of slipping I took the car straight in to the nearest agents, Sargent and Brooker of East Grinstead. They took less than a day over the job and charged me £18, which seems fair at today's prices.

Apart from things mechanical, tyres have naturally had to be replaced. The standard tyres were ordinary crossply Pirellis and the handling was outstandingly good, especially on wet roads. I tried a similar Fiat on Pirelli radials but found the increase in road noise a little tiresome, while there was no noticeable improvement in roadholding. I usually buy Dunlops, but because the car handled so well on the standard tyres I decided on a repeat performance. I ordered a pair of Pirellis for the rear wheels and months later I was in danger of falling foul of the police for worn treads, in spite of repeated telephone calls. Just in time, the two tyres arrived, and at 15,000 miles the bald ones were replaced. I immediately ordered a pair for the front end, but 4000 miles later I could wait no longer, in spite of the usual telephone routine. So, I took a pair of Firestone from stock and, to my intense joy, the delicate balance of the little car has not been upset in the least.

With crossply tyres, there are a few "sandpaper" textures on the road surface which make a rushing sound, but these are infrequently met and there is no bump-thump. As with most rear-engined cars, there is some pitching on bumpy roads, but although this is noticeable at first, one gets used to it. Indeed, I could scarcely convince myself that the car still pitches except by watching the headlamp beams on the trees. This apart, the ride is outstandingly good for such a small car.

The front seats are very comfortable, with enough leg-room for the tallest driver. Provided that the people in front are not greedy, the rear seating can really be used by adults. Preferably the rear passengers should not be tall, as the head room is limited, but a single grown-up can be quite well accommodated and of course children would be at ease for long journeys—like my dogs. The front luggage boot is quite useful, because the battery and spare wheel are cleverly stowed, and the car is not sensitive to extra weight here.

As I am in the lucky position of driving many fast cars, 150 mph motoring is no novelty to me and the speed of the tiny Fiat should be of little interest. Nevertheless, I do admire the way it buzzes along so willingly at 80 to 90 mph and its acceleration is quite lively if the big rev counter is allowed to go well round the dial. Almost incredibly, the speedometer is just about dead accurate by careful timing, an unheard of virtue in these corrupt days. The latest version of the car, with a more highly tuned 903 cc engine and radial ply tyres on wide wheels, is a little faster and has better acceleration but is less refined, which most people would gladly accept for the higher performance.

The body is very well made and finished and it is extremely tough, being quite heavy for its size. Its only fault concerned the two metal straps restricting the opening of the doors, both of which wore and allowed the paint to be marked before I saw anything amiss. This was corrected at the 18,000 miles service.

Worth every penny

The Fiat 850 Coupe is an expensive little car, but worth every penny for the pleasure it gives. One could have a much bigger car for the money, but for my work its small size is a great advantage especially for parking in Paris and other continental cities; the excellent steering lock gives a smaller turning circle than any front-drive car can boast. I think that a small luxury car should have a more sophisticated heating and ventilation system, but in other respects it is well furnished. It is rather like having a beautiful watch that gives pleasure every time you look at it. I admit that for travelling in England nowadays I would rather have a chauffeur-driven limousine, but as a piece of equipment for my job this Fiat has proved almost ideal.

FAST IT AIN'T

. . . BUT IF YOU WANT A "CUTE," "LITTLE," CAR THAT HAS AN **HONEST** 55 CUBIC INCHES AND GETS AN **HONEST** 32 MILES TO THE GALLON — WELL, THEN, MAYBE YOU OUGHTA THINK ABOUT A FIAT 850 RACER

BY PAUL VAN VALKENBURGH

PHOTOS/BILL RUSSOM

SCG ROAD TEST

THE FUTURE EVERYDAY RUNABOUT COMMUTER-CAR may not be far away. As a matter of fact one may be sitting only a few blocks away right at this instant. The prognosticators are telling us that transportation survival in the cities depends on the evolution of tiny, two-passenger vehicles with miniature low-emission engines . . . stylish but space-saving, so that we can re-divide four freeway lanes into three, and be able to park two for one. American prognosticators are envisioning this. The Europeans are *doing* it.

I'm sorry to admit that under the inundating propaganda of VW, it has taken me this long to discover Fiat. I've been noticing them for years — Angie has one, Barb has one, Judy has one . . . and our mail runs heavily toward information on them. But since the Fiat folk haven't done anything new or exotic in the past few years there hasn't been cause for a road test. Now, with merely a new top and a few extra horses on their old 850 Spider, we finally have a good excuse to review their case.

This car has by far the smallest engine of any car we've had the guts to test in the last couple of years, at 55 *honest* cubic inches. The Subaru had it beat with a mere (and we really mean *mere*) 22 cubic inches, but that baby buggy struck such fear in the hearts of our death-defying drivers that we sent it home with a cookie and a note to its mother. But for Fiat's 903 cc's — think about that, hardly bigger than a good motorcycle — it really does nicely. For being only *one-eighth* the displacement of the grosser Stingray it's at least a third of the value . . . and more, in tight spatial or financial situations. Surprisingly, it doesn't take long to conclude that just about every car we test has "adequate" horsepower for its purpose, and the 850's 64 is not an exception. If you're not in a hurry, you soon learn to concentrate on avoiding stop signs and red lights, and when you simply *must* move out, you can floor it and redline in every gear without guilt or fear. Actually, with the super-low gear ratios we spent a lot of time at redline — even on the freeway in fourth gear. The acceleration feels dreadfully slow, and

yet it out-performed a lot of bigger test cars such as Citroen, Cortina, Ro 80 and all the VWs including the 1600. Unbelievable? Well, maybe we ought to compare it to VW.

With a $2500 price tag, the 850 Racer falls right on the Karmann Ghia, Volkswagen's idea of a sports car. Fiat, however, has concentrated on squeezing a lot more performance out of a smaller package. Not only does the 850 engine win with 64 hp to 53, but it has much less vehicle to push. Overall dimensions show it to be about 8 percent smaller than Volks, and weight is correspondingly about 14 percent less. It *is* tiny. It is *not* a car to get angry in and launch an offensive against anything else on the road but a pedestrian — and then with discretion.

The small size naturally means a short wheelbase, which at 79 inches can't prevent a lot of pitching and bounding over road roughness, but it still manages to have plenty of room for people, one suitcase and engine work. Like VW, they have sacrificed footroom for a narrow track width, and the impinging left front wheel well only leaves room for twinkle-toes on the pedals. If you tire of resting your left foot back on the wheelhouse, you can stretch it out to the footrest *under* the clutch pedal. In a crisis, however, no matter *where* your feet are, they'll get caught under *some* bloody thing — brake pedal, upholstery, steering column — and take about five crashing minutes to get sorted out and work right.

The seats are about right and headrestful, but the steering wheel and seat belt were designed for a 300-pound orangutan with the afore-hinted size 4-AAA feet. Ever since Nuvolari, the Italians have been booby over arms-out driving, which is fine, except that the wheel isn't vertical enough and you have to get out of your seat to reach the top of it. To allow for this, our 850 came with a seven-league (minimum length) seat belt that could be looped through the door handle, around the shifter, over the steering column, and still not be snug. Perhaps in case of a rollover the passengers are just supposed to be thrown out and dragged along at a safe distance. All levity aside, though, the interior is otherwise quite nice, except for lacking a dimming rearview mirror, and having a weird radio that switches stations on whim and receives unintelligible sounds from other planets.

The basic vehicle layout — with engine overhung out back as in a VW — favors space but is not conducive to good transient response. Resultant high polar moment of inertia on such a short wheelbase tends to make the car over-react to steering and throttle inputs, and the tail quite often wags the dog. During steady-state cornering, as on our skidpad, non-steady actions — particularly "throttle-off" — produce the expected sudden, final oversteer. As with the other tail-engine designs, though, the oversteer progresses slowly enough that it can be caught and negated with reverse lock and/or more throttle. Just mind the front/rear tire pressure differential, Bucko, and everything will come out OK. Maximum lateral acceleration capability is quite good at 0.77 g, with a modicum of understeer to the limit. Tire to weight ratio is a strong determinant in this test, and with a near record low weight of 1670 pounds running wet, practically any tire can stick it down.

The braking test showed the same thing. When front/rear force distribution is correct for the surface we happen to be stopping on, retardation is limited only by the tires and, to a much lesser extent, "feel," or the ability to prevent lockup. The 850 is very well braked from all three standpoints, and therefore produces 0.87 g, right in there with the best lightweight over-tired sports cars.

Aerodynamics is very important to such a lightweight, but less so because of its limited top speed. Side-wind gusts and passing truck blasts are noticeable, and may move the car over a half lane, but the directional stability feels better than would be indicated by excessive, avoidable aerodynamic lift front and rear. Air drag, however, is second lowest only to the 850's cousin, the Abarth Scorpion, with 230 pounds total at 100 mph. We extrapolate the measured drag to 100 for reference, but for your purposes, halve the force for a more reasonable 70 mph.

All factors, except for a very low gear ratio, point toward good mileage: small engine, light weight, low air drag, high compression, 4-speed standard, radial tires — and the Racer produces. Congratulations to Fiat for a new road test record of 32 mpg.

One last, hopefully insignificant comment. The fuel filler neck is located in the engine room, directly above the exhaust pipes. I'm pretty sure spilled gasoline won't ignite, but neither pump jockeys nor I are *that* sure. At the very least, make damn sure you shut off the engine when filling.

In sum, we would recommend the car to anyone who wants the image of a sports car but can't pay the price for performance. We think the 850 Racer is worth the near $2600 asked for it on the West Coast, as long as the car's eye-catching lines, fun potential and low upkeep are uppermost in the buyer's mind. But then, for that price — consider the alternatives.

FIAT 850 RACER

PRICE
Base ....$2515 (F.O.B. West Coast)
As tested $2700
With options ......Delivery, tax and license,
AM-FM radio, luggage rack, guard kit

ENGINE
Type ....4-cylinder, in-line, water-cooled,
cast-iron block, aluminum head
Displacement ....55.1 cu. in. (903 cc)
Horsepower ....64 hp @ 6400 rpm
Torque ....47.7 lbs.-ft. @ 4000 rpm
Bore & stroke ....2.56 in. x 2.68 in.
(65 mm x 68 mm)
Compression ratio ....9.5 to 1
Valve actuation ....Ohv, pushrod
and rocker arm
Induction system ....Single 2V Weber
Exhaust system .....Steel headers, 4 into 1
Electrical system ....12-volt alternator,
point distributor
Fuel ....Premium
Recommended redline 6500

DRIVE TRAIN
Clutch ....Single dry plate
Transmission ......Gear Ratio Overall Ratio
  1st Synchro ......3.63 ......17.71
  2nd Synchro ......2.05 ......10.01
  3rd Synchro ......1.40 ......6.84
  4th Synchro ......0.96 ......4.69
Differential ....Ring and pinion, 4.88 ratio

CHASSIS
Frame ....Unitized,
rear engine, rear drive
Front suspension ....Independent with
upper swinging arms,
transverse-mounted leaf springs,
telescopic shocks; stabilizer bar
Rear suspension ....Independent with
swinging arms and coil springs,
telescopic shocks, stabilizer bar
Steering ....Worm and helical gear,
3.5 turns,
turning circle 31.5 feet
Brakes ....Front disc, rear drum,
9.5-in. dia. front,
8.0-in. dia. rear
Wheels ....13-in. dia.; 5-in. wide
Tires ....Pirelli 155 SR 13,
pressures F/R: 20/26 (rec.), 24/30 (test)

BODY
Type ....Unitized, 2-door, 2-passenger
Seats ....Front bucket, rear boot (3 cu. ft.)
Windows ....2 manual, 2 vents
Luggage space ....Front trunk, 4.5 cu. ft.
Instruments ....120 mph speedo,
8000 rpm tach
  Gauges: ....oil pressure, fuel, temp
  Lights: ....ignition, door ajar

WEIGHTS AND MEASURES
Weight .....1670 lbs. (curb), 1895 lbs. (test)
Weight distribution F/R 40%/60%
Wheelbase ....79.0 in.
Track F/R ....46.5 in./47.5 in.
Height ....48.0 in.
Width ....59.0 in.
Length ....148.0 in.
Ground clearance ....5.3 in.
Oil capacity ....3.5 qt.
Fuel capacity ....8 gal.
Coolant capacity ....8 qt.

MISCELLANEOUS
Weight/power ratio
(curb/advertised) ....26.1 lbs. per hp
Advertised hp/cu. in. 1.16
Speed per 1000 rpm (top gear) ....14.2 mph
Warranty ....12 months/12,000 miles

AERODYNAMIC FORCES AT 100 MPH

CORNERING CONDITIONS

PERFORMANCE

Acceleration ....0-30 (4.8 sec.), 0-60 (16.1 sec.)
0-quarter mile (20.1 sec., 65.9 mph)

Top speed ....92 mph (est.) at 6500 rpm (rpm limited)

Braking ....Distance from 60 mph: 137 ft. (0.87 g av.)
Number of stops to fade: Not attainable
Stability: Good
Maximum pitch angle: N.A.

Handling ....Maximum lateral: 0.77 g right, 0.77 g left
Maximum roll angle: 3.9°
Reaction to throttle, full: More understeer; off: Oversteer

Speedometer	30.0	40.0	50.0	60.0	70.0	80.0
Actual mph	29.0	38.5	48.5	58.5	68.5	78.5

Mileage ....Average: 32.6 mpg
Miles on car: 3500-5200

Aerodynamic forces at 100 mph:
  Drag ....230 lbs. (includes tire drag)
  Lift F/R ....170 lbs./210 lbs.

TEST EXPLANATIONS

Fade test is successive maximum g stops from 60 mph each minute until wheels cannot be locked. Understeer is front minus rear tire slip angle at maximum lateral on 200-ft. dia. Digitek skidpad. Autoscan chassis dynamometer supplied by Humble Oil.

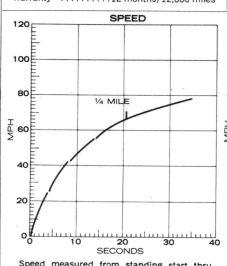

SPEED

Speed measured from standing start thru ¼ mile to maximum shown. Shift points indicated by line breaks.

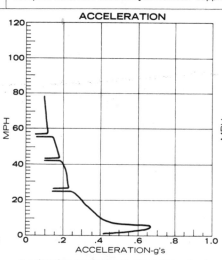

ACCELERATION

Acceleration measured in "g's" from standing start to speed shown. Shift points indicated by "spikes" on graph.

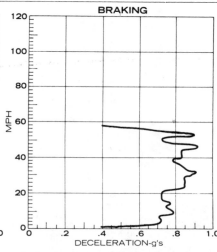

BRAKING

Brakes applied at 60 mph with maximum force, but using pedal "feathering" technique to prevent wheel lockup.

"A PERSON WHO LIKES TO DRIVE WILL ENJOY THIS CAR," SAYS OUR OWNER-REPORTER. SERVICE IS STILL A PROBLEM, HE FEELS, AND THERE ARE SOME DISAPPOINTING FEATURES LIKE BAD CHROME AND SOME RUSTING

Headlights were redisinged to comply with Federal Safety Regulations, but still blend with original design. Bumper protection is minimal.

It was about the beginning of June when our faithful Corvair began to show the ill effects of the 40,000 or so very hard driving miles we had put on the odometer during the previous year. First, the transmission began to emit strange but very expensive sounding noises; then the throwout bearing joined in with a plaintive cry each time the clutch was engaged or disengaged (come to think of it, the clutch did not sound any too good either). Finally, the engine drastically increased its rate of oil consumption.

All this plus the fact that the body shop had not straightened the frame completely from the time whrn we had put the car into a guard rail at about 60 miles per hour while we were foolishly trying to demonstrate our skills as a driver led us to make the decision to buy a new car.

Early in the game the choice of replacement transportation came down to two cars, the Fiat 850 Spider and the Renault R-10, both rear-engined and both under $2100.

Since the new car, like the old one, would be our second car and would be used mainly in our work as a journalist, we decided we wanted a small, economical, "fun-type" car.

While our better half went for the Renault as the more practical of the pair, we fell in love with the Fiat's no-nonsense black on white instruments and the wood (at least we think it is wood) steering wheel. Besides which, we really went for the Bertone styling.

Thus, one day after the Corvair keys had been turned over to the nice man along with a suitable amount of cash, a spanking new green Fiat 850 Spider appeared in the driveway.

Now this is a moment of truth in the life of any new car owner for it is

850 Fiat SPIDER

By BILL OURSLER

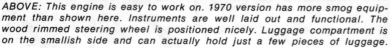

ABOVE: This engine is easy to work on. 1970 version has more smog equipment than shown here. Instruments are well laid out and functional. The wood rimmed steering wheel is positioned nicely. Luggage compartment is on the smallish side and can actually hold just a few pieces of luggage.

850 Fiat

only after the car is brought home that the thought sinks in that it is really yours. With this thought comes the recognition of all those little faults in the car which were either unnoticed or else repressed when the little dear belonged to the other fellow, your local friendly dealer.

The first thing which caught our eye was the ill-fitting rubber matting in the not-too-generous luggage space up front. In fact, about all that can be accommodated there is our camera gear and a small overnight bag. Secondly, we found that the seats were a lot less than really comfortable as they did not provide any support for the small of the back.

The drive from the dealer's place to our house convinced us that the shift linkage was not the most positive we had encountered over the years. First gear was (and still is) extremely difficult to engage.

Our first time in the rain with the car convinced us that not only were the non-radial tires, which come as standard equipment, not the greatest'

things on a wet surface, but also the windshield wipers were too slow even at their fastest setting.

Moreover, the engine from the very first and despite tuneups has displayed an eagerness to run on after being shut off.

As for the controls, the most important switches are easily reached and readily identifiable through the international picture language, but the heater knobs are hidden underneath the dashboard while the choke is nestled in the console between the seats on the driver's side of the handbrake. Finally there is a pull-type handle which, as our wife discovered to her surprise one day, operates a hand throttle. This, like the choke, is not marked.

Although we have found many things wrong with the car, we have spent most of our time in it appreciating the reasons why we bought the car.

Without hesitation, we can say that it is one of the most fun cars we have driven in a long time. Its handling is

beautiful even though it has a semi-swing axle arrangement in the rear, and the brakes have little trouble bringing the car to a halt.

Despite the size of the engine, acceleration was better than fair, and although the tach needle usually rested on the far side of the dial, the engine seemed to be able to handle the high revs without a sweat.

Having driven the car throughout the past winter, several good and bad features have made themselves very clear to us.

Although we had a large amount of snow in New England this past winter, the rear engine lication helped so much that snow tires were not needed and, indeed, were not fitted. The heater is great. On many days we had to turn it down, and it was adequate even in below-zero weather. The car is tight. Like Fiats of the past, the top and its fit are among the best in the business. Finally, the mechanical aspects of the car including the engine and drive train and the electrical system stood up well un-

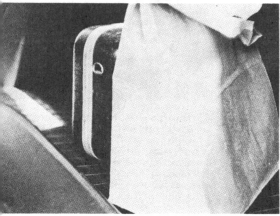

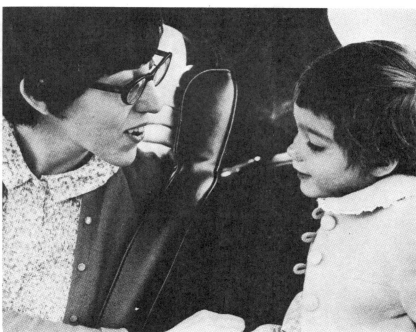

LEFT AND ABOVE: The top stows on the parcel shelf normally. There is lots of room on it when the top is raised. Author's wife, Janice, arranges daughter Jean in her seat on this parcel shelf which id ideal for seating a child of her size. A grownup just wouldn't fit back there.

SPIDER

der the abuse of the winter.

In fact, the engine at 20,000 miles still shows good compression, and the transmission, except for a weakness in the synchromesh ring on second gear which causes it to be slow to engage, is in excellent shape. The brakes still work well, and the battery shows little sign of weakening.

Unfortunately, the same praise can not be given to either the body or the chrome of the car. Fiat chrome just has to be the worst in the business. Almost every piece had started to pit even before the winter set in, and pieces which were replaced pitted again within a short time.

If you buy a Fiat, find a good rechroming place; you are going to need it. The body, on the other hand, started to develop rust spots by mid-winter as the salt and water and winter crud worked their way into and through the various nooks and crannies.

By spring, the entire bottom half of the vehicle had to be repainted. This was caused not only by the rust but

also by the wearing of paint in spots where stones had been kicked up by the tires. Wings can be added to the wheel wells where the tires protrude to cure this problem.

The tires, which had not been rotated but had been balanced when the front end was aligned, were replaced because of wear at about the 19,000 mile mark.

The generator was also replaced about this time after it for some mysterious reason had burned itself out.

At this point it would be well to mention the car's weakest point, the Fiat dealer, himself. Unfortunately, most of the dealers we encountered knew little about the car or how to maintain it which is inexcusable and especially so since the car is a relatively simple machine.

Nevertheless, they seem either not to care, to be totally incompetent or to be ignorant (and sometimes all three) when it comes to service. These are traits which they share with other car dealers of all makes, both im-

ported and domestic, but since Fiat's reputation has been tarnished in the past by poor workmanship, and quality control, it is something which they can not afford to display if they hope to grab a large share of the import market.

To sum up, why should a prospective buyer choose this car? The answer is in the nature of the beast.

The 850 Spider is basically a specialty car in that it is a two-seater with limited luggage space and good short distance performance and comfort. It is not the car to take the whole family cross country to Aunt Millie's, but it is a car which the person who likes to drive can enjoy.

In short, it is a fairly well-made, refined version of the basic British sports car. While not perfect for everyone, it is one of the best designs in its class and a good buy for those looking to combine practicality and fun in driving. Now if they could just fix those minor annoyances and get those dealers working, they would really be in business. ●

SPECIAL! COMMUTERS: $1600 AND UNDER

The Honda 600 and Fiat 850. Two sedans that answer a question Detroit hasn't asked yet. **By Chuck Koch.**

Above: With a 2-cylinder air-cooled engine displacing 598cc, the Honda 600 delivered excellent fuel economy and surprisingly good performance. Below: The Fiat 850, although its performance figures were better than the Japanese competition, also outpriced its Eastern rival by $300.

Urban travel is perhaps the most difficult problem in modern society. With population figures spiraling ever upwards, there has been a proportionate increase in the number of automobiles inhabiting our roads, and whereas it once took only a few minutes to commute from the suburbs to the city, it can now consume more than an hour for the same distance.

There is no surprise at the public outcry against overcrowded streets but, no one is willing to give up his personal means of transportation to help assuage the problem. The solution, therefore, has fallen to the automobile manufacturers and they have responded by offering the public smaller cars. First it was the compacts of the '60s, then a new breed arrived on the scene, the sub-compact. Now, no sooner than we see the Vega and Pinto, foreign auto makers offer a different species; the mini-car, pocket vehicle which may be the ultimate answer. Small vehicles designed for short distance travel with minimum space on crowded highways.

The Honda 600 and Fiat 850 sedans are perfect examples of this new genre of the automobile. They are both extremely small, very maneuverable in all traffic situations, easy to maintain and require gasoline refills only at infrequent intervals. But, the new American sub-compacts can also claim size, ease of maintenance and economy as virtues. However, what they cannot claim, and what is so appealing about the Fiat and Honda, is a price tag under $1,600.

Although the two cars share a common goal, to get you from point A to point B with a minimum of fuss and frustration, along with similar specifications like curb weights less than 1,550 pounds, wheelbases in the 79 inch range, unitized bodies, 32-foot turning diameters and almost equal performance figures, the Honda and Fiat are very dissimilar.

The Honda, for example, has a 598cc 2-cylinder air-cooled engine which looks a lot like a motorcycle engine until you discover a differential and cooling fan not included on the 2-wheelers. It is a front-engine, front-wheel-drive unit which produces 36 hp at 6,000 rpm and

158

FIAT 850

Top left: For a car with small exterior dimensions, Fiat featured good-sized trunk space. Above: Fiat's 843cc 4-cylinder engine produces 42 hp at 5,300 rpm and while not fast, the 29.4 mpg fuel consumption figure is a welcomed consideration in today's tight economy. Left: Although by means roomy, interior is comfortable with a simple dashboard design.

31.8 lbs-ft of torque at 4,000 rpm. The Honda has a 4-speed all synchromesh transmission and a 6.23:1 final drive ratio. The front suspension is independent through MacPherson struts, coil springs, and tube shocks. Rear suspension components are a beam axle, transversely-mounted leaf springs, and tube shock absorbers. The Honda has front disc brakes and rear drums while tire size is 5.20-10.

Fiat, on the other hand, has taken a different engineering tack to fulfill the needs of commuters. The 850 sedan, like its sporty cousin the 850 Spyder, incorporates a rear-engine, rear-wheel-drive set up. The Fiat's 4-cylinder engine displaces 843cc, produces 42 hp at 5,300 rpm and 44 lbs-ft of torque at 3,600 revs. Fiat suspension also differs from Honda's in that it is independent both front and rear. Upper swinging arms, semi-elliptic springs and a stabilizer bar compose the front suspension while hydraulic shocks, swinging arms and a stabilizer bar are used in the rear. The braking system is 4-wheel drums with 5.50-12 tires.

With the placement of the engines and drive-units both cars have, they do not suffer from the driveshaft mound syndrome, therefore, giving occupants a little more room. Actually, though, the room is there anyway, unless you sit in the back seat for extended trips.

HONDA 600

Above: Two-cylinder Honda 600 engine looks a lot like a motorcycle power plant until you discover a differential and cooling fan attached. Top right: As in the Fiat, the Honda's interior is simple and direct. Strange positioning of shift lever does cause problems during gear changes. Right: Trunk space in the Honda is sadly lacking with a smallish cubicle sufficing.

In most small cars the occupants have a feeling that their feet are riding on the front bumper. Not so in the Fiat or Honda. Maybe it's the high seating position of the Fiat or the seemingly endless expanse of glass in the Honda. There is ample arm and leg room for front seat occupants in both cars and the driver is afforded an excellent view of the road in all directions. It even gets a little scary when you see this big Cadillac coming at you from the rear when before you couldn't see that portion of the road from inside a Detroit automobile.

Due to the overall size of the Honda and Fiat, some of the normal Detroit creature comforts are not possible. The seats in the Honda are only comfortable up to a point and the strange positioning of the gear shift lever, up high under the dashboard, combined with its close placement to the driver allows you to pull a quick speed shift with your kneecap. Also, everytime the transmission is shifted a rather loud and disconcerting "gerchunk" issues from the unit. The Fiat has its interior failings also. They center mainly around the operating controls of the car. The clutch, brake, and gas pedals are located too close to each other. This often leads to the error of stepping on both the brake and accelerator at the same time. If you are lucky you'll avoid wedging your foot between the two pedals. The shift lever is long, which cuts down on reach distances, but you get the feeling during shifts that your calf is going into second gear. Other than those quirks, the Honda and Fiat have good interior design.

Instrument packages in both cars are very simplistic and extremely easy to read. In the Fiat, one huge dial suffices for the gauge cluster and includes the speedometer with calibrations showing shift points, a gas gauge and fuel reserve indicator, idiot lights for temperature, oil pressure, and amperage, along with turn signal lights, high beam indicator, and so forth. The Honda has two round dials containing necessary instruments placed directly behind the steering wheel. On the right is the speedometer which also has shift point indicators while the left dial contains the fuel gauge, battery discharge warning and lights for turn signals, high beams and parking brakes. Regrettably, no oil pressure light is included. All operating controls on both cars are extremely easy to reach and the all-too-normal confusion of too many buttons does not exist in these vehicles.

When you get down to a discussion on the styling of the Fiat and Honda, you have to bear in mind the old cliche that "function is beauty." If that statement is true, then these two cars must be the most beautiful machines ever produced, for their design is purely functional: basic box. There are no huge banks of headlights, overbearing grille work or tons of shining chrome. These fixtures would only be superfluous to the cars' basic job, that of commuting in traffic. The Honda resembles a dehydrated station wagon with a high — 52.4-inch — roofline which ex-

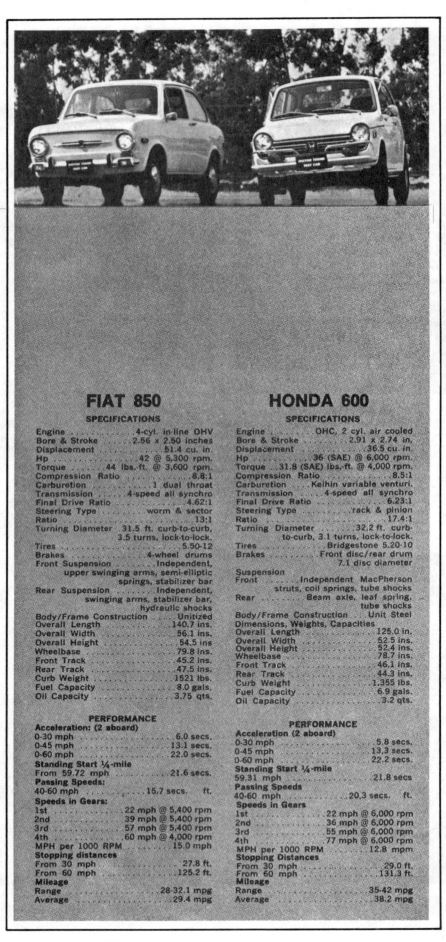

FIAT 850
SPECIFICATIONS

Engine	4-cyl. in-line OHV
Bore & Stroke	2.56 x 2.50 inches
Displacement	51.4 cu. in.
Hp	42 @ 5,300 rpm.
Torque	44 lbs.-ft. @ 3,600 rpm.
Compression Ratio	8.8:1
Carburetion	1 dual throat
Transmission	4-speed all synchro
Final Drive Ratio	4.62:1
Steering Type	worm & sector
Ratio	13:1
Turning Diameter	31.5 ft. curb-to-curb, 3.5 turns, lock-to-lock.
Tires	5.50-12
Brakes	4-wheel drums
Front Suspension	Independent, upper swinging arms, semi-elliptic springs, stabilizer bar
Rear Suspension	Independent, swinging arms, stabilizer bar, hydraulic shocks
Body/Frame Construction	Unitized
Overall Length	140.7 ins.
Overall Width	56.1 ins.
Overall Height	54.5 ins
Wheelbase	79.8 ins.
Front Track	45.2 ins.
Rear Track	47.5 ins.
Curb Weight	1521 lbs.
Fuel Capacity	8.0 gals.
Oil Capacity	3.75 qts.

PERFORMANCE
Acceleration: (2 aboard)

0-30 mph	6.0 secs.
0-45 mph	13.1 secs.
0-60 mph	22.0 secs.

Standing Start ¼-mile

From 59.72 mph	21.6 secs.

Passing Speeds:

40-60 mph	15.7 secs. ft.

Speeds in Gears:

1st	22 mph @ 5,400 rpm
2nd	39 mph @ 5,400 rpm
3rd	57 mph @ 5,400 rpm
4th	60 mph @ 4,000 rpm
MPH per 1000 RPM	15.0 mph

Stopping distances

From 30 mph	27.8 ft.
From 60 mph	125.2 ft.

Mileage

Range	28-32.1 mpg
Average	29.4 mpg

HONDA 600
SPECIFICATIONS

Engine	OHC, 2 cyl. air cooled
Bore & Stroke	2.91 x 2.74 in.
Displacement	36.5 cu. in.
Hp	36 (SAE) @ 6,000 rpm.
Torque	31.8 (SAE) lbs.-ft. @ 4,000 rpm.
Compression Ratio	8.5:1
Carburetion	Keihin variable venturi.
Transmission	4-speed all synchro
Final Drive Ratio	6.23:1
Steering Type	rack & pinion
Ratio	17.4:1
Turning Diameter	32.2 ft. curb-to-curb, 3.1 turns, lock-to-lock.
Tires	Bridgestone 5.20-10
Brakes	Front disc/rear drum 7.1 disc diameter
Suspension	
Front	Independent MacPherson struts, coil springs, tube shocks
Rear	Beam axle, leaf spring, tube shocks
Body/Frame Construction	Unit Steel
Dimensions, Weights, Capacities	
Overall Length	125.0 in.
Overall Width	52.5 ins.
Overall Height	52.4 ins.
Wheelbase	78.7 ins.
Front Track	46.1 ins.
Rear Track	44.3 ins.
Curb Weight	1,355 lbs.
Fuel Capacity	6.9 gals.
Oil Capacity	3.2 qts.

PERFORMANCE
Acceleration (2 aboard)

0-30 mph	5.8 secs.
0-45 mph	13.3 secs.
0-60 mph	22.2 secs.

Standing Start ¼-mile

59.31 mph	21.8 secs

Passing Speeds

40-60 mph	20.3 secs. ft.

Speeds in Gears

1st	22 mph @ 6,000 rpm
2nd	36 mph @ 6,000 rpm
3rd	55 mph @ 6,000 rpm
4th	77 mph @ 6,000 rpm
MPH per 1000 RPM	12.8 mpm

Stopping Distances

From 30 mph	29.0 ft.
From 60 mph	131.3 ft.

Mileage

Range	35-42 mpg
Average	38.2 mpg

tends back until a rather abrupt slash sends it plummeting to rear bumper level. The only hint of style in the car is a windshield slanted a "rakish" 31 degrees from the vertical position. This, combined with a slightly lowered front end profile, lends the honest-to-goodness illusion of speed. Although originating in the fatherland of automobile styling, the Fiat has only a sloping rear window, suggestive of a fastback GT car, and flared wheel wells as concessions to modern design while the remainder of the car sticks to the functional box look.

Speed is also a duty of function. While a figure of 150 mph may sound impressive, on a Group 7 race car it would mean nothing. That is the way you must look at the Honda and Fiat. They are not fast cars, but they are not meant to be. Even with this in mind, it is a good feeling to know that both cars are quite comfortable when traveling at freeway speeds. Both can handle a smooth 70 mph without difficulty and it is possible to coax them above 75 mph on occasion. Their only downfall lies in inclement weather. The slightest breeze, coupled with the cars' light weight, narrow track, and short wheelbase, causes both cars, particularly the Honda, to wander in traffic lanes. It is nothing serious, but you do get an insecure feeling when the wind blows. Despite this slight failing, the ride qualities in both cars are good, maybe a little rough, but stable under normal conditions.

Performance figures for the cars are, of course, not at all spectacular. In fact,

it almost seems inappropriate to quote them, but they do allow some insight into the machines and their functions.

Surprisingly, the Fiat and Honda, despite their small displacements and prodigious lack of power, show a fair amount of pep on the track. In acceleration runs the Honda, with a much lower drive ratio, was faster to 30 mph, 5.8 seconds to the Fiat's 6.0. Once above this speed, however, the Fiat came on to record a 13.1 time to 45 mph and 22.0 to 60 mph while the Honda droned to times of 13.3 and 22.2 at the same speeds. In the quarter mile runs, the Fiat got down to 21.6 seconds and 59.72 mph with the Honda registering a 21.8 e.t. at 59.31 mph. Passing speed honors also went to the Fiat with 15.7 seconds from 40 to 60 mph while the Honda required 20.3. Sure, you're not going to suffer whiplash everytime the accelerator is depressed, but you will get mileage figures of 29 mpg for the Fiat and an astonishing 38 mpg average by the Honda. What more can a commuter car do?

Handling characteristics are as dissimilar as the cars, with different engine placements and drive units this is only to be expected. The Honda, with its front-wheel-drive and beam axle rear suspension, exhibits decided understeer when cornering, a normal reaction for a power train of this sort. Under hard cornering the front wheels just plow across the turn while the inside rear wheel elevates itself a good 4 inches off the road surface. The rear-engine Fiat, on the other hand, enters a corner with initial understeer and as you begin to accelerate out of the turn, final oversteer is encountered. Both cars had body roll during cornering, but it is

not the sort to be upsetting although the driver feels he must exert a certain amount of body english in order to negotiate the turn.

Steering response on each car is fairly good with the Fiat feeling a little front heavy despite its engine location. It has a 13:1 ratio in the worm and sector steering unit with 3.5 turns lock-to-lock at the wheel. The Honda's rack and pinion steering claims a 17.4:1 ratio and 3.1 turns lock-to-lock. One disappointing, and unexplained fact is the width of both cars' turning circles; 32.2 feet for the Honda and 31.5 feet by the Fiat. Somehow compared to the VW's 36 feet, this doesn't seem plausible for automobiles with such short wheelbases.

After driving the Honda and Fiat for two weeks in Los Angeles traffic and after seeing what they could do when really pushed, we came away thinking that these two cars fulfill their function beautifully. The Fiat 850 and Honda 600 sedans have everything a commuter could possibly want, small size, ease of driving, low maintenance cost, and an inexpensive list price. When you swoop into the ultra-low-buck class, even price differences of a hundred dollars are sufficiently significant to bracket vehicles in different classes so you can't compare the Honda and Fiat head-to-head. By logic of its lower price, Honda is a better investment. By ride and space the Fiat is more sensible, if that enters into it at all. The only other problem is convincing those drivers of big cars that this is the solution to our immediate traffic problems. Besides, in their way, they bring back some of the fun of driving we've crowded out of our lives.   /MT

FIAT 850S

(Continued from page 90)

over my test course soon put them out of my mind.

An average of 52.75 m.p.h. was once reserved for sports cars and fast saloons; but such were the Fiat's handling and braking that I was able to keep the foot down longer than with higher-powered machinery — rather in the same manner that a

1500c.c. racer can make up on a 2500c.c. on twisty circuits.

The hillclimb time of 2min. 38sec. and a quarter-mile at 22.2sec. are quite remarkable — and the 850S's circuit and climb results shaded the outstanding Viva figures I ran off about a year ago.

So—will the 850S appeal to Australians? I'll be surprised if it doesn't suit them very well, both as family car and a fun-to-drive machine for Dad, when he feels so inclined. It

has looks, finish, room, economy, long legs and spirit—but it has a hard road to hoe against established competitors.

That 12 months' lag, especially, has put it in a difficult situation, for now it must compete against the recently released 998c.c. hydrolastic Mini Deluxe—a big advance on the normal Morris 850, and priced only £1 above the Fiat's tag of £832 tax-paid.

Still, I wish it luck, for it's a game little wildcat.   •

FIAT 850 SPIDER

CONTINUED FROM PAGE 124

Except for the three light toggles and wiper switch, most on-off knobs are scattered pretty haphazardly, where there happened to be space I would judge. The drop-down glove bin is not a success, mostly due to flimsy construction, and the alloy wheel is very pretty but a following

sun reflects off its spokes. I'd paint mine matt black.

And we're off. At 54 SAE hp (the same output as the T-Type MG 1250s) this is a very quick 850, and for town use or wandering the byways, one that is quite hot enough. For passing, however, it lacks torque. This is a condemnation of the size as such, not the Fiat-tuned version which remains the nicest 850 I've driven. Cars are just getting

larger these days and you need more sheer engine volume to keep up safely.

At its red line of 6200 rpm, the Spider is definitely buzzy but obviously willing to go all day. With the top down and that rear deck catching the wind it is hard to excede the red line in top anyway, giving you a couple of miles over 80. With the top up you have to watch the tach like a hawk. The im-

850 SPECIAL

FIAT South Africa's "baby" — the 850 Special — is a pretty and capable little car. It is bargain-priced at R1 450 (only three other cars are obtainable at under R1 500, new), and of the cars in this class, it is way out front in equipment and performance.

The 850 Special — an uprated version of the earlier 850 Super — is popular as a runabout and second car, and is often praised by owners for its practical features and operating economy.

Overseas it is also available in handsome coupé form, and it is good news that this 850 Special Coupé has also become available in the Republic now, in limited volume, priced at R1 980.

CONVERTIBLE SEDAN

Essential features of the 850 Special are that it is a two-door, rear-engined, rear-wheel-drive light car, with a rear seat which folds down to create a utility space of considerable size — something over half a cubic meter, or 20 cu. ft.

The interior is tidy, with well-shaped individual front seats, a centre console with oddments tray, heater, windscreen washers and parcel shelf for both driver and front-seat passenger. The front luggage trunk has a useful capacity and interior release control, the lid opening forward for safety.

Ventilation inlets include well-placed swivelling ducts at centre on the fascia, and hinged rear side windows to allow through-flow.

DRIVER CONTROLS

A sporty-looking simulated wood-rim steering wheel is fitted, and the four-speed gearbox — a very good one — is controlled by a sports-type shift on the floor console.

Instrumentation is rather basic — a metric speedometer and odometer, with fuel and temperature gauges plus warning lights.

With an engine that revs freely to 6 500 rpm a rev-counter is normally required, but its absence can perhaps be excused on such a low-priced model. One could be fitted, with some adaptation, but in normal driving the revs are very audible and this tough little engine is not likely to be pushed too far.

The metric speedometer is reasonably accurate, with a slight over-reading error, and it is supplemented with a strip reading in mph, which can be removed once the driver is accustomed to metrics.

There is one irritating feature in the instrumentation: a very "loud" pilot light which appears to have only one function: telling the driver that parking and/or driving lights are switched on. This bright green "idiot light" cannot be switched off, and becomes most irksome in night driving: Remedy: disconnect it, or cover it with plastic tape.

PERFORMANCE ENGINE

This high-compression, 843-cm³ engine is a sweet little motor, proving tough and willing on test. With 9·3 compression ratio, it is rated for 98-octane fuel. It might have been running on a slight retard on our 93-octane, but it gave flashing performance and showed no signs of distress.

It is a fairly vocal motor, becoming noisy at higher revs, but gentle-running at about-town speeds — though 3rd gear is often needed in urban areas. It uses a twin-choke downdraught carburettor, either Weber or Holly/Weber (they are interchangeable) and free-flow exhaust manifold to get the breathing necessary for a peak of 6 400 revs.

Although the rear panel can be removed to improve it, we rate engine access as "very poor" because of such things as an oil dipstick which hides between the exhaust branches to invite burnt fingers, an oil filler which can only be used via a long-spout funnel, and water filler which is similarly inaccessible — though with a sealed cooling system this filler is not often used. Little things like working on the carburettor or changing a thermostat would be quite an operation on this car.

On the other hand, though the bonnet panel is small, distributor and timing controls are well placed for servicing, and with the correct tools, plug changing would not be too bad.

GEARING AND WHEELS

Another distinction for the 850 Special: the only car in its class with radial-ply tyres on semi-wide-rim wheels. Standard tyres are 145 x 13 radials, but as the rims are 4½J, we would be inclined to fit 155's on replacement.

This would reduce the car's under-gearing, which is rather pronounced at 20·9 km/h 1 000 rpm (13·0 mph), giving more range, less noise and even better fuel economy. We found that the car only just goes to 100 km/h in 3rd, for instance.

Although the car has only a mild oversteer tendency, Fiat seems to be sensitive about this, and specifies a big front/rear differential in tyre pressures to promote understeer. We increased front pressures by a fair amount for this Test, without any handling defects arising, and would suggest 1·5 bars (22 lb) front and 1·9 (28 lb) rear for normal purposes — that is, a differential of 0·4 bars instead of the specified 0·7 — with small increases for high-speed and/or loaded driving.

PERFORMANCE

Like most rear-engined cars — and particularly when fitted with radials — the Fiat 850 Special is little inclined to spin driving wheels on a fast start from rest, but the clutch takes this extra load cheerfully, and performance is quite exceptional for a car of this engine capacity.

It goes to 100 km/h in 18·1 sec, or, by our disappearing standards, to 60 mph in 17·5 sec, covering the 400 m (¼ mile) sprint in 20·5 sec, and will go on to a true maximum speed of 130 km/h (80·8 mph).

(continued overleaf)

SPECIFICATIONS

ENGINE:

Cylinders	4 in line, rear-mounted
Carburettor	Twin-choke Holly/Weber
Bore	65·0 mm (2·56 in.)
Stroke	63·5 mm (2·50 in.)
Cubic capacity	843 cm³ (51·6 cu. in.)
Compression ratio	8·3 to 1
Valve gear	Ohv, pushrods
Main bearings	Three
Aircleaner	Paper element
Fuel rating	98-octane
Cooling	Water, sealed system
Electrics	12-volt DC

ENGINE OUTPUT:

Max. bhp SAE	38·8 kW (52 bhp)
Max. bhp net	35·0 kW (47 bhp)
Peak rpm	6 400
Max. torque/rpm	58·6 N.m/3 800 (43·5 lb.ft.)

TRANSMISSION:

Forward speeds	Four
Synchromesh	All
Gearshift	Floor console
Low gear	3·636 to 1
2nd gear	2·055 to 1
3rd gear	1·409 to 1
Top gear	0·963 to 1
Reverse gear	3·615 to 1
Final drive	5·125 to 1
Drive wheels	Rear
Tyre size	145 radials on 4½J x 13 rims

BRAKES:

Front	Discs
Rear	Drums

Total lining area	N/S
Boosting	Nil
Handbrake position	Between seats

STEERING:

Type	Worm and sector
Lock to lock	3·2 turns
Turning circle	9·63 m (31·5 ft.)

MEASUREMENTS:

Length overall	3·575 m (140·7 in.)
Width overall	1·425 m (56·5 in.)
Height overall	1·385 m (54·5 in.)
Wheelbase	2·027 m (79·8 in.)
Front track	1·148 m (45·0 in.)
Rear track	1·207 m (47·8 in.)
Ground clearance	0·019 m (7·5 in.)
Licensing weight	693 kg (1 525 lb)

SUSPENSION:

Front	Independent
Type	Transverse leaf spring, anti-roll bar
Rear	Independent
Type	Coils and semi-trailing arms, anti-roll bar

CAPACITIES:

Seating	4/5
Fuel tank	30 litres (6·5 gal)
Luggage trunk	0·17 m³ (6·0 cu. ft. approx.)
Utility space	0·57 m³ (20·0 cu. ft. approx.)

SERVICE DATA:

Sump and filter capacity	3·3 litres (5·8 pints)
Change interval	10 000 km (6 000 miles)
Gear diff capacity	2·05 litres (3·6 pints)
Change interval	30 000 km (18 000 miles)
Air filter change	10 000 km (6 000 miles)
Greasing points	Two
Greasing interval	2 500 km (1 500 miles)

(These basic service recommendations are given for guidance only, and may vary according to operating conditions. Inquiries should be addressed to authorised dealerships.)

TYRE PRESSURES:
Radial ply: Front 1·2 to 1·7 bars (18–24 lb)
Rear 1·8 to 2·2 bars (26–32 lb)

WARRANTY:
Six months or 6 000 miles.

BASIC PRICES:

Coast and Reef	R1,450

PROVIDED TEST CAR:
Fiat South Africa, Alberton, Transvaal.

STANDARD EQUIPMENT:
Heater/demister with blower, windscreen washers, sports steering wheel, centre console, disc front brakes, radial-ply tyres on semi-wide-rim wheels, rubber-faced bumper overriders, headlamp flasher, roof grab-handles with coat hooks, door pockets, dipping rearview mirror, steel sump guard, chromed exhaust tailpipe.

PERFORMANCE

MAKE AND MODEL:
Make . . . . Fiat
Model . . . . 850 Special

PERFORMANCE FACTORS:
Power/mass (kg/kW) . . . . . 19·8
Frontal area (m³) . . . . 1·97
km/h/1 000 rpm (top) . . . . 20·9
(Calculated on licensing mass, gross frontal area, gearing and net power output.)

INTERIOR NOISE LEVELS:
	Min.
Idling	54·0
60 km/h	74·5
80 km/h	79·5
100 km/h	82·0
Full throttle	See graph

(Measured in decibels, "A" weighting, averaging runs both ways on a level road; "Minimum" with car closed.)

ACCELERATION FROM REST:
0–50	4·7
0–60	6·3
0–70	9·1
0–80	11·9
0–90	15·0
0–100	18·1
0–110	25·8
0–120	36·4
400 m	20·5

OVERTAKING ACCELERATION:
	3rd	Top
40–60	4·7	9·4
60–80	5·4	8·7
80–100	6·8	10·9
100–120	—	19·0

(Measured in seconds, to true speeds, averaging runs both ways on a level road, car carrying test crew of two and standard test equipment.)

MAXIMUM SPEED:
True speed . . . . 130·0 km/h
Speedo reading . . . . . 137·0 km/h
Calibration:
Indicated	40	60	80	100	120
True speed	42	59	78	97	115

FUEL ECONOMY (litres/100 km in brackets):
60 km/h . . . . 17·4 km/l (5·8)
80 km/h . . . . 14·5 km/l (6·9)
100 km/h . . . . . . 12·5 km/l (8·0)
Full throttle . . . . . . See graph
(Measured in kilometres per litre, averaging runs both ways on a level road.)

BRAKING TEST:
From 80 km/h:
First stop . . . . 2·6
Tenth stop . . . . 3·6
Average . . . . 3·07
(Measured in sec, with stops from true speeds at 30-sec intervals on a good bituminised surface.)

GRADIENTS IN GEARS:
Low gear . . . . 1 in 3·2
2nd gear . . . . 1 in 4·7
3rd gear . . . . 1 in 6·7
Top gear . . . . 1 in 11·3
(Tabulated from Tapley (x gravity) readings, car carrying test crew of two and standard test equipment.)

GEARED SPEEDS:
Low gear . . . . 36·1 km/h
2nd gear . . . . 63·6 km/h
3rd gear . . . . 92·3 km/h
Top gear . . . . 136·0 km/h
(Calculated to true speeds, at engine peak rpm — 6 400.)

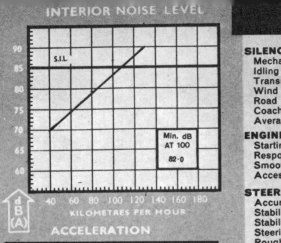

INTERIOR NOISE LEVEL

S.I.L.

Min. dB AT 100
82·0

dB(A) / KILOMETRES PER HOUR

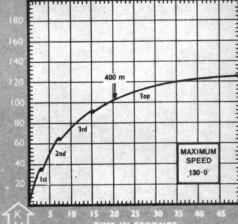

ACCELERATION

400 m

Top

3rd

2nd

1st

MAXIMUM SPEED
130·0

KMH / TIME IN SECONDS

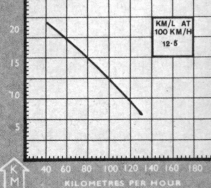

FUEL CONSUMPTION

KM/L AT 100 KM/H
12·5

KML / KILOMETRES PER HOUR

ENGINE SPEED

MAXIMUM TORQUE

Top

3rd

2nd

1st

KMH / REVS. PER MINUTE

TEST REPORT

SILENCE LEVELS:
Mechanical . . . . Poo
Idling . . . . Poo
Transmission . . . . Goo
Wind . . . . Fa
Road . . . . Goo
Coachwork . . . . Goo
Average . . . . Fa

ENGINE:
Starting . . . . Goo
Response . . . . Goo
Smoothness . . . . Fa
Accessibility . . . . . Very Poo

STEERING:
Accuracy . . . . Goo
Stability at speed . . . . . Goo
Stability in wind . . . . . . Fa
Steering effort . . . . Very Goo
Roughness . . . . Goo
Road feel . . . . Goo
Centring action . . . . . . Poo
Turning circle . . . . Goo

BRAKING:
Pedal pressure . . . . Goo
Response . . . . Very Goo
Fade resistance . . . . . . Goo
Directional stability . . . . Goo
Handbrake position . . . Very Goo
Handbrake action . . . Very Goo

TRANSMISSION:
Clutch action . . . . . Very Goo
Pedal pressure . . . . . . Goo
Gearbox ratios . . . . . . Goo
Final drive ratio . . . . . . Poo
Gearshift position . . . Very Goo
Gearshift action . . . Very Goo
Synchromesh . . . . Very Goo

SUSPENSION:
Firmness rating . . . . Very Goo
Progressive action . . . Very Goo
Roadholding . . . . Goo
Roll control . . . . . . Excelle
Tracking control . . . . . . Fa
Pitching control . . . . . . Goo
Load ability . . . . Goo

DRIVER CONTROLS:
Hand control location . . . . Goo
Pedal location . . . . Fa
Wiper action . . . . Goo
Washer action . . . . . . Goo
Instrumentation . . . . . . Fa

INTERIOR COMFORT:
Seat design . . . . Goo
Headroom front . . . . . . Goo
Legroom front . . . . . . Goo
Headroom rear . . . . . . Po
Legroom rear . . . . Fa
Door access . . . . Fa
Lighting . . . . Goo
Accessories fitted . . . . . Fa
Accessories potential . . . . Fa

DRIVING COMFORT:
Steering wheel position . . . Goo
Steering wheel reach . . . Goo
Visibility . . . . . . Very Goo
Directional feel . . . . . . Fa
Ventilation . . . . Fa
Heating . . . . . . Very Goo

COACHWORK:
Appearance . . . . Goo
Finish . . . . Goo
Space utilization . . . Very Goo
Trunk capacity . . . . . . Goo
Trunk access . . . . Fa

TEST CONDITIONS:
Altitude . . . . At sea lev
Weather . . . . Fine and wa
Fuel used 93-octa
Test car's odometer . . . . 5 710 k

Its capabilities are best illustrated by a comparison (in Imperial measures) with the standard 850 Super Road Test (CAR May, 1967):

			850	850S
0–40	..	..	9·6	**7·3**
0–50	..	..	14·7	**11·7**
0–60	..	..	25·0	**18·1**
0–70	..	..	47·5	**29·3**
¼ Mile	..	..	22·2	**20·5**
Speed	..	..	76·0	**80·8**

It also has strong overtaking ability, but with torque coming in only over 3 000 rpm, 3rd gear is needed at speeds below 60 km/h (38 mph).

FUEL ECONOMY

A 30-litre fuel tank is pretty small, but when the car is capable of well on the sunny side of 10 kilometres per litre at cruising speeds, it goes a long way. All Fiat models are strong on economy, and this one is no exception.

With reasonable driving, owners are likely to get 12–15 km/l over, say, a year's driving. For those who have not quite caught up yet, that would be 35–40 mpg: either way, a highly-satisfactory figure.

STOPPING ABILITY

The front disc brakes on the 850 Special (again, it is the only car in its price/engine capacity class to be fitted with them) are so good that, even with radial-ply tyres and without boosting, it is possible to lock front wheels in a hard stop.

This is easily controlled, and we were able to get very sound stopping times with this firm-handling little car: an average of just over 3 sec for 10 stops from 80 km/h. with just a shade of fade developing toward the end, and from 120 km/h — which is a severe test for any touring car — in 4·3 sec.

VENTILATION AND NOISE

The ventilation system is as good or better than any car in this class, and only one other car in this class has a heater as standard equipment.

Wind noise is not high, and with the radials, road noise drops to a very low level for a light car.

The only real source of noise is the engine, and then only if the available revs are used. At cruising speeds, the decibels rise to just above speech interference level, but about town and on expressways, the car is smooth and quite reasonably quiet. Quite possibly, the quietest in its class — so what are we fussing about?

DATA AT 120

Min. noise level	87·5 dBA
0–120 through gears . .	36·4 sec
Economy at 120 . 10·7 km/l (9·4 litres/	
	100 km)
Braking from 120	4·3 sec
Reserve power . .	0·032 (x gravity)
Max. gradient (top) . . .	1 in 31·2
Speedo error	4·2% over
Speedo at true 120	115
Rpm at 120 (top)	5 720

HANDLING AND LOAD

This is a firm-handling car with strong, all-independent suspension, "tame" swing axles which do not cause problems, and anti-roll bars front and rear. The body is very stable in cornering, and the handling dependable on radials: oversteer can be created by using power.

The suspension is load-capable and yet comfortable, primarily because of its strong progressive action.

SUMMARY

The Fiat 850 Special is not to be compared directly with GT cars costing R500 and upwards more, but it runs them a close second in general capability.

Like all the modern Fiats, it is a car which shows imagination in design and engineering, and high standards in manufacture and equipment. It is a drivers' car, yet very easy to drive.

It derives from the almost-legendary Fiat 500, 600 and 750 models, and is the greatest of them all. ●

IMPERIAL DATA

Major performance features of this Road Test are summarised below in metric measures:

PERFORMANCE FACTORS:

Power/mass (lb/bhp) . . .	32·4
Frontal area (sq. ft.) . . .	21·2
Mph/1 000 rpm (top) . . .	13·0

ACCELERATION FROM REST (in seconds):

0–30	4·7
0–40	7·3
0–50	11·7
0–60	17·5
0–70	29·3
¼ Mile	20·5

MAXIMUM SPEED (mph):

True speed	80·8

FUEL CONSUMPTION:

30	55·8
45	43·6
60	35·8
75	30·2

GEARED SPEEDS:

1st gear	22·4
2nd gear	39·5
3rd gear	57·6
Top gear	84·5

The neat appearance is enhanced by rubber-faced overriders and radial-ply tyres on semi-wide rims.

Engine access is through this narrow aperture: oil dipstick (left) is in a hot-spot position.

The front luggage trunk locks from inside, and its depth gives useful capacity.

Sports-type simulated woodrim wheel, centre console and moulded rubber mats are good interior features.

Fiat 850T Utility

Brief Test

Big-hearted, frugal friend of large impecunious families, teams or firms; clever engineering prevents the Fiat minibus from being a misery to drive or a mobile traffic jam

DO you want to get that coach-driver feeling without spending too much money on it? Well, you could do worse than try the Fiat 850T Utility. For £1,004 you get seven, maybe eight, seats besides your own. You get all-independent suspension. You get a rear engine, just like many of the modern coaches. You get a high driving position right at the front of the vehicle, three big doors and a little one.

Lest it all goes to your head, the 850T is based on the little 850 saloon. The forward-control, bus-type body gives that generous seating capacity, yet allows the length to be kept to just over 12ft. Combined with a remarkably tight turning circle, it means that this big-looking vehicle can be slotted into ridiculous-looking parking spaces.

Apart from that, it is only 4ft 10in. wide, which makes it much better than you would think for squeezing through narrow gaps. Oddly enough, if it were bigger, it might also be cheaper. Had it the room for 12 seats, the 850T would carry no purchase tax; but with

only nine, it means £202 for the Chancellor....

The Japanese make vehicles in this class based on their tiny 360 c.c. cars, which probably robs the 850T of the title of Smallest Bus in the World. The interesting thing, however, is the way the Fiat slots into the European traffic pattern without drama.

It is *not* impossibly slow. Its standing-start acceleration times compare well with those we have on file for the Mini Traveller. In part this is achieved by what are euphemistically termed "Alpine" gear ratios, which means that first, second and third are low and close, while top is high and wide, so to speak. The whole effect is magnified by the engine, which is a low-compression (7.3 to 1) version of that used in the 850 Coupé — i.e., it is actually 903 c.c. — and which is almost the only Fiat engine *not* willing to be revved until the driver's nerve gives out. A screaming limit of 5,500rpm gives the princely maximum speed of 18mph in first gear, followed by 32mph in second, and 46mph in third. Top gear gave us a mean 64mph, and the incredible commotion which

Above left: Generous top hatch opens to give access to the engine. The rear panel opens too; accessibility is good. Above right: Rear door is for luggage only; the luggage platform makes a convenient table or bench if you are working near the vehicle. Below left: Driving position is bus-like, but none the worse for that; neatly-shrouded spare wheel takes up some of the front passenger's legroom. Below right: Middle row of seats folds forward to give access to the rear or to create a load platform

ensued the only time we hit a true 70mph (downhill) more or less ensures that you will stay legal.

The gearchange, and indeed the controls as a whole, are good. The change itself is light, precise and spring-loaded into third/top, so that it almost changes itself when you are racing taxis away from the lights. Steering is by Fiat's beloved worm and roller, with a sense of vagueness which is due more to the chassis than to the system. Actually, straight-line stability is by no means bad, but the driver can never quite stop making small corrections to maintain course.

The brakes are rather less reassuring. At times, slipping the 850T into neutral when approaching a hold-up almost gives the impression that it is accelerating again; but a really hefty shove on the brake pedal soon brings results. It is not, however, a progressive enough system to be used with finesse. A skilled driver can do better by relying on the lower gears alone, using the brakes only when coming to a complete stop.

Apart from its small size and clever gear ratios, the Fiat's other great secret for speedy traffic-penetration is the driver's high sitting position. This gives him an eye level somewhere between that of bus and taxi, quite sufficient to see over the roofs of mere cars and anticipate the traffic pattern. All-round visibility is good, and the vehicle seems not to mist up inside despite the apparent lack of any form of ventilation.

Heating is primitive. Water flows, via a simple tap, into a front radiator whose airflow depends on forward movement — there is no fan. For all that, it is effective in terms of quantity of heat once the 850T is moving at more than a crawl.

For the average driver, the 850T is something that must be learned. Seated as one is right at the front of the vehicle, one tends to cut corners rather viciously until one learns to run the nose wide, almost "going past" the turning and then hauling the beast round. In tight corners, the two well-placed wing mirrors help a lot.

Within limits, the vehicle handles well. At normal speeds it simply goes round corners. The unusual driving position upsets any normal judgment of niceties like understeer — in fact, almost everything feels like oversteer. Real oversteer does eventually set in and there is little doubt that the 850T could be deliberately rolled. Warning signs are plentiful, however, and on wet roads the back wheels are much more likely simply to slide. In practical terms, the vehicle is never limited by its handling in ordinary traffic situations. Trying conclusions with a well-driven Mini down a country lane might be something else altogether.

One fact of life underlined by the 850T is that a very upright driving position caters for a much wider variety of drivers without the need for adjustment. Our largest driver took it to MIRA with no complaint beyond the hardness of the seat and the shortness of the cushion; yet there is no adjustment of any kind provided. The ride is better than might be expected, although the short wheelbase gives rise to some pitching. With a heavy load aboard, the ride improves almost as much as the performance suffers. Roll angles are never large.

Although, for *Autocar*, the 850T was something of a "joke" test, there was no denying the practicality of the vehicle. For a man with a large family and a limited budget, or firms needing an eight-seat minibus, it has strong attractions — not least of which is a fuel consumption of 29mpg, running on 91 octane (or lower, if you can find it). But perhaps the most significant thing of all was that we actually *enjoyed* driving it. . . . ☐

Left: The side door (one only, on the left) is very large. The rear-mounted engine makes it impossible to fit a full back door. Below: Neat in appearance, the 850T is actually very compact, smaller than it looks in both length and width; while the turning circle is very good

PERFORMANCE CHECK

Maximum speeds

Gear	mph		kph		rpm	
	850T	Special	850T	Special	850T	Special
Top (mean)	64	80	103	129	5,160	5,850
(best)	66	84	106	135	5,300	6,110
3rd	46	70	74	113	5,500	7,200
2nd	32	45	51	72	5,500	7,200
1st	18	26	29	42	5,500	7,200

Standing ¼-mile	850T	24.4 sec	53 mph
	Special	21.3 sec	62 mph
Standing kilometre	850T	47.6 sec	62 mph
	Special	40.8 sec	72 mph

Acceleration,

850T	6.7	11.9	21.1	40.2	—	—
Special	5.0	8.5	12.9	19.0	32.6	—
Time in seconds	0					
True speed mph	30	40	50	60	70	80

Indicated speed mph 850T	31	41	51	61	—	—
Indicated speed mph Special	32	42	52	62	72	82

Speed range, Gear Ratios and Time in seconds

Mph	Top		3rd	
	850T	Special	850T	Special
0-20				
10-30	14.7	—	8.4	9.5
20-40	15.3	16.3	9.3	9.0
30-50	18.2	16.6	—	9.4
40-60	30.5	19.4	—	11.2
50-70	—	26.3	—	—

Fuel Consumption

Overall mpg	850T	29.0 mpg	(9.7 litres/100km)
	Special	29.0 mpg	(9.7 litres/100km)

NOTE: "Special" denotes performance figures for Fiat 850 Special tested in *AUTOCAR* of 3 October 1968.

Wally Pratt owns what looks like a Fiat 600. But the scorpion badges give the game away: this is a 65 bhp Abarth 850TC, in which Wally, aged 72, has won over 200 trophies. He talked to John Simister

STING

N THE TAIL

I n the middle of Wally Pratt's sitting room mantlepiece is a scale model of a Fiat 600. It's painted blue, the same blue as his front door. On top of some shelves to the right is a larger model of a Fiat 600, this time in clear Perspex. Look still further to the right and there's a Fiat that's larger still. In fact it's a real one, sitting in the road outside. It, too, is blue.

Wally Pratt bought it in 1968 from Paul Huxford, when it was three years old. It's his everyday transport and has covered 185,000 miles. "So what," you think. "That's only 8409 miles a year."

True enough. The point is, though, that Wally has during those 185,000 miles collected around 200 trophies – gained through a list of sprint and hillclimb class wins, as well as outright championship titles – as long as both your arms and your legs as

well. In club-level competition, Wally's Fiat and Wally's skill have been an unbeatable combination.

In a Fiat 600D? Actually, no. The scorpion badges give the lie to the sting in this particular Fiat's tail: it's a Fiat Abarth 850 TC. They used to race around European saloon circuits with their engine lids propped open, doing to the larger cars what racing Minis did in Britain. With around 65 bhp in a car weighing 597 kg (11.8 cwt), it's not hard to see how.

There's another interesting thing about Wally Pratt. He's 72 years old, and made his racing debut (in another Fiat Abarth) at the age of 50. It was an auspicious debut; he won the Abarth trophy (his favourite one) in 1965 for his racing successes. "I used to write to Carlo Abarth and tell him what I'd been doing," says Wally.

The Abarth trophy, cast in bronze and signed by Carlo himself, lives in a red presentation

The sting in the tail: 65 bhp worth of Abarth-camshafted engine with Weber progressive twin-choke carb. The cars used to race with the engine lids propped open

box. That makes it easy to find among silver-plated cups as numerous as a high-mileage sales rep's Esso glasses. Not to mention shields, plaques and even a brandy flask in the shape of a Bugatti radiator. Some are really quite valuable; "This is a solid silver one," says Wally, holding a particularly shining example. Behind him is a glass-fronted cabinet containing trophies three-deep.

Wally Pratt used to be a technician in the Ministry of Defence. So he's technically-minded and a good engineer. He keeps a freshly-built spare engine in the room in his flat that he uses as a workshop, a room full of useful pieces of Fiat that give off an oily aroma. The diminutive engine he shows me is built around a Fiat 850 block –

Among Wally's proudest possessions are over 200 cups and trophies, arranged three-deep in their own cabinet

"much stronger than the original 767 cc engine".

A similar engine sits in the back of BCG 590C, having long since ousted the 29 bhp unit that Fiat intended for the pint-sized 600D. The 847 cc engine block (slightly overbored from the original 843 cc) contains an Abarth camshaft actually developed for use in the 903 cc Fiat 127 engine; the pushrods this actuates operate standard valves with Abarth springs. The ports were gas-flowed by Wally himself; on the inlet side they are fed by a Weber 28/36 DCD progressive twin-choke carburetter (a favourite of 1960s tuners because every setting can be altered), while the exhaust ports lead into an Abarth fabricated manifold and free-flow exhaust system.

The four-speed transmission is standard, so are the worm-and-sector steering and the all-drum brakes. In layout, the same applies to the transverse leaf front suspension (the bottoms of the kingpin carriers are attached to each end of the leaf) and the swing-axle system at the rear. But the little Fiat sits three inches lower on its springs than it did when it left the Turin factory, imparting some aggressive-looking negative camber to the rear wheels. These, and their counterparts at the front, are Cromodora items shod with 165/60 HR13 Dunlop D3s; Wally has various other wheel/tyre combinations lurking in the darker recesses of his flat. To accommodate this generous rubber, the rear wheel arches are very slightly flared out.

Dampers are by Koni. "J. W. E. Banks, the importers, were good to me," says Wally. "I sent the dampers up to them for reconditioning, and they came back with everything replaced. And they didn't charge me a penny." This is what happens when you're an institution like Wally is.

The classes have changed, now, so instead of the up-to-one-litres Wally now has to compete with the likes of 1300 cc Novas, Fiestas and Alfasuds – not to mention the odd hot Mini. "You see, in the one-litre class I used to win everything, not wishing to be big-headed you understand. I beat most things in the next class up, too. I need a bigger engine now. The 1050 engine in the Autobianchi A112 Abarth. But they're like gold dust."

So what was it that made Wally take up motor sport in mid-term, so to speak? "Well, I needed

It's the scorpion (left) that gives the game away; otherwise the Fiat (above) looks amazingly standard. Wheels (right) are Cromodora items shod with 165/60 HR13 Dunlop D3s; wheelarches are slightly flared to accommodate these and other combinations

some excitement. I started doing some marshalling, but I got fed up with watching and decided to have a go. I'd done some motorcycle racing earlier – one of those over there is a motorcycling trophy."

So hardly the Nigel Mansell approach for laid-back Wally. But the awards came thick and fast. He used Fiat Abarths right from the start, having developed a liking for small Fiats after owning a pre-war Topolino. "Before this one I had a white 1000 TC, but it was left-hand drive and I couldn't get on with it. I had some others, too, a dark blue one, another white one, and an Allemano coupé which I got from Radbourne's (the Abarth importers). But that wasn't quick enough.

"I've done full seasons every year from 1968 to now. I eased off a bit last year, though, and did all the classic car shows. I'd done all the sprints, all the hillclimbs, all the venues – it gets a bit boring. So I thought I'd try something different. At one show they promised me a table for all the trophies, but there was nothing. So I had the trophies on the

bonnet, on the roof, inside the car, everywhere. People were picking up those tankards there and pretending to drink out of them. I won't do the shows again. I'm registered for all the championships this year: ACSMC, LCAMC, ASEMC, BARC and so on…

"There, that's a picture of my grandfather on a Hansom cab. He was called Wally Pratt as well. He was a Hansom cab driver." Driving is obviously in the blood. We go outside to the small blue Fiat for a demonstration run. It starts easily, settling down to a smooth tickover with the characteristic note of a rear-engined car. It seems tractable and docile as we move off, though there's an underlying hardness to the exhaust note.

"Oh yes, it revs well," says Wally as he applies more throttle. At around 4000 rpm the note gets harder and the unsilenced Weber begins to snort enthusiastically. It's also very smooth, as tiny "fours" so often are. As the Fiat is a rear-engined car, does Wally have any difficulty getting it off the line? "Not really. I just let the clutch in when the

engine sounds about right."

Wally is obviously capable of moderating his right foot when he needs to, though. One year his Fiat won the Fiat Motor Club economy run. But despite the Abarth's impressive finishing record, it has had its off days. "It had a partial seizure at Greenham Common once. But the last time was on my way to a sprint at North Weald. A valve seat shattered. Ruined the piston and the head. But I was mobile again by 5 pm with my other engine fitted."

The suspension is firm, and on taking the wheel I find that the handling is taut. Combined with the Fiat's small dimensions, this makes this competition car an ideal traffic companion. I can see clearly why Wally doesn't feel the need for any other form of transport. Besides, after 19 years Wally is rather attached to his baby bombshell. Will he keep it indefinitely? "Someone suggested I should be buried in it…"

Meanwhile, Wally will continue to demolish the opposition with his 100 mph Fiat Abarth 850 TC. "It's something to do, isn't it." I hope I'm like that when I'm 72.

FUNSIZE FIAT

The Fiat 850 in all its forms is a rarity these days but there is a strong following for them in the Fiat Motor Club. Story by Mike Taylor

Outside Italy when did you last see a Fiat 850 saloon, let alone an 850 coupé or Spider? I certainly hadn't seen one for a long, long time before arranging this meeting with three members of the Fiat Motor Club. Louise Raphael, Chris Lake and David Carpenter are great devotees of the 850 and they convinced me of the true merit of these small cars overlooked by many in their search for interesting, practical, reliable and relatively inexpensive Classic transport. In the course of my day with the Fiats and their owners I learned more of the cars' appeal and fascinating history.

Fiat (Fabbrica Italiana Automobili Torina) goes back to 1899 and by the Fifties had grown to be Europe's most profitable and largest car manufacturer, producing mainly mass-market saloons.

The foundation for the Fiat 850 series of models can be traced back to the early Fifties when Engineering Chief Dr Giacosa and his staff finalised the concept for a four-seat, two-door family saloon with a water-cooled 633cc four-cylinder 22bhp engine. Significant to the basic layout of the drivetrain was that the engine location was behind the centre line of the rear wheels, driving forward to the four-speed gearbox which was positioned ahead of this centre line. Moreover, the suspension was fully independent all-round giving a good ride quality and, despite its size, interior room was far in advance of the opposition for this class of car.

The little Fiat, known as the 600, set new standards for driveability and economy and, as more and more were sold, it gained a reputation for reliability, too. Taking into account the cars built in other countries as well, some 2.5 million of these vehicles were sold – an impressive figure.

In 1960 the engine was increased to 767cc by enlarging the bore and stroke dimensions which boosted the power to 29bhp. However, by this time the 600 was beginning to show its age. Through some lack of advanced product planning, Fiat had no entirely new model on the stocks. As a result, a new model was created using the basis of the 600. Based on a two-door unit construction body, the replacement was some 14.5in longer overall, although the wheelbase was just one inch longer. The suspension design followed the same principle as the existing model – independent all-round with transverse front springs and semi trailing arms and coil springs at the rear. Indeed, there were few major differences. The petrol tank was moved from the front to a point just behind the rear seat and in order to create the necessary extra space the old sweeping tail of the 600 was given 'notchback' styling. The bore was increased yet again, producing an engine size of 843cc which developed just 34bhp. Porsche-type synchromesh was added to the gearbox.

By the early Sixties sales of the 850 saloon were strong and tuning experts like Carlo Abarth had demonstrated that the Fiat engine could be made to perform out of all recognition. With such healthy demand, it was decided to add a fixed-head coupé and an open sports version to the range, the coupé to be styled in-house, the sports (Spider) to be styled and manufactured by Bertone whose chief (and at that time, only) stylist was Giorgetto Giugiaro, the actual shaping of the Spider being undertaken by Marcello Gandini who went on to style the Lamborghini Miura!

Both Coupé and Spider utilised the saloon's floorpan structure together with the same engine, transmission and final drive, save for the fact that the compression ratio was increased and a Weber twin choke carburettor added to push up power by 10bhp on the Coupé and 12bhp on the Spider. The road wheels were increased to 13in to accommodate the front disc brakes.

In reply to criticism concerning lack of power in the little Coupé and Spider, three years later Fiat introduced the 850 Sport Coupé and the 850 Sport Spider. The 843cc engine was increased to 903cc (by lengthening the stroke)

which in turn pushed the power up to 52bhp at 6,500rpm although, surprisingly, the gearing was left unaltered. Wider section tyres were the only outward acknowledgement of the higher performance potential. Trim differences on the Coupé included rubber bumper over riders (this modification being shared with the new Spider model), a rear spoiler and twin driving lights.

So much of the basic mechanics of the Coupé and Spider was based on the Fiat saloon that when the 850 saloon was replaced by the 127 Hatchback in March 1971, it clearly wouldn't be long before the sports models would be replaced. The crunch came later that year when Fiat introduced the 128 Sports Coupé. The Spider, however, had no direct replacement, Fiat filling the gap for an open car with the X1/9 Targa.

Louise Raphael has owned several

Fiats both at home and abroad. "My love affair with Fiat began in the States when I bought a 124 Special. It was much maligned by everyone around me at the time. Being a Briton in America I was determined to preserve my 'Europeanism' and not drive an American car. I saw the 124 for sale and bought it because I'd always liked Fiats. I then thought about buying an X1/9 but came back to the UK."

Back in Britain Louise then bought a Polski Fiat, based on the Fiat 125. Comparing that with her 124, she says of the Polski that it was built like a tractor, "a much heavier, sturdier car although the two were very similar inside".

After this Louise began looking around for a Fiat 600 but saw an 850 saloon advertised and decided to buy that instead. "It was in very good condition although it needed some work

on the engine. I had just began to do that when a Mercedes ran into the back, causing considerable damage. Luckily, while I was in the process of fighting the insurance company I came across my current 850 Saloon at an attractive price, so that is now my day-to-day transport."

But why Fiats? "Mainly because I now know them well enough to be confident to attempt maintenance myself. I'll undertake servicing myself, changing oil and plugs, but when it comes to the bodywork I'd rather give that to a specialist because if you don't know what you're doing I think you can easily make a mess of it." Among the car's attractions are its almost Mini-like handling and nippy performance. Economy, too, is a consideration. However, when it comes to the dreaded problem of rust, Louise says that, yes,

she is aware of the problem ("one bad rust area is below the front bumper"). However, she feels that if rust is treated as soon as it appears, that's half the battle. "I'm now thinking about buying an 850 Coupé," she says.

"My parents always had Fiat cars, so it was natural that it was the car I learnt to drive in," says Chris Lake, owner of the charming little cherry red 850 Coupé pictured here. "They had a VW Beetle but when the Fiat 128 won the 'Car of the Year' award, the Beetle was sold and replaced by a Fiat 128 and, through brand loyalty, they've stuck with Fiat.

"When I came to choose a car for myself it was simply familiar ground. My first car was a Fiat 127. It was very cheap and very rusty. In fact, so much so that the boot refused to open. Then I traded that in for another 127, then on to a 128. After that, I had a 124 Sports

From left, Chris Lake with the Coupé, David Carpenter with the Spider and Louise Raphael with the Saloon

FUNSIZE FIAT

Coupé which was far too expensive to run, so I sold it and bought another 128. I then happened to be leafing through the pages of a magazine, saw the 850 Coupé for sale, went along to have a look and bought it."

After four years of ownership Chris is just as enthusiastic about it, maintaining that, aesthetically, the 850 Coupé cannot be faulted whichever way one looks at it. "In fact, when I went to see the car I had no idea what a Fiat 850 Coupé really was," continues Chris. "Having bought it I used it for three years while I was still a student and it never let me down. I paid £300 for the car with 31,000 miles on the clock. It has now done 48,000 and it still has the original clutch, gearbox and brakes."

Chris has had the sills replaced and the bodywork resprayed. That said, mechanically, the car has not needed any work at all, underlining Chris's faith in Fiat engineering. "Of course, it is serviced. But during the winter months when I was away at university the car was left out in the snow but it never failed to start first time."

Chris came to hear about his other two 850 Coupés through the Fiat Motor Club. The first was given to him when someone began talking to him at the Alexandra Palace Show. The car was languishing in a garden and was holding up urgent work on a house extension. The second Coupé was bought from another club member who had intended to restore it but had subsequently given up. "Both cars started easily," says Chris, "despite having been left outside."

"I've always been interested in cars," says David Carpenter, owner of the very pretty little Bertone-built 850 Spider soft top and a self-confessed lover of Italy and things Italian, especially Fiat. "My first was a Fiat Topolino which I bought in 1954. From then on it's always been Fiats. We bought an 850 Coupé when they first came out and kept that until the family outgrew it. Then came an 1100R Estate and later still a 128 3P which we still run today, 14 years and 140,000 miles later, along with a Uno 70SX. In 1974 I managed to buy a rather rusty 850 Coupé for £15 – which will illustrate its condition – and after running it for a few years I took it off the road with the intention of restoring it. I'm still hoping to find the time! In fact, I'd just made a start on the Coupé when the opportunity arose to buy the Spider, so the Coupé project has been shelved yet again.

"The irony of the Spider is that even when we were on holiday in Italy at the time when the car was new, I can never recall actually seeing one there," continues David. "My car was advertised in the pages of the October '87 issue of the Fiat Club magazine under the heading of 'spares and restoration' and I assumed it was probably just a lot of spares. I looked closer at the ad and found it was a Southampton telephone number. Finally, it turned out that the car was stored in a paddock only a quarter of a mile from my house."

"Despite the overhang, the proportions are as near perfect as you can get"

David says that although the car was complete, it had a lot of superficial rust and two small holes behind the rear wheelarch. With a little haggling, however, he finally managed to buy the car for £600. "Luckily, in the same issue of the magazine, another engine and gearbox were advertised. These I also bought and after a lot of work, which included fitting the other engine, I was able to have the car running by the summer of last year."

Initial body repairs to the car were done by David himself although more recently he has taken the car to a local professional body repair specialist who guarantees his work against rust for six years. David is waiting to see how well this work on the offside rear wing lasts before spending more money. Meanwhile, the car's original lilac paintwork has been covered by a coat of Ferrari red which David applied by hand. "I think it looks a million dollars. I can't afford a Ferrari, so this is the closest I shall ever get," says David wistfully.

With its narrow, tall lines the Fiat 850 Saloon was never intended to be anything other than functional, so it comes as no surprise that from most angles the car conveys a somewhat ungainly feel, largely because it lacks a balance of proportion like, say, the Mini. The high waist and hunched hindquarters do little to help. Comparing the Fiat to, say, the Hillman Imp of the same period, the Italian saloon lacks the crisp lines of the Rootes product.

Inside the car, Fiat's preoccupation with functionality in their small saloon is all too evident. Plain vinyl seats and a black sheet steel dashboard (save for the single instrument binnacle ahead of the driver) was Fiat's answer to designing the interior of an economically-priced mass-market saloon.

Surprisingly, it works – and works well. The seats are comfortable and the driver soon becomes accustomed to the upright driving position with its off-set pedal cluster. The speedo can be seen easily and is set in just the right position with petrol and coolant gauges on either side.

The steering is pleasantly light with little feedback from road irregularities, added to which the car is blessed with a good lock making town manoeuvering easy. Clutch action is smooth, although the gearchange movement is over-long with a 'rubbery' feel – something the driver has to get used to.

At town driving speeds the engine feels willing. However, even at low revs there is a degree of noise penetration which discourages any enthusiatic use of the gears. It's a plodder rather than a screamer. In view of the fact that the engine is actually located behind the rear wheels, ride quality is surprisingly good. Understandably, there is a trace of fore and aft pitching, although roll on corners is well damped. Potholes are

handled with nonchalance, adding to the car's appeal. Sensible with a capital 'S' is how best to describe the Fiat 850 Saloon.

Next, I drove Chris Lake's 850 Coupé, a 1970 MkII model. As Chris says, the in-house Fiat styling is elegant and passes the test of time. The use of chrome trim is well controlled and the clever flick-up line of the rear side windows stops the fastback shape from looking as though the car is sitting on its haunches.

This hint of up-market elegance is carried through to the interior. Ahead of the driver are two clear large dials for speed and engine revs, while the standard Fiat steering wheel has been replaced by a sporty woodrim type. Gone, too, are the basic but comfy saloon seats. In their place are well contoured recliners with good support and plenty of rearward travel for the long-legged driver.

The 903cc engine with its 52bhp (DIN) delights in being revved. Certainly, there is sufficient power to give the car spirited performance, although there is sufficient torque that the driver is not constantly having to use the gears to get the best from the car. As in Louise's saloon, the delightfully smooth clutch and light, responsive steering give confidence and pleasure and the Coupé's disc/drum brakes are well up to coping with the car's 90 + top speed. That said, there is still the same slightly 'rubbery' feel to the stick with its long travel from gear to gear.

Noise from the engine is not obtrusive, even when using higher revs, and with its directional steering and little roll on corners the Fiat Coupé can be enjoyed to the full. However, fore and aft pitching is more obvious than in the saloon, thereby upsetting an otherwise well-balanced ride.

Stylish and sporting, the 850 (or should we say 903?) Coupé is fun and satisfying without ruining your bank balance.

Finally, my turn came to drive David Carpenter's sleekly beautiful 850 Spider. From almost every angle it looks 'just right' and doubtless the majority of owners, past and present, bought their Spiders on looks alone – performance notwithstanding. Like the Coupé, the Spider owes its appeal to shape rather than added embellishment or stick-on stripes. Despite the large overhang at the rear to accommodate the engine, the proportions are as near perfect as you can get.

Bertone has cast his spell over the interior, too, with a well-planned dash carrying the speedo and tachometer with supplementaries for battery condition, temperature and fuel states. Ahead of the passenger is an impressive large glove box with a stout-looking grab handle. The seats are set low in the cockpit yet give good support with plenty of legroom should the driver need it.

Compared with the Coupé, the Spider's soft top stowed neatly away in the rear, engine noise – particularly

Above: variations on a rear-engined theme; both Bertone (Spider) and Fiat (Coupé) achieved excellent lines for the sports models, though the saloon, for practical reasons, was somewhat dumpy

The 1970 Mark II Sport Coupé has an air of elegance inside and out that belies its humble origins

The 850 Saloon (this is a Mark II) is a nippy and compact car which exudes cheerful practicality

FUNSIZE · FIAT

when free use is made of the revs – is far more intrusive. Moreover, David's car was suffering from a slight drive-line vibration which acted as a further deterrent to indulgent use of the gears.

The Spider also benefits from Fiat's light, directional steering and smooth clutch, together with just the right degree of action from the disc/drum brakes. But, again, the gearchange is marred by its long movement. Unfortunately, especially since this is the most sporting of the trio, the pitching characteristic is even more pronounced, giving a degree of discomfort when driving over less than smooth surfaces.

Without doubt, the Spider is a very pretty car and its looks are its greatest attraction. Treating the three cars as one (although the little Bertone-styled Spider is very rare so there's little chance of seeing one for sale in the columns of the magazines), the first aspect to consider when buying is the bodywork. If rust is allowed to take a firm hold in the sill section, it can not only destroy the sills themselves but also creep back towards the centre of

"People buy them as a cheap form of transport and they become neglected"

the car eating its way through the floorpan. Equally important is the area at the rear of the front wings where moisture causes rot to attack the whole of the inner wing and 'A' post sections. "I think that has to be *the* most important area to check on an 850 since it is structural and if the car is badly rotted, it's probably not worth saving," says Chris candidly. Rust can also take hold in the section around the head-lights, the wheelarches, and in the bottoms of the doors. It's also worth inspecting the battery compartment, which is located in the front boot, since spillage of acid can have a nasty effect on the paintwork and if this happens, rust will start. "I've seen cars where the boot floor and the battery box have completely rotted away," warns Chris.

Unfortunately, the availability of body panels is not that good for these Fiat models. This is where the Club can

help," adds Chris. "Both the Saloon and the Coupé were built by Fiat and rust-proofed while in the process of manufacture. Whether their system was good or bad, who can say? The Spider, however, was assembled by Bertone whose rust-proofing processes were probably less effective."

Model Years
1964 – late '68 Series I 850 Saloon
1965 – late '68 Series I 850 Coupé (designed & built by Fiat)
1965 – late '68 Series I 850 Spider (designed & built by Bertone)
Late '68 – early '71 Series II Saloon
Late '68 – '73 850 Sport Coupé
Late '68 – '73 850 Sport Spider
Late '68 – '74 Saloon (built under licence in Spain as Seat)

As for the mechanicals, Chris says that in normal use the 850 engine is a very strong, reliable unit although the Saloon is reckoned to be the more reliable since the Coupé is tuned to give greater performance which the average owner probably takes delight in using. "When the engine starts to wear, the tell-tale signs are usually an increase in oil consumption," says Chris, "caused by worn valve guides." As with most rear-engined cars, it is important to ensure that the fan belt is in good condition because the fan itself is crucial to the cooling of the engine. Should the engine be allowed to overheat the cylinder head can warp causing the gasket to blow.

Another area which Chris says can cause problems is the carburettor – and in particular the twin choke version fitted to the Coupé. This can sometimes prove troublesome if dirt is allowed to enter the fuel system.

The clutch is more than up to handling the power output from the Coupé engine, although Chris says that the shortfall in the design of the gearbox is the synchromesh on second gear which, after a high mileage, can become weak. But Chris is quick to point out that the box was strong enough to take the 200 or so bhp developed in the Abarth-tuned cars.

While the braking system and wheel bearings hold no special horrors in day-to-day operation, the kingpins on the front suspension have grease nipples which should receive their usual diet of lubricant from the grease gun every 3,000 miles. However, Chris suspects that some owners, blissfully unaware of this maintenance detail, allow the joints to become dry causing rapid wear. In the case of the Saloon, people buy them as a cheap form of transport and they become neglected simply through lack of attention.

Practical and economical, the Fiat 850 Saloon is a treasure for the owner who demands sensible motoring from his Classic car. In contrast, the elegance of the Coupé and Spider speaks for itself. Nowadays, values are increasing. ◬

Bertone's Spider has a timeless style which sadly was never officially available in right-hand drive. The interior was also by Bertone. Below, the 903cc engine